Statistics for Social Science and Public Policy

Advisors:
S.E. Fienberg   W. van der Linden

Springer
New York
Berlin
Heidelberg
Hong Kong
London
Milan
Paris
Tokyo

Statistics for Social Science and Public Policy

Paul De Boeck
Mark Wilson, Editors

Explanatory Item Response Models

A Generalized Linear and Nonlinear Approach

With 50 Figures

 Springer

Paul De Boeck
Department of Psychology
K.U. Leuven
Tiensestraat 102
B-3000 Leuven
Belgium
Paul.DeBoeck@psy.kuleuven.ac.be

Mark Wilson
Graduate School of Education
University of California, Berkeley
Berkeley, CA 94720-1670
USA
mrwilson@socrates.berkeley.edu

Editorial Board

Library of Congress Cataloging-in-Publication Data
Explanatory item response models : a generalized linear and nonlinear approach / [edited
    by] Paul De Boeck, Mark Wilson.
        p. cm. — (Statistics in social sciences and public policy)
    Includes bibliographical references and index.
    ISBN 0-387-40275-6 (alk. paper)
        1. Social sciences—Statistics—Databases. 2. Item response theory. 3. Psychometrics. I.
Boeck, Paul de. II. Series.
    HA32.E95   2004
    150'.1'5195—dc22   2004040850

ISBN 0-387-40275-6   Printed on acid-free paper.

Printed in the United States of America.   (MVY)

9 8 7 6 5 4 3 2 1   SPIN 10935354

Springer-Verlag is a part of *Springer Science+Business Media*

springeronline.com

To Jano, for all the ways that you help to make things work, and for all the ways that you make things worthwhile (MW)

Preface

This edited volume gives a new and integrated introduction to item response models (predominantly used in measurement applications in psychology, education, and other social science areas) from the viewpoint of the statistical theory of generalized linear and nonlinear mixed models. Moreover, this new framework allows the domain of item response models to be co-ordinated and broadened to emphasize their *explanatory* uses beyond their standard *descriptive* uses.

The basic explanatory principle is that item responses can be modeled as a function of predictors of various kinds. The predictors can be (a) characteristics of items, of persons, and of combinations of persons and items; they can be (b) observed or latent (of either items or persons); and they can be (c) latent continuous or latent categorical. Thus, a broad range of models can be generated, including a wide range of extant item response models as well as some new ones. Within this range, models with explanatory predictors are given special attention, but we also discuss descriptive models. Note that the 'item responses' that we are referring to are not just the traditional 'test data,' but are broadly conceived as categorical data from a repeated observations design. Hence, data from studies with repeated-observations experimental designs, or with longitudinal designs, may also be modeled.

The intended audience for this volume is rather broad. First, the volume is meant to provide an introduction to item response models, starting from regression models, although the introduction is at a quite compact and general level. Second, since the approach is so general, many different kinds of models are discussed, well-known models as well as less well-known models, and even previously-unknown models, all from the same perspective, so that those already well familiar with psychometrics may also find the volume of interest to them. Third, the volume also has practical purposes for those already practicing in the field: (a) the regression-based framework that is presented makes it easier to see how models can be estimated with software that was not originally designed with item response models in mind, and (b) one can formulate and estimate new models, tailor-made to the measurement and explanatory purposes one has in mind. In this way, we hope to give practitioners a flexible tool for their work.

We see this volume as being suitable for a semester-long course for advanced graduate students in measurement and psychometrics, as well as a reference for the practicioner. Each chapter is followed by a set of exercises designed (a) to give the reader a chance to practice some of the computer analyses and (b) to point out some interesting perspectives and extensions arising in the chapter. In order to make the task easier for the reader, a unified approach to notation and model description is followed throughout the chapters, and a single data set is used in most examples to make it easier to see how the many models are related. The volume includes a chapter that describes the principal computer programs used in the analyses, and at the end of most chapters one can find command files and enough detail for a representative set of analyses, with the intent that the reader can carry out all computer analyses shown in this volume. A website associated with this volume, has been installed (`http://bear.soe.berkeley.edu/EIRM/`) – it contains all data sets used in the chapters, the command files for all analyses, sample output, and (sample) answers to the exercises. Part I of the volume gives an introduction to the framework. In Chapter 1, starting from the linear regression model, two basic ideas are explained: How linear models can be generalized using a nonlinear link function, and how individual differences can be incorporated, leading to generalized linear and nonlinear mixed models (GLMMs and NLMMs). In Chapter 2 we illustrate the concepts of descriptive and explanatory measurement using four basic item response models: the Rasch model, the latent regression Rasch model, the linear logistic test model (LLTM), and the latent regression LLTM. Chapter 3 describes the extension to models for polytomous data. The general statistical background of the models is explained in more depth in Chapter 4.

In Part II, these models are generalized to other and more complicated models that illustrate different ways that models can be explanatory by incorporating external factors. In this part, we concentrate on three types of predictors: (a) Models with explanatory person predictors, including multilevel models with person groups as predictors (Chapter 5); (b) models with explanatory item predictors, including multilevel models with item groups as predictors (Chapter 6); and (c) models with explanatory person-by-item predictors, including models for differential item functioning (DIF) and so-called dynamic models with responses from one or more other items as predictors (Chapter 7).

In some situations it can make sense to consider models that deal with 'unknown' predictors or predictors with values that are 'not known *a priori.*' These are together called internal factors, because the values of the predictors are derived from the data, instead of being given as external information. This is the basis for Part III. In this part, Chapter 8 and Chapter 9 deal with models with so-called latent item predictors. In Chapter 8 bilinear models with item slopes ('discrimination' parameters) are discussed, for example the two-parameter logistic model. Multidimensional models are also discussed in this chapter. In Chapter 9 bilinear models where item parameters are a function of other item parameters are discussed – the so-called models with internal restrictions on difficulty (MIRID). In general, independent of the model under consideration, some dependence between the item responses may remain. This is the issue of local item dependence. In Chapter 10, different ways to model remaining dependence are presented. An assumption in all models in the previous chapters is that, if predictor weights are random, a normal distribution applies to these weights. This assumption is relaxed in Chapter 11 on mixture models.

The volume closes with a final part where there is a chapter on estimation methods and software (Chapter 12). This chapter includes examples of how to use a wide variety of computer programs to estimate models in the Chapters.

There are some topics that the reader might have expected to be included in this volume that we have not included. For example, in pursuit of our theme of explanatory rather than descriptive item response models, we have not explored the topic of the estimation of person parameters, a topic that is mainly of interest in descriptive measurement. In a similar vein, we have not discussed issues in conditional maximum likelihood estimation, as, at present, this seems less useful to explanatory measurement than other formulations. Except in passing, we have not considered response formats involving response times and counts: We see these as being most promising forms of response data for response modeling, but did not include them at this point due to (a) the relative rarity of models for such data in the item response modeling literature, and (b) our own relative inexperience with such data formats. Although we make frequent use of some statistical model testing techniques, we do not include an in-depth account of such techniques, although a general discussion is given in Chapter 4.

Paul De Boeck, Leuven, Belgium
Mark Wilson, Berkeley, California, USA
December 29, 2003

Contents

Contributors

Derek Briggs,
School of Education, University of Colorado, Colorado, USA.

Paul De Boeck,
Department of Psychology, K.U.Leuven, Belgium.

Karen Draney,
Graduate School of Education, University of California, Berkeley, California, USA.

Steffen Fieuws,
Biostatistical Center, K.U.Leuven (U.Z. St.-Rafaël), Belgium.

Rianne Janssen,
Department of Psychology and Department of Educational Sciences, K.U.Leuven, Belgium.

Michel Meulders,
Department of Psychology, K.U.Leuven, Belgium.

Geert Molenberghs,
Center for Statistics, Limburg University Center, Belgium.

Stephen Moore,
Graduate School of Education, University of California, Berkeley, California, USA.

Insu Paek,
Harcourt Educational Measurement, Texas, USA.

Deborah Peres,
Graduate School of Education, University of California, Berkeley, California, USA.

Frank Rijmen,
Department of Psychology, K.U.Leuven, Belgium.

Jan Schepers,
Department of Psychology, K.U.Leuven, Belgium.

Dirk Smits
Department of Psychology, K.U.Leuven, Belgium.

Bart Spiessens,
Biostatistical Center, K.U.Leuven (U.Z. St.-Rafaël), Belgium.

Francis Tuerlinckx,
Department of Psychology, K.U.Leuven, Belgium.

Wim Van den Noortgate,
Department of Educational Sciences, K.U.Leuven, Belgium.

Geert Verbeke,
Biostatistical Center, K.U.Leuven (U.Z. St.-Rafaël), Belgium.

Wen-Chung Wang,
National Chung Cheng University, Taiwan.

Mark Wilson,
Graduate School of Education, University of California, Berkeley, California, USA.

Yiyu Xie,
Graduate School of Education, University of California, Berkeley, California, USA.

Notation

Indices

p for persons, $p = 1, \ldots, P$;
i for items, $i = 1, \ldots, I$;
k for item predictors, $k = 0$ or $1, \ldots, K$,
(or alternatively for fixed-effect predictors);
j for person predictors, $j = 0$ or $1, \ldots, J$,
(or alternatively for random-effects predictors);
h for person-by-item predictors, $h = 1, \ldots, H$;
g for groups, $g = 1, \ldots, G$;
r for latent predictors, $r = 1, \ldots, R$;
m for categories, $m = 1, \ldots, M$, or $m = 0, \ldots, M - 1$;
(including quadrature nodes).

Data

Y is used for the data, with Y_{pi} denoting the response of person p to item i.

Predictors

X for item predictors (X_{ik}),
(or alternatively for predictors with fixed effects);
Z for person predictors (Z_{pj}),
(or alternatively for predictors with random effects);
W for person-by-item predictors (W_{pih});
α for latent predictors (α_{ir} or α_{pr}).

Effects (Weights, Coefficients)

β for fixed effects of item predictors (β_k),
θ for random effects of item predictors (commonly θ_{pk}),
ϑ for fixed effects of person predictors (ϑ_j),
ζ for random effects of person predictors (commonly ζ_{pj}),
δ for fixed effects of person-by-item predictors (δ_h),
γ for random effects of person-by-item predictors (commonly γ_{ph}),
ε for remaining continuous random terms when predictors are used.

Model

π_{pi} for the probability of a $Y_{pi} = 1$ (binary data),
π_{pim} for the probability of $Y_{pi} = m$ (multicategorical data),

η_{pi} and η_{pim} for the transformed π_{pi} and π_{pim}, respectively, based on the link function.

Comments

1. By convention, the πs and ηs are used without an indication of the random variables they are conditioned upon. The conditioning should be clear from the context. It is mentioned in an explicit way when the values are marginal values.

2. Most random effects are effects that are random over persons, so that a subscript p is used. The same symbol (e.g., θ) is also used when the effects are random over items or groups, but the subscripts are adapted (into i and g, respectively).

3. Depending on the chapter, more specific and adapted notation is used. As an example, in Chapters 1, 3, and 4, the notation for predictors and their indices is somewhat different and more consistent with the statistical literature (as in parentheses above). There are other differences that are chapter specific.

Part I: Introduction to the framework

Chapter 1

A framework for item response models

Paul De Boeck
Mark Wilson

1.1 Introduction

This volume has been written with the view that there are several larger perspectives that can be used (a) to throw light on the sometimes confusing array of models and data that one can find in the area of item response modeling, (b) to explore different contexts of data analysis than the 'test data' context to which item response models are traditionally applied, and (c) to place these models in a larger statistical framework that will enable the reader to use a generalized statistical approach and also to take advantage of the flexibility of statistical computing packages that are now available.

1.1.1 Measurement or explanation?

Suppose that we have been asked to analyze some data from a typical educational achievement test. We note parenthetically that we could as easily have chosen to consider an example from a psychological experiment on, say, attitudes, or from a developmental study of some sort of growth using categorical observations. We will return to discuss these somewhat different contexts in the next section, but for now, we will confine ourselves to this 'testing' context, as it is familiar to most people, if only from their own educational experiences.

There are two very general types of scientific questions that might arise concerning this type of data. One type of question pertains to how well the test can serve as providing a 'measure' of the examinees' proficiency on the underlying variable that the test is designed to measure – commonly called the 'latent' variable. Such questions center around the use of the test at the level of the individual examinees. We will refer to the approach as the *measurement* approach, as it seeks to describe the performance of the individual examinees on the test.

In contrast, without being interested in the measurement of the individual examinees, one could also consider a very different type of scientific question, which seeks to relate the item responses on the test to other variables, which might include variables that pertain to the examinees (person predictors), or variables that pertain to the items (item predictors). We will refer to item response models that follow this approach as *explanatory*, as the intention is to explain the item responses in terms of other variables. An interesting example of this occurs when one seeks to investigate the relationship between the examinees' performance on the test and their previous training. Another would be to consider design variations in the items that make up the test, to see if performance on the items depends on, say, item features that are related to the cognitive processes that are involved. Here, the level of interpretation in these scientific questions is not the individual examinee, but rather the general inferences that can be made about the relationship of certain variables across the set of examinees. For example, one might be interested in testing a psychological theory, without any interest in a further use of the measurement of individual examinees. It is evident that the two approaches, the descriptive measurement approach and the explanatory approach, can be combined. Thus, explanation is seen as complementary to measurement.

1.1.2   Test data, repeated observations data, and longitudinal data

In this volume then, we will be emphasizing the possibilities of explanatory uses of item response models, and thus not only the more usual descriptive approaches that tend to predominate in practice. In doing so, we also wish to emphasize that the item response models we will be exploring can be used in a wide range of data analysis contexts. In particular, we will look beyond the traditional 'test data' context for item response models, and also examine applications that are in the contexts of (a) experiments with repeated observations, and (b) longitudinal data. The reason for looking beyond 'test data' is that experiments with repeated observations and longitudinal designs share two important features with test data: More than one observation is made for each person, and observations are made for more than one person. Note that commonly the term 'repeated measurements' is used, but we will avoid that term here, as we see it as important to make a distinction between 'observations' and 'measurements.'

Consider the first of these additional contexts: *experiments with repeated observations*. Such observations come from an experiment with factors that are manipulated within persons. The corresponding situation is called a *within-subjects design* in the psychological literature, because the manipulated factors vary *within* individuals. These factors are termed the *design factors* of the observations. When the persons are all drawn from one population and undergo the same treatment(s), the design is a *single-sample design*. When they are drawn from different populations, for example, males and females, and/or undergo different treatment(s), the design is a *multiple-sample design*. Another term for the latter is the *split-plot design* (Kirk, 1995).[1] For example (an example that we will expand upon in later sections), two sets of frustrating situations could be presented to a group of participants in an experiment, situations where one would likely feel that oneself was to blame for the frustration –'self-to-blame situations'– and situations where one would likely feel that another person was to blame for the frustration –'other-to-blame situations.' These could be followed by, say, questions on verbal aggression with a number of response categories. In this example, self-to-blame versus other-to-blame is a manipulated factor and, hence, a design factor. The experiment has a single-sample design.

Consider now the second of these additional contexts: These observations may also come from studies with a *longitudinal design* – repeated observations of the same dependent variable at regular (or irregular) time intervals. The time of observation and other variables related to time may be considered *covariates* one wants to relate to the observations. Equally, person properties may figure in models for longitudinal data.

Note that one could well take either approach described above in analyzing data from these two additional contexts – repeated observations data could be treated in a measurement way, de-emphasizing the role of design factors or covariates. Equally, data from these two contexts could be treated in an explanatory way, given that data on suitable explanatory variables were available (design factors or covariates).

Returning to the test data context, we can now see that the repeated observations may be responses to the items from a test instrument (thinking of this class broadly as being composed of instruments such as achievement and aptitude tests, attitude scales, behavioral inventories, etc.). Since a test typically consists of more than one item, test data are repeated observations. Test data are just a special case, but a prominent one in this volume. We have found it refreshing to think of test data as being repeated observations that have to be explained from properties that co-vary with the observations. These properties have been termed design factors and covariates for the contexts of experiments and longitudinal data, respectively, but from now on both terms will be used interchangeably, and will also be used for test data contexts.

This broader perspective can make testing less exclusively a matter of measuring, but also a way of testing theories. Note that tests with a test design (Embretson, 1985) may be considered as experiments with a within-subjects design, because the design implies that item properties are varied within the test, just as design factors are manipulated in an experiment.

---

[1]Kirk (1995) describes the design as one for different samples from the same population but with a different treatment.

1.1.3 Categorical data

An important and distinctive feature of the data we will deal with is their categorical nature. The simplest case of a categorical variable is a binary variable. In many tests there are only two response categories, and in other tests there are more but they are recoded into, say, 1 and 0, because one is interested only in whether the responses are correct or not, or whether the persons agree or disagree with what the item states. This is why measurement models for *binary data* are the more popular ones. However, in other cases, there may be more than two response categories which are not recoded into two values. In a similar way, observations in general can be made in two or more categories. For more than two categories, the data are called *polytomous* or *multicategorical*.

Observation categories can be ordered or unordered. The categories can be ordered because of the way they are defined, as in a rating scale format; or they can be ordered based on a conception from the investigator. The corresponding data are *ordered-category data*. Examples of categories that are ordered by definition are categorical degrees of frequency (often, sometimes, never), of agreement (strongly agree, agree, disagree, strongly disagree), and of intensity (very much, moderately, slightly). Examples of categories that are ordered on the basis of a conception would be response alternatives for a multiple-choice item where these alternatives can be ordered on their correctness. Observational categories can also be unordered, because nothing in the category definition is ordinal and because one has no idea of how the categories relate to some underlying dimension. The difference between such categories is only nominal and therefore these are called nominal categories, and the corresponding data are called *nominal-category data*. For example, in a scenario-based test on emotional intelligence four responses may be presented for each problem and it may not be clear in advance which response is the most intelligent one and what the order of the other responses is with respect to emotional intelligence. The models and applications in this volume mainly include the first two cases of data being categorical: binary data and ordered-category data. However, binary data will play a more important role in the introduction, since the models for binary data can be extended for other types of categorical data. See Chapter 3 for the extension to multicategorical data, including nominal-category data.

1.1.4 A broader statistical perspective

The broader statistical perspective that we adopt in this volume is that item response models are members of a class of models that is larger than their traditional applications to item responses may suggest. It turns out that most extant item response models are special cases of what are called *generalized linear* or *nonlinear mixed models* (GLMMs and NLMMs) (Mc-

Culloch & Searle, 2001). The GLMM and NLMM perspective has several advantages over the standard approach, and is quite simple in its core conceptualization, which is based on the familiar linear regression model, although it is not necessarily simple in how it is applied to a specific situation. We see it as being straightforward because the similarities and differences between models can be described in terms of the kinds of predictors (e.g., item predictors and person predictors) and the kinds of weights (i.e., fixed or random) they have in the prediction of the observations.

Perhaps the most important feature of the broader statistical approach is that it facilitates an implementation of the explanatory perspective described above. Additional important advantages we see are (a) that the approach is a general one and therefore also flexible, and (b) that the approach connects psychometrics strongly to the field of statistics, so that a broader knowledge basis and literature become available. Finally, the availability of generalized statistical software makes the implementation of new models developed for specific situations much more straightforward than it has been in the past, where specific-purpose programs could be used only under less general circumstances. Examples of general software are the NLMIXED procedure from SAS (SAS Institute, 1999), and WIN-BUGS (Spiegelhalter, Thomas, Best & Lunn, 2003). See Chapter 12 for an overview and discussion.

GLMMs and NLMMs are an appropriate way to model repeated categorical data, binary data as well as, by extension, ordered-category data and nominal-category data. They can give a broader perspective on the modeling and analysis of data, from tests, experiments, and longitudinal studies, a perspective that goes beyond the common practices in psychology and educational measurement.

1.2   Example data set on verbal aggression

We will make use of an example data set (Vansteelandt, 2000) throughout this volume, in order to give a concrete basis for the models to be presented. This data set is available at the website given in the Preface. The data are responses of persons to questions about verbal aggression (see Table 1.1). They can be considered as test data or as experimental data. The instrument is a behavioral questionnaire, or one may also call it a personality scale or an attitude scale. All items refer to verbally aggressive reactions in a frustrating situation. For example, one item is: "A bus fails to stop for me. I would curse." And the possible responses are: "yes," "perhaps," or "no." They define a set of three ordered response categories. Because the data are responses to items, one may consider the data as being exemplary of a broad type arising from a measurement scenario: Types of instruments like this include achievement and aptitude tests, attitude scales, personality scales, etc. On the one hand, a traditional way to analyze data like this is, after a numerical coding of the responses (e.g., yes=2, perhaps=1, and no=0), to consider the sum as a measure of a person's tendency to react with verbal aggression. On the other hand, because a design is built into the items, the data may also be considered data from a psychological experiment. The experimental design has four factors (see Table 1.1).

The first design factor is the *Behavior Mode*. A differentiation is made between two levels: wanting to do, termed *Want* (i.e., wanting to curse, wanting to scold, or wanting to shout) and actual doing, termed *Do* (i.e., cursing, scolding, or shouting). The reason for the distinction is that we don't always do what we might want to do. The discrepancy between the act and the action tendency is an indication of behavioral inhibition. We expect that for a behavior with a negative connotation, one would be less likely to do than to want, precisely because of this inhibition. In principle, one can also do something one didn't want to do, but the data show that this occurs less often.

The second design factor is the *Situation Type*. This factor has two levels: situations in which someone else is to blame, termed *Other-to-blame*, and situations in which oneself is to blame, termed *Self-to-blame*. The two other-to-blame situations that were presented are: "A bus fails to stop for me" (Bus), and "I miss a train because a clerk gave me faulty information" (Train), and the two self-to-blame situations that were presented are: "The grocery store closes just as I am about to enter" (Store), and "The operator disconnects me when I had used up my last 10 cents for a call" (Call). The reason for including this design factor was that we expect people to display more verbal aggression when someone else is to blame. Note that an additional design factor, the specific situations that are asked about (two of each – see Table 1.1), is nested within this second factor.

The third design factor is the *Behavior Type*, and it has three levels: *Curse*, *Scold*, and *Shout*. These three behaviors were chosen because they represent two behavioral aspects: the extent to which they ascribe blame (Blaming), and the extent to which they express frustration (Expressing): cursing and scolding were classified as blaming, and cursing and shouting were classified as expressive (i.e., note that the Dutch word that was used for 'shout' in the original instrument is 'het uitschreeuwen,' which is primarily expressive).

Because multiple observations are made for all participants, we have repeated observations data. The factors are manipulated within the set of items to be responded to by all participants. The *item design* is a $2 \times 2 \times 3$ design with two specific situations in each cell, leading to 24 items in total. There is also a minimal person design, based on *Gender* (F and M) and on the *Trait Anger* (TA) score. The design for the persons is not shown in Table 1.1.

All items of the test and the factors of the experiment are presented in Table 1.1. The order in the table was not the order of presentation. In fact, the items were presented to the respondents in a random order, mixed with other items of a similar type.

TABLE 1.1. The 24 verbal aggression items categorized according to their design.

Items	Situation type	Behavior
Behavior Mode: Want		
A bus fails to stop for me. I would want to curse.	*Other-to-blame*	*Curse*
A bus fails to stop for me. I would want to scold.		*Scold*
A bus fails to stop for me. I would want to shout.		*Shout*
I miss a train because a clerk gave me faulty information. I would want to curse.		*Curse*
I miss a train because a clerk gave me faulty information. I would want to scold.		*Scold*
I miss a train because a clerk gave me faulty information. I would want to shout.		*Shout*
The grocery store closes just as I am about to enter. I would want to curse.	*Self-to-blame*	*Curse*
The grocery store closes just as I am about to enter. I would want to scold.		*Scold*
The grocery store closes just as I am about to enter. I would want to shout.		*Shout*
The operator disconnects me when I had used up my last 10 cents for a call. I would want to curse.		*Curse*
The operator disconnects me when I had used up my last 10 cents for a call. I would want to scold.		*Scold*
The operator disconnects me when I had used up my last 10 cents for a call. I would want to shout.		*Shout*
Behavior Mode: Do		
A bus fails to stop for me. I would curse.	*Other-to-blame*	*Curse*
A bus fails to stop for me. I would scold.		*Scold*
A bus fails to stop for me. I would shout.		*Shout*
I miss a train because a clerk gave me faulty information. I would curse.		*Curse*
I miss a train because a clerk gave me faulty information. I would scold.		*Scold*
I miss a train because a clerk gave me faulty information. I would shout.		*Shout*
The grocery store closes just as I am about to enter. I would curse.	*Self-to-blame*	*Curse*
The grocery store closes just as I am about to enter. I would scold.		*Scold*
The grocery store closes just as I am about to enter. I would shout.		*Shout*
The operator disconnects me when I had used up my last 10 cents for a call. I would curse.		*Curse*
The operator disconnects me when I had used up my last 10 cents for a call. I would scold.		*Scold*
The operator disconnects me when I had used up my last 10 cents for a call. I would shout.		*Shout*

An extract of the actual data for the 24 items is shown in Table 1.2. As noted above, the three categorical responses were coded as 2 (yes), 1 (perhaps), and 0 (no). There were 316 respondents in total. The first three and the last one are shown in Table 1.2; see the first column for their number. Of the respondents 243 were females (F), and 73 were males

(M). We also had information about the Trait Anger (TA) score of the respondents, as derived from a personality inventory: the State-Trait Anger Expression Inventory (STAXI; Spielberger, 1988; Spielberger & Sydeman, 1994). The mean STAXI score in the example data set is 20.00 and the standard deviation is 4.85.

TABLE 1.2. Part of the verbal aggression data set ('CSS' is Curse, Scold, Shout).

	Want				Do			
Person	Bus CSS	Train CSS	Store CSS	Call CSS	Bus CSS	Train CSS	Store CSS	Call CSS
001	000	000	001	200	101	100	100	222
002	000	000	000	000	000	000	100	000
003	111	101	100	000	011	001	000	100
⋮								
316	111	101	001	000	000	000	000	000

Although the models to be discussed in this volume are models for repeated observations categorical data, for didactic purposes, we will consider the data as if they were continuous. Later on in this chapter they will be treated as categorical, after a dichotomization in order to obtain binary data. Later on in the volume, and especially in Chapter 3 on models for multicategorical data, the data will be treated in agreement with their true nature: as ordered-category data. The reason for treating the data first as continuous data is because we want to start from familiar models for continuous data to explain some principles of modeling. The reason for dichotomizing the data later in the chapter is that we want to introduce the models for categorical data in their simplest (binary data) form.

1.3   The person side of the data

The data matrix in Table 1.2 has two sides: a person side and an item side. When looking at the person side of the data, it can be noted that some persons have a higher sum score than others. For example, person 1 and person 3 have a sum score of 13 and 10, respectively, while person 2 and person 316 have a sum score of 1 and 6, respectively. The most likely general reason why the sum scores differ is that some people tend to be more verbally aggressive than others. Therefore, it seems reasonable to use the inventory as a measurement tool or test for the propensity to verbal aggression, and the sum score derived from the inventory as a measure of that propensity.

In general, tests are used for the measurement of individual-difference variables, and often the sum score or a transformation of the sum score is used as the measurement result. The test is a *measurement tool*, and its score is a so-called operational definition of the construct one wants to measure. Constructs are also called latent variables or latent traits. In the example, the construct is the propensity to verbal aggression.

Measurement is of interest for several reasons. The first reason we will consider is *evaluation* of the individual. Suppose, in our example, that we have experience and evidence that from a score of 25 on, people tend not to be able to control their verbal aggression. Someone with a score of 25 or higher may then be evaluated as too aggressive, and may therefore be given the recommendation to follow a course of training for self-control, and after the training a new evaluation could be made. In a similar way, educational achievement tests can be used to evaluate whether or not students have achieved what might be expected from a curriculum. The evaluation can be individual or collective (a class, a school, a district), and again some action may be recommended. A second reason is *prediction*. For example, suppose it is possible to predict interpersonal conflicts in a job on the basis of the verbal-aggression score. One could apply the test to obtain an expectation regarding interpersonal conflicts. In a similar way as an evaluation, a prediction can also lead to a recommendation and action. A third reason is *explanation*. If the measurement is made for reasons of explanation, one may want to correlate the measure to potential causal or consequential variables. For verbal aggression, two such causal factors could be Gender and Trait Anger. Perhaps Gender as such does not have a causal role, but its effect may stem from associated variables, possibly related to the learned roles of males and females in our society. Trait Anger is the tendency to feelings of anger, and it may be hypothesized that anger is an activating source of verbal aggression. An example of a consequential variable would be how much the person is liked by others. An explanation may be also the basis for a recommendation or action.

When we talk of 'explanation' as a possible reason for measurement, then this is accomplished with a two-step procedure, with measurement as a first step, followed by correlating derived test scores with external variables in a second step, in order to explain the test scores or to explain the external variable(s) from the test scores. Alternatively, a one-step procedure can be used, where the external variables are directly incorporated in the model to explain the data. The models we will discuss in this chapter are all based on a one-step procedure, with a direct modeling of the effect external variables have. When we refer to the 'explanatory' approach in this volume, a one-step procedure is what is meant.

1.3.1 Classical test theory

The traditional way of looking at test scores is through *classical test theory* (CTT, Lord & Novick, 1968). According to this theory, test scores result from the combination of a true score and an error term. The assumption is that the score we observe is partly due to an underlying latent variable, and partly due to an error term:

$$Y_{pu} = \theta_p + \varepsilon_{pu}, \tag{1.1}$$

where Y_{pu} represents the test score of person p $(p = 1, \ldots, P)$ on occasion u, an index for the occasions on which the person could be tested; θ_p represents the underlying latent trait for person p; and ε_{pu} represents the error term for person p on occasion u.

The error term ε_{pu} has an expected value of zero, is normally distributed and is unrelated to the true score: $E(\varepsilon_{pu}) = 0$, $\varepsilon_{pu} \sim N(0, \sigma_\varepsilon^2)$, and $\rho_{\varepsilon\theta} = 0$. As a result, the expected value of Y_{pu}, $E(Y_{pu})$, is θ_p. That is, in the long-run, one expects to observe an average score that equals the true score, but for particular observations, Y_{pu} is randomly distributed around θ_p with variance σ_ε^2. In the verbal aggression example, it is assumed that there is a true propensity for verbal aggression, which is denoted by θ_p, and that the observed sum score Y_{pu} is a reflection of this true score, except for an error term.

Note that relying on the sum score makes it sound like we are back in the single-observation context, but note that $Y_{pu} = \Sigma_i^I Y_{piu}$, which is the sum of the item scores Y_{piu}, $i = 1, \ldots, I$ on the occasion u – i.e., we have subsumed the repeated observations into a single score. This move allows one to apply all the 'usual suspects' in terms of statistical analysis. But it is also somewhat disturbing that the actual responses are not being analyzed – one might wonder what was lost in the process of reducing the data from a vector of responses for each person (i.e., the set of Y_{piu}) to a single score Y_{pu}.

Note also that the index u is not always used, because in fact there may be only one observation made for person p and item i. One can differentiate between Y_{pu} and $Y_{pu'} (u \neq u')$ only when more than one observation of Y_p is made. For reasons of simplicity we will from now on omit the index u for all observations, but conceptually the index has a necessary role.

1.3.2 Item analysis

Within the traditional CTT perspective, item analysis is a notable exception to the focus on the sum scores Y_p. Here the unmodeled Y_{pi} are investigated to check whether they are appropriate for a contribution to the measurement of the underlying construct. The traditional aspects of the results that one looks at are: the degree of difficulty (proportion correct, proportion of "yes" responses), item-total correlation (the correlation between the item and the sum score), and the coefficient of internal consistency. This last coefficient is an estimation of the reliability of the sum, for example, coefficient alpha, which is a lower bound for the reliability. Items with a negative correlation with the total score go against the general tendency of the test – those with a low correlation add little to the test. Such items are not good indicators of the construct and they affect the reliability of the test; they therefore are usually eliminated. Also items with extreme degrees of difficulty are less informative, and therefore are often eliminated. Apart from this quality check, items are commonly not of interest, and therefore not directly modeled.

None of the items in the verbal aggression data have extreme difficulty, or a low correlation with the total score. The correlations vary from .31 to .60. The internal consistency is rather high (Cronbach's $\alpha = .89$). There is no item with the property that when you eliminate it, you obtain a higher coefficient of internal consistency. Therefore, all items may be considered as reasonably good indicators of the verbal aggression tendency.

Whereas for test data the person side often predominates, in an experimental context, individual differences are not of interest as such, but only in an indirect way as something to be controlled for (as will be explained in the next paragraph), or when one has a hypothesis of individual differences in the effect of a manipulated factor. In longitudinal studies one is commonly interested in individual differences in the change rate and in other aspects of change and development.

1.4   The other side of the data – the item side

One can take a totally different view of the data than that described in the previous section. This is the view that is most commonly taken for experimental and longitudinal designs. From this other perspective one would look at the columns of the data matrix in order to investigate whether they relate to covariates of the repeated observations, such as manipulated factors in an experimental study, and time and time covariates in a longitudinal study. In our example this would mean that we want to find out what the effect is of Want vs Do, of Other-to-blame vs Self-to-blame, and of Behavior Type, or the behavioral features (Expressing and Blaming), without being much interested in the measurement of individuals. Thus the same data can be used for this other purpose, and consequently measurement concerns are not so important.

For test data we will call the covariates or design factors of the repeated observations *item predictors* because they refer to the items of the test. Item predictors either stem from an *a priori* item design, or they relate to an unplanned variation of the items. When the test is intentionally constructed on the basis of item properties, these properties and the way they are combined in items might be considered the elements of the 'test blueprint.' An example of unplanned variation would be variation based on properties derived from a post-hoc content analysis of the items in an extant test.

Table 1.1 shows the design of the example study in terms of *a priori* item properties. This design is the basis for looking at the item side of the data matrix in Table 1.2, in order to answer questions regarding the effect of the item properties. In the next paragraph, we note three patterns that can be observed on the item side of the matrix.

First, the means for wanting (the first 12 items) versus doing (the last 12 items) are .77 and .59, respectively. This makes sense because not all verbally aggressive tendencies (wanting) will be expressed (doing). Second, the mean item scores (over all persons) on the Other-to-blame and Self-to-blame subtests (composed of the items 1 to 6 and 13 to 18, and the items 7 to 12 and 19 to 24, respectively) are .84 and .52, respectively. These values make sense too, because when someone else is being the source of the frustration, this contributes more to anger feelings than when oneself is to blame.

Third, note that the means of the items for the two blaming behaviors (items 1, 2, 4, 5, 7, 8, etc.) versus the non-blaming behavior (items 3, 6, 9, etc.) are .81 and .41, respectively and the means for the two expressive behaviors (items 1, 3, 4, 6, 7, 9, etc) versus the non-expressive behavior (items 2, 5, 8, etc.) are .68 and .66, respectively. This means that cursing (blaming and expressive) is more common than scolding (blaming), while the latter is in turn more common than shouting (expressive). The larger mean for blaming is expected because blaming is an action tendency associated specifically with frustration and anger.

What one can learn from 'the other side' of the data matrix nicely complements what one can learn from the person side. The person side yields test scores and relations of these scores with other variables, from which we can infer possible sources of individual differences. The item side tells us about general effects that are independent of individual differences. For example, the quick look at means over sets of items carried out in the previous paragraph illustrated that (a) people inhibit their verbally aggressive tendencies to a certain degree, (b) verbal aggression occurs more often if others are to blame, and (c) blaming is a more likely response than expressing one's frustration, but the combination of both is the most frequent response. Even more could be learned if the interactions between the properties were also studied, but this is beyond the scope of what we want to explain in this chapter.

All these effects of item properties give us an idea about the factors that play in verbal aggression in general. Therefore, the combination of an analysis of the person side with an analysis of the item side can contribute to our understanding of the meaning of the test scores. This is an instantiation of how explanation is complementary to measurement.

1.5   A joint analysis of the two sides

Following the discussion above, we could carry out two relatively straight-forward analyses of the data. These are briefly explained in the paragraphs below to introduce the reasons why a joint analysis of the two sides (person plus item) is preferable.

First, we can derive scores for each individual on each design factor. For example, for the Behavior Mode design factor, we could compute a subscore for the want-items and another for the do-items, and then we can carry out a two-sample t-test to see if the two subscore means are significantly different. This is simplistic because the subscores are in fact correlated (i.e., they come from the same individuals), and this correlation is not taken into account in the t-test analysis. As a consequence, the faulty t-test would be conservative (assuming the correlation is positive). Taking into account the correlation of the subscores by applying a paired t-test means that one is taking into account systematic individual differences, which are the basis for the correlation. Without such individual differences and the correlations that follow from these, there would be no need for the one-sample t-test.

Second, we can derive the mean score per item over persons, so that 24 item means are obtained. These 24 item means can function as the dependent variable in a linear regression with the design factors as the predictors. This is also simplistic, since it assumes that there are no individual differences in the regression weights: in the slopes and/or the intercept. A better way of analyzing would be to allow for these individual differences.

Hence, a more appropriate way of approaching the data is a combined analysis, one that captures the individual differences, while still estimating and testing the effects of the item properties. If there were no reliable individual differences, then the two separate approaches just mentioned would be less problematic. However, it is quite plausible that when the repeated observations data come from different individuals, individual differences will occur. Another way of saying the same is that the data are likely to be *correlated data*. The structure of the data is called a *clustered* structure, with each person forming a cluster of data. All data from the same individual share a common source and are therefore considered as correlated. If one wants to have a model for the complete data, correlated data or repeated observations data with individual differences may not be dealt with from just the item side. In a similar way, if there are reliable differences between items, and one wants to have a model for the complete data, one may not look just at the person side – again both sides need to be considered.

However, for some purposes, one may have a restricted interest in just the person side of the data, for example, when sum scores are used to 'measure' a construct such as a trait or state of some kind (cognitive, personality). As will be explained in Chapter 4, there are also approaches that under certain conditions allow one to isolate the item side of the data matrix, in order to estimate and test the effects of item properties. These are the so-called marginal models. However, these approaches require either assumptions regarding the person side or a basis that prevents the person side from interfering with the estimates for the item side.

1.6   The linear regression perspective

1.6.1   Individual linear regressions

In order to develop the linear regression perspective while taking into account individual differences, let us assume we carry out a different individual regression analysis on *each* of the 316 persons. We will call this the *individual* regressions approach. As will be explained, this is not the best way to proceed, but we are discussing this method for illustrative purposes. This method has actually been used, for example, by Sternberg (1977, 1980) for the study of intelligence, to find out how much separate cognitive processes contribute to a person's response time. Each process was represented by an item property and the regression weights of these properties per individual were interpreted as the times used by the individuals to execute the different processes. In our example, for each individual there are 24 observations on the dependent variable, one for each item. The predictors in the regression are the design factors that are manipulated, the same design factors for all individuals: Behavior Type, Behavior Mode, and Situation Type. Because Behavior Type has three levels, technically it requires two predictors, so that in fact there will be four item predictors.

Suppose the predictors are defined as in Figure 1.1. The method of coding the predictors in Figure 1.1 is called *contrast coding*. Each predictor defines a contrast between the levels of a design factor, so that the sum of the weights over the levels is zero (e.g., 1/2, 1/2, -1). The alternatives to contrast coding are *dummy coding* and *effect coding*. For a discussion of the types of coding and an interpretation of the effects, see Cohen and Cohen (1983). The contrast coding we use is one with centering on the mean of all observations (of person p, because we follow an individual regressions approach). This means that the mean of each of the predictors is zero. This is so in our case because the number of observations is equal over the levels of a factor. For a discussion of centering, see Raudenbush and Bryk (2002). Note that two of the contrast predictors (Blaming and Expressing) are not independent.

For contrast coding with centering on the overall mean, the overall mean of the observations is the reference level that is used to define the effects. Because this basic level is incorporated in all estimated values of the observations for all combinations of predictors, one may consider this basic

Behavior Mode
predictor 1 $(X_{do-want})$ Do = 1   Want = −1

Situation Type
predictor 2 $(X_{other-self})$ Other-to-blame = 1   Self-to-blame = −1

Behavior Type
predictor 3 (X_{blame}) Curse, Scold = 1/2   Shout = −1
predictor 4 $(X_{express})$ Curse, Shout = 1/2   Scold = −1

FIGURE 1.1. Coding scheme for the item response predictors.

level as the effect that all items share. This is equivalent to saying that it is the effect of an additional predictor with a value of 1 for all items. We will call this predictor the *constant predictor*. The coding of all items according to their predictors, including the constant predictor, defines the *design matrix* X of items by predictors. Each row of the matrix represents an item, each column represents an item predictor (including the constant predictor), and each cell contains the value of the corresponding item on the corresponding predictor.

Note that we could have defined one more predictor: namely the specific situation (i.e., Bus or Train, Store or Call) nested within Situation Type. Not using this predictor means that the expected value of the observations is the same for the two situations within the same type, and that possible differences in the observed values are to be attributed to the error term.

For each single person p one can use the observations per item, Y_{pi} as the dependent variable, so that the regression equation for each person p reads as follows:

$Y_{pi} =$
$\mu_p X_{i\ constant}$ the overall mean for person p
$+$ plus the effect of
$\beta_{p\ do-want} X_{i\ do-want}$ Do vs Want for person p
$+\beta_{p\ other-self} X_{i\ other-self}$ Other-to-blame vs Self-to-blame for person p
$+\beta_{p\ blame} X_{i\ blame}$ Blaming vs not blaming for person p
$+\beta_{p\ express} X_{i\ express}$ Expressing vs not expressing for person p
$+$ plus
ε_{pi} an error term for person p and item i.

The Xs are the predictors. Their values are displayed in Figure 1.1, except for those of $X_{constant}$ (=1 for all items). The βs are the weights of the item predictors, and when multiplied with the corresponding X-value, they are the deviations from the overall mean created by the predictor value. The weight of the constant predictor is the overall mean μ_p.

We can write the above expression more compactly if we use an index k

for the different predictors above: $k = 0$ for the constant predictor, $k = 1$ for the do-want predictor, etc. The individual regression approach implies that a separate regression holds for each person:

$$Y_{pi} = \sum_{k=0}^{K} \beta_{pk} X_{ik} + \varepsilon_{pi}, \qquad (1.2)$$

with Y_{pi} as the observed response variable, functioning as the dependent variable;

$k, k = 0, \ldots, K$ as an index for the item predictors;

X_{ik} as the value of predictor k for item i, and $X_{i0} = 1$ for all values of i – predictor $k = 0$ is the constant predictor;

β_{pk} as the regression weight of predictor k for predicting the responses of person p;

β_{p0} is the intercept, $\beta_{p0} = \mu_p$ is the mean of the person (because of the centered contrast coding);

ε_{pi} as the error term for person p and item i.

It is assumed that ε_{pi} has an independent normal distribution with mean 0, and variance σ_ε^2, the same for all persons and items.

1.6.2   Results of individual regressions

The linear regressions for all of the individuals were calculated using the contrast coding just explained. The results for a few persons are shown in Table 1.3. For the first person, the multiple R turns out to be .58, and for the second person a multiple R of .42 is obtained. As can be seen, the regression weights and the constant seem to differ depending on the person (but see further for a discussion on this point).

Figure 1.2 shows the slopes of just one of the factors, Do vs Want, for all 316 persons. For each person, the mean of the do-items is shown on the right, and the mean for the want-items on the left. The difference is twice the regression weight. Figure 1.2 illustrates how this approach results in many regression lines, one for each person. As expected, most lines in Figure 1.2 decrease from left to right, because people tend to do less than they want. As noted earlier, there may be exceptions, and examples actually do occur in Figure 1.2, but the general trend is a decreasing one. It is difficult to tell just from an inspection of the figure whether the individuals differ in a reliable way as to their slope. One would like to have a technique that gave one guidance as to what constitutes important individual differences, and what does not.

Suppose for the argument, that the major difference between the persons is not the discrepancy between Do and Want, but the value of the intercept, and that the effects of the four predictors are actually fixed over persons. As we will see later, this is not an uncommon assumption. That there are individual differences in the intercept is nicely illustrated in Table 1.3, but

TABLE 1.3. Regression weights for each person in the sample (only a few are shown).

Predictor	Overall Mean (Constant)	Do vs Want	Other- vs Self- to-blame	Blaming	Expressing
Person 1	.54	-.29	-.21	.25	.42
Person 2	.04	-.04	.04	.08	.08
Person 3	.42	.08	.08	.00	.17
Person 4	.62	-.04	.04	.25	.25
...	...				
Person 13	.58	.00	.00	.67	.42
...	...				
Person 316	.25	.25	.08	-.08	.08

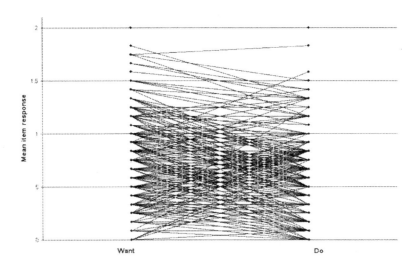

FIGURE 1.2. Slopes of Do vs Want for 316 persons.

the support for the assumption of equal slopes for all individuals is not evident from the same table nor from Figure 1.2, as some large individual differences appear. However, it is difficult to tell whether the variation reflects unreliable variation around a truly fixed slope, or reliable individual differences instead. This illustrates the need for an approach that goes beyond individual regressions.

1.6.3   An alternative: linear mixed models

There are three related problems with the approach of individual regressions. First, if one wants to derive the mean and the variance of the weights, a two-step procedure is required. The initial step is to carry out individual regression analyses, and the last step is to calculate the mean and variances of the weights. Second, one cannot incorporate simplifying assumptions regarding the variation of weights. These assumptions may stem from substantive theory, and can be used to test such a theory, for example a theory on the location of individual differences. The assumptions may also stem from statistical theory. For example, the assumption of normal distributions often provides a basis for standard statistical tests. Third, the individual regressions approach is not based on a joint model for the data, which is required if one is interested in joint probabilities of responses, and in associations between these responses. As a consequence, not all information in the data is used for the estimation.

The individual regressions as described above are actually only one of three alternatives. This first alternative was labeled *separate* regressions by Kreft and de Leeuw (1998). A second strategy that has been used is called the *total* or *pooled* regression approach by the same authors. This is where the data from all of the individuals are pooled together, and a single regression equation is estimated for all of the individuals in the data matrix. Thus, in our example, for the total regression, there is one regression equation and 316×24 observations of the dependent variable. Both the separate regressions and the total or pooled regression lack the perspective that persons may be sampled from a population.

There is a third regression approach, called the *random coefficients approach* by Kreft and de Leeuw (1998), where the regression weights depend on the person, and the persons are considered as sampled from a population. This is commonly called a *hierarchical* or *multilevel* regression approach. The modeling occurs at the different levels simultaneously: within and between persons. Under these circumstances, the regression weight at the individual level is called a *random coefficient* or random effect, sampled from the distribution that corresponds to the population the person is sampled from. The most common assumption is that the distribution is a normal distribution.

Models with a mixing of fixed effects (that do not vary over persons) and random effects (that do vary over persons) are called *mixed models*. When the mixed model is a linear model, it is then called a *linear mixed model* (LMM) (Verbeke & Molenberghs, 2000). The fixed effects are also population effects. They apply to the population average and to each individual separately. However, this feature may not be generalized to the category of generalized linear mixed models to be introduced later. This is stressed in Chapter 4. A description and discussion of the LMM is given in Section 1.6.4 and more extensively in Chapter 4. This model has the advantages of being a combined and simultaneous model for the two sides of the data matrix, and of allowing the combination of fixed and random effects. Because of this flexibility, it is the model we prefer to continue with at this point.

Note that one can reason in an analogous way for items as for persons, so that also for the items three approaches can be followed: (1) separate analyses for each item – i.e., set up a regression analysis for each of the 24 items separately, with 316 observations for each, and with predictors such as Gender and Trait Anger; (2) a total or pooled regression with the same two predictors; and (3) a linear mixed model with again the same two person predictors.

In its most general formulation both item predictors *and* person predictors may be included in a LMM. This is a very interesting line to pursue, but we will delay further elaboration until Chapter 2, in the context of generalized linear mixed models.

1.6.4   Formulation of the linear mixed model

The linear mixed model formulation resembles the formulation for the individual linear regression model in Equation 1.2, but now (1) a distinction is made between two kinds of predictors: predictors with fixed weights (fixed effects) and predictors with (individual-specific) random weights (random effects), and (2) a distribution is specified for the individual regression weights. Two different symbols are used for the predictors: X for predictors with a fixed effect, and Z for predictors with a random effect, and correspondingly two kinds of indices are needed: k for X, and j for Z.

The general formulation of a linear mixed model in *scalar notation* is the following:

$$Y_{pi} = \sum_{k=0}^{K} \beta_k X_{ik} + \sum_{j=0}^{J} \theta_{pj} Z_{ij} + \varepsilon_{pi}, \qquad (1.3)$$

with k $(k = 0, \ldots, K)$ as an index for predictors with a fixed effect;
j $(j = 0, \ldots, J)$ as an index for predictors with a random effect;
X_{ik} as the value of predictor k for item i (for $k = 0$, $X_{i0}=1$ for all i);
Z_{ij} as the value of predictor j for item i (for $j = 0$, $Z_{i0} = 1$ for all i);
β_k as the fixed regression weight of predictor k, an overall intercept for $k = 0$, and predictor-specific effects for $k = 1, \ldots, K$;
θ_{pj} as the random regression weight of predictor j for person p, a person-specific *intercept* for $j = 0$, and person-specific *slopes* for $j > 0$, jointly following a multivariate normal distribution (for a further specification, see below);
ε_{pi} as the error term for person p and item i (for a further specification, see below).
We assume here and in the following that, for each person, responses on

the same set of items are available. This is not a condition for the models to apply, but it largely simplifies the notation.

Regarding the notation and further specification, we note the following:

1. One can split a random effect into two parts: its mean and the deviation from that mean. The mean of the effects can be considered as a fixed effect, and the deviations from the mean as random effects, so that the mean of the random effects (i.e., the deviations) is zero. Also, a fixed effect can be considered a random effect with zero variance. Therefore, it is a conceptually interesting option to consider the X-set and the Z-set as equivalent, unless indicated differently. This is the option we have followed for general formulation purposes.

2. It is assumed that the *random effects* are each normally distributed: $\theta_{pj} \sim N(0, \sigma_j^2)$, and that jointly they follow a multivariate normal distribution $\boldsymbol{\theta}_p \sim N(\mathbf{0}, \boldsymbol{\Sigma})$, $\mathbf{0}$ denoting a vector of zeros, and $\boldsymbol{\Sigma}$ denoting the $J \times J$ covariance matrix of the random effects. The variance of the random intercepts is denoted by σ_0^2 (since $j = 0$) or σ_θ^2 if there are no other random effects. The common practice of fixing the mean of the random effects to zero is not really a restriction, because, as mentioned above, the mean itself can be included as a fixed effect.

3. It is assumed that the error terms, ε_{pi}, each follow a normal distribution with mean zero, and that jointly per person they follow a multivariate normal distribution, $\boldsymbol{\varepsilon}_p \sim N(\mathbf{0}, \boldsymbol{\Omega})$, $\mathbf{0}$ denoting a vector of zeros, and $\boldsymbol{\Omega}$ denoting a $I \times I$ covariance matrix, the same for all persons. It is commonly assumed that $\boldsymbol{\Omega}$ is diagonal, and very often also that all diagonal values are equal (i.e., σ_ε^2). The assumption that the error terms are not correlated from one item to another (i.e., $\boldsymbol{\Omega}$ being diagonal) is called *local item independence*.

4. As we have noted above, it is a convention in the literature on mixed models (e.g., Davidian & Giltinan, 1995; McCulloch & Searle, 2001; Verbeke & Molenberghs, 2000) to denote predictors with a fixed effect as Xs, and predictors with a random effect as Zs. Thus far, X and Z are presented as item predictors, but, in principle, their value may change with the persons as well. If the value of the predictors depends on the person, a subscript p needs to be added for the Xs and Zs in Equation 1.3. In Equation 1.3 we have denoted the corresponding effects by βs and θs. In the statistical literature, the random effects are commonly denoted by b, but we chose θ for reasons of conformity with the notation for item response models. The βs are overall fixed effects, whereas the θs vary at random over persons and therefore have a person subscript.

The formulation of a linear mixed model *in matrix notation* is the following:

$$\boldsymbol{Y}_p = \boldsymbol{X}\boldsymbol{\beta} + \boldsymbol{Z}\boldsymbol{\theta}_p + \boldsymbol{\varepsilon}_p, \tag{1.4}$$

where $\boldsymbol{Y}_p$ is an $I \times 1$ vector of observations Y_{pi};
$\boldsymbol{X}$ is an $I \times K$ matrix, the design matrix for the fixed effects;

β is a $K \times 1$ vector of fixed regression weights;

Z is an $I \times J$ matrix, the design matrix for random effects;

θ_p is a $J \times 1$ vector of random regression weights per person p;

and ε_p is an $I \times 1$ vector of error terms.

We have omitted the subscript p for X and Z, assuming for reasons of simplicity these matrices do not differ from person to person, but as mentioned, the more general formulation would be one with X_p and Z_p.

1.6.5 Application of the linear mixed model

A linear mixed model was tried out for the verbal aggression data with three response categories (0, 1, 2), including all four predictors from Figure 1.1 and the constant predictor (and making the common assumptions described in Section 1.6.4). These five predictors were used both as predictors with a fixed effect and as predictors with a random effect (as X and as $Z, k = 0, \ldots, 4; j = 0, \ldots, 4$). The results are displayed in Table 1.4.

TABLE 1.4. Results of the linear mixed model (verbal aggression data).

	Fixed effect (Mean effect)	Variance[a] of random effect	Correlation of random effects[b]			
			1	2	3	4
0. Constant	.68***	.13***		.45***	.26***	
1. Doing vs Wanting	-.09***	.02***				
2. Other-to-blame vs Self-to-blame	.16***	.02***				
3. Blaming behavior	.37***	.09***				
4. Expressing behavior	.20***	.05***		-.20*	.57***	

Note a: The significance of the variance is tested with a Wald test, which is conservative because the variance has a lower bound of zero. For a discussion of this issue, see Chapter 2 and Verbeke and Molenberghs (2000).
Note b: Only significant correlations are shown.
*: p<.05, **: p<.01; ***: p<.001.

All predictors seem to have a significant effect. The mean is significantly different from zero (.68). People want to be more verbally aggressive than they say they would actually be (-.09). They tend to be more verbally aggressive when someone else is to blame (.16), when the behavior one considers is of a blaming kind (.37), and when it is of an expressive kind (.20). Note that the effects of the orthogonal design factors equal half of the differences between the means reported in Section 1.4. The effect of all four predictors seems to vary over persons. The largest variance is found for the intercept. This variation reflects the overall level of the tendency to be verbally aggressive. Further, some people show a larger discrepancy between doing and wanting than others do (variance of .02), and some people are more sensitive than others to other-to-blame situations (variance of .02) and finally, some people tend to blame and express more than others (variances of .09 and .05, respectively).

Some of the random effects are correlated to other random effects. First, the general tendency to be verbally aggressive (the random intercept) is positively correlated with a verbally aggressive sensitivity to situations where others are to be blamed for (.45), and also with the tendency for blaming others (.26). Second, being expressive in one's verbal aggression is positively correlated with blaming as a reaction (.57), and is negatively correlated with the verbally aggressive sensitivity to situations others are to be blamed for (-.20). In other words, the two behavior styles (blaming and expressing one's frustration) are positively correlated, but they are differentiated in terms of their other correlates. The blaming style goes with the general tendency to be verbally aggressive, but the expressive style does not, and is associated instead with a sensitivity for situations where one is one's own source of frustration (based on the negative correlation).

It is remarkable that all effects vary over persons, which implies that the data are five-dimensional in terms of individual differences. However, remember that the data are ordered-category data with only three categories, which is far from being continuous data. In a linear mixed model, the data are treated as if they were continuous, so that we may not really trust the outcome of the analysis (but see Chapter 10 for similar results when the data are treated as categorical). This application was only meant to be illustrative of a model that, albeit inappropriate for our data, can be generalized to deal with categorical data (see Section 1.7).

1.6.6   Multilevel modeling

As mentioned above, the structure of the linear mixed model is in fact a multilevel structure (see also Chapter 5). The levels refer to levels of nested clusters. In the context of the verbal aggression data, the lowest-level clusters are the pairs of persons and items. For these data, there is only one observation per cluster. It is typical of test data that only one observation is made for each pair of a person and an item. The second level of clustering is the persons. Each person is a cluster, or in other words, each person is a grouping of the observations for the various items. In other applications, clusters of persons can also occur (i.e., schools, regions; see Chapter 5).

Each level has its own clusters and because these clusters may induce variation between observations, each level also has its own sources of variation. Take the example of a linear mixed model for the verbal aggression data, with only the intercept as a random effect (θ_{p0}) but no random slopes (i.e., $\sigma_j^2 = 0$ for $j > 0$). On the within-person level there are two sources of variation: the error term, ε_{pi}, which is a source of random variation, and the effect of the item predictors, β_k, a source of fixed variation, the same for all individuals. On the person level the intercept, θ_{p0}, is a source of random variation, and when Gender and Trait Anger are included as person predictors, then there are also sources of fixed variation at the level of the persons. The level above the persons, the population they belong to, is not a source of variation. It could be, if the study were to be repeated with various groups. In total, there are two sources of random variation and two sources of variation due to fixed effects. The sources of random variation are the error term and the random intercept, and they each play on a different level. The error term ε_{pi} represents the unexplained variation at the within-person level, whereas the random intercept represents the unexplained variation at the person level. The two sources of fixed variation are the item predictors and the person predictors (each with fixed effects).

It is typical of multilevel models that different levels are taken into account, and that the effects can be tied to specific levels. If one wants to disentangle the components of variance that correspond to the effects and to the different levels, one is required to build a model with a correct specification of the effects on the different levels, and to estimate the model at all levels simultaneously in order to avoid confounding one level with another. Linear mixed modeling addresses the issues of multilevel modeling; in fact, it is a specific type of multilevel modeling. For the link between multilevel modeling and mixed models, see among others Goldstein (2003), Longford (1993), Raudenbush and Bryk (2002), and Snijders and Bosker (1999).

1.6.7 Analysis of variance

Linear mixed models can be seen as a generalization of a common model for the analysis of variance. When the intercept is the only random effect, as suggested earlier in the example, the resulting model is the same as one that is used in the traditional analysis of variance (ANOVA) procedure for repeated observations under the assumption of *compound symmetry*.[2] The compound symmetry model is the standard model for repeated observations ANOVA (Davis, 2002), and is formally designed for observations on continuous variables rather than the categorical observations under consideration here. The model has the important assumption of a homogeneous covariance structure: equal variances for all items, and equal correlations between all items (between all repeated observations).

This can be understood as follows. The variance per item (repeated observations) is simply the sum of the random-intercepts variance and the error variance, and therefore it is equal for all items (repeated observations): $\sigma_\varepsilon^2 + \sigma_\theta^2$. Since all items (repeated observations) share the random-

---

[2]In fact, sphericity rather than compound symmetry is the more general condition for the F tests of the repeated observations ANOVA model to be valid, but Davis (2002) and Wallenstein (1982) conclude that it is hard to imagine that the sphericity condition would be met but not the compound symmetry condition, so that in practice the required assumption is compound symmetry.

intercepts value and have an independent error term with equal variances, the correlation is equal for all pairs of items (repeated observations). The expected correlation between items i and i' is the ratio of the random-intercepts variance divided by the sum of this variance and the error variance: $\rho_{ii'} = \sigma_\theta^2/(\sigma_\theta^2 + \sigma_\varepsilon^2)$, as in the formula of the reliability coefficient.

Because of the assumptions of equal variance and equal correlation, this model is quite restrictive. We will see that the analogue of compound symmetry is also used in some of the item response models to be explained later, for example in the Rasch model and all other models of Chapter 2. It is remarkable that these models, which are often considered as too restrictive, are in this respect equivalent with a common practice in the analysis of variance. In contrast with its random-intercepts variant, the most general formulation of the linear mixed model implies a high flexibility, one that can overcome the limitations of the classical repeated observations ANOVA model. This is because not just the intercept but also other regression weights can be defined to be random effects, each with their own variance and with an unrestricted joint covariance structure. As will be discussed, there are also item response models with the same flexibility.

1.6.8 Two points of view

Note that an analysis along the lines described above in the description of repeated observations ANOVA does not require an estimation of the individual intercepts or any interest in the individual differences. For example, from an experimental point of view, one is interested in the effects of the manipulated factors, and not in the individual differences. The only reference to individual differences is that the correlation of the items (because of repeated observations) is taken into account in the analysis of variance, in order to obtain a more appropriate confidence interval and a (often more powerful) significance test of the effect. The approach can be used in a way that is free of any measurement of individual differences, or, we might say as a 'measurement-free' approach, notwithstanding the recognition that these differences exist and play a role in testing the significance of the effects.

The other point of view is where one concentrates precisely on individual differences and the measurement of individuals. It is possible to estimate the random intercept for each person, for example, in order to relate the intercepts to an external variable. When contrast coding with centering on the overall mean is used for the predictors, then the estimation of the random intercept is analogous to the estimation of the true score in classical test theory. In the example, the random intercept is an indicator of the overall tendency to react with verbal aggression, something one might be interested in measuring for any number of reasons.

From a measurement point of view, the advantage of combining the measurement of individuals with estimating the effects of the design factors is that one is informed about the design factors that affect the variable one is measuring. Knowledge of these effects contributes to the interpretation of one's measurements, and may be seen as the basis for internal construct validity (Embretson, 1983; Wilson, 2005). From a general research point of view, the combination of both is an opportunity to understand the data and the phenomena that at play, and to test theories about these phenomena, while integrating the two main paradigms Cronbach (1957) has described for research in psychology: the experimental paradigm and the correlational paradigm (Wilson & Adams, 1992).

1.7   Modeling binary data

Thus far we have treated the example data as though they were continuous. However, they are not, since they are in fact ordered-category data. The linear mixed model cannot be applied to categorical data, because the linear model has a continuous error term that requires continuous outcomes and, hence, does not respect the boundaries of a categorical variable. However, it is possible to generalize the linear model to one that can handle categorical data. In order to illustrate this, we will discuss the case of binary data as the simplest type of categorical data. As will be shown in Chapter 3, the extension to multiple categories is not very difficult.

Although a general formulation of the linear mixed model was given earlier in this chapter, we will continue here with the *random-intercepts model* (the one that corresponds to the classical repeated observations ANOVA model). The reason for this limitation is not only didactical, but also it will turn out that the first item response models we want to discuss (in Chapter 2) are also random-intercepts models. In the following we will stick for a while to the random-intercepts case:

$$Y_{pi} = \sum_{k=0}^{K} \beta_k X_{ik} + \theta_{p0} Z_{i0} + \varepsilon_{pi}. \tag{1.5}$$

The model in Equation 1.5 has multiple fixed slopes ($\beta_1, \ldots, \beta_k, \ldots, \beta_K$), an overall intercept β_0, and a random deviation from the overall intercept (θ_{p0}). This model is the starting point to introduce models for categorical data, and, in particular, to introduce item response models.

1.7.1   The linear random-intercepts model as an underlying model for binary data

In this section, we give a heuristic argument that illustrates how to extend the LMM to a more general model that deals with categorical data. Readers familiar with this argument, which is built upon Lord and Novick's (1968) discussion (see also Thissen and Orlando, 2001) or who wish to proceed to the general formulation, may skip to the next section. A similar argument is developed in Chapter 3.

Suppose that the binary data Y_{pi} stemmed from the dichotomization of a continuous covert variable, denoted as V_{pi}. Then we could use the model of Equation 1.5 for this V_{pi}, which after dichotomization yields Y_{pi}. A model for the binary variable Y_{pi} implies that the probability that $Y_{pi} = 1$, denoted by π_{pi}, can be derived from the distribution of V_{pi} in some way. The reasoning behind a common way to think of π_{pi} is as follows:

1. Assuming that V_{pi} follows Equation 1.5, implies the assumption that V_{pi} is normally distributed. Let us denote the mean, the expected value of V_{pi}, as η_{pi}. The variance, σ_ε^2, is equal for all pairs (p, i). The dichotomization is realized by the use of a cut-off value c, defined so that $Y_{pi} = 1$ if $V_{pi} > c$, $Y_{pi} = 0$ otherwise. The probability that $Y_{pi} = 1$, π_{pi}, is determined as $\Pr(V_{pi} > c)$. Figure 1.3a gives a graphical representation of this idea for person 1 and item i, where $g(\cdot)$ denotes a density function. In a similar way Figure 1.3b shows the distributions for three pairs (persons 1, 2, and 3, paired with item i), with dotted lines for the distributions of the two added pairs. For $(2, i)$ the distribution is located somewhat more to the left $(\eta_{2i} < \eta_{1i})$ and for $(3, i)$, the distribution is located somewhat more to the right $(\eta_{1i} < \eta_{3i})$. One can easily see that the probability of a one increases from $p = 2$ to $p = 1$ to $p = 3$, or $\pi_{2i} < \pi_{1i} < \pi_{3i}$.

2. To determine the probability that $Y_{pi} = 1$, we need to specify values for σ_ε^2 and c. However, the choice of an origin and unit for the continuum on which the V_{pi} vary is without consequences. This means that the cut-off value and the means are identified only up to a linear transformation. The value of π_{pi} is invariant under linear transformations of the V-scale. Therefore, we can choose $c = 0$, and $\sigma_\varepsilon^2 = 1$. See Figure 1.3c for an illustration of a linear transformation. In fact, only the location has changed (from $\eta_{1i} = 0$ to $c = 0$) but in principle also the widths of the distributions would change if we had not started with $\sigma_\varepsilon = 1$ in the top left-hand panel. Thus, one interpretation of π_{pi} is the probability that the value of 0 is exceeded under the normal distribution of V_{pi} with mean η_{pi} and $\sigma_\varepsilon^2 = 1$.

3. The cut-off value $c = 0$ corresponds with a value of $-\eta_{pi}$ under the standard normal distribution (i.e., $(0 - \eta_{pi})/1$). This means that under this distribution, the cumulative probability of $-\eta_{pi}$ is $(1 - \pi_{pi})$, so that under the same distribution the cumulative probability of η_{pi} is π_{pi}.

It follows from the argument above that the cumulative normal distribution function, also called the standard *normal-ogive* function, maps η_{pi} into π_{pi} and that the inverse function maps π_{pi} into η_{pi}. As a consequence, we can transform π_{pi} into η_{pi} in order to obtain the mean of the hypothetical underlying V_{pi}. The function for this latter mapping is the probit link function, $\eta_{pi} = f_{\text{probit}}(\pi_{pi})$. It is the inverse of the normal-ogive function $\pi_{pi} = f_{\text{probit}}^{-1}(\eta_{pi})$, shown in Figure 1.3d. Note that the normal-ogive func-

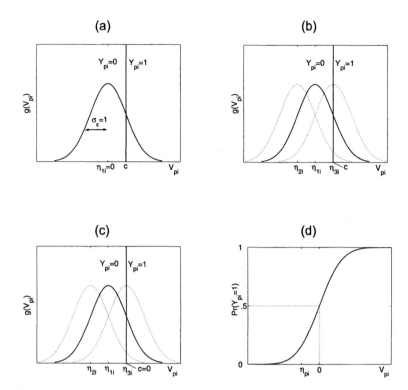

FIGURE 1.3. Illustrations of the distribution of V_{pi}. The four panels are denoted by 1.3a, 1.3b, 1.3c (densities) and 1.3d (cumulative).

tion as used does not imply a normal distribution of the persons, but only a normally distributed V_{pi} (and ε_{pi}) for each given pair of a person p and item i (Lord & Novick, 1968; Thissen & Orlando, 2001).

1.7.2 The normal-ogive random-intercepts model for binary data

The previous line of reasoning implies two kinds of variables: the binary variable Y_{pi} and the continuous variable V_{pi}. For the latter, Equation 1.5 is used (substituting V_{pi} for the continuous Y_{pi} in that equation for the linear model):

$$V_{pi} = \sum_{k=0}^{K} \beta_k X_{ik} + \theta_{p0} Z_{i0} + \varepsilon_{pi}, \qquad (1.6)$$

and $Y_{pi} = 1$ if $V_{pi} > 0$, $Y_{pi} = 0$ otherwise.

From the dichotomization and the independence of the error terms, it follows (a) that Y_{pi} has an independent Bernoulli distribution with mean

π_{pi} and variance $\pi_{pi}(1 - \pi_{pi})$, and (b) that Equation 1.6 without the error term ε_{pi} is a model for η_{pi} and thus for $f_{\text{probit}}(\pi_{pi})$:

$$\eta_{pi} = \sum_{k=0}^{K} \beta_k X_{ik} + \theta_{p0} Z_{i0}, \tag{1.7}$$

with $\theta_{p0} \sim N(0, \sigma_\theta^2)$. Thus, $\pi_{pi} = f_{\text{probit}}^{-1}(\sum_{k=0}^{K} \beta_k X_{ik} + \theta_{p0} Z_{i0})$. By convention we do not show the conditional nature of π_{pi} and η_{pi} (conditional on θ_{p0}, also not in the following when π_{pi} and η_{pi} may be defined conditionally on other random variables).

This, then, is the *normal-ogive random-intercepts model*. The model has three components: the first to connect Y_{pi} to π_{pi}, the second to connect π_{pi} to η_{pi}, and the third to connect η_{pi} to the Xs and Z_0.

First, the component that relates Y_{pi} to π_{pi} is the *distributional* or *random component*. Formally, $Y_{pi} \sim \text{Bernoulli}(\pi_{pi})$, and all Y_{pi}s are independent. Remember that π_{pi} is the probability of $Y_{pi} = 1$ given θ_{p0}. Figure 1.4 gives a graphical representation of the random component. This figure and the following two are pieces of a larger representation that will be introduced at the end of this section. The wiggly line symbolizes the distribution of Y_{pi} given π_{pi}. Dotted circles (or ellipses) represent random variables (including effect parameters) and elements that are a function of these such as π_{pi} and η_{pi}.

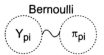

FIGURE 1.4. The random component.

Second, the component that links the expected value of the binary observations, π_{pi}, to the expected value of the underlying continuous variable, η_{pi}, is the *probit link function*. Formally, $\eta_{pi} = f_{\text{probit}}(\pi_{pi})$. Figure 1.5 gives a graphical representation of the link function.

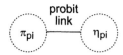

FIGURE 1.5. The link function.

Third, the component that links η_{pi}, the expected value of the underlying continuous variable, to the predictors, Xs and Z_0, is the *systematic component*. Formally,

$$\eta_{pi} = \sum_{k=0}^{K} \beta_k X_{ik} + \theta_{p0} Z_{i0}. \tag{1.8}$$

The function value, η_{pi}, is called the *linear predictor* of Y_{pi} in the statistical literature. Since in this volume we will often use the term 'predictor' for the Xs and Zs, this statistical terminology could be confusing, and hence we will use the term *linear component*. Figure 1.6 gives a graphical representation of the linear component.

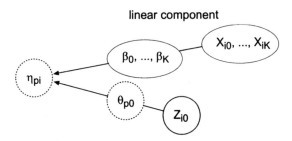

FIGURE 1.6. Graphical representation of the linear component.

The arrows in Figure 1.6 represent the linear effects of the predictors, and the circle and the ellipse on the arrows represent the size of the effects. As can be seen, θ_{p0} is represented with a dotted circle, in agreement with the convention that was made earlier regarding random effects. The Xs and Z_0, and the βs have fixed values (known and unknown, respectively); they are not random variables, and hence they are represented within a solid line. Together, Figures 1.4, 1.5, 1.6 define the elements of the more complex Figure 1.7 that represents the whole normal-ogive random-intercepts model with its three components. This kind of graphical representation will also be used in many of the following chapters, but not in all. For some of the models we will discuss the graphical representation would be too complicated for what it illustrates.

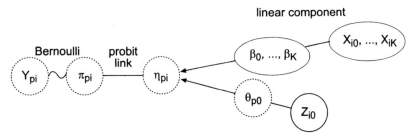

FIGURE 1.7. Graphical representation of the normal-ogive random-intercepts model.

Without the independence assumption, the variance of the observations may be larger or smaller than what can be expected on the basis of independent Bernoulli distributions. In case of positive dependence, the variance will be larger, and in case of negative dependence, it will be smaller. When the variance is larger than $\pi_{pi}(1 - \pi_{pi})$, it is called *overdispersion*. Overdispersion stems from neglected sources of variance and therefore from neglected predictors or random effects. Overdispersion is a sign that the model is incomplete. For a further explanation, see Section 1.7.4.

1.7.3   The logistic random-intercepts model

A popular alternative for the probit link is the *logit link*: $\eta_{pi} = f_{\text{logit}}(\pi_{pi})$, or $\eta_{pi} = \log(\pi_{pi}/(1 - \pi_{pi}))$. The function value of $f_{\text{logit}}(\cdot)$ is the natural logarithm of (in this chapter) the probability of a 1-response divided by the probability of a 0-response. This function leads to a value that, when multiplied by 1.7, approximates the result of the probit link quite well: $1.7 f_{\text{logit}}(\pi_{pi}) \approx f_{\text{probit}}(\pi_{pi})$ (Birnbaum, 1968; Camilli, 1994).

The logistic model is no longer based on an underlying *normally* distributed error term, ε_{pi}. The error term is now a *logistic error term*. Its distribution has a larger variance and somewhat heavier tails than the standard normal distribution. For the best approximation of the standard normal distribution, one should divide by 1.7 which implies that the effects are multiplied by 1.7. This explains the multiplicative factor.

The popularity of the logit link is based on the fact that it is the canonical link for the binomial (and Bernoulli) distribution, while the probit link is not (see Chapter 4 for an explanation of the canonical link). The logit link has a very simple mathematical form, the logarithm of the odds, and is also easy to interpret. A discordant feature is that the logistic model with random effects involves two different kinds of distributions: the logistic distribution for the error term, ε_{pi}, and the normal distribution for the person random effects, θ_{p0}.

The resulting model is the *logistic random-intercepts model*. It differs from the normal-ogive model only because it has a different link function, which has consequences for the error term of the hypothetical underlying continuous variable.

1.7.4   Scaling issues

The normal-ogive and the logistic models are scaled in a particular way. The fixed effects (βs) and the variance of the random effect (σ_θ^2) are expressed relative to σ_ε (to σ_ε^2 in case of σ_θ^2), the standard deviation of the error term of the hypothetical underlying continuous variable. Because of the hypothetical nature of this continuous variable, the value of σ_ε is fixed to a value that is determined by convention (see Section 1.7.1).

A first consequence of this relative way of expressing effects is that a different convention leads to a different scale for the effects. This explains the multiplicative factor to approximate the normal-ogive effect values from a logistic model. One can see the logistic model as one with a different convention (a larger σ_ε).[3] When the effects are expressed relative to a larger σ_ε, then they are of course expressed in smaller values.

A second consequence of this relative way of expressing effects is that the scale is reduced when a source of variation is not included in the model. Such non-included effects become part of the error term. Since σ_ε has a fixed value by convention, the effects that are included will be expressed through reduced values. This is for example the case for the fixed effects when the random intercepts are not included. The reduction factor is not easy to determine, but for the logistic random-intercepts model it is known to be $15\pi/16\sqrt{3}$ or 1.7 (divide by 1.7 to obtain the reduced values) (see Chapter 4).

1.7.5   Item response models

The normal-ogive random-intercepts model and its logistic variant are in fact two well-known item response models. This can be seen from the following:

1. The random intercept, $\theta_{p0}Z_{i0}$ from Equation 1.5, corresponds to the *person parameter*, often denoted as θ_p, and often called 'ability.'

2. When the item predictors are dummy variables meant to identify the items ($X_{ik} = 1$ if $i = k$, and $X_{ik} = 0$ if $i \neq k$), then the fixed effects, the $\Sigma_k^K \beta_k X_{ik}$ term from Equation 1.5, corresponds to the *item parameter*, further denoted as β_i ($\Sigma_k^K \beta_k X_{ik} = -\beta_i$), and often called 'item difficulty.' It is a convention that a negative sign is used for β_i:

$$\eta_{pi} = \theta_p - \beta_i, \qquad (1.9)$$

so that π_{pi} depends on the difference between θ_p and β_i, the difference between the person's 'ability' θ_p and the item's 'difficulty' β_i. Because $K = I$ item predictors are used for I items, the constant predictor must be omitted to render the model identifiable.

3. The normal ogive in Figure 1.3d was constructed to map (for a varying error term) V_{pi} into π_{pi} for a given value of θ_p (for the particular value chosen in Figure 1.3d, $\eta_{pi} < 0$). However, when θ_p increases so that η_{pi} becomes 0, then, following Equation 1.9, θ_p would be equal to β_i. Thus, β_i is the point on the scale that indicates the value of θ_p for which $\eta_{pi} = 0$,

---

[3]The standard logistic distribution, with mean 0 and scale parameter 1, is the distribution used for the logistic error term. It has a variance of $\pi^2/3$ or 3.29. However, the best approximation of the standard normal distribution is not obtained dividing by $\pi/\sqrt{3}$ but by $(15/16)(\pi/\sqrt{3})$ or 1.7.

and hence, $\pi_{pi} = .5$. The curve that maps θ_p into π_{pi} for a given β_i is shown in Figure 1.8 for the logistic model. A curve that maps θ_p into π_{pi} for a given item is called an *item characteristic curve* (ICC), or *item response function* (IRF). The value of β_i locates the curve. Depending on the value of β_i, the IRF is located more to the left or more to the right. The underlying continuum is the common continuum for θ, β, and the V_{pi}, but in the IRF, θ_p, not V_{pi}, is mapped into π_{pi} for a given value of β_i.

4. For the logistic model, the IRF is different from a corresponding normal-ogive model because of the different link function. The main difference is that the logistic IRF is less steep, because of the larger variance σ_ε^2.

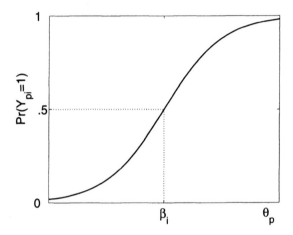

FIGURE 1.8. Item response function for the logistic random-intercepts model.

The resulting item response models are one-parameter item response models: the Rasch model when a logit link is used, and its normal-ogive equivalent (with 'uniform slope') if the probit link is used. They are called one-parameter models because the items have only one parameter each: the fixed effect of the corresponding item indicator. The one-parameter models differ from the two-parameter models and the three-parameter models in that the latter require two or three item parameters, respectively, to describe the IRF. In the two-parameter models, an item-specific weight is used for the random intercepts so that the slope of the IRF depends on the item, and in the three-parameter model, in addition the lower asymptote of the IRF depends on the item.

For an orientation in the literature of item response models (since 1990), one can consult one or more of the following publications: Bond and Fox (2001) (introductory) and Fischer and Molenaar (1995) for the Rasch model, and, for item response models beyond the Rasch model, see Baker (1992), Bock (1997), Boomsma, van Dijn, and Snijders (2001), Embretson and

Reise (2000), Hambleton, Swaminathan, and Rogers (1991), McDonald (1999), Thissen and Wainer (2001), and van der Linden and Hambleton (1997). They differ in generality and technicality, and in the variety of what they offer. For the combination of a broad overview and an in-depth discussion, the edited books by Fischer and Molenaar (1995) and van der Linden and Hambleton (1997) are to be recommended.

1.8 Generalized linear mixed models

Models that require a transformation in the form of a link function before the observations are related to predictors through a linear function are called *generalized linear models* (GLM) (McCullagh & Nelder, 1989). They are 'generalized' because the freedom of a transformation is allowed before the linear function applies. If such a model includes one or more random effects, it is called a generalized linear *mixed* model (GLMM) (Breslow & Clayton, 1993; Fahrmeir & Tutz, 2001; McCulloch & Searle, 2001).

The GLMMs are a broad category of models, of which the random intercepts probit and logit models are just two instances. Other functions may be considered for the link function, and other parameters besides the intercept may be random instead of fixed. It was only for didactic reasons and to prepare for Chapter 2 that we have concentrated on random-intercepts models. The item response models that will be discussed in the next chapter are also random-intercept models, and therefore GLMMs, but in later chapters many other item response models will be discussed from a GLMM perspective. For a similar view, see Mellenbergh's (1994) generalized linear item response theory (GLIRT) and the generalized latent trait models proposed by Moustaki and Knott (2000). A similar approach is described for a multilevel context by Goldstein (2003), Kamata (2001), Raudenbush and Bryk (2002), and Snijders and Bosker (1999). For an introductory presentation of GLMMs in a context of repeated observations similar to the context of item response models, see Agresti, Booth, Hobert, and Caffo (2000).

All generalized linear mixed models have three components, just as for the random-intercepts models which are a special case of a GLMM.

1. The *random component* describes the distribution function of Y_{pi} with μ_{pi} as the mean of the distribution (μ_{pi} is conditional on the random effects). In the models for binary data the independent Bernoulli distribution is used when only one observation is made for each pair of p and i. In that case $\mu_{pi} = \pi_{pi}$. The Bernoulli distribution is a binomial distribution with $n = 1$. When more than one observation is made per pair of p and i, the binomial distribution applies, with n equal to the number of observations. For count data, the Poisson distribution is appropriate. If Y_{pi} is a continuous variable, then one can, in principle, again make use of the normal

distribution for the error term. When $Y_{pi} = \mu_{pi} + \varepsilon_{pi}$, with ε_{pi} being normally distributed, the Y_{pi} are called Gaussian outcomes. Binary data are clearly not Gaussian outcomes.

2. The *link function* connects the expected value of the observed variable to the linear component η_{pi}, $\eta_{pi} = f_{\text{link}}(\mu_{pi})$, with $f_{\text{link}}(\cdot)$ as the link function. Thus far we have encountered two link functions: the probit link and the logit link, yielding normal-ogive models and logistic models, respectively, but also other links are possible. For example, for count data, a logarithmic link is commonly used.

3. The *linear component* defines η_{pi} as a linear function of the predictors, the Xs and Zs. In mixed models there are two types of predictors: those with a fixed weight (the Xs) and those with a random weight (the Zs). The general formulation of the linear component of a GLMM can be written as:

$$\eta_{pi} = \sum_{k=0}^{K} \beta_k X_{ik} + \sum_{j=0}^{J} \theta_{pj} Z_{ij}, \qquad (1.10)$$

with a multivariate normal distribution for the θs and means equal to zero and a covariance matrix Σ: $\boldsymbol{\theta}_p \sim N(\mathbf{0}, \boldsymbol{\Sigma})$. In *matrix notation* this is:

$$\boldsymbol{\eta}_p = \mathbf{X}\boldsymbol{\beta} + \mathbf{Z}\boldsymbol{\theta}_p. \qquad (1.11)$$

See Equations 1.3 and 1.4 for similarities with Equations 1.10 and 1.11, and Section 1.6.3 for an explanation of the right-hand side matrices and vectors of Equation 1.11. The error does not appear in Equations 1.10 and 1.11, because they are expressions for expected values. Again the subscripts p are omitted for X_{ik} and $\mathbf{X}$, Z_{ij} and $\mathbf{Z}$, without excluding they can depend on p.

As has been foreshadowed in this chapter, later chapters will see alterations on the basic pattern of the random-intercepts models. We will also go one step further and also present models that go beyond the GLMM framework, because they cannot be formulated with a linear component, but require a nonlinear component instead, for example, item response models with item discriminations (Birnbaum, 1968). Models of this type are called nonlinear mixed models (NLMM) (e.g., Davidian & Giltinan, 1995; Vonesh & Chinchilli, 1997). When the nonlinear aspect of a model stems from the link function, as in a GLMM, the model is called 'generalized linear' (GLMM), but when the nonlinearity stems from η_{pi} not being linear in the parameters, it is no longer called 'generalized linear,' but rather 'nonlinear' (NLMM). A nonlinear component is then substituted for the linear component.

A description of a general framework for item response models as illustrations of GLMMs and NLMMs is given by Rijmen, Tuerlinckx, De Boeck, and Kuppens (2003). The features of a GLMM can be graphically represented as in Figure 1.9. The graphical representation shows the three parts of the model, from the left to the right: the random component (denoted with the wiggly line) connecting Y_{pi} and μ_{pi} through a distribution function of some kind; the link function (denoted with a straight line) connecting μ_{pi} to η_{pi}; and finally the linear component, connecting η_{pi} to its linear predictor sets X and Z, through β_k's and θ_{pj}'s, respectively. As can be seen, the general formulation includes a random intercept as well as random slopes (since $j = 0, .., J$).

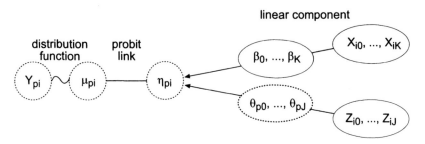

FIGURE 1.9. Graphical representation of a GLMM.

1.9   Philosophical orientation

The approach that we have adopted throughout this volume, and the one that has motivated the introduction in the previous sections of this chapter, is based on a certain philosophical position regarding the relationship between the disciplines of measurement and statistics. On the one hand, there is a long history of statistical methods being used as a basis to test hypotheses in social sciences. Almost invariably, these hypotheses relate to general effects of design factors one is interested in because of theoretical or exploratory reasons, as in experimental psychology. The statistical analysis that is being conducted under this perspective we have labeled *explanatory analysis*, because the principal aim is to explain the dependent variable on the basis of the design factors under consideration. Of course, from a more general view, one might call this an instantiation of 'data analysis' or 'statistical modeling.' On the other hand, there is another perspective, also with a long history, that aims instead to measure individuals (and, consequently, items) on one or more constructs (or latent variables), which are sometimes theoretically derived, sometimes not. Here the purpose of using the measures is very often descriptive, in order to assign numbers to the persons (and the items), and only in a next step explanation is considered, if at all. In the introduction, we have mentioned prediction and evaluation in the next step as alternative reasons to measure. The measurement that is being conducted in this perspective will be labeled *descriptive measurement*, even when meant for explanation, prediction or evaluation in the next step. In many cases when we need to know an individual's measure, the measure is used as the basis for some action regarding that individual, based on an explanation, prediction, or evaluation.

Under the perspective of an *explanatory* analysis (but not for a descriptive measurement), one might prefer to ignore the individual differences that are the traditional target of measurement, and historically this has been common. However, there are well-established reasons why one should not, hence, one should seek to control for individual differences. On the contrary, under the perspective of descriptive measurement, measuring individual differences is the prime objective of the effort, without any necessary interest in systematic effects that may explain the observations. On the surface, the two perspectives seem to be in conflict, but in fact they can be combined into what we will call *explanatory measurement*.

Our thesis is that a common core of statistical models can be used under either or both of these perspectives, as well as under their combination. With item response models being framed within the broad family of GLMMs and NLMMs, these models can be used either primarily for explanatory analysis, or primarily for descriptive measurement, or for both – i.e., for 'explanatory measurement' – depending on one's theoretical and practical research purposes. For example, for many practical purposes descriptive measurement suffices, and for many theory-testing purposes, an explanatory analysis suffices. But we believe that for both kinds of purposes, explanatory measurement can provide important improvements – this will be explicated in Chapter 2 and the chapters that follow.

1.10   Exercises

1. Sternberg (1977) uses response times for verbal analogy problems as a dependent variable. The analogy problems have a format such as 'A relates to B as C to ?.' The response times seem to increase linearly with the number of feature differences between A and B. Suppose that this number is one of the predictors (called X_{AB}) in an individual linear regression analysis. What is the meaning of the weight (β_{AB}) of this predictor?

2. Why might it be a problem to analyze responses on a 4-point scale (from 1 to 4) as continuous data using the LMM? What if it were a 7-point scale?

3. Formulate the LMM as a GLMM. In other words, define the random component, the link function, and the linear component.

4. When you know η_{pi} and σ_ε^2 (mean and variance of V_{pi}, respectively), can you then express the variation of V_{pi} on the probability scale, indi-

cating the 95% confidence interval, with π_{pi} as the expected value, for the normal-ogive model and (approximately) for the logistic model? How can you reconcile this continuous variation when expressed on the probability scale with the fact that the observations are binary?

5. In the general description of the GLMM, π_{pi} is replaced with μ_{pi} (the expected value of Y_{pi} given the random effects). Why is this? When does it hold that $\pi_{pi} = \mu_{pi}$?

1.11 References

Agresti, A., Booth, J., Hobert, J.P., & Caffo, B. (2000). Random-effects modeling of categorical data. *Sociological Methodology, 30*, 27–80.

Baker, F.B. (1992) *Item Response Theory: Parameter Estimation Techniques*. New York: Marcel Dekker.

Birnbaum, A. (1968). Some latent trait models and their use in inferring an examinee's ability. In F.M. Lord & M.R. Novick (Eds), *Statistical Theories of Mental Test Scores* (pp. 395–479). Reading, MA: Addison-Wesley.

Bock, R.D. (1997). A brief history of item response theory. *Educational Measurement : Issues and Practice, 16*, 21–33.

Bond, T., & Fox, C. (2001). *Applying the Rasch Model: Fundamental Measurement in Human Sciences*. Mahwah, NJ: Lawrence Erlbaum.

Boomsma, A., van Dijn, M.A.J., & Snijders, T.A.B. (Eds) (2001). *Essays and Item Response Theory*. New York: Springer.

Breslow, N.E., & Clayton, D.G. (1993). Approximate inference in generalized linear mixed models. *Journal of the American Statistical Association, 88*, 9–25.

Camilli, G. (1994). Origin of the scaling constant $d = 1.7$ in item response theory. *Journal of Educational and Behavioral Statistics, 19*, 293–295.

Cohen, J., & Cohen, P. (1983). *Applied Multiple Regression/correlation Analysis for the Behavioral Sciences (2nd ed.)*. Hillsdale, NJ: Lawrence Erlbaum.

Cronbach, L.J. (1957). The two disciplines of scientific psychology. *American Psychologist, 12*, 672–684.

Davidian, M., & Giltinan, D.M. (1995). *Nonlinear Models for Repeated Measurement Data*. London: Chapman & Hall.

Davis, C.S. (2002). *Statistical Methods for the Analysis of Repeated Measurements*. New York: Springer.

Embretson, S.E. (1983). Construct validity: Construct representation versus nomothetic span. *Psychological Bulletin, 93*, 179–197.

Embretson, S.E. (Ed.) (1985). *Test Design: Developments in Psychology and Psychometrics*. New York: Academic Press.

Embretson, S.E., & Reise, S. (2000). *Item Response Theory for Psychologists*. Mahwah, NJ: Lawrence Erlbaum.

Fahrmeir, L., & Tutz, G. (2001). *Multivariate Statistical Modeling Based on Generalized Linear Models (2nd ed.)*. New York: Springer.

Fischer, G.H., & Molenaar, I. (Eds) (1995). *Rasch Models Foundations, Recent Developments and Applications*. New York: Springer.

Goldstein, H. (2003). *Multilevel Statistical Models (3rd ed.)*. London: Arnold.

Hambleton, R.K., Swaminathan, H., & Rogers, H.J. (1991). *Fundamentals of Item Response Theory*. Newbury Park, CA: Sage.

Kamata, A. (2001). Item analysis by the hierarchical generalized linear model. *Journal of Educational and Behavioral Statistics, 38*, 79–93.

Kirk, R.E. (1995). *Experimental Design. Procedures for the Behavioral Sciences (3rd ed.)*. Pacific Grove, CA: Brooks/Cole.

Kreft, I., & de Leeuw, J. (1998). *Introducing Multilevel Modeling*. London: Sage.

Longford, N.T. (1993). *Random Coefficient Models*. London: Oxford University Press.

Lord, F.M., & Novick, M. (1968). *Statistical Theories of Mental Test Scores*. Reading, MA: Addison Wesley.

McCullagh, P., & Nelder, J.A. (1989). *Generalized Linear Models (2nd ed.)*. London: Chapman & Hall.

McCulloch, C.E., & Searle, S.R. (2001). *Generalized, Linear, and Mixed Models*. New York: Wiley.

McDonald, R.P. (1999). *Test Theory*. Hillsdale, NJ: Lawrence Erlbaum.

Mellenbergh, G. (1994). Generalized linear item response theory. *Psychological Bulletin, 115*, 300–307.

Moustaki, I., & Knott, M. (2000). Generalized latent trait models. *Psychometrika, 65*, 391–441.

Raudenbush, S.W., & Bryk, A.S. (2002). *Hierarchical Linear Models: Applications and Data Analysis Methods*. Thousand Oaks, CA: Sage.

Rijmen, F., Tuerlinkx, F., De Boeck, P., & Kuppens (2003). A nonlinear mixed model framework for item response theory. *Psychological Methods, 8*, 185–205.

SAS Institute (1999). *SAS Online Doc (Version 8)* (software manual on CD-Rom). Cary, NC: SAS Institute Inc.

Snijders, T., & Bosker, R. (1999). *Multilevel Analysis*. London: Sage.

Spiegelhalter, D., Thomas, A., Best, N. & Lunn, D. (2003). BUGS: Bayesian inference using Gibbs sampling. MRC Biostatistics Unit, Cambridge, England. www.mrc-bsu.cam.ac.uk/bugs/

Spielberger, C.D. (1988). *State-Trait Anger Expression Inventory Research Edition. Professional Manual.* Odessa, FL: Psychological Assessment Resources.

Spielberger, C.D., & Sydeman, S.J. (1994). State-trait anxiety inventory and state-trait anger expression inventory. In M.E. Maruish (Ed.), *The Use of Psychological Tests for Treatment Planning and Outcome Assessment* (pp. 292–321). Hillsdale, NJ: Lawrence Erlbaum.

Sternberg, R.J. (1977). Component processes in analogical reasoning. *Psychological Review, 84*, 353–378.

Sternberg, R.J. (1980). Representation and process in linear syllogistic reasoning. *Journal of Experimental Psychology: General, 109*, 119–159.

Thissen, D., & Orlando, M. (2001). Item response theory for items scored in two categories. In D. Thissen & H. Wainer (Eds), *Test Scoring* (pp. 73–140). Mahwah, NJ: Lawrence Erlbaum.

Thissen, D., & Wainer, H. (Eds) (2001). *Test Scoring.* Mahwah, NJ: Lawrence Erlbaum.

van der Linden, W.J., & Hambleton, R.K. (Eds) (1997). *Handbook of Modern Item Response Theory.* New York: Springer.

Vansteelandt, K. (2000). Formal models for contextualized personality psychology. Unpublished doctoral dissertation, K.U.Leuven, Belgium.

Verbeke, G., & Molenberghs, G. (2000). *Linear Mixed Models for Longitudinal Data.* New York: Springer.

Vonesh, E.F., & Chinchilli, V.M. (1997). *Linear and Nonlinear Models for the Analysis of Repeated Measurements.* New York: Dekker.

Wallenstein, S. (1982). Regression models for repeated measurements. *Biometrics, 38*, 849–853.

Wilson, M. (2005). *Constructing Measures: An Item Response Modeling Approach.* Mahwah, NJ: Lawrence Erlbaum.

Wilson, M., & Adams, R.J. (1992). A multilevel perspective on the 'two scientific disciplines of psychology'. Paper presented in a Symposium on the Two Scientific Disciplines of Psychology at the XXV International Congress of Psychology, Brussels.

Chapter 2

Descriptive and explanatory item response models

Mark Wilson
Paul De Boeck

2.1 Introduction

In this chapter we present four item response models. These four models
are comparatively simple within the full range of models in this volume,
but some of them are more complex than the common item response models. On the one hand, all four models provide a measurement of individual
differences, but on the other hand we use the models to demonstrate how
the effect of person characteristics and of item design factors can be investigated. The models range from descriptive measurement for the case
where no such effects are investigated, to explanatory measurement for the
case where person properties and/or item properties are used to explain
the effects of persons and/or items.

In the following sections of this chapter we will concentrate on logistic
models, but all that is said also applies to normal-ogive models if the logit
link is replaced with the probit link. The models we will discuss are all
GLMMs with random intercepts and fixed slopes.

2.1.1 The intercept or person parameter

Typically, the intercept in an item response model is one that varies at
random over persons. It is therefore called the *person parameter*. In the
notation for item response models, it is commonly denoted by θ_p. It is
assumed in this chapter that θ_p is normally distributed with mean zero:
$\theta_p \sim N(0, \sigma_\theta^2)$.

The random intercept or person parameter fulfills the function that is
often the main reason why people are given a test. Person parameters provide a measurement of latent variables such as abilities, achievement levels, skills, cognitive processes, cognitive strategies, developmental stages,
motivations, attitudes, personality traits, states, emotional states or incli-
nations. A general term that we will use for what is measured in a test
is *propensity*. Alternatively, another conception of the person parameter is
that it can also be (a) a fixed parameter, and/or (b) more than one person

parameter (i.e., in a multidimensional model). We will elaborate on these possibilities only later. For now, it suffices to know that the random intercept is a person parameter and that the estimate for an individual person is considered a measurement of the propensity expressed in the test.

As a measurement tool, item response models of the type we are discussing provide more than ordinal quantification. However, an important alternative approach is to restrict quantification to ordinal numbers. Ordinal item response models are often also called nonparametric item response models (Junker & Sijtsma, 2001; Sijtsma & Molenaar, 2002). The important asset of nonparametric models is that they make no assumptions regarding the item response functions, except for monotonicity assumptions. Thus, they are more flexible than parametric item response models. However, the family of nonparametric models has been developed mainly for measurement purposes. It is not yet fully elaborated for explanatory purposes to investigate the effect of person properties and item properties (such as factors in an experimental design). Thus, in this volume, we will concentrate on parametric models.

2.1.2 The weights or item parameters

As in Chapter 1 we will denote the item predictors by an X, with subscript k $(k = 1, \ldots, K)$ for the predictors, so that X_{ik} is the value of item i on predictor k. The most typical predictors in an item response model are not real item properties as in Chapter 1, but item *indicators*. This means that as many predictors are used as there are items, one per item, so that $X_{ik} = 1$ if $k = i$, and $X_{ik} = 0$ if $k \neq i$. For example, for a set of six items, the predictor values would be as follows:

item 1:	1	0	0	0	0	0	item 4:	0	0	0	1	0	0
item 2:	0	1	0	0	0	0	item 5:	0	0	0	0	1	0
item 3:	0	0	1	0	0	0	item 6:	0	0	0	0	0	1.

In typical item response modeling applications, the weights of these predictors are fixed parameters since they do not vary over persons. These weights are the slopes of the binary indicators (see Figure 2.1). The values of these indicator weights are called the *item parameters*, commonly denoted by β_i. Since each item has its own predictor, the subscript i is used instead of k.

2.1.3 Resulting models

The resulting equation for the linear component η_{pi} is the following:

$$\eta_{pi} = \beta_i + \theta_p, \tag{2.1}$$

with $\beta_i = \sum_{k=1}^{K} \beta_k X_{ik}$. As noted in Chapter 1, η_{pi} is $\eta_{pi}|\theta_p$, but here and in the following we will omit the conditional notation for η_{pi} (and π_{pi}). Since all X_{ik} with $i \neq k$ equal 0, only one term of this sum has a non-zero value. It is a common practice to reverse the sign of the item parameter, so that the contribution of the item is negative and may be interpreted as the item difficulty in the context of an achievement test. The resulting equation is:

$$\eta_{pi} = \theta_p - \beta_i. \tag{2.2}$$

In order to convey some intuitions about the intercept and coefficients used above, we give, in Figure 2.1 a graphical representation of Equation 2.2 for person p and the kth predictor. The value of X_{ik} is represented on the x-axis. X_{ik} can have two values: 0 and 1. For $k = i$, the value is 1 for item i, and 0 for all other items. This simply means that item i makes no contribution for other items. Note that the intercept of the regression line is the value of θ at $X_{ik} = 0$. Also note that the difference between $X_{ik} = 1$ and $X_{ik} = 0$ is 1, and the difference between the η_{pi} for $X_{ik} = 1$ and $X_{ik} = 0$ is $-\beta_i$, hence the slope of the line (i.e., the regression weight) is also $-\beta_i$. Other persons will have a parallel line, but the intercepts of the line will vary (and we have assumed they follow a normal distribution). Figure 2.1 does not give the full picture since it represents the effect of only one predictor, the item indicator $k = i$. Figure 2.1 is also somewhat imaginary in the sense that our item indicators can have only two values, while the line connecting the two points suggests that intermediate values can also exist.

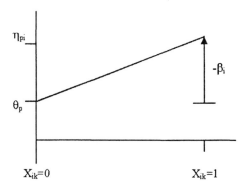

FIGURE 2.1. Linear function for one item predictor in the Rasch model. (Note that in this case $\beta_i < 0$.)

The resulting model of Equation 2.2 (or, equivalently, 2.1) is the Rasch model (Rasch, 1960). The Rasch model is a model that is descriptive for both the person side and the item side of the data matrix. It describes variation in the persons through a person parameter θ_p, which is a random variable as presented here. And it describes the variation in the items through fixed individual item parameters.

2.2   Four item response models

The primary aim of this chapter is to illustrate the distinction between a *descriptive* approach and an *explanatory* approach in the context of item response modeling. In the course of illustrating the distinction, we will present four item response models one of which is the Rasch model from Equations 2.1 and 2.2. The four models differ in whether they are descriptive or explanatory at the person side and the item side.

The four models we have selected to present below are logistic random-intercepts models and therefore belong to the Rasch tradition, but this does not mean we are in this volume restricting our possible models to that approach. In the Rasch tradition, which might also be called *prescriptive measurement* (Rasch, 1960; Fischer & Molenaar, 1995), models include no interactions between persons and items, but just main effects of persons and items – specifically, the random intercept, θ_p, is not weighted depending on the item. If there were such interactions, then the effect of a person parameter would depend on the items, and therefore, by implication, in the inferential step, the measurement outcome would necessarily also depend on the items that are included. This prescriptive measurement approach is only one of two measurement approaches that are commonly followed with item response models (Thissen & Orlando, 2001; Wilson, 2003). The alternative approach might be termed *empirical* in that one seeks to modify the model to fit the data more closely – specifically, the model is expanded by weighting the random intercept by an item parameter α_i (Birnhaum, 1968). Such a model is called the *two-parameter logistic model* (2PL model) Thus, in the empirical tradition, relatively more items will fit the model than in the prescriptive tradition, although there will be items that do not fit well under either tradition.

The basis for selecting these particular models for this second introductory chapter is that they are building blocks which can serve as the basis for the very extensive expansion of the models in the remainder of this volume, and which will include, as one aspect, adding the second item parameter α_i, typical of the empirical tradition. After the model formulation and discussion for each of the four models below, an application will be discussed, making use of the dichotomized example data from Chapter 1.

Table 2.2 shows four types of models, depending on the types of predictors that are included. There are two kinds of item predictors: item indicators, and item properties. And there are also two kinds of person predictors: person indicators, and person properties. Look first at the top left-hand corner of the 2×2 layout of Table 2.1. When each person has his/her own unique effect, unexplained by person properties, and when each item has its own unique effects, unexplained by item properties, we will refer to the model as *doubly descriptive*. Such a model describes the individual effects of the persons and of the items (hence, doubly descriptive), without explaining either of these effects. The Rasch model is an example.

TABLE 2.1. Models as a function of the predictors.

Item predictors	Person predictors	
	Absence of properties	Inclusion of properties (person properties)
Absence of properties	doubly descriptive	person explanatory
Inclusion of properties (item properties)	item explanatory	doubly explanatory

Doubly descriptive models are mostly sufficient for measurement purposes, and are those most commonly seen in practice.

However, if the person parameter is considered to be a random effect, then there may be unwanted consequences if the effect of certain person properties is not taken into account. If a normal distribution is assumed, the result is that the normal distribution no longer applies for the entire subset of persons, but only for subsets of persons who share the same person property values. For example, if gender has an effect, then not one normal distribution applies but two, differentiated by the gender of the person. Thus, when person properties are included in the model to explain the person effects, then the models will be called *person explanatory* (top right-hand corner of Table 2.1).

In a similar way, when item properties are included to explain the item effects, the models will be called *item explanatory* (bottom left-hand corner of Table 2.1). Finally, when properties of both kinds are included, the models will be called *doubly explanatory* (bottom right-hand corner of Table 2.1). See Zwinderman (1997) and Adams, Wilson and Wu (1997) for similar taxonomies and short descriptions of the models. In the verbal aggression example data set from Chapter 1, we have information on person properties as well as on item properties, so that the two types of explanatory models (person and item) can be illustrated.

2.2.1 Summary and notation

A summary of the four models to be explained is given in Table 2.2. The following notation is used in the table and will be followed also in the remainder of this chapter. θ_p is used for the random person parameter, with mean zero and variance σ_θ^2. When person properties are included in the model, the symbol ε_p is used for the unexplained part of the person contribution, with mean zero and variance σ_ε^2. The person properties are denoted with capital Z. The subscript j is used for these predictors, $j = 1, \ldots, J$.

TABLE 2.2. Summary of the four models.

| | | $\eta_{pi} =$ | | |
Model	Person part	Item part	Random effect	Model type
Rasch model	θ_p	$-\beta_i$	$\theta_p \sim N(0, \sigma_\theta^2)$	Doubly descriptive
Latent reg Rasch model	$\sum_{j=1}^{J} \vartheta_j Z_{pj} + \varepsilon_p$	$-\beta_i$	$\varepsilon_p \sim N(0, \sigma_\varepsilon^2)$	Person explanatory
LLTM	θ_p	$-\sum_{k=0}^{K} \beta_k X_{ik}$	$\theta_p \sim N(0, \sigma_\theta^2)$	Item explanatory
Latent reg LLTM	$\sum_{j=1}^{J} \vartheta_j Z_{pj} + \varepsilon_p$	$-\sum_{k=0}^{K} \beta_k X_{ik}$	$\varepsilon_p \sim N(0, \sigma_\varepsilon^2)$	Doubly explanatory

This is a deviation from the GLMM notation where Z is used for predictors with a random effect. The GLMM notation is the notation that is followed in Chapter 4 on the statistical background of this volume and in Chapter 3 on multicategorical data also because that chapter relies more directly on the general GLMM framework. Rather than distinguishing between the predictors on the basis of whether they have a fixed or random effect, we use here a different notation for person predictors and item predictors, because they lead to quite different item response models and because in these models persons and items are not treated in an equivalent way, as will be explained in Sections 2.4.1, 2.5.1, and 2.6.1. This leaves the X for the item predictors, with subscript k, $k = 1, \ldots, K$. Where the effects of person predictors are considered fixed, they are denoted by ϑ_j, and the fixed effects of item predictors by β_k. The random intercepts may be considered the effect of a constant predictor (Z_{p0}, or alternatively X_{i0}).

2.3 A doubly descriptive model: the Rasch model

2.3.1 Formulation of the model

The *Rasch model* was defined earlier in Equations 2.1 and 2.2. We will use Equation 2.2 to obtain an expression for the odds, or $\pi_{pi}/(1-\pi_{pi})$. If on both sides of Equation 2.2 the exponential form is used, then $\exp(\eta_{pi}) = \exp(\theta_p - \beta_i)$. Since $\eta_{pi} = \log(\pi_{pi}/(1 - \pi_{pi}))$, and $\exp(\theta_p - \beta_i) = \exp(\theta_p)/\exp(\beta_i)$, it follows that

$$\pi_{pi}/(1 - \pi_{pi}) = \exp(\theta_p)/\exp(\beta_i). \qquad (2.3)$$

Equation 2.3 is the *exponential form* of the Rasch model. As a way to understand Equation 2.3, interpret $\exp(\theta_p)$ as an exponential measure of the ability of person p when taking an achievement test, and interpret

$\exp(\beta_i)$ as an exponential measure of the difficulty of the item i from that test. Then the formula expresses the ratio of the success probability π_{pi} to the failure probability $(1 - \pi_{pi})$ as the ratio of a person's ability to the difficulty of the item.

The intuition reflected in the formula, in an achievement context, is that ability allows one to succeed, while difficulty makes one fail, and that the ratio of both determines the odds of success. Figure 2.2a gives a schematic presentation of this intuitive idea. The figure shows two rectangles on a balance beam – if one weighs more than the other, then the balance will tip that way. Physical balance beams tip one way as soon as the weight on that side is larger than the weight on the other side. Imagine now that tipping one way or the other way in an achievement context is probabilistic as follows. The white rectangle represents the ability and the gray rectangle the difficulty. The ratio of ability to difficulty is 2/1, so that the ratio of the success probability to the failure probability is also 2/1.

From the odds equation, one can derive the equation for the probability. If the numerator on each side of Equation 2.3 is divided by the sum of the numerator and the denominator, it follows that $\pi_{pi}/(\pi_{pi}+(1-\pi_{pi})) = \exp(\theta_p)/(\exp(\theta_p)+\exp(\beta_i))$, and thus that $\pi_{pi} = \exp(\theta_p)/(\exp(\theta_p)+\exp(\beta_i))$. When the numerator and denominator of the latter are each divided by $\exp(\beta_i)$, then the familiar equation for the probability of a 1-response is obtained:

$$\pi_{pi} = \exp(\theta_p - \beta_i)/(1 + \exp(\theta_p - \beta_i)). \tag{2.4}$$

The intuition behind this alternate formula for the Rasch model is that there are two competing responses each of which has a certain attractiveness. Let us denote the attractiveness of $Y_{pi} = 0$ as A and the attractiveness of $Y_{pi} = 1$ as B. The probability of a response may then be considered the ratio of its attractiveness to the sum of the two attractiveness values, or $\pi_{pi} = B/(A+B)$. This is an example of the well-known Bradley-Terry-Luce choice rule: the probability of an alternative depends on the ratio of the attractiveness of that alternative to the sum of the attractiveness values of all alternatives. In Equation 2.4, $A = 1$, and $B = \exp(\theta_p - \beta_i)$. The value of 1 for A is an arbitrarily chosen convention (i.e., the value of π_{pi} is invariant under multiplicative transformations of the attractiveness values, so that one may as well set A equal to 1).

The intuition behind Equation 2.4 is presented in Figure 2.2b. The two attractiveness values are each represented by a section of a rectangle: the gray section for the 0-response, and the white section for the 1-response. The probability of each response is the proportion of the corresponding section in the rectangle. The white section is twice as large as the gray section, so that the resulting probability of a 1-response is $2/(2+1) = .67$.

The link between Figure 2.2a and Figure 2.2b is that the two rectangles of the upper part are first shrunken in equal proportions, and then put next to one another to form one long rectangle. This is a legitimate operation

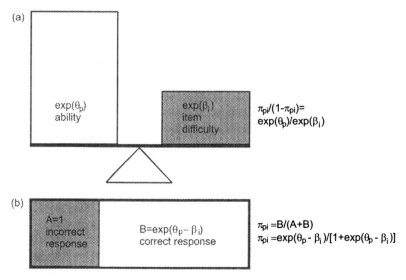

FIGURE 2.2. Illustration of two ideas behind two different formulations of the Rasch model: (a) odds formula, and (b) probability formula.

since π_{pi} is invariant under multiplicative transformations of the rectangles. The transformation illustrates that both $\exp(\theta_p)$ and $\exp(\theta_p - \beta_i)$ may be understood as the attractiveness of a 1-response, and both $\exp(\beta_i)$ and 1 as the attractiveness of a 0-response, depending on whether or not one divides by $\exp(\beta_i)$.

A third metaphor is one of a hurdler (the person) and a series of hurdles (the items). The hurdler is seen as having the ability to leap over hurdles of a certain height (the ability is indicated by θ_p), and the series of hurdles have heights indicated by the series of item difficulties $(\beta_1, \ldots, \beta_I)$. When the hurdler's ability is equal to the height of the hurdle, the leap is successful, with a probability of .50. When the hurdler's ability is different than the height of the hurdle, the leap is successful, with a probability dependent on the difference between them (when the difference is positive, the probability will be greater than .50, and when it is negative, it will be less than .50). This metaphor is possibly better-suited to achievement and ability contexts than other such as attitude variables, but similar interpretations in such contexts are also possible.

In a fourth metaphor, one can represent the heights of the hurdles (the item difficulties) as points along a line, and the ability of the person as a point along the same line. The amount determining the probability of success is then the difference between the two locations, or $(\theta_p - \beta_i)$. This representation is sometimes called an 'item map' or 'construct map.' A generic example is shown in Figure 2.3, where the students are shown on the left-hand side, and the items on the right-hand side. This representation has been used as a way to enhance the interpretability of the results from item response model analyses. Segments of the line can be labeled as exhibiting particular features, for both the persons and the items, and the progress of say, students, through this set of segments, can be interpreted as development in achievement. The placement of the person and item locations in a directly linear relationship has been the genesis of an extensive methodology for interpreting the measure (Masters, Adams, & Wilson, 1990; Wilson, 2003; Wilson, 2005; Wright & Stone, 1979).

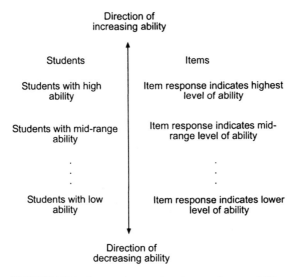

FIGURE 2.3. A generic construct map for an ability.

Item response function

Item response functions or item characteristic curves are item specific functions that map the value of θ_p into the corresponding probability π_{pi}, given the value of β_i. Figure 2.4 shows the item response functions of three items. The shape of Rasch item response functions is the same for all three items, but the location is different. All curves are equally steep, because θ_p is not weighted depending on the item. For all items $\pi_{pi} = .50$ when $\beta_i = \theta_p$, which indicates that β_i locates the curve on the θ-scale.

Graphical representation

The Rasch model is graphically represented in Figure 2.5, following the conventions introduced in the previous chapter. The figure shows the item parameter β_i as the effect of the corresponding item indicator X_{ik} (for $k = i$, the other item indicators are not shown since they don't have an effect), and it shows the person parameter θ_p as the random effect of the constant predictor Z_{p0}. Note that in GLMM notation Z is used for predictors with a random effect, while our notation Z is used for person predictors.

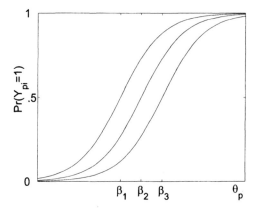

FIGURE 2.4. Item response functions for three items.

Incidentally, the Z_{p0} in Figure 2.5 corresponds with both conventions. It is a constant predictor with a random effect, and it may be considered a person predictor as well, one with a value of 1 for all persons.

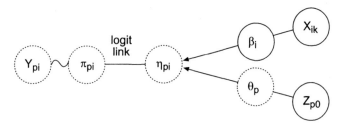

FIGURE 2.5. Graphical representation of the Rasch model. (Note that $k = i$.)

Local independence

An important feature of the model is the so-called *local (or conditional) independence* assumption, meaning that for any response vector $\boldsymbol{y}_p =$ $(y_{p1}, \ldots, y_{pI})'$ (with y_{pi} being the realization of Y_{pi}, ($y_{pi} = 1$ or 0)), the conditional probability of the whole vector is the product of the conditional probabilities of each response. This implies that, for all pairs of items i and i' $(i \neq i')$: $\Pr(Y_{pi} = y_{pi} \ \& \ Y_{pi'} = y_{pi'}|\theta_p) = \Pr(Y_{pi} = y_{pi}|\theta_p) \times$ $\Pr(Y_{pi'} = y_{pi'}|\theta_p)$. Under this assumption, θ_p is the only source of dependence (or correlation) between items – hence, for a given value of θ_p the observations are independent, which means that one dimension or latent trait, θ_p, explains all inter-item correlations. The assumption of local independence underlies all four models in this chapter, and also all models in this volume, except for models with a residual dependence part (see Chapters 7 and 10 for an explanation of that).

Parametrization

Note that the parameters in the above equations appear in two forms: the *exponential form*, using $\exp(\theta_p)$ and $\exp(\beta_i)$, as in Equation 2.3, and the *logarithmic form*, using θ_p and β_i, as in Equation 2.4. We will use the logarithmic form, which is also the most common form. Four different but equivalent parametrizations are possible based on the signs of the person and item expressions:

(1) $\theta_p - \beta_i$;

(2) $\theta_p + \beta_i^*$, with $\beta_i^* = -\beta_i$;

(3) $-\theta_p^* - \beta_i$, with $\theta_p^* = -\theta_p$; and

(4) $\beta_i^* - \theta_p^*$.

The difference between the four is that in some contexts, one of them might work better in terms of interpretation. For example, taking the difference between the item parameter and the person parameter (fourth parametrization) could be useful for the verbal aggression example if the person parameter is seen as a personal aggression threshold (θ_p^*) and the item parameter as the inductive power of the situation-behavior pair (β_i^*). The probability of a verbally aggressive response then grows with the difference between the inductive power of the situation-behavior pair and the personal threshold. In general, the two subtraction parametrizations (1 and 4) lend themselves to metaphors of comparison and competition (e.g., ability and difficulty), and are compatible with the intuitions mentioned above whereas the two addition formulations (2 and 3) are suitable for an intensification metaphor.

Identification

The model as formulated in the previous equations would have an *identification problem* if the mean of the person parameters was not restricted to be zero. The exponential parameters and logarithmic parameters are identified only up to a multiplicative or additive constant, respectively. If one multiplies all exponential parameters with a constant c, then the odds in Equation 2.3 do not change, and if one adds a constant c to all logarithmic parameters, then the probability in Equation 2.4 does not change. Different conventions exist to solve this problem. For instance, one can set the mean θ_p equal to 0, which is the solution we have chosen for this volume, or one can set either a particular β_i or the mean of the β_i equal to 0, which are the most common tactics if θ_p is not considered a random effect.

Variants

The Rasch model exists in three variants named after the formulation of the likelihood to be maximized (Molenaar, 1995). There are three likelihood formulations for the model: the joint maximum likelihood formulation (JML), the conditional maximum likelihood formulation (CML), and the marginal maximum likelihood formulation (MML). The labels of the three formulations refer to a maximization of the likelihood function for estimation purposes. The likelihood function is the probability of the data as a function of the parameters, and, in the case of CML, also of the sufficient statistics for the person parameters. It has been common to consider the three different formulations as no more than three estimation tools, but they can also be considered as being based on different models, as explained in Chapter 12 of this volume. We will follow here the MML formulation, meaning that we assume that the person parameters are sampled from a distribution, so that only the parameters of that distribution (and not the individual person parameters) enter the likelihood that is maximized. If the distribution is the normal distribution, these parameters of the distribution are the mean and the variance. In all applications up to Chapter 10, the normal distribution will be used for person parameters. Other distributions can also be used – for example a histogram distribution can be particularly flexible (Adams, Wilson, & Wu, 1997; de Leeuw & Verhelst, 1986; Follmann, 1988).

MML formulation and estimation of person parameters

For the MML formulation, a more complete way of presenting the model is

$$\pi_{pi} = \exp(\theta_p - \beta_i)/(1 + \exp(\theta_p - \beta_i)),$$
$$\theta_p \sim N(0, \sigma_\theta^2), \tag{2.5}$$

with σ_θ^2 being the variance of the θ_p, and assuming local independence. The corresponding marginal likelihood for a full response pattern (y_p as the realization of Y_p) is

$$\Pr(Y_p = y_p)$$
$$= \int_{-\infty}^{+\infty} \prod_{i=1}^{I} (\exp(y_{pi}(\theta_p - \beta_i))/(1 + \exp(\theta_p - \beta_i)))g(\theta_p|\psi)d\theta_p, \tag{2.6}$$

with $g(\theta_p|\psi)$ as the normal density of θ_p with parameters ψ (μ_θ and σ_θ^2). For all persons together, the marginal likelihood is the product of the corresponding integrals. The marginal likelihood will not be repeated for the next three models, since one can simply adapt Equation 2.6 based on the equation for π_{pi}. To estimate the model, we need to estimate only the structural parameters $\beta_1, \ldots, \beta_I$, and σ_θ^2 (the mean of the distribution is fixed at 0). Therefore, the estimation of θ_p requires a further step beyond the model estimation. A common method for this second step is to calculate empirical Bayes estimates; see Bock and Aitkin (1981), Adams, Wilson and Wang (1997), or Wainer et al. (2001) for a discussion of the concept within the context of item response modeling. These estimates are maximum likelihood estimates given the item responses of the person and the assumed normal distribution with estimated (or fixed) mean and variance. For a discussion and some interesting results on the estimation of person parameters for the Rasch model, see Hoijtink and Boomsma (1995) and Warm

(1989). The issue of estimating person parameters is the same for all four models in this chapter, and in general for all models with a random person parameter.

Comments and literature

The Rasch model is a doubly descriptive model, since it yields only estimates of the individual item and individual person effects. Its great asset is that if it is valid, the person effect does not depend on the item, which is an attractive measurement quality and corresponds to certain notions of what it means to measure (Rasch, 1961). When the ultimate goal is to assign a number to each person in order to measure the person's latent trait, the Rasch model is an excellent model. However, there may be complications in the data that it does not incorporate, and when it comes to *understanding* the responses in terms of person and item properties, the model itself does not help.

The Rasch model is also called the one-parameter logistic (1PL) model because it has only one parameter per item. We will not use this terminology for the Rasch model, since a model with unequal but fixed item weights (discriminations) is also a one-parameter logistic model (OPLM, Verhelst & Glas, 1995). The Rasch model was first described by the Danish mathematician and statistician Rasch (1960, 1961, 1967), and it became known in the psychometric literature thanks to work by Fischer (1968, 1974, 1981) in Europe and Wright (1968, 1977) in the United States. For a history of the Rasch model, see Wright (1997). For a description and discussion of recent developments in the Rasch model and related models, see Fischer and Molenaar (1995) and Rost (2001). A recent introduction has been written by Bond and Fox (2001). A good description of the life and work of Rasch is given by Andersen and Olsen (2001).

2.3.2 Application of the Rasch model

After a dichotomization (i.e., 2 and 1 are mapped to 1), the example data set is analyzed with the NLMIXED procedure of SAS (SAS Institute, 1999), in order to estimate the Rasch model in its MML formulation. The options we chose for all four models discussed in this chapter are: Gaussian quadrature for numerical integration, with 20 quadrature points without adaptive centering (with centering on 0), and Newton Raphson as the optimization method. When adaptive centering was used, essentially the same results were obtained for all four models as with the nonadaptive method – however, it took much longer to run the analysis. For a discussion of estimation methods, see Chapters 4 and 12, and for a discussion of software, see Chapter 12. The use of the NLMIXED procedure of SAS is described in Section 2.8.1.

We will not test this model and the other models with respect to their absolute goodness of fit. Instead we will do two other things. First, we will report the value of three indices: the deviance, the Akaike information criterion (AIC) (Akaike, 1974), and the Bayesian information criterion (BIC) (Schwarz, 1978), with the aim to compare the four models from this chapter on these fit indices. The deviance is $-2\log(L)$, with L being the maximum of the likelihood function given the estimated model. The AIC and BIC are information criteria derived from the deviance, but with a penalty included for the number of parameters: $AIC = -2\log(L) + 2N_{par}$, and $BIC = -2\log(L) + \log(P)N_{par}$, with N_{par} being the number of parameters (for the persons, only the variance is counted as a parameter), and P being the number of persons (see also Bozdogan, 1987; Read & Cressie, 1988). Lower values of the deviance, the AIC, and the BIC indicate a better fit. As a comparison makes sense only when at least one other model is involved, we will start using these indices only in the discussion of the results from the second model; see Section 2.4.2.

Second, we will use significance tests of the likelihood-ratio type and Wald tests. For nested models, we can use *likelihood-ratio tests* (LR tests). The LR test is based on the ratio of two likelihoods. The first likelihood (L_1) belongs to a model that is nested in a second, more general model. The second likelihood (L_2) belongs to this more general model. When the models are estimated with a maximum likelihood method, then minus two times the logarithm of the likelihood ratio, $-2\log(L_1/L_2)$, or the difference between the deviances, is asymptotically distributed as a χ^2 with a number of degrees of freedom (df) equal to the difference between the number of parameters of the two models. Further, we will also use *Wald tests* (Wald, 1941) to determine whether the difference of an estimate with zero is statistically significant. The asymptotic normality of the parameter estimates is the basis for dividing the parameter estimate by its standard error, in order to obtain a statistic that is approximately distributed as a standard normal. For a discussion of adaptations one may consider for this test, depending on the estimation method that is followed, see Verbeke and Molenberghs (2000). The LR test does not apply when one wishes to compare a model with one or more parameters fixed at a boundary value to a model in which these parameters are not fixed but free. For example, the regular LR test does not apply when comparing a model with the person variance fixed to zero and another model where the variance is estimated. For a model with one variance parameter fixed to zero (model 1, likelihood is L1) and a model where that variance is estimated (model 2, likelihood is L2), the LR statistic $-2\log(L1/L2)$ follows a mixture of a $\chi^2(0)$ and a $\chi^2(1)$ distribution (Verbeke & Molenberghs, 2000). Therefore, the regular LR test (which would use $\chi^2(1)$ as the difference in number of parameters is one) is conservative and in fact the p-values must be halved. Given the asymptotic equivalence of the Wald test for a given parameter value and the likelihood-ratio test to test whether the parameter is needed, the Wald test may also be considered conservative. Thus, if the p-value of the Wald test (as shown by NLMIXED) is smaller than the critical value, then the correct *p*-value certainly is smaller also.

Results

Person variance

The estimated *person variance* is 1.98 on the logit scale. The standard error (SE) of the variance estimate is .21, meaning that the individual differences are statistically significant, with $p < .001$. In general, to interpret an effect a on the logit scale, one should multiply the odds by $\exp(a)$. In order to translate this effect into an effect on the probability, the probability of .50 can be used as a reference value. The size of the person effects can be examined by considering the effect of one standard deviation of θ. Based on Equation 2.3, the odds increase by a factor 4.08 when θ increases by one standard deviation (i.e., 4.08 is $\exp(\sqrt{1.98})$). To illustrate this, suppose a person has a probability of .50 of responding with a 1 ("yes" or "perhaps") on the first item, then someone with a θ-value that is one standard deviation higher has a probability of .80.

Item parameters

The estimated *item parameters* vary from −1.75 to +2.97 on the logit scale, with an average value of .16. The estimates of the item parameters are given in Table 12.3 (Chapter 12). Note that, because of the subtraction in the model equations, lower values of the item parameters imply higher probabilities (i.e., are 'easier' to endorse). The average item value is only slightly higher than the mean of the persons (fixed at zero to identify the model). This means that the average person has a probability of about .50, or more exactly .46, to endorse the average item (responding "yes" or "perhaps"). Note that the effect on the average person is not the average effect, as will be explained in Chapter 4.

Discussion

The rationale of the Rasch model is in the first place to measure persons – in this case, to measure the tendency of individual persons to react with verbal aggression. When used for that purpose, the 24 items relating to only four situations are a rather narrow basis for a reliable measurement (but note that Cronbach's $\alpha = .89$). One way to estimate the reliability of the estimates is to derive the standard error (SE) of each of the person parameters. However, since we want to concentrate on the model and not so much on its application for measurement, we will not follow up the reliability of the person measurement at this point (but see Hoijtink & Boomsma, 1995). Instead we will switch to models that can explain person variance and/or item parameters.

2.4 A person explanatory model: the latent regression Rasch model

2.4.1 Formulation of the model

The second model that we consider is the *latent regression Rasch model*. It includes person properties to explain the differences between persons with respect to verbal aggression. Including person properties as predictors is a possibility in GLMMs that we mentioned in Chapter 1, but we did not elaborate on this point there. Recall that person predictors are denoted by Z, and the predictor subscript with j, while the fixed effect is denoted by ϑ. The model differs from the Rasch model in that θ_p is now replaced with a linear regression equation (see also Table 2.2):

$$\theta_p = \sum_{j=1}^{J} \vartheta_j Z_{pj} + \varepsilon_p, \qquad (2.7)$$

so that

$$\eta_{pi} = \sum_{j=1}^{J} \vartheta_j Z_{pj} + \varepsilon_p - \beta_i, \qquad (2.8)$$

in which Z_{pj} is the value of person p on person property j ($j = 1, \ldots, J$),
ϑ_j is the (fixed) regression weight of person property j,
ε_p is the remaining person effect after the effect of the person properties is accounted for, $\varepsilon_p \sim N(0, \sigma_\varepsilon^2)$, which may be considered as the random effect of Z_{p0}, the random intercept.
Note that the ϑ_j that is used in Equation 2.7 as a symbol for the regression weight of a person property is a symbol that differs from θ_p, which is used as the person parameter.

This model is called here the 'latent regression Rasch model', because one can think of the latent person variable θ_p as being regressed on external person variables (Adams, Wilson, & Wu, 1997) such as, for the verbal aggression example, Gender and Trait Anger.

The external person variables are considered as variables with fixed values. When observed person properties are used, the fact that they may include error is ignored in this model (i.e., any errors in the Zs are not modeled). An alternative solution would be a regression on the latent variable that underlies the observed properties (Fox & Glas, 2003; Rabe-Hesketh, Pickles, & Skrondal, 2001). For example, the latent variable underlying the Trait Anger score can function as a latent predictor for the verbal aggression propensity. However, this solution is not part of the latent regression Rasch model formulation in this chapter. In principle, it can be incorporated in the present framework through a multidimensional model with a criterion θ being a function of predictor θs. Depending on the model this may require restrictions on the covariance structure of the θs. For example, when θ_1 has an effect on both θ_2 and θ_3, then this has consequences for the correlation between θ_2 and θ_3.

Graphical representation

Figure 2.6 gives a graphical representation of the latent regression Rasch model. The difference with Figure 2.5 is that the person parameter θ_p is explained in terms of person properties (the Zs) and their effects (the ϑs), and that the unexplained part or error term is the random effect of the constant predictor. One can also connect the two right-most arrows directly to η_{pi}, omitting θ_p, in correspondence with Equation 2.8.

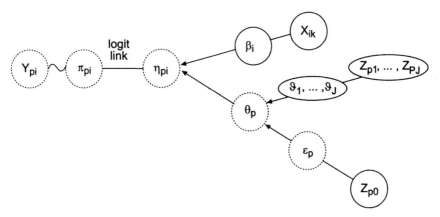

FIGURE 2.6. Graphical representation of the latent regression Rasch model. (Note that $k = i$.)

Literature

The latent regression Rasch model was first described by Verhelst and Eggen (1989) and Zwinderman (1991). This latter author used the term 'generalized Rasch model for manifest predictors' for the global model, and 'structural model' for the latent regression part of the model. Similar models have been presented by Mislevy (1987) for the 2PL or Birnbaum model. For a rather brief but thorough discussion of this model in the broader context of the models of this chapter, see Zwinderman (1997).

2.4.2 Application of the latent regression Rasch model

Two person properties will be used in the application ($J = 2$): the Trait Anger score ($j = 1$) and Gender ($j = 2$). A *dummy coding* is used for Gender, with a 1 for males, and a 0 for females. Of the 316 respondents 243 are males, and 73 are females. For Trait Anger, the raw score is used as a person property; as reference points, the mean score is 20.00 and the standard deviation is 4.85. The use of the NLMIXED procedure for this application is described in Section 2.8.2.

Table 2.3 shows the goodness of fit of the latent regression Rasch model, and also of the Rasch model. The lower the value of these indices, the better the fit of the model. One should of course take into account the number of parameters to make an evaluation, which is why the AIC and the BIC are important criteria. As explained earlier, the penalty for number of parameters is larger in the BIC. It can be noted from Table 2.3 that

TABLE 2.3. Goodness-of-fit indices for the four models.

Model	deviance	AIC	BIC
Rasch	8072	8122	8216
latent regression Rasch	8060	8114	8215
LLTM	8232	8244	8266
latent regression LLTM	8220	8236	8266

the latent regression Rasch model has a better fit than the Rasch model, although the difference is rather small, especially for the BIC. Based on a LR test, the difference is significant ($\chi^2(2) = 12.6$, $p < .01$) meaning that the goodness of fit of the Rasch model is lower.

Person property effects and residual person variance

There are a number of ways to express the results indicated by the estimated parameters. We mention several of them in the following paragraphs.

The estimated *effect of Trait Anger* is .057 on the logit scale, with a *SE* of .016, so that the effect is highly statistically significant ($p < .001$). The value of .057 is the change one would expect, given a change of one unit on the Trait Anger score – it corresponds to a multiplication of the odds ratio by 1.06. An alternative framework is provided by the standard deviation. An increase of one standard deviation (SD) in Trait Anger (instead of one unit) represents a multiplication of the odds by 1.32, and the difference between $-2SD$ and $+2SD$ represents a multiplication of the odds by 3.02. The effect of $+1SD$ on a .50 probability is to raise this probability to .57.

The estimated *effect of Gender* is .29 on the logit scale, with a *SE* of .20, so that the effect is not statistically significant. Males are not significantly more inclined to verbal aggression than females, but the odds for male students are nevertheless 1.34 times larger than the odds for female students. The effect of being male on a probability of .50 is to raise this probability to .57.

Since Trait Anger and Gender explain part of the original person variance, the *residual person variance* may be expected to be lower than the one estimated with the Rasch model. The estimated value of the person variance is 1.84, with a SE of .19, so that we must conclude that the individual differences that are not explained by Trait Anger and Gender are still highly statistically significant ($p < .001$). We note that the person variance is smaller than it was for the Rasch model.

In comparison with the residual person variance, the variance that is explained by Trait Anger is rather small: the variance of Trait Anger multiplied by the squared effect of Trait Anger is $(4.85^2 \times .057^2 =).08$, which is 4% when added to the residual person variance. This percentage represents a correlation of .20 between Trait Anger and the verbal aggression propensity as measured in a small set of specific situations. This low correlation is not surprising since typically situational behavior is not correlated higher than approximately .20 to .30 with trait measures (Mischel, 1968). The variance explained by Gender is even much smaller: the variance of Gender multiplied with the squared effect of Gender is $(.42^2 \times .29^2 =).02$, which is not significant. Thus, in terms of effect size, the effect of Trait Anger is small to moderate and the effect of Gender is small to vanishing.

Item parameters

The estimated *item parameters* vary from $-.57$ to $+4.16$. To interpret these values one needs to know the actual mean of the person effects. This mean is the result of adding three terms: (1) the mean of the normal distribution of ε (which is zero), (2) the average Trait Anger score (20.00) times the Trait Anger effect (.057), and (3) the average of Gender (the proportion of males: .23) times the effect of Gender (.29). The sum of these three terms is 1.20. When this reference value of 1.20 is subtracted from the original range ($-.57$ to $+4.16$), the result is -1.77 to $+2.96$, which is very close to the range obtained with the estimates from the Rasch model. This short discussion demonstrates how the parameter values are identified only up to an additive constant.

2.5   An item explanatory model: the LLTM

2.5.1   Formulation of the model

In the third model, the *linear logistic test model* (LLTM), item properties are used to explain the differences between items in terms of the effect they have on η_{pi}, and therefore on π_{pi}. The model differs from the Rasch model in that the contribution of item i is reduced to the contribution of the item properties and the values they have for item i (see also Table 2.2):

$$\eta_{pi} = \theta_p - \sum_{k=0}^{K} \beta_k X_{ik}, \qquad (2.9)$$

in which X_{ik} is the value of item i on item property k ($k = 0, \ldots, K$), and β_k is the regression weight of item property k. Comparing Equation 2.9 with the corresponding equation for the Rasch model (see Equation 2.2), one can see that the item parameter β_i is replaced with a linear function:

$$\beta'_i = \sum_{k=0}^{K} \beta_k X_{ik}. \tag{2.10}$$

Note that in general β'_i will not equal β_i as the prediction will not be perfect.

Because the mean of the person distribution is fixed to zero, a property with a value of 1 for all items is needed (a constant predictor) to act as the intercept in Equation 2.10. Hence, we need an item predictor for $k = 0$, with $X_{i0} = 1$ for all values of i, so that β_0 is the item intercept. An alternative is to estimate the mean of the θ_p, and to omit the contribution of the constant predictor, so that in Equations 2.9 and 2.10 k would run from 1 to K. These remarks apply also to the fourth model; see Section 2.6.1.

The model in Equation 2.9 is called the 'linear logistic test model' (LLTM; Fischer, 1973) because the model is based on a logit link and on a linear combination of item properties in the linear component, and because it was first used for test data. Instead of estimating individual item effects, the effects of item properties are estimated. The term 'logistic' in the label of the model does not mean that the principle of a linear combination of item properties cannot be used for normal-ogive models. Substituting a probit link instead of a logit link is all that is needed to obtain the normal-ogive equivalent of the LLTM.

The LLTM also allows for interactions between the item properties. If one is interested in the interaction between two item properties, their product can be added as an additional item property.

Graphical representation

A graphical representation of the LLTM is given in Figure 2.7.

The difference between Figure 2.5 for the Rasch model and Figure 2.7 for the LLTM is that the contribution of each item is explained through the item properties (the Xs) and their fixed effects (the βs from 1 to K, and a constant β_0, the effect of the constant item predictor). The constant predictor is represented twice, as X_{i0} and Z_{p0}, because it is also used twice: for the fixed LLTM intercept (β_0) and for the random intercept (θ_p).

Comments and literature

Note that there is no error term in Equations 2.9 and 2.10 and hence, the prediction is assumed to be perfect. The model implies that the item effects can be perfectly explained from the item properties, that β_i from the Rasch model equals β'_i from Equation 2.10. This is a strong assumption, and it

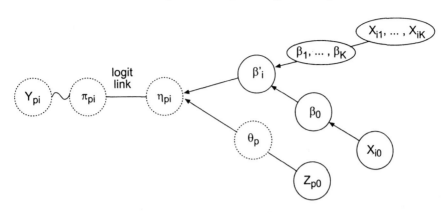

FIGURE 2.7. Graphical representation of the LLTM.

makes the model highly restrictive. But this constraint may be relaxed in more complex models. In Chapter 6, models are presented with an error component added to Equations 2.9 and 2.10.

The LLTM was developed by Fischer (1973, 1983). For an early application of regressing the item parameters on item properties, although the latter were not incorporated in the model, see Scheiblechner (1972). Fischer (1977) has presented a LLTM for multidimensional items, and later he described a general framework for designs with multidimensional items and different points in time, possibly with different subsets of items for different occasions (Fischer, 1989). For an overview of LLTM developments, see Fischer (1995).

2.5.2   Application of the LLTM

Three item properties are used in the LLTM for the verbal aggression data: Behavior Mode, Situation Type, and Behavior Type. The three properties are coded into four X-variables ($k = 1$ to 4), complemented with the constant item predictor ($k = 0$). We chose the coding given in Figure 2.8.

Behavior Mode
predictor 1   Do $= 1$ Want $= 0$

Situation Type
predictor 2   Other-to-blame $= 1$ Self-to-blame $= 0$

Behavior Type
predictor 3   Curse, Scold $= 1/2$ Shout $= -1$
predictor 4   Curse, Shout $= 1/2$ Scold $= -1$

FIGURE 2.8. Coding scheme for the LLTM

Note that the coding scheme as presented in Figure 2.8 differs from the one used for the simple linear regressions in Chapter 1, since, except for the Behavior Type, dummy coding is used. This illustrates how alternative coding schemes are possible. For the Behavior Type, contrast coding with centering on the overall mean is used as in Chapter 1, because we are still interested in the effect of the behavioral features (Blaming, Expressing) in comparison with the mean. However, we will also report the estimates using dummy coded factors for Behavior Type: one for Curse versus the other two behaviors, and one for Scold versus the other two behaviors (Shout is the reference level). The Behavior Mode is coded as a dummy variable: Do is coded as 1, and Want as 0. Also the Situation Type is coded as a dummy variable, with Other-to-blame coded as 1, and Self-to-blame as 0. In order to include an intercept, an item predictor is added with a value of one for all items ($k = 0$).

The goodness-of-fit values of the LLTM are given in Table 2.3. The values are clearly inferior to those of the previous models. The LR test comparing the LLTM to the Rasch model is significant $\chi^2(19) = 159.6$ ($p < .001$), meaning that the goodness of fit of the LLTM is lower. The reason is that the 24 parameters for item effects are now reduced to only five, corresponding to the five item predictors (including the constant predictor). But see our discussion below regarding the estimates, where we conclude that the item properties have a very high explanatory value. This illustrates how choosing to use an explanatory model can be at the cost of a statistically significant lower goodness of fit even when the explanation is rather successful. See Chapter 6 for a solution to this by defining the item parameters as a random variable. As for the other models, we first discuss the results regarding the person variance.

Person variance

The estimated *person variance* is 1.86, with a SE of .20 and thus significant ($p < .001$). Note that the variance is smaller than for the Rasch model (where it was 1.98). This illustrates how the estimates for the person mode are slightly affected by a different approach for the item mode (explanatory instead of descriptive). This phenomenon can be explained as a scaling effect (Snijders & Bosker, 1999, pp. 227–228), which was also discussed in Chapter 1. The effect is due to the less than perfect explanation of the item parameters on the basis of the item properties (see next paragraph).

Item property effects

We no longer have estimates of the individual item parameters but instead we have estimates of the effects of the item properties. To find out the effect per item, the sum of the effects of the corresponding item property variables must be made, as will be illustrated below.

The estimated *effect of the Behavior Mode* is .67, with a SE of .06, so that this effect is also highly statistically significant ($p < .001$) – when going from wanting to doing, the odds are reduced to about half of their value for wanting. The odds decrease with (are divided by) a factor of about two, more precisely 1.96. If the probability of wanting were .50, then the reduction would yield a probability of .34.

The estimated *effect of the Situation Type* is -1.03, with a SE of .06, so that the effect is highly statistically significant ($p < .001$). The effect implies that when others are to blame, verbal aggression is more common than when oneself is to blame. When others are to blame, the odds increase by a factor 2.80. The effect on a probability of .50 would be to raise it to .74.

Recall that for the *effect of the Behavior Type* two predictors were used. The effect of the first (Curse and Scold vs Shout) is -1.36, with a SE of .05; and the effect of the second (Curse and Shout vs Scold) is $-.70$, with a SE of .05. Both effects are highly statistically significant ($p < .001$). From these effects it may be concluded that for the situations under investigation the blaming aspect of a behavior has a larger effect on its occurrence than the expression aspect. When both effects are combined, the values for the three behaviors are: $-1.36/2 - .70/2 = -1.03$ for Curse, $-1.36/2 + .70 = .02$ for Scold, and $1.36 - .70/2 = 1.01$ for Shout. Using odds to describe the effect size, the odds of cursing are 2.86 times higher than those of scolding, and the odds of scolding are in turn 2.69 times higher than those of shouting. The odds roughly increase with a factor of almost three when going from shouting to scolding, and when going from scolding to cursing. If the probability of scolding were .50 in a given situation, then the corresponding probabilities of cursing and shouting would be .74, and .27, respectively. Equivalent results are obtained with the dummy coding. The effects are -2.04 (SE is .07) for Curse, and $-.99$ (SE is .07) for Scold. Finally, the estimated effect of the *constant predictor* is .31, the estimation of the fixed intercept using the coding scheme of Figure 2.8. Given the mixed coding (contrast coding and dummy coding) this effect has no easy interpretation.

In order to reconstruct the individual item parameters from the LLTM, one has to add up the effects that correspond to the four item property variables and the constant. For example, the reconstructed parameter for "A bus fails to stop for me. I would want to scold" is .02 (Scold) + .00 (Want is the reference level) -1.03 (Other-to-blame) $+.31$ (constant) $= -.70$. The parameter as estimated on the basis of the Rasch model is $-.57$. The correlation between the item parameters as estimated with the Rasch model and the parameters as reconstructed from the LLTM is .94. Thus, although the LLTM fits significantly worse in a statistical sense, it does very well in explaining the item parameters, so that we may say it has a large effect size in this respect.

2.6 A doubly explanatory model: the latent regression LLTM

2.6.1 Formulation of the model

Finally, one can carry out both of the previous extensions by combining Equations 2.7 and 2.10 into the equation for the Rasch model (Equation 2.2), assuming that β_i' is used in place of β_i. This yields the *latent regression LLTM*, a model that is explanatory for both the person mode and the item mode (see also Table 2.2):

$$\eta_{pi} = \sum_{j=1}^{J} \vartheta_j Z_{pj} + \varepsilon_p - \sum_{k=0}^{K} \beta_k X_{ik}. \tag{2.11}$$

As for the previous models, the model of Equation 2.11 has two parts: a person contribution and an item contribution. The person contribution is explained in terms of person properties and has an error term, while the item contribution is explained in terms of item properties and does not include an error term. This asymmetric construction is not a necessity, as will be seen in Chapter 6.

The model in Equation 2.11 is a GLMM with both person predictors and item predictors, each having a fixed effect, and a random intercept, which is the error term of the person contribution. The previous three models in this chapter can be obtained from Equation 2.11. Two kinds of modifications are needed to obtain the other three models: (a) to obtain the LLTM, the Zs are omitted, so that ε_p can be expressed as θ_p; and (b) to obtain the latent regression Rasch model, the Xs are just the item indicators ($X_{ik} = 1$ if $i = k$, $X_{ik} = 0$ otherwise, and $K = I$), so that for $k = i$ it holds that $\beta_k X_{ik} = \beta_i$, and for $k \neq i$ it holds that $\beta_k X_{ik} = 0$. For the Rasch model both modifications are needed. Alternatively, these three models can be seen as being built up by adding complications to the basic building block of the Rasch model.

Graphical representation

Figure 2.9 gives a graphical representation of the latent regression LLTM. The difference with Figure 2.5 (the Rasch model) is that in Figure 2.9 for the latent regression LLTM both the contribution of each item and of each person is explained through properties, item properties with a fixed effect β_k, and person properties with a fixed effect ϑ_p, respectively. For the items, the effect of the constant predictor is β_0, while for the persons the effect of the constant predictor is a random effect, which appears as an error term ε_p. This is why both X_{i0} and Z_{p0} are included in the representation. Note that the circles containing β_i' and θ_p are not needed. A direct connection of the arrows from the Xs and the Zs to η_{pi} is a more parsimonious but perhaps less interpretable representation.

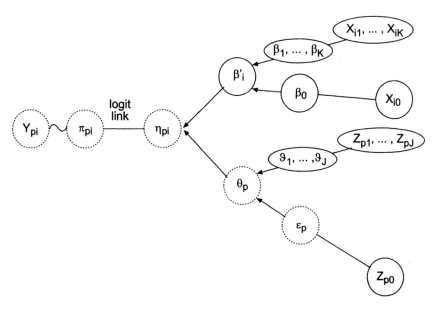

FIGURE 2.9. Graphical representation of the latent regression LLTM.

Literature

The latent regression LLTM is simply a combination of the latent regression idea with the LLTM, and this is why we call this combined model here the 'latent regression LLTM'. It is described theoretically in Zwinderman (1997), and Adams, Wilson and Wu (1997).

2.6.2   Application of the latent regression LLTM

The fit indices for the latent regression LLTM are given in Table 2.3. The goodness of fit is slightly better than for the LLTM, for the same reasons that the latent regression Rasch model had a slightly better goodness of fit than the Rasch model. The LR test comparing the latent regression LLTM to the LLTM is significant ($\chi^2(2) = 12.6$, $p < .001$). We will not note the specific effect estimates here, as the estimated *person property effects* are about the same as those obtained with the latent regression Rasch model, and also the estimated *item property effects* are about the same as those obtained with the LLTM.

It is noteworthy that the *residual person variance*, after the estimated effect of Trait Anger and Gender is accounted for, amounts to 1.73 in the latent regression LLTM, while it was 1.84 in the corresponding latent regression Rasch model. Again, the more flexible the model is for the estimation of the item effects, the larger the variance is of the (residual) person effects, as could be expected from the scaling effects discussed earlier.

2.7   Enlarging the perspective

The four models we have presented are chosen to illustrate the contrast between descriptive and explanatory models. They are only an introductory selection. In order to cover the broad variety of item response models, we need an enlargement of the perspectives. In principle the extensions can relate to the three parts of a GLMM: the random component, the link function, and the linear component.

Regarding the first two parts, the extension of the models to multi-categorical data has consequences for the link function and the random component. We will not go as far as extending the models also to count data, however, which would require a logarithmic link and a Poisson distribution for the random component. Regarding the linear component, the extensions concern not only the type of predictors and the type of effects, but also the linear nature of the component, since some of the item response models are not generalized linear mixed models but nonlinear mixed models. Examples of nonlinear mixed models are the two- and the three-parameter logistic models (2PL and 3PL models), and the multidimensional two-parameter models. Finally, the assumption of local independence will be relaxed.

For all these models, the parameters can either be descriptive parameters or explanatory parameters. Explanatory parameters are effects of properties, or in other words, of external variables. Descriptive parameters are either random effects or fixed effects of predictors that are not properties but indicators. This distinction, which is at the basis of the presentation of four models in this chapter, will be extrapolated in the following chapters.

Chapter 3 discusses extensions to multicategorical data. Other extensions are presented from Part II on. Chapter 4 describes more thoroughly than the previous chapters the statistical background for this volume.

2.8   Software

2.8.1   Rasch model (verbal aggression data)

The basic options that were used are described in Section 2.3.2. In later chapters, the basic options are reported in the sections on software.

Code

```
PROC NLMIXED data=aggression_dich method=gauss
technique=newrap noad qpoints=20;
PARMS b1-b24=1 sd0=1;
beta= b1*x1+b2*x2+b3*x3+b4*x4+b5*x5+b6*x6+b7*x7
+b8*x8+b9*x9+b10*x10+b11*x11+b12*x12+b13*x13+b14*x14
+b15*x15+b16*x16+b17*x17+b18*x18+b19*x19+b20*x20
```

```
+b21*x21+b22*x22+b23*x23+b24*x24;
ex=exp(theta-beta);
p=ex/(1+ex);
MODEL y ~ binary(p);
RANDOM theta ~ normal(0,sd0**2) subject=person;
ESTIMATE 'sd0**2' sd0**2;
RUN;
```

Comments

1. The data set is called **aggression_dich** (see website mentioned in the Preface). The data matrix contains the data in one long string and the values of the design factors corresponding with each observation (see Chapter 12).

2. In the **PARMS** statement, the parameters are introduced together with their initial values.

3. Next, the formula for the probability is built up from two ingredients: **beta** and **theta**. The **beta** part is based on the 24 item indicators (**x1** to **x24**) and their weights (**b1** to **b24**). The **theta** part is just a single term (θ_p, but see the software for the next application). With the basic ingredients of **theta** and **beta**, the formula for the probability is constructed. Instead of building up the formula in steps, one can as well give the formula in one step.

4. In the **MODEL** statement, it is specified that the observations follow a Bernoulli distribution (**binary**) with parameter **p** (π_{pi}).

5. In the **RANDOM** statement the distribution of **theta** is specified, over persons (**subject=person**), with mean zero and a variance that is the squared value of **sd0** (σ_θ). The value that is estimated is therefore the *SD* and not the variance.

6. This is why an **ESTIMATE** statement is added, so that also the variance is estimated, with label 'sd0**2' (the label may differ from the symbol in the software; e.g., **vartheta** would be another label).

7. The code for the LLTM will not be shown, but is analogous: **x1** to **x24** is replaced with **x1** to **x5** (the coded design factors) with their weights.

2.8.2 *Latent regression Rasch model (verbal aggression data)*

The options are the same as for the Rasch model.

Code

```
PROC NLMIXED data=aggression_dich method=gauss
technique=newrap noad qpoints=20;
PARMS b1-b24=1 sd0=1 g1-g2=0;
theta=eps + g1*anger + g2*male;
beta= b1*x1+b2*x2+b3*x3+b4*x4+b5*x5+b6*x6+b7*x7
+b8*x8+b9*x9+b10*x10+b11*x11+b12*x12+b13*x13+b14*x14
+b15*x15+b16*x16+b17*x17+b18*x18+b19*x19+b20*x20
+b21*x21+b22*x22+b23*x23+b24*x24;
ex=exp(theta-beta);
p=ex/(1+ex);
MODEL y ~ binary(p);
RANDOM eps ~ normal(0,sd0**2) subject=person;
ESTIMATE 'sd0**2' sd0**2;
RUN;
```

Comments

The two differences with the estimation of the Rasch model are:
1. theta is now defined as a sum of the Gender effect, the Trait Anger effect, and a random term eps, in correspondence with how theta is defined in the latent regression Rasch model. The person properties are anger and male (the Zs), and their weights g1 and g2 (the ϑs).
2. It is now the distribution of eps that is defined, instead of the distribution of theta.

2.9   Exercises

1. Why is no intercept (β_0) used in the Rasch model?

2. Redraw Figure 2.5 for a model with fixed person effects and random item effects.

3. How should one interpret the intercept in the LLTM? Suppose the intercept would be fixed to zero, while the mean of the θ-distribution is free. What would be the consequence of this? How do β_0 and the mean of θ relate to one another?

4. Suppose that for Do vs Want not a dummy coding would have been used but contrast coding (Do $= 1$, Want $= -1$). What would then have been the weight of this predictor?

5. θ_p can be removed from Figure 2.6. How would the new figure look

like then? Would ε_p be the random intercept? If yes, how can an error term be the measure of a latent trait, and how would the trait be defined?

2.10   References

Adams, R.J., Wilson, M., & Wang, W. (1997). The multidimensional random coefficients multinomial logit model. *Applied Psychological Measurement, 21*, 1–23.

Adams, R.J., Wilson, M., & Wu, M. (1997). Multilevel item response models: An approach to errors in variables regression. *Journal of Educational and Behavioral Statistics, 22*, 47–76.

Akaike, M. (1974). A new look at the statistical model identification. *IEEE Transactions on Automatic Control, 19*, 716–723.

Andersen, E.B., & Olsen, L.W. (2001). The life of Georg Rasch as a mathematician and as a statistician. In A. Boomsma, M.A.J. van Duijn & T.A.B. Snijders (Eds), *Essays on Item Response Theory* (pp. 3–24). New York: Springer.

Birnbaum, A. (1968). Some latent trait models and their use in inferring an examinee's ability. In F.M. Lord & M.R. Novick (Eds), *Statistical Theories of Mental Test Scores* (pp. 394–479). Reading, MA: Addison-Wesley.

Bock, R.D., & Aitkin, M. (1981). Marginal maximum likelihood estimation of item parameters: An application of the EM algorithm. *Psychometrika, 46*, 443–459.

Bond, T., & Fox, C. (2001). *Applying the Rasch Model: Fundamental Measurement in Human Sciences.* Mahwah, NJ: Lawrence Erlbaum.

Bozdogan, H. (1987). Model selection for Akaike's information criterion (AIC). *Psychometrika, 53*, 345–370.

de Leeuw, J., & Verhelst, N. (1986). Maximum-likelihood estimation in generalized Rasch models. *Journal of Educational Statistics, 11*, 183–196.

Fischer, G.H. (1968). Neue Entwicklungen in der psychologischen Testtheorie. In G.H. Fischer (Ed.), *Psychologische Testtheorie* (pp. 15–158). Bern: Huber.

Fischer, G.H. (1973). The linear logistic test model as an instrument in educational research. *Acta Psychologica, 3*, 359–374.

Fischer, G.H. (1974). *Einführung in die Theorie Psychologischer Tests.* Bern: Huber.

Fischer, G.H. (1977). Linear logistic trait models: Theory and application. In H. Spada & W.F. Kampf (Eds), *Structural Models of Thinking and Learning* (pp. 203–225). Bern: Huber.

Fischer, G.H. (1981). On the existence and uniqueness of maximum-likelihood estimates in the Rasch model. *Psychometrika, 46,* 59–77.

Fischer, G.H. (1983). Logistic latent trait models with linear constraints. *Psychometrika, 48,* 3–26.

Fischer, G.H. (1989). An IRT-based model for dichotomous longitudinal data. *Psychometrika, 54,* 599–624.

Fischer, G.H. (1995). Linear logistic models for change. In G.H. Fischer & I. Molenaar (Eds), *Rasch Models. Foundations, Recent Developments and Applications* (pp. 157–201). New York: Springer.

Fischer, G.H., & Molenaar, I. (1995) (Eds), *Rasch Models. Foundations, Recent Developments, and Applications.* New York: Springer.

Follmann, D.A. (1988). Consistent estimation in the Rasch model based on nonparametric margins. *Psychometrika, 53,* 553–562.

Fox, J.P., & Glas, C.A.W. (2003). Bayesian modeling of measurement error in predictor variables using item response theory. *Psychometrika, 68,* 169–191.

Hoijtink, H., & Boomsma, A. (1995). On person parameter estimation in the dichotomous Rasch Model. In G.H. Fischer & I. Molenaar (Eds), *Rasch Models. Foundations, Recent Developments and Applications* (pp. 53–68). New York: Springer.

Junker, B., & Sijtsma, K. (2001). Nonparametric item response theory. Special issue. *Applied Psychological Measurement, 25.*

Masters, G.N., Adams, R.A., & Wilson, M. (1990). Charting of student progress. In T. Husen & T.N. Postlewaite (Eds), *International Encyclopedia of Education: Research and Studies. Supplementary Volume 2.* (pp. 628–634) Oxford: Pergamon Press.

Mischel, W. (1968). *Personality Assessment.* New York: Wiley, 1968.

Mislevy, R.J. (1987). Exploiting auxiliary information about examinees in the estimation of item parameters. *Applied Psychological Measurement, 11,* 81–91.

Molenaar, I. (1995). Estimation of item parameters. In G.H. Fischer & I. Molenaar (Eds), *Rasch Models. Foundations, Recent Developments and Applications* (pp. 39–57). New York: Springer.

Rabe-Hesketh, S., Pickles, A., & Skrondal, A. (2001). *GLLAMM Manual.* Technical Report 2001/01. Department of Biostatistics and Computing, Institute of Psychiatry, King's College, University of London.

Rasch, G. (1960). *Probabilistic Models for Some Intelligence and Attainment Tests.* Copenhagen, Denmark: Danish Institute for Educational Research.

Rasch, G. (1961). On general laws and the meaning of measurement in psychology. *Proceedings of the Fourth Berkeley Symposium on Mathematical Statistics and Theory of Probability* (Vol. IV, pp. 321–333). Berkeley, CA:

University of California Press.

Rasch, G. (1967). An informal report on a theory of objectivity in comparisons. In L.J.Th. van der Kamp & C.A.J. Vlek (Eds), *Psychological Measurement Theory* (pp. 1–19). Proceedings of The NUFFIC international summer session. Leiden: University of Leiden.

Read, T.R.C., & Cressie, N.A.C. (1988). *Goodness-of-fit Statistics for Discrete Multivariate Data.* New York: Springer.

Rost, J. (2001). The growing family of Rasch models. In A. Boomsma, M.A.J. van Duijn & T.A.B. Snijders (Eds), *Essays on Item Response theory* (pp. 25–42). New York: Springer.

SAS Institute (1999). *SAS OnlineDoc (Version 8)* (software manual on CD-ROM). Cary, NC: SAS Institute.

Scheiblechner, H. (1972). Das Lernen and Lösen komplexer Denkaufgaben. *Zeitschrift für Experimentelle und Angewandte Psychologie, 3,* 456–506.

Schwarz, G. (1978). Estimating the dimension of a model. *The Annals of Statistics, 6,* 461–464.

Sijtsma, K., & Molenaar, I. (2002). *Introduction to Nonparametric Item Response Theory.* Thousand Oaks, CA: Sage.

Snijders, T., & Bosker, R. (1999). *Multilevel Analysis.* London: Sage.

Thissen, D., & Orlando, M. (2001). Item response theory for items scored in two categories. In D. Thissen & H. Wainer (Eds), *Test Scoring* (pp. 73–140). Mahwah, NJ: Lawrence Erlbaum.

Verbeke, G., & Molenberghs, G. (2000). *Linear Mixed Models for Longitudinal Data.* New York: Springer.

Verhelst, N.D., & Eggen, T.J.H.M. (1989). Psychometrische en statistische aspecten van peilingsonderzoek (PPON rapport 4). Arnhem: Cito.

Verhelst, N.D., & Glas, C.A.W. (1995). The one parameter logistic model. In G.H. Fisher & I. Molenaar (Eds), *Rasch Models. Foundations, Recent Developments, and Applications* (pp. 215–237). New York: Springer.

Wainer, H., Vevea, J.L., Camacho, F., Reeve, B.B., Rosa, K., Nelson, L., Swygert, K., & Thissen, D. (2001). Augmented scores – "Borrowing strength" to compute scores based on small numbers of items. In D. Thissen & H. Wainer (Eds), *Test Scoring* (pp. 343–387). Mahwah, NJ: Lawrence Erlbaum.

Wald, A. (1941). Asymptotically most powerful tests of statistical hypotheses. *Annals of Mathematical Statistics, 12,* 1–19.

Warm, T.A. (1989). Weighted likelihood estimation of ability in item response models. *Psychometrika, 54,* 427–450

Wilson, M. (2003). On choosing a model for measuring. *Methods of Psychological Research - Online, 8*(3), 1-22.

Wilson, M. (2005). *Constructing Measures: An Item Modeling Approach.* Mahwah, NJ: Lawrence Erlbaum.

Wright, B. (1968). Sample-free test calibration and person measurement. *Proceedings 1967 Invitational Conference on Testing* (pp. 85–101). Princeton: ETS.

Wright, B. (1977). Solving measurement problems with the Rasch model. *Journal of Educational Measurement, 14*, 97–116.

Wright, B. (1997). A history of social science measurement. *Educational Measurement: Issues and Practice, 16*, 33–52.

Wright, B., & Stone, M. (1979). *Best Test Design.* Chicago, IL: MESA.

Wu, M.L., Adams, R.J., & Wilson, M. (1998). *ACERConquest.* Hawthorn, Australia: ACER Press.

Zwinderman, A.H. (1991). A generalized Rasch model for manifest predictors. *Psychometrika, 56*, 589–600.

Zwinderman, A.H. (1997). Response models with manifest predictors. In W.J. van der Linden & R.K. Hambleton (Eds), *Handbook of Modern Item Response Theory* (pp. 245–256). New York: Springer.

Chapter 3

Models for polytomous data

Francis Tuerlinckx
Wen-Chung Wang

3.1 Introduction

In the first two chapters of this volume, models for binary or dichotomous variables have been discussed. However, in a wide range of psychological and sociological applications it is very common to have data that are polytomous or multicategorical. For instance, the response scale in the verbal aggression data set (see Chapters 1 and 2) originally consisted of three categories ("yes," "perhaps," "no"), but it was dichotomized to illustrate the application of models for binary data. In aptitude testing, the response is often classified into one of several categories (e.g., wrong, partially correct, fully correct). In attitude research, frequent use is made of rating scales with more than two categories (e.g., "strongly agree," "agree," "disagree," "strongly disagree"). Other examples are multiple-choice items, for which each separate choice option represents another category. In a typical discrete choice experiment, the subject is faced with a choice between several options (e.g., several brands of a product in a marketing study).

Each of the previous examples is characterized by the fact that the outcome variable has more than two response categories. Analyzing such data requires the use of a model that can adequately handle the additional information that is supplied by the greater number of response categories. Dichotomizing the scale often leads to a loss of information about the response process and less precise inferences about the scientific question of interest.

An important feature of multicategorical data, which was not relevant for binary items, is whether the response categories are ordered or not. If the categories are not ordered, we say they are nominal; in the other case, the categories are called ordinal. If the categories are ordinal, the model should be one that takes this information into account.

Each item has M_i possible response categories ($m = 0, \ldots, M_i - 1$), and the response of the person falls into one of those categories. A different kind of analysis is needed if the person can choose simultaneously more than one category but we will not consider such data here (see Agresti & Liu, 2001). In this general setup the number of response categories can change over items. For a person p and item i with M_i (ordered or unordered) response categories, there is a set of M_i probabilities $\{\pi_{pim}, \ m = 0, \ldots, M_i - 1\}$ describing the chance for person p to respond on item i in each category and the M_i probabilities sum to one.

Historically, one of the first mixed models for polytomous data was proposed in an educational measurement context by Rasch (1961; see also Andersen, 1995). Rasch's model was the predecessor of a whole family of educational measurement models for polytomous data (Andrich, 1978, 1982; Fischer & Parzer, 1991; Fischer & Ponocny, 1994; Glas & Verhelst, 1989; Masters, 1982). A restricted version of Bock's nominal response model (without discrimination parameters; Bock, 1972) can also be seen as a member of this Rasch model family. A common feature of these models is that they are based on baseline-category or adjacent-categories logits (see below). The random coefficients multinomial logit model (Adams & Wilson, 1996; Adams, Wilson, & Wang, 1997) encompasses many members of the Rasch model family. A different type of mixed model for polytomous data is Samejima's graded response model (Samejima, 1969), based on cumulative logits. In econometrics, a mixed-effects version of the multinomial logit model for discrete (unordered) choice data (Luce, 1959; McFadden, 1974) was introduced in the early 1980s (Boyd & Mellman, 1980; Cardell & Dunbar, 1980). Surprisingly, the intensive study of mixed models for polytomous data in statistics began relatively late (Ezzet & Whitehead, 1991; Harville & Mee, 1984; Hedeker & Gibbons, 1994; Jansen, 1990; McCullagh & Nelder, 1989; for a review, see Agresti, 1999). Polytomous data can also be analyzed from a structural equations model perspective (Bartholomew, Steele, Moustaki, & Galbraith, 2002) but this approach is more related to traditional factor analysis models and therefore it will not be covered here.

We will first introduce a general model, called the multivariate generalized linear mixed model, from which specific models for polytomous data will be derived. Our treatment of these models is inspired by the approach of Fahrmeir and Tutz (2001). Some of the models will be discussed more in detail, including applications to the verbal aggression data.

3.2   The multivariate generalized linear mixed model

When a sample of persons respond to a set of polytomous items, two kinds of correlated multivariate data result. First, and as in the other chapters, the responses to the different polytomous items are dependent as a consequence of the clustered structure of the data (i.e., items nested within persons). Second, the response to a single polytomous item in itself can be seen as a multivariate dependent response. Although counterintuitive at first sight, this fact is essential to cast models for polytomous data in the GLMM framework.

We will now discuss an extension of the previously presented models in order to deal with polytomous data. The extension will be discussed first for the GLM (without a random effect) and, in a second step, for the GLMM (with a random effect).

3.2.1 Data

If the response of person p to item i falls in category m, then $Y_{pi} = m$ $(m = 0, 1, \ldots, M_i - 1)$. Clearly, $M_i = 2$ refers to the binary case. However, a fundamental difference between binary and polytomous data is that the latter is actually a multivariate or vector-valued random variable while the former is univariate. To see this, one can recode the random variable Y_{pi} into a random vector consisting of zeros and ones, denoted as $\boldsymbol{C}_{pi}$ with length $M_i - 1$ (the length is one less than the number of categories). The components of a realization $\boldsymbol{c}_{pi}$ of the random vector $\boldsymbol{C}_{pi}$ are defined as follows:

$$c_{pim} = \begin{cases} 1 & \text{if } Y_{pi} = m, \quad m = 1, \ldots, M_i - 1, \\ 0 & \text{otherwise.} \end{cases} \tag{3.1}$$

This response vector is a dummy coded or indicator version of the poly- tomous outcome variable. For simplicity, we discard the first category 0 because this leads to the simplest formulation of subsequent models, but, in principle, any other category could be chosen as the reference category. Hence, the response to a polytomous item with M_i response categories is actually a vector of $M_i - 1$ distinct, nonredundant but correlated binary responses. In the binary case, the vector $\boldsymbol{C}_{pi}$ has only one component and therefore the outcome variable is essentially univariate and does not differ from Y_{pi}.

As an illustration of the preceding, consider the data set on verbal ag- gression. In the original study, 316 participants could choose one of three re- sponse options ("no," "perhaps," and "yes") indicating whether they would react in the way described by the item in a given situation. Hence, in this data set M_i equals 3 for all 24 items $(i = 1, \ldots, 24)$ and the responses "no," "perhaps," and "yes" are scored 0, 1, and 2, respectively. For example, if person p responds with "perhaps" to item i, then $Y_{pi} = 1$. The vector of multivariate observations for each person-item combination, $\boldsymbol{c}_{pi}$, has two components $(M_i - 1 = 2)$. The possible data patterns are: (0,0) when re- sponding "no," (1,0) when responding "perhaps," and (0,1) when respond- ing "yes." For simplicity, we will continue to work with $M_i = M = 3$ in the explanation of the models. The adaptation of the material to the case of a greater number of categories or a varying number of categories over the items is straightforward.

3.2.2   Multivariate extension of the generalized linear model

Modeling data with a GLM requires an answer to three questions (see McCullagh & Nelder, 1989, and McCulloch & Searle, 2001). (1) What is the specific distribution of the data? (2) What transformation of the mean will be modeled linearly? (3) Which predictors will be included in the model? The first question refers to the distributional or random component of the model, the second to the link function, and the third to the linear component. Because for polytomous data the response is multivariate, we extend the univariate GLM framework to the multivariate case so that *multivariate generalized linear models* are obtained (MGLM). The three parts of a MGLM (distribution, link function, linear predictor) will be treated successively.

The distribution

As mentioned, c_{pi} is a vector of length 2 with all components except one equal to zero, or all equal to zero. The appropriate distribution for this random vector is the multivariate Bernouilli distribution (a multinomial distribution with total count equal to one):

$$
\begin{aligned}
\Pr(Y_{pi} = m) &= \Pr(C_{pi} = c_{pi}) \\
&= \pi_{pi1}^{c_{pi1}} \pi_{pi2}^{c_{pi2}} (1 - \pi_{pi1} - \pi_{pi2})^{(1 - c_{pi1} - c_{pi2})},
\end{aligned}
\tag{3.2}
$$

where π_{pim} $(m = 1, 2)$ is the probability of responding in category m for person p on item i and $1 - \pi_{pi1} - \pi_{pi2} = \pi_{pi0}$. The mean of the multivariate Bernouilli distribution is actually the vector of the marginal probabilities $\pi'_{pi} = (\pi_{pi1}, \pi_{pi2})$. The variances of each of the univariate components are $\pi_{pim}(1 - \pi_{pim})$ and the covariance between the two components equals $-\pi_{pi1}\pi_{pi2}$ (see Fahrmeir & Tutz, 2001). The distribution of the MGLM belongs to the multivariate exponential family.

The link function

The vector-valued link function f_{link} transforms the vector of means of the multivariate Bernouilli distribution π_{pi} into a vector η_{pi} with the same dimension:

$$
f_{\text{link}}(\pi_{pi}) = \left(\begin{array}{c} f_{\text{link } 1}(\pi_{pi}) \\ f_{\text{link } 2}(\pi_{pi}) \end{array} \right) = \left(\begin{array}{c} \eta_{pi1} \\ \eta_{pi2} \end{array} \right) = \eta_{pi}.
\tag{3.3}
$$

In general, if an item has M categories, the link function has $M - 1$ components, equal to the number of nonredundant probabilities.

In the polytomous case, there are a number of possible choices for link functions. All link functions discussed in this chapter are generalizations of the simple logit link that was introduced for binary data (except for Exercise 4 where the probit link is used). A detailed discussion of the link functions will be given in Section 3.4. For the moment, we confine ourselves to a general account of these logit link functions. Each logit is defined as the logarithm of the ratio of the probability of responding in a subset A_m of all categories, relative to the probability of responding in a disjoint subset B_m of all categories. Formally, this is represented as follows:

$$f_{\text{link } m}(\boldsymbol{\pi}_{pi}) = \log\left(\frac{\pi_{pi}(A_m)}{\pi_{pi}(B_m)}\right), \qquad (3.4)$$

where A_m and B_m are two disjoint subsets of the response categories (the union of A_m and B_m does not necessarily include all categories). In the binary case, there is only one way to form two disjoint subsets: A_1 for the category scored as 1 and B_1 for the category scored as 0 (the reference category). However, with polytomous data, there are in total four different ways, three of which will be discussed extensively in this chapter.

A component of the link function is called the 'binary building block' of models for polytomous items (Thissen & Steinberg, 1986) and it can be interpreted as a measure of the attractiveness of subset A_m relative to subset B_m. The attractiveness will be modeled as a linear function of the predictors. The choice of a particular link function will determine the interpretation of the regression coefficients of the linear predictor. The inverse of the link function is called the response function: $f_{\text{link}}^{-1}(\boldsymbol{\eta}_{pi}) = \boldsymbol{\pi}_{pi}$. It will be used to express the probabilities as a function of the predictors.

The linear predictor

Since the vector-valued link function in Equation 3.3 has $M - 1 = 2$ components, we need to equate it to a two-component vector of linear combinations of the predictors. Suppose we measured K predictor variables, denoted as $X_1, \ldots, X_k, \ldots, X_K$; the predictors can be item, person, or logit predictors, or any combination of them. An observed value for person p, item i and logit m on the kth variable is denoted as X_{pimk}. The reason for using the term *logit predictor*, instead of the more intuitive label 'category predictor,' will be explained in Section 3.3. For the moment it suffices to say that a predictor that varies over the $M-1$ different logits (or nonredundant categories) can be included in the model.

All measurements for the combination of person p and item i can be collected in a predictor matrix $\boldsymbol{X}_{pi}$ with two rows (for the three categories) and K columns. Each column refers to one of the K variables. A particular row in this predictor matrix is denoted as $\boldsymbol{X}'_{pim}$. The I matrices $\boldsymbol{X}_{pi}$ can be stacked in the predictor matrix $\boldsymbol{X}_p$ (for person p) and all P predictor matrices can be stacked in the super predictor matrix $\boldsymbol{X}$. In Section 3.3 the predictor matrix will be treated in more detail.

The vector of regression coefficients is denoted by $\boldsymbol{\beta}$. Multiplying $\boldsymbol{X}_{pi}$ with $\boldsymbol{\beta}$ results in the vector of linear predictors $\boldsymbol{\eta}_{pi}$. However, we will consider the negative of the product of $\boldsymbol{X}_{pi}$ with $\boldsymbol{\beta}$, because it is a tradition in the item response modeling literature and because the interpretation of some of the parameters will be more straightforward after a random effect is added (see below):

$$\boldsymbol{\eta}_{pi} = \begin{pmatrix} \eta_{pi1} \\ \eta_{pi2} \end{pmatrix} = \begin{pmatrix} -\sum_{k=1}^{K} \beta_k X_{pi1k} \\ -\sum_{k=1}^{K} \beta_k X_{pi2k} \end{pmatrix}$$

$$= \begin{pmatrix} -\boldsymbol{X}_{pi1}'\boldsymbol{\beta} \\ -\boldsymbol{X}_{pi2}'\boldsymbol{\beta} \end{pmatrix} = -\boldsymbol{X}_{pi}\boldsymbol{\beta}. \tag{3.5}$$

We have made no explicit reference to the intercept in the model formulation but it can be defined easily by including a column of ones $\boldsymbol{X}_0$ in the predictor matrix $\boldsymbol{X}$ and assigning it a regression coefficient β_0 (with the restriction that the columns should be linearly independent, see below).

3.2.3 Multivariate extension of the generalized linear mixed model

It is often the case that psychological data, and data from the social sciences in general, are the outcome of repeated observations on the same individuals. Such data are commonly characterized by response dependencies within the same person and by systematic differences between persons. One way to take into account within-subject correlation and between-subject heterogeneity is to add a person-specific random effect θ_p to the linear predictor described in Equation 3.5. Adding a random effect to the MGLM results in a *multivariate generalized linear mixed model* (MGLMM; Agresti, 2002; Hartzel, Agresti, & Caffo, 2001). Equation 3.5 now becomes:

$$\boldsymbol{\eta}_{pi} = \begin{pmatrix} Z_{pi1}\theta_p \\ Z_{pi2}\theta_p \end{pmatrix} - \begin{pmatrix} \boldsymbol{X}_{pi1}'\boldsymbol{\beta} \\ \boldsymbol{X}_{pi2}'\boldsymbol{\beta} \end{pmatrix} = \boldsymbol{Z}_{pi}\theta_p - \boldsymbol{X}_{pi}\boldsymbol{\beta}, \tag{3.6}$$

where it is assumed that $\theta_p \sim N(0, \sigma_\theta^2)$, for $p = 1, \ldots, P$. The vector $\boldsymbol{Z}_{pi} = (Z_{pi1}, Z_{pi2})'$ is the predictor vector for the random effect. The $P \times I$ random-effect predictor vectors $\boldsymbol{Z}_{pi}$ can be stacked below each other into a super random-effects predictor matrix $\boldsymbol{Z}$. For almost all models discussed in this chapter $\boldsymbol{Z}$ will be a column vector of all ones ($\boldsymbol{Z} = \boldsymbol{Z}_0$); therefore, these models are random-intercepts models because θ_p is a person-specific deviation from the general intercept. Moreover, all MGLMMs in this chapter are unidimensional because only a single random effect is considered.

The MGLMM in Equation 3.6 rests on the assumption of conditional independence or local stochastic independence (as it is often called in the item response modeling literature). This means that, conditionally upon the random effect θ_p, the responses on the items are independent. Therefore, θ_p explains both the within-person dependence and the between-person heterogeneity.

As has been emphasized in the first two chapters, there are two possible interpretations for the random intercept θ_p: a descriptive and an explanatory one. A descriptive perspective on the random effect is most common in a measurement context in which one wants to measure a latent dimension or propensity (e.g., an ability, or a personality trait), in order to locate a person p on the unobserved dimension. The corresponding location is denoted as θ_p. From the explanatory perspective, the researcher wants to explain the between-person variability σ_θ^2 by including predictors into the model. Ideally, one wants the unexplained variability between persons to be as small as possible. To distinguish between the descriptive and explanatory approaches, we use two symbols for the random effect, depending on the situation: θ_p is used if no person covariates are included in the model (i.e., if no attempt is made to explain between-person heterogeneity), while ε_p is used if person covariates are included. Despite the differences, the two approaches are often complementary.

3.3   Predictor matrices and model building

In this section we will illustrate how different models for polytomous data can be built by specifying the predictor matrix. It will be shown that one of the great advantages of the MGLMM framework is the flexibility the researcher has to construct a model that is tailor-made for her or his purposes.

A MGLMM contains two predictor matrices: X and Z. We will use X for the fixed-effects predictor matrix and Z for the random-effects predictor matrix, in conformity with the general GLMM notation as used in Chapter 4 because we start from the same general framework. This is in contrast with the notation in the other chapters on specific types of models, where X and Z denote the item predictor matrix and the person predictor matrix, respectively. We will not use the graphical representations that were introduced in Chapters 1 and 2, because the multivariate nature of the models is a serious complication for this kind of representation.

Predictor types

Apart from the intercept, the predictors that are included in the predictor matrix X can be classified into seven groups: item predictors, person predictors, logit predictors, and the four combinations of them. Person and item predictors are discussed in the previous chapters and person-by-item predictors will be discussed in detail in Chapter 7 of this volume. A logit predictor has the same value in all rows of the predictor matrix referring to the same component of the vector-valued link function. Interactions between a logit predictor and any of the other predictors are also possible. For instance, an item-by-logit predictor has constant values for all rows in the predictor matrix referring to the same combination of an item with a specific component of the link function. Similar definitions apply to person-by-logit and person-by-item-by-logit predictors. Examples of some of these predictors will follow below.

In this volume, we have chosen to use the term 'logit predictor' instead of 'category predictor.' The latter may seem more appealing but we believe that it may cause confusion. There are two main reasons to opt for the term 'logit predictor.' First, although the data come with M categories, there are only $M-1$ corresponding components of the link function in any model for polytomous data. Consequently, there are only $M-1$ rows in the predictor matrix available for a person-item pair and thus the predictor values can only attain $M-1$ different values for a person-item pair. In the models we discuss, the components of the link functions are all some form of logits and therefore we have chosen this term. Second, each component of the link function (i.e., each logit) is modeled as a function of the predictors. As expressed in Equation 3.4, the logits determine the attractiveness of a subset of the categories A_m compared to another subset B_m. Different choices of these subsets are possible and they are not always directly linked with a single category.

Item-by-logit interaction model

The process of finding a suitable inferential model for data should start in the first place with a fairly general tentative model (Ramsey & Schafer, 2001) that can be refined or expanded in the course of the analysis. With categorical data, a reasonable point of departure is to consider a model with dummy variables for items and logits and interactions between them. In analogy with the predictor matrix of a multiple regression model for fitting a full two-way analysis-of-variance (ANOVA) model, this is a model with main effects for the factors Item (with I levels) and Logit (with $M-1$ levels) and an interaction between them. There are several ways in which the predictor matrix can be set up to represent such a model, but the common approach in item response modeling is to define $I(M-1)$ indicator variables that take the value 1 for all rows that refer to a specific item-by-logit combination, and zero otherwise. For example, if a person p responds to three items having each three categories (and thus two logits), the predictor matrix X_p would be as shown in Table 3.1.

Hence each separate item-by-logit combination will have a corresponding parameter (to be discussed in the next session) and the predictor matrix contains item-by-logit predictors (because the values on these predictors are different for different items and logits within persons but not over persons). Without person predictors, a model with interactions between the item and logit indicators is the most general model one can fit. Because of its generality, we will call this model the *full item-by-logit model*. If no more information about the items or categories is available, the full item-by-logit

TABLE 3.1. Predictor matrix for a full item-by-logit model for three items each having three categories (interactions between items and logits).

Item	Logit	X_1	X_2	X_3	X_4	X_5	X_6
1	L_1	1	0	0	0	0	0
1	L_2	0	1	0	0	0	0
2	L_1	0	0	1	0	0	0
2	L_2	0	0	0	1	0	0
3	L_1	0	0	0	0	1	0
3	L_2	0	0	0	0	0	1

interaction model is often the only reasonable model that can be fit.

Item response models that allow for item-by-logit interactions are Bock's nominal response model (NRM or nominal model; Bock, 1972), Masters' partial credit model (PCM; Masters, 1982), and Samejima's graded response model (GRM; Samejima, 1969). Note however that the original formulations of the GRM contain item-specific discrimination parameters that have to be estimated from the data and that, in the NRM, these discrimination parameters may vary both over items and over logits within items. Discrimination parameters are considered in Chapter 8 and we will work in this chapter only with models without discrimination parameters.

Item and logit main effects

The next step of the inferential process will often consist of simplifying the full item-by-logit model, if possible. For example, if the same response options are used for all items (as in the verbal aggression data set), it makes sense to assess the fit of a model with only item and logit main effects (the item and logit main-effects model). Item main-effects parameters determine the general location of the items on the latent variable continuum θ_p, while logit parameters determine the position of the different categories relative to the item location. The main-effects predictor matrix $\boldsymbol{X}_p$ for person p can be constructed by including I item indicators and $M - 2$ logit indicators (an explanation for the latter count will be given shortly). An example for three items with each three categories is given in Table 3.2.

The indicators X_1, X_2, and X_3 refer to the item main effects and X_4 to the logit main effect; hence the latter is a logit predictor because its value changes over logits within person-item pairs but not over persons and items. At first sight, the predictor matrix for the full item-by-logit model in Table 3.1 and for the item and logit main-effects model in Table 3.2 seem unrelated but that is not the case. The main-effects model predictor matrix can be derived from the full item-by-logit model predictor matrix

TABLE 3.2. Predictor matrix for an item and logit main-effects model for three
items each having three categories (no interactions between items and logits).

Item	Logit	X_1	X_2	X_3	X_4
1	L_1	1	0	0	0
1	L_2	1	0	0	1
2	L_1	0	1	0	0
2	L_2	0	1	0	1
3	L_1	0	0	1	0
3	L_2	0	0	1	1

by a simple reparametrization of the latter. Thus, the main-effects model
is nested within the full item-by-logit model. Therefore, their relative fit
can be compared with a likelihood-ratio (LR) test. The main-effects model
is referred to in the item response modeling literature as the rating scale
model (RSM; Andrich, 1978, 1982) when the adjacent-categories logit link
is used (see below). However, with other link functions, the same principle
can be applied.

In the main-effects predictor matrix, there are as many item location
parameters as items but there is only one logit main-effects parameter (despite the fact that there are two logits). The reason is that adding a dummy
variable that corresponds to the second logit would render a predictor matrix that is not of full rank. For RSMs, a different identification constraint
is traditionally used. For instance, Andrich (1978) formulated the model in
such a way that each item, except the first, has a separate location parameter and there are $M - 1$ logit-specific parameters (the location of the first
item is therefore set to zero). The total number of parameters in both versions of the model is the same and they will fit equally well. Furthermore,
we have used for all predictors a dummy coding scheme because that was
most natural, but other coding schemes may be more appropriate in other
situations.

Including properties of items and categories

In a subsequent step in the analysis, other item and logit predictors than
mere indicators of the different items and logits can be considered. These
lead to a more parsimonious inferential model with a greater explanatory
power. Both item and logit properties can be used as predictors. The use of
item properties is illustrated in the previous chapters. In a similar way one
can include logit properties in the predictor matrix. For example, consider a
discrete choice study where a participant has to choose repeatedly between
three transportation modes (bicycle, train, and car). Then their prices are

included in the model as a predictor. We will see that the appropriate link function (the baseline-category logit link) for such data is one where each component of the function indicates the attractiveness of a single category (train or car) relative to the reference category (e.g., bicycle). Therefore, only the relative price of a train or car trip compared to the price of a bicycle trip is relevant in the model. In practice one subtracts the price of a bicycle trip from the price of a train trip or car trip. Finally, it is also possible to include item-by-logit predictors, or logit-specific item predictors.

Person predictors

The inclusion of person predictors in the model is analogous to what has been described in Chapter 2. They are easily inserted as extra columns in the predictor matrix. However, an additional extension with polytomous data is possible by constructing a person-by-logit predictor. In that case the person predictor has a separate regression coefficient for each logit. As a caveat, we note that including person-by-logit predictors is not always reasonable or free of interpretational difficulties for ordinal data, as we will show in Section 3.5.

3.4   Specifying the link function

The choice of the link function determines the specific type of model and it has important consequences for the interpretation of the results. For binary data, there was only one possible logit link function, but for polytomous data, one has the choice between several generalized logit functions. Each link function defines in a different way how the categories are classified into the two subsets A_m and B_m to form the mth logit (see Equation 3.4). Three common logits for polytomous data are discussed here: (1) the adjacent-categories logits, (2) the cumulative logits, and (3) the baseline-category logits. The first two link functions are for ordinal data, the last one is mainly used for nominal data. All three generalized logits simplify to the regular univariate logit if the data have only two categories.

There are two ways of introducing the different link functions. The first focuses on the partitioning of the categories into subsets A_m and B_m and on the interpretation of the parameters. In a second approach, one assumes an unobserved behavioral process that takes place when a person responds to an item. It can then be shown that the unobserved behavioral process leads to the same model as a particular link function, but now the parameters have a meaningful interpretation in terms of the latent process. In our presentation, we will emphasize the first approach of the link functions, but we will mention the behavioral process in some cases because it can be illuminating.

For illustrative purposes, we consider in the explanation of the link functions an item i with three categories (as in the verbal aggression data set) and the fixed-effects predictor matrix $\boldsymbol{X}$ corresponding to a full item-by-logit model as in Table 3.1. Thus for item i, there are two logit-specific parameters β_{i1} and β_{i2}.

3.4.1 Adjacent-categories logits

The mth adjacent-categories logit is the logit of responding in category m versus in category $m-1$. Therefore, A_m and B_m equal $\{m\}$ and $\{m-1\}$, respectively. The link function and structural component of the model become:

$$
\begin{aligned}
f_{\text{link } 1}(\boldsymbol{\pi}_{pi}) &= \log\left(\frac{\pi_{pi1}}{1-\pi_{pi1}-\pi_{pi2}}\right) = \log\left(\frac{\pi_{pi1}}{\pi_{pi0}}\right) \\
&= Z_{pi1}\theta_p - \boldsymbol{X}'_{pi1}\boldsymbol{\beta} = \theta_p - \beta_{i1}, \qquad (3.7) \\
f_{\text{link } 2}(\boldsymbol{\pi}_{pi}) &= \log\left(\frac{\pi_{pi2}}{\pi_{pi1}}\right) = Z_{pi2}\theta_p - \boldsymbol{X}'_{pi2}\boldsymbol{\beta} = \theta_p - \beta_{i2}.
\end{aligned}
$$

From Equation 3.7, it can be seen that the random-effects predictor matrix $\boldsymbol{Z}$ is a long vector of ones.

In adjacent-categories logit models, the attractiveness of a higher category relative to the adjacent lower one is modeled and it is precisely this paired adjacent-categories comparison that recognizes the ordering of the categories. Indeed, we see that if θ_p increases, the attraction of the upper category in each adjacent-categories logit increases too.

It follows from Equation 3.7, that category m and $m-1$ are equally attractive if $\theta_p = \beta_{im}$. Thus β_{im} refers to the value of θ_p where the probabilities of responding in category m and $m-1$ are equal. For this reason the parameters in a full item-by-logit adjacent-categories logit model are called *category crossing parameters* or *intersection parameters*. These parameters indicate the points on the latent continuum for which the probabilities of responding in the two adjacent categories are equal.

Inverting the link function gives an expression for the probabilities to respond in each of the categories:

$$
\begin{aligned}
\Pr(Y_{pi} = 0) &= \frac{1}{1 + \exp(\theta_p - \beta_{i1}) + \exp(2\theta_p - \beta_{i1} - \beta_{i2})}, \\
\Pr(Y_{pi} = 1) &= \frac{\exp(\theta_p - \beta_{i1})}{1 + \exp(\theta_p - \beta_{i1}) + \exp(2\theta_p - \beta_{i1} - \beta_{i2})}, \qquad (3.8) \\
\Pr(Y_{pi} = 2) &= \frac{\exp(2\theta_p - \beta_{i1} - \beta_{i2})}{1 + \exp(\theta_p - \beta_{i1}) + \exp(2\theta_p - \beta_{i1} - \beta_{i2})}.
\end{aligned}
$$

This model is the well-known *partial credit model* (PCM; Masters, 1982), which is an adjacent-categories logit model with interactions between items and logits. The model is applied in aptitude testing to allow for partially crediting the correctness of the response, but it can be applied in many other areas too, such as attitude measurement.

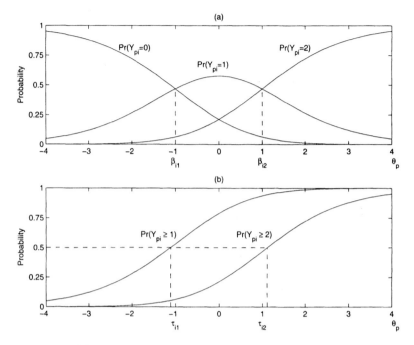

FIGURE 3.1. (a) Category response functions, and (b) cumulative probabilities for the partial credit model.

The PCM can be displayed graphically by plotting the probabilities of responding in each of the categories as a function of θ_p; these plots are called *category response functions*. This is shown in panel (a) of Figure 3.1 for $\beta_{i1} = -1$ and $\beta_{i2} = 1$. One can see from the figure that the category response functions for categories 0 and 1 intersect at $\beta_{i1} = -1$ and those for categories 1 and 2 intersect at $\beta_{i2} = 1$. A figure such as Figure 3.1 is helpful for the interpretation. In the example of Figure 3.1 response 0 is the most likely one below β_{i1}, response 1 between β_{i1} and β_{i2}, and response 2 above β_{i2}. Note that if $\beta_{i2} < \beta_{i1}$, then the interpretation changes, with response 1 not being the most likely at any point. This might be interpreted as indicating a problem with the middle response category, but that is only true if there is some theoretical basis to require that each category must be most likely at some value of θ_p (and this is a rare, and strong, theoretical assumption).

As an alternative, Wu, Adams and Wilson (1998) considered the cumulative probabilities $\Pr(Y_{pi} \geq 1)$ and $\Pr(Y_{pi} \geq 2)$, shown in panel (b) of Figure 3.1. The thresholds, τ_{i1} and τ_{i2}, are the points on the θ_p continuum at which the cumulative probabilities equal .5. No matter what the order of the βs is, the cumulative probability curves will always be ordered along the θ_p continuum and they do not intersect. Working with these cumulative probabilities avoids undue emphasis on the possibility that some response categories may not be the most likely (which becomes quite common as the number of categories increase). We must note however that because of the adjacent-category logits, the cumulative probabilities do not have a simple functional form that can be used to assess easily the effect of predictors.

Because Equation 3.7 has the simple form of a Rasch model, it is tempting to consider the parameter β_{im} as the difficulty of the mth step in the solution process. However, as pointed out by Molenaar (1983; see also Tutz, 1990), this is an erroneous interpretation, since the value of β_{im} in the step process interpretation is also determined by the difficulty of step $m + 1$. By conditioning on being in category m or $m - 1$, one restricts the attention to responses that did not get into a higher category than m. What is true is that β_{im} governs the relative probability of a response in category m or the category $m - 1$: Simple manipulation of Equation 3.8 gives $\pi_{pi1}/\pi_{pi0} = \exp(\theta_p - \beta_{i1})$ and $\pi_{pi2}/\pi_{pi1} = \exp(\theta_p - \beta_{i2})$. Thus one can see β_{im} as expressing the relative difficulty of category m compared to category $m - 1$ (Masters, 1982). A behavioral process interpretation for the adjacent-categories logit model will be given when the baseline-category logit model is discussed.

As one starts to move away from the tentative full item-by-logit model, restrictions are placed on the category crossing parameters. A first step is that only main effects of items and logits are allowed in the model, so that the *rating scale model* (RSM; Andrich, 1978, 1982) is obtained with β_{im} being decomposed as follows:

$$\beta_{i1} = \beta_i,$$
$$\beta_{i2} = \beta_i + \lambda, \tag{3.9}$$

where β_i denotes the item location (also the position where the category response curves 0 and 1 cross), and λ is the position of the intersection of categories 1 and 2 relative to β_i. Hence, the category crossings are at the same distance apart from each other for all items.

In a next step, predictors with explanatory potential can be included in the model (if they are available). In such cases, the category crossing parameters β_{im} are regressed on a set of explanatory item predictors. This is the *linear PCM* or facets model (Fischer & Ponocny, 1994; Glas & Verhelst, 1989; Linacre, 1989). An even more restrictive model results when the item location parameters β_i from a RSM (Equation 3.9) are regressed on explanatory item predictors. This is the *linear RSM* (Fischer & Parzer, 1991; Linacre, 1989). These models will be illustrated in the analysis of the verbal aggression data in Section 3.5.

3.4.2   Cumulative logits

The mth cumulative logit is the logit of responding in category m or a higher category versus a lower category than category m. Thus A_m and B_m equal $\{m, \ldots, M-1\}$ and $\{1, \ldots, m-1\}$, respectively. For three categories, the link function becomes:

$$
\begin{aligned}
f_{\text{link } 1}(\boldsymbol{\pi}_{pi}) &= \log\left(\frac{\pi_{pi1} + \pi_{pi2}}{1 - \pi_{pi1} - \pi_{pi2}}\right) = \log\left(\frac{\pi_{pi1} + \pi_{pi2}}{\pi_{pi0}}\right) \\
&= Z_{pi1}\theta_p - \boldsymbol{X}'_{pi1}\boldsymbol{\beta} = \theta_p - \beta_{i1}, \\
f_{\text{link } 2}(\boldsymbol{\pi}_{pi}) &= \log\left(\frac{\pi_{pi2}}{1 - \pi_{pi2}}\right) = \log\left(\frac{\pi_{pi2}}{\pi_{pi0} + \pi_{pi1}}\right) \\
&= Z_{pi2}\theta_p - \boldsymbol{X}'_{pi2}\boldsymbol{\beta} = \theta_p - \beta_{i2}.
\end{aligned}
\tag{3.10}
$$

Hence, each cumulative logit contains the ratio of two cumulative probabilities: $\Pr(Y_{pi} \geq m)/\Pr(Y_{pi} < m)$. Thus, in models based on the cumulative logit, one models the tendency for person p to respond to item i in category m or higher rather than in a lower category as a linear combination of item-by-logit indicators and the person-specific random effect θ_p. If θ_p increases, the probability of responding in a higher category increases also. In the item response modeling literature, models of this type have been called *graded response models* (GRM; Samejima, 1969). In the statistics literature, the fixed-effects versions of these models are known as *proportional odds models* (McCullagh, 1980; the reason for this name becomes clear when we discuss the parameter interpretation in Section 3.5). As for the adjacent-categories logits, we assume that the random-effects predictor matrix contains only ones.

From Equation 3.10, one can derive that the probability of responding in category m or higher equals:

$$
\begin{aligned}
\Pr(Y_{pi} \geq 1) &= \frac{\exp(\theta_p - \beta_{i1})}{1 + \exp(\theta_p - \beta_{i1})}, \\
\Pr(Y_{pi} \geq 2) &= \frac{\exp(\theta_p - \beta_{i2})}{1 + \exp(\theta_p - \beta_{i2})}.
\end{aligned}
\tag{3.11}
$$

Thus, the cumulative probability of responding in category m or higher has the same structural form as the Rasch model. The category probabilities $\Pr(Y_{pi} = m)$ can be derived from these cumulative probabilities as follows:

$$
\begin{aligned}
\Pr(Y_{pi} = 0) &= 1 - \Pr(Y_{pi} \geq 1), \\
\Pr(Y_{pi} = 1) &= \Pr(Y_{pi} \geq 1) - \Pr(Y_{pi} \geq 2), \\
\Pr(Y_{pi} = 2) &= \Pr(Y_{pi} \geq 2).
\end{aligned}
\tag{3.12}
$$

In order for $\Pr(Y_{pi} = 1)$ not to be negative, an inequality constraint has to be imposed on the parameters: $\beta_{i1} < \beta_{i2}$, for all $i = 1, \ldots, I$. Note that this well illustrates that, although we have used the same symbols for the parameters for the cumulative logit and adjacent-categories logit models, β_{i1} and β_{i2} are inherently different under the two formulations.

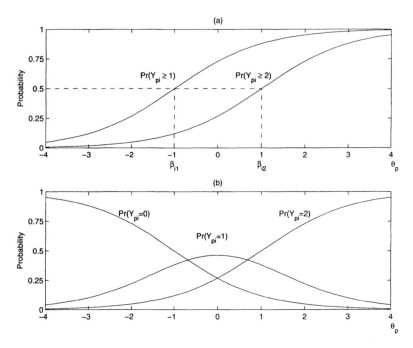

FIGURE 3.2. (a) Cumulative probabilities for the graded response model, and (b) category response functions.

In panel (a) of Figure 3.2, we show the cumulative probabilities for the GRM with $\beta_{i1} = -1$ and $\beta_{i2} = 1$. Panel (b) of Figure 3.2 contains the category response functions for the GRM. Although we have chosen similar parameter values as for the graphical representation of the PCM (see Figure 3.1), the two parameter sets cannot be compared because the two models are not related. However, it can be seen that the trace lines in Figure 3.2 are very similar to the corresponding trace lines in Figure 3.1 despite the different nature of the models. An important dissimilarity with the PCM is that in the GRM the middle category is always dominant for a certain region of the θ_p continuum because of the order restriction that is placed on the βs while that does not have to be the case for the PCM.

For the GRM, it is illuminating to derive the model from a behavioral process perspective, which goes back to Thurstone (1927). Suppose that each time a person p responds to an item i (with 3 categories), a new unobserved variable V_{pi} is elicited (see Chapter 1). The distribution of V_{pi} is logistic with mean θ_p and variance $\frac{\pi^2}{3}$. The logistic distribution is bell-shaped, like the normal, but its tails are somewhat heavier and wider. In Figure 3.3 the unobserved logistic distributions for three persons are shown. In the full item-by-logit model, the two item-specific fixed-effects parameters, β_{i1} and β_{i2} act now as thresholds or cut points in generating the response of the person in the following way:

$$
\begin{aligned}
Y_{pi} = 0 &\iff V_{pi} \leq \beta_{i1}, \\
Y_{pi} = 1 &\iff \beta_{i1} < V_{pi} \leq \beta_{i2}, \\
Y_{pi} = 2 &\iff V_{pi} > \beta_{i2}.
\end{aligned}
$$

To show how the probabilities in Equation 3.11 follow from this process, we derive $\Pr(Y_{pi} = 2)$. First, we note that $O_{pi} = V_{pi} - \theta_p$ is a random variable with a logistic distribution with mean 0 and variance $\frac{\pi^2}{3}$. The derivation then goes as follows:

$$
\begin{aligned}
\Pr(Y_{pi} = 2) &= \Pr(V_{pi} > \beta_{i2}) = \Pr(O_{pi} + \theta_p > \beta_{i2}) \\
&= 1 - \Pr(O_{pi} \leq \beta_{i2} - \theta_p) = 1 - \frac{\exp(\beta_{i2} - \theta_p)}{1 + \exp(\beta_{i2} - \theta_p)} \\
&= \frac{\exp(\theta_p - \beta_{i2})}{1 + \exp(\theta_p - \beta_{i2})}.
\end{aligned}
$$

Thus we find the same probabilities as obtained from the cumulative logit link formulation. In this threshold approach, the inequality constraint on the GRM parameters, $\beta_{i1} < \beta_{i2}$, has a meaningful interpretation because it requires that the second cut-off has to be placed on the right of the first cut-off. Note that the same model follows if one assumes that the latent random variable V_{pi} has a logistic distribution with mean $\theta_p - \beta_{i1}$ while the thresholds are 0 and $\beta_{i2}^* = \beta_{i2} - \beta_{i1}$. Just as for the PCM, a rating scale version of the GRM may be constructed too: $\theta_p - \beta_i$ is the mean of the underlying logistic distribution and the thresholds are located at 0 and γ ($\gamma > 0$) for all items. Again, one can incorporate into the model more meaningful and explanatory predictors (as illustrated in Section 3.5). We remark that the latent variable motivation is not a requirement to use or interpret the GRM; the cumulative logits are the crucial part of the model. However, the latent variable conceptualization may facilitate the model-building task in some cases.

3.4.3   Baseline-category logits

The logits discussed above take into account the ordering of the response categories. However, with nominal data, it is more appropriate to use a model based on the baseline-category logits. The mth baseline-category logit is the logit of responding in category m versus baseline category 0. Thus, A_m and B_m equal $\{m\}$ and $\{0\}$, respectively. The baseline category

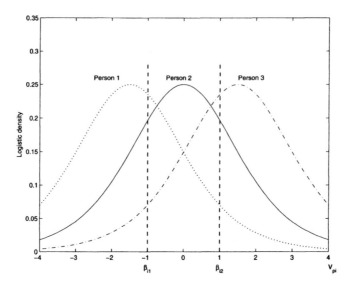

FIGURE 3.3. The elicited logistic distribution for three persons.

is arbitrary but category 0 is often a reasonable choice. The link function is defined as:

$$\begin{aligned}
f_{\text{link }1}(\boldsymbol{\pi}_{pi}) &= \log\left(\frac{\pi_{pi1}}{1 - \pi_{pi1} - \pi_{pi2}}\right) = \log\left(\frac{\pi_{pi1}}{\pi_{pi0}}\right) \\
&= Z_{pi1}\theta_p - \beta_{i1}, \\
f_{\text{link }2}(\boldsymbol{\pi}_{pi}) &= \log\left(\frac{\pi_{pi2}}{1 - \pi_{pi1} - \pi_{pi2}}\right) = \log\left(\frac{\pi_{pi2}}{\pi_{pi0}}\right) \qquad (3.13) \\
&= Z_{pi2}\theta_p - \beta_{i2}.
\end{aligned}$$

The random-effects predictor matrix will be specified below to relate the baseline-category logit model to other models and to illustrate its use.

Solving for the response probabilities gives:

$$\begin{aligned}
\Pr(Y_{pi} = 0) &= \frac{1}{1 + \exp(Z_{pi1}\theta_p - \beta_{i1}) + \exp(Z_{pi2}\theta_p - \beta_{i2})}, \\
\Pr(Y_{pi} = 1) &= \frac{\exp(Z_{pi1}\theta_p - \beta_{i1})}{1 + \exp(Z_{pi1}\theta_p - \beta_{i1}) + \exp(Z_{pi2}\theta_p - \beta_{i2})}, \quad (3.14) \\
\Pr(Y_{pi} = 2) &= \frac{\exp(Z_{pi2}\theta_p - \beta_{i2})}{1 + \exp(Z_{pi1}\theta_p - \beta_{i1}) + \exp(Z_{pi2}\theta_p - \beta_{i2})}.
\end{aligned}$$

This model is a constrained version of the nominal response model in item response modeling (Bock, 1972); it is also known as the *multinomial mixed logit model* in econometrics (Train, 2003) or simply the *baseline-category logit model* (Agresti, 2002).

From the set of Equations 3.14 it can be derived that the PCM is a special case of the nominal model if the random-effects predictor matrix is specified as follows: $Z_{pi1} = 1$ and $Z_{pi2} = 2$. Moreover, the parameter β_{i2} in Equation 3.14 is now the sum of the two category crossing parameters from the PCM. The relation between the PCM and the nominal model can also be shown by expressing the baseline-category logits in terms of the adjacent-categories logits. The first logit under both schemes is already equal (compare Equations 3.7 and 3.13) and for the second baseline-category logit the derivation is as follows:

$$\log\left(\frac{\pi_{pi2}}{\pi_{pi0}}\right) = \log\left(\frac{\pi_{pi1}}{\pi_{pi0}}\right) + \log\left(\frac{\pi_{pi2}}{\pi_{pi1}}\right).$$

Alternative specifications of the random-effects predictor matrices can be constructed as in the *ordered partition model* of Wilson and Adams (1993) and the PCM for null categories (categories which no person has chosen; Wilson & Masters, 1993).

The behavioral process interpretation that leads to the nominal model is a random utility maximization(RUM) process. In short, it means that each category has an associated utility and the category with the highest utility is chosen by the person. Technically, a so-called extreme-value distribution (we will not discuss this distribution in detail, see Train, 2003) is elicited for each category when a person responds to an item. The mean of the distribution for the reference category equals zero, but for the other two it is equal to the corresponding right-hand sides of Equation 3.13. These distributions represent the random utilities for the categories. A draw from each distribution is taken and the category with the maximum utility is chosen (the person acts as a rational utility maximizer). In a baseline-category logit model, the systematic part of the category-specific utility distribution (the mean) is modeled as a function of the predictors.

Because adjacent-categories logit models are a special case of baseline-category logit models, a RUM perspective is also valid for adjacent-categories logit models. The main difference with the more general baseline-category logit models is that the adjacent-categories logit model constrains the ordering of the extreme-value distributions in a special way. For a person with very small value of θ_p, the ordering of the three distributions (labeled by the corresponding categories) will be 2, 1, and 0. This means that for such a person category 0 has the largest probability of being chosen. For a person with a large positive value of θ_p, the ordering will be the reverse (0, 1, 2), meaning that category 2 has the largest chance of being chosen. Such a reversal of the orderings of the distribution is not necessarily true for the nominal model.

Despite the fact that the baseline-category model as it is presented in this chapter is more general than the adjacent-categories logit model, its applicability is limited. The reason is that it is often difficult to specify *a priori* a random-effects predictor matrix (except for the case in which the categories are clearly ordered and the PCM can be defined). For this reason, the baseline-category logit model is usually defined with an unknown or latent random-effects predictor matrix for which the entries have to be estimated. These unknown values are called the discrimination parameters (see Chapter 8). In the most general case, it is assumed that the discrimination parameters may vary both within items (over logits) and over items. Such a model can then be compared to a more restricted one, for instance a PCM with an *a priori* determined random-effects predictor matrix. The test of the restricted model against the full one assesses the explicitly presumed ordering of the categories in the PCM.

In this chapter we will restrict the focus to models without discrimination parameters and therefore we do not consider the general version baseline-category logit model further. Because the restricted version without discriminations is not so useful, it will not be discussed either.

3.5   Application of models for polytomous data

In this section we apply the two models for ordered polytomous items to the verbal aggression data set. The main focus will be on the adjacent-categories logit models but we will briefly outline some results using cumulative logit models. Software code to estimate some of the presented models in SAS is given in Section 3.8.

3.5.1   Adjacent-categories logit models

As a first model we consider the PCM (Masters, 1982), which is a model with interactions between indicator predictors for items and logits. Consequently, each item has two category crossing parameters. The deviance of the model, and its AIC and BIC values, can be found in Table 3.3 in the PCM row. The estimated standard deviation of the random-effects distribution is .95 $(SE = .05)$. We do not present the estimates for all category crossing parameters numerically but graphically. We could plot the category response curves for each item as a function of θ_p (see Figure 3.1). But for this application, we have chosen to display the data in a different way, as in Figure 3.4. First, we ordered the items according to the expected response they elicit in the population from lowest or 'easiest' (bottom of the figure) to highest or 'most difficult' (top of the figure).[1] Then we use a different shade of gray to mark the regions in which a certain category is most likely: light gray for category 0, medium gray for category 1 and

---

[1]The expected response for a polytomous item can be computed as follows: $\sum_{m=0}^{2} m \int_{-\infty}^{\infty} \Pr(Y_{pi} = m)\phi(\theta_p|0, \sigma_\theta^2)d\theta_p$, where $\phi(\theta_p|0, \sigma_\theta^2)$ represents the normal probability density for θ_p with mean 0 and variance σ_θ^2.

dark gray for category 2. Each item is represented by a separate bar and the item numbers can be found on the left side. At the right side, we list the item features (Behavior Mode, Situation Type, Behavior Type). The vertical solid lines indicate the mean of the random-effects distribution together with the intervals of $+1\sigma_\theta$ to $-1\sigma_\theta$ (containing about 68% of the population) and $+2\sigma_\theta$ to $-2\sigma_\theta$ (containing about 95% of the population). In Figure 3.4, most bars contain three shades of gray so that for those items

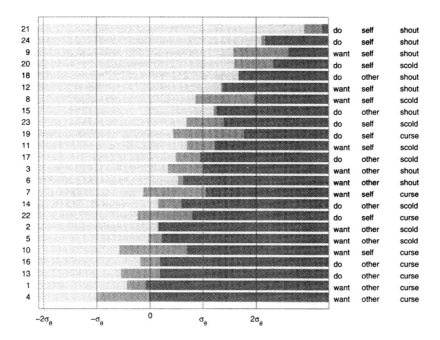

FIGURE 3.4. Graphical presentation of the PCM estimates for the items together with the item features (verbal aggression data).

all three categories are the most likely ones at some point (an exception is item 18). Relating the item features with the item difficulties, we see that situations where oneself is to blame are the most difficult ones. There is also a tendency that shouting is associated with the most difficult items, scolding with the intermediate ones and cursing with the easier ones. For doing versus wanting, the results are less clear but in the first half of the items 8 out of 12 are about doing, which suggests it is more difficult than wanting. The effects of the item predictors will be investigated in more detail below.

Next, the PCM is extended with two person predictors which are regressed on θ_p:

$$\theta_p = \beta_{\text{Gender}} Z_{p\text{ Gender}} + \beta_{\text{Trait Anger}} Z_{p\text{ Trait Anger}} + \varepsilon_p, \qquad (3.15)$$

where Z_p Trait Anger and Z_p Gender stand for the Trait Anger score and Gender of person p (Z_p Gender $= 0$ for women, Z_p Gender $= 1$ for men), respectively. The quantity ε_p now plays the role of random effect. The software code to estimate this model can be found in Section 3.8.1. By including these two person predictors in the PCM, the estimated standard deviation for the random-effects distribution, slightly drops to .92 ($SE = .05$). (A model with an interaction between Trait Anger and Gender did not result in a significant improvement of the fit.) As can be seen in Table 3.3, the model with person predictors, the PCM(person) in Table 3.3, results in a lower AIC and BIC. Also a LR test comparing the first two models turns out to be significant ($\chi^2(2) = 29, p < .001$). The regression coefficients for Trait Anger and Gender are estimated at .06 ($SE = .01$) and .28 ($SE = .12$), respectively. For both regressors, the coefficients differ significantly from zero ($p < .01$ for Gender, and $p < .001$ for Trait Anger, using a Wald test).

The interpretation of effects of the person predictors is based on the adjacent-categories odds. For instance, for Gender, we can conclude that, holding everything else constant, the odds of responding "perhaps" vs "no" (or the odds of responding "yes" vs "perhaps") are $\exp(.28) = 1.3$ times larger for men than for women. Hence, men are a little bit more inclined to express high levels of verbal aggression than women. The 95% CI shows a wide range of plausible effect sizes: It ranges from a little more than 1.0 to 1.6. The positive regression coefficient for Trait Anger indicates that higher Trait Anger is associated with higher levels of verbal aggression. More precisely, an increase of 1 SD in Trait Anger ($SD = 4.85$) multiplies the odds of responding "perhaps" rather than "no" (or "yes" rather than "perhaps") with $\exp(4.85 \times .06) \approx 1.3$ (the 95% CI ranges from 1.2 to 1.4). A plot of the category crossing parameters looks similar as the one in Figure 3.4, except that the plot is shifted to the right when the vertical lines remain in place. The explanation of this observation is left as an exercise.

The regression coefficients estimated with the PCM can be compared with those obtained from estimating the latent regression Rasch model (see Chapter 2). The values of the estimated coefficients are almost exactly equal to each other, but the corresponding standard errors are about 60% larger with the dichotomized data. For instance, the effect of Gender was not significant in the dichotomized data set, while it is significant with polytomous data (although the range of plausible effects is still very large). The comparison shows that the loss in information by dichotomizing the data translates into larger standard errors for the estimated regression coefficients.

The third model we estimated is the RSM without person predictors. We could make a similar graphical presentation for the RSM as for the PCM (see Figure 3.4). The most important difference with Figure 3.4 would be that the medium gray rectangles are of equal length for all items. Because this model is nested within the PCM without person predictors, we can

TABLE 3.3. Deviance, AIC, and BIC of several adjacent-categories logit models (verbal aggression data).[a]

Model	N_{par}	Deviance	AIC	BIC
PCM	49	641	739	923
PCM(person)	51	612	714	906
RSM	26	693	745	842
RSM(person)	28	664	720	825
PCM(person,item)	13	819	845	894

Note a: A value of 12000 should be added to each of the numbers in the columns Deviance, AIC and BIC.

perform a LR test to compare both models. The LR test is significant ($\chi^2(23) = 52, p < .001$) so that the goodness of fit of the RSM must be considered inferior to the goodness of fit of the PCM. That comes not as a surprise, given the large variability in the lengths of the medium gray bars in Figure 3.4. As shown in Table 3.3, the conclusion that the PCM fits better is also supported by the lower AIC for the PCM, but not by the BIC, which is lower for the RSM (recall that the BIC penalizes more heavily for the number of free parameters). If the person predictors Trait Anger and Gender are included in the RSM (RSM(person) in Table 3.3), the fit of the RSM improves but it still falls short against the corresponding PCM ($\chi^2(23) = 52, p < .001$). The estimated regression coefficients for the person predictors are equal to those obtained under the PCM and their interpretation is unaffected.

For the application of both the PCM and the RSM, the effect of the person predictors was constrained to be equal for the two adjacent-categories logits ("perhaps" versus "no" and "yes" versus "perhaps"). This is perfectly reasonable in a model for ordered data. Assume that Trait Anger was allowed to have a separate influence on the two logits and that the regression coefficient for the first logit was positive and that for the second one was negative. In such a case, the categories are still ordered with respect to the random intercept ε_p but not with respect to Trait Anger. That is because an increase in Trait Anger leads to an increase in the odds of responding "perhaps" rather than "no," but to a decrease in the odds of responding "yes" rather than "perhaps." Therefore, person predictors were restricted to have the same effect on all logits if the data are ordered. When the categories are not ordered, as in a pure baseline-category model, this causes no problems.

Because the PCM with person predictors was the most satisfying model, the item predictors that code for the item features are included in the PCM in a next step. The items in the verbal aggression data set can be classified according to three categorical item features: Behavior Mode (Want vs Do), Situation Type (Other-to-blame vs Self-to-blame) and Behavior Type (Curse, Scold, Shout). Based on these features, the following item predictors are defined:

$$
\begin{aligned}
X_{pim1} &= 1 \quad \text{if the item concerns Do and 0 otherwise,} \\
X_{pim2} &= 1 \quad \text{if the item concerns Other-to-blame and 0 otherwise,} \\
X_{pim3} &= 1 \quad \text{if the item concerns Curse and 0 otherwise,} \\
X_{pim4} &= 1 \quad \text{if the item concerns Scold and 0 otherwise.}
\end{aligned}
$$

Note that the item predictors are based on a different coding than in Chapter 1 or 2 (i.e., dummy coding for all predictors). In the PCM with explanatory item predictors, the category crossing parameters of the original PCM are decomposed as follows (for all i):

$$
\begin{aligned}
\beta_{i1} &= \delta_{10} + \delta_{11}X_{pi11} + \delta_{12}X_{pi12} + \delta_{13}X_{pi13} + \delta_{14}X_{pi14}, \\
\beta_{i2} &= \delta_{20} + \delta_{21}X_{pi21} + \delta_{22}X_{pi22} + \delta_{23}X_{pi23} + \delta_{24}X_{pi24},
\end{aligned}
$$

where δ_{m0} is the specific intercept for the mth logit (the two intercepts are constant over items) and δ_{mk} is the regression weight of predictor k for the mth logit. More generally, the mth logit pertaining to person p and item i is modeled as $\boldsymbol{X}'_{pim}\boldsymbol{\delta}$, where

$$
\begin{aligned}
\boldsymbol{X}'_{pi1} &= (1, X_{pi11}, \ldots, X_{pi14}, 0, 0, \ldots, 0), \\
\boldsymbol{X}'_{pi2} &= (0, 0, \ldots, 0, 1, X_{pi21}, \ldots, X_{pi24}), \\
\boldsymbol{\delta}' &= (\delta_{10}, \delta_{11}, \ldots, \delta_{14}, \delta_{20}, \delta_{21}, \ldots, \delta_{24}).
\end{aligned}
$$

The model has only $5 \times 2 + 2 + 1 = 13$ parameters in total: the 10 regression weights of the item properties (one for each combination of a predictor, the intercept included, with a logit), the two weights of the person predictors, and the variance of the random effect. The goodness of fit of this model is given in Table 3.3 on the PCM(person, item) row. The estimated standard deviation of the random-effects distribution is .90 ($SE = .22$), which is smaller than that for the regular PCM. A similar effect is reported in Chapter 2 when going from the Rasch model to the LLTM. As expected, the model has a higher deviance and the LR test is significant when comparing it to the PCM with person predictors and item-by-logit predictors ($\chi^2(38) = 207, p < .001$). Also, the AIC and BIC indicate that the model fits the data worse than the original PCM with only person predictors (see Table 3.3).

The estimates for the regression coefficients can be found in Table 3.4. The contributions of all predictors are significant. The interpretation of the coefficients is as follows. Holding everything else constant, going from wanting to doing decreases the odds of responding "perhaps" rather than "no" by about 40% ($\exp(-\delta_{11}) = \exp(-.54) \approx .6$, 95% CI from .5 to .7) and the odds of responding "yes" rather than "perhaps" by 30% ($\exp(-\delta_{21}) = \exp(-.35) \approx .7$, 95% CI from .6 to .8). This conclusion is supported by Figure 3.4, where there is a tendency for do-items to be more difficult. The effects are clearer for the Situation Type. Going from a self-blame situation to an other-blame situation and holding everything else constant doubles the odds of responding "perhaps" rather than "no" ($\exp(.69) \approx 2.0$, 95% from 1.7 to 2.5), and increases the odds of "yes" vs "perhaps" by a factor of 2.6 ($\exp(.97) \approx 2.6$, 95% CI from 2.3 to 3.1). This conclusion is clearly supported in Figure 3.4 because of the notable tendency of self-blame items to be situated among the most difficult ones. For the last two variables (cursing and scolding) similar interpretations can be made (in those cases all odds increase, because the effects have to be interpreted as going from shouting to another reaction, and shouting is the least favorable reaction; see also Figure 3.4). All effect sizes correspond to those reported in Chapter 2 of this volume for the binary model, even though a different coding for the predictors was used. The interpretation of the effects of the person variables Trait Anger and Gender is not affected.

TABLE 3.4. Estimated regression coefficients for the PCM with person and (logit-specific) item predictors (verbal aggression data).

Predictor	Coefficient	Estimate	SE
Trait anger	$\beta_{\text{Trait Anger}}$	.05	.01
Gender	β_{Gender}	.27	.12
Intercept	δ_{10}	1.89	.22
	δ_{20}	1.96	.23
Behavior Mode (Do)	δ_{11}	.54	.06
	δ_{21}	.35	.07
Situation Type (Other-to-Blame)	δ_{12}	-.69	.06
	δ_{22}	-.97	.08
Behavior Type (Curse)	δ_{13}	-1.68	.08
	δ_{23}	-.93	.10
Behavior Type (Scold)	δ_{14}	-.80	.07
	δ_{24}	-.50	.10

3.5.2   Cumulative logit models

In this section we illustrate briefly how to estimate cumulative logit models and how to interpret the results. Only the GRM with person and item predictors is estimated and it is shown that the conclusions are very similar to those obtained with the adjacent-categories logit model. The SAS code for this model is given in Section 3.8.2.

The regression of the person predictors on θ_p is already defined in Equation 3.15. To understand the inclusion of the item predictors Behavior Mode, Situation Type and Behavior Type, we refer to the latent process interpretation of the GRM. For the encounter of person p with item i, a draw V_{pi} from a logistic distribution with mean $\theta_p - \beta_{i1}$ is realized. If V_{pi} is smaller than 0, then $Y_{pi} = 0$; if V_{pi} is larger than $\beta_{i2}^* = \beta_{i2} - \beta_{i1}$, then $Y_{pi} = 2$ ($\beta_{i2}^* > 0$); otherwise, if V_{pi} falls in between these bounds, $Y_{pi} = 1$. The item parameters β_{i1} and β_{i2} are decomposed as follows (the definition of β_{i2}^* is also given):

$$
\begin{aligned}
\beta_{i1} &= \delta_0 + \delta_1 X_{pi11} + \delta_2 X_{pi12} + \delta_3 X_{pi13} + \delta_4 X_{pi14}, \\
\beta_{i2} &= \delta_0 + \delta_1 X_{pi11} + \delta_2 X_{pi12} + \delta_3 X_{pi13} + \delta_4 X_{pi14} + \lambda, \quad (3.16) \\
\beta_{i2}^* &= \beta_{i2} - \beta_{i1} = \lambda,
\end{aligned}
$$

where $X_{pi11}, \ldots, X_{pi14}$ are defined as in the coding scheme used for the PCM. Thus, $\boldsymbol{X}_{pi1}' = (1, X_{pi11}, \ldots, X_{pi14}, 0)$, $\boldsymbol{X}_{pi2}' = (1, X_{pi11}, \ldots, X_{pi14}, 1)$ and $\boldsymbol{\delta}' = (\delta_0, \delta_1, \ldots, \delta_4, \lambda)$. In this model, the location of the latent distribution is regressed on the item properties, while the boundaries are constant over items (at 0 and $\lambda > 0$). In other words, we have regressed the two cumulative logits in the same way on the item predictors allowing for an additional logit-specific effect λ for the second logit. If logit-by-item interactions were allowed, the inequality constraint on the thresholds would lead to a complicated system of linear inequalities on the regression weights. However, finding parameter estimates that satisfy a system of linear inequalities calls for more advanced optimization routines than those implemented in the software for fitting GLMMs and NLMMs. The model we fit has four parameters less than the PCM (person, item) model from Table 3.3, because the effect of the item predictors is not logit-specific.

Nevertheless, the fit is slightly better than for the corresponding model in Table 3.3 (PCM(person, item)). The deviance of the model is 817 (vs 819), the AIC is 835 (vs 845) and the BIC is 869 (vs 894). The parameter σ_ε is estimated at 1.22 ($SE = .06$); the remaining parameter estimates can be found in Table 3.5. The estimates for the person predictors are somewhat larger in magnitude than for the adjacent-categories logit model, but the corresponding standard errors are also larger. This phenomenon is to be expected (Agresti, 2002), because the effects in the adjacent-categories logit model are defined locally (i.e., on the logits of two adjacent categories) while in the cumulative logit model, they are defined globally (i.e., on the entire scale).

TABLE 3.5. Estimated regression coefficients for the GRM with person and item predictors (verbal aggression data).

Predictor	Coefficient	Estimate	SE
Trait anger	$\beta_{\text{Trait Anger}}$	.07	.01
Gender	β_{Gender}	.34	.16
Intercept	δ_0	1.71	.29
Behavior Mode (Do)	δ_1	.63	.05
Situation Type (Other-to-blame)	δ_2	-1.08	.05
Behavior Type (Curse)	δ_3	-1.86	.06
Behavior Type (Scold)	δ_4	-.95	.06

For the interpretation of the effects, one has to evaluate the corresponding changes in the cumulative odds when a given predictor changes with one unit, holding all other predictors constant (this is also called the cumulative odds ratio). For example, going from wanting to doing, with everything else held constant, almost halves the cumulative odds of giving a more positive response rather than a more negative one (i.e., "yes" or "perhaps" rather than "no," and "yes" rather than "perhaps" or "no"; $\exp(-\delta_1) = .53$, the 95% CI ranges from .48 to .58). The fitted model can be called a random-effects proportional odds model because going from wanting to doing changes both cumulative odds in the same way (i.e., the effects are independent of which of the two cumulative logits we consider).

3.6   Choice of a logit link function

Before discussing the considerations that lead to the choice of a certain link function, we must note that, besides the three logit link functions we discussed in this chapter, there is a fourth, less common type: the continuation-ratio logit. In this link function the attractiveness of category m relative to any category that is higher than m is modeled: $A_m = \{m\}$ and $B_m = \{m+1, \ldots, M-1\}$. The way the link function is defined already indicates that models based on the continuation-ratio logit are especially suited for ordered data. Continuation-ratio logit models with a random effect and item-by-logit interactions result in the so-called sequential or stepwise Rasch models as described by Tutz (1990, 1997).

There are a few considerations that are helpful to make a choice between logit link functions. First, there is the tradition within a particular domain of research. For instance, in educational measurement applications, ordinal data are usually modeled using adjacent-categories logits, while the cumulative logits are more common in biostatistical applications.

Second, the adjacent-categories logits are to be preferred to test the ordering of categories. If one is in doubt about the exact ordering of the response categories, a formal test of the presumed ordering is helpful. We have seen that the adjacent-categories logit models are a special case of the baseline-category logit models and if one allows for logit-specific discrimination parameters, a LR test for comparing the adjacent-categories logit model with a less restrictive baseline-category logit model yields a test of the ordering of the categories. The cumulative logit models impose an ordering and the model cannot be compared with the baseline-category logit model.

A third consideration is the interpretation of the parameters. Generally, the cumulative logit model is the easiest to interpret for ordinal data because of the proportional odds property (see above). Another interpretational advantage of the cumulative logit models is that if adjacent categories are merged into a new category, this does not affect the estimates of the remaining parameters (invariance under grouping), while this is not true for the baseline-category logit models or adjacent-categories logit models (Jansen & Roskam, 1986; McCullagh, 1980).

Fourth, substantial features in the data may lead to a certain choice. For instance, if the response process can be thought of as being sequential, the continuation-ratio logit model is to be preferred. An item where continuation-ratio logit can be applied is the following: "Have you ever suffered from a psychiatric illness?" with response categories "no," "yes, but never hospitalized," and "yes, and I was hospitalized." The first step in the responding to such a question is to decide whether one has suffered from a psychiatric illness and the second step is whether one was hospitalized given that one does have such an illness.

3.7   Concluding remarks

In this chapter we have presented some common models that can be used to analyze polytomous data. It is shown that the principles in model construction, estimation and testing that applied to models for binary data carry over without much difficulty to the polytomous case. However, polytomous data are more complex and that leads to more flexibility when setting up the model (see Section 3.6 on the choice of the link function).

All extensions for models for binary data that are proposed throughout the volume can also be applied to the models presented in this chapter. Here we mention a few important modifications explicitly. First, we may abandon the unidimensionality assumption and introduce multiple random effects (among others, see Hartzel, et al., 2001; Tutz & Hennevogl, 1996; for multidimensional extensions of models for binary data, see Chapter 8, this volume). Besides the simplest extension in which the intercept is made random over persons, also regression slopes of predictors may be allowed to vary over persons.

A second extension is the already mentioned possibility of including discrimination parameters (for models for binary data with discrimination parameters, see Chapter 8, this volume). The discrimination parameters may vary over items: For full item-by-logit cumulative logit models, this leads to the original GRM (Samejima, 1969) and for the adjacent-categories logits to the PCM with a discrimination parameter (Muraki, 1992). However, for the nominal model, we can go one step further because it is also natural to consider discrimination parameters that vary over the logits of a single item and between items as in the original model proposed by Bock (1972). Models with discrimination parameters can be used to test a hypothesis about a certain *a priori* ordering of the categories by comparing the fit of a model for ordered categories and a more relaxed model in which there is no restriction that requires the categories to be ordered in a certain way.

Third, when the conditional independence assumption does not hold in the data, one can extend the models from this chapter with the techniques presented in Chapters 7 and 10. Moreover, the framework for differential item functioning (DIF) described in Chapter 7 is easily adapted to models for polytomous data.

3.8   Software

All models considered in this chapter were estimated using the procedure NLMIXED from SAS. For two of the models discussed in Section 3.5, the program code is given here. We recommend that you first read Chapter 12 on software, particularly the parts on NLMIXED.

The SAS code may also seem a little bit unfamiliar. That is because for polytomous outcome variables NLMIXED does not have a standard distribution implemented. Therefore, the user has to specify the contribution to the loglikelihood of an observation through the statement MODEL y ~ general(ll), where ll stands for the log of the probability of the observed response for a person-by-item combination.

All models were estimated using nonadaptive Gaussian quadrature with 20 nodes to approximate the integral over θ_p. For all estimated models, the starting values were set to zero for the regression coefficients and to .5 (for PCMs and GRMs) or 1.5 (for RSMs) for the standard deviations because convergence proved to be faster if the starting value were set at these values (compared to the standard value of 1). We specified the optimization algorithm to use the Newton–Raphson technique.

3.8.1   Partial credit model with person predictors (verbal aggression data)

Code

```
PROC NLMIXED data=aggression_poly method=gauss
technique=newrap noad qpoints=20;
PARMS b1_1-b1_24=0 b2_1-b2_24=0 g1-g2=0 sd=.5;
theta=eps+g1*anger+g2*male;
beta1=b1_1*x1+b1_2*x2+b1_3*x3+b1_4*x4+b1_5*x5
+b1_6*x6+b1_7*x7+b1_8*x8+b1_9*x9+b1_10*x10
+b1_11*x11+b1_12*x12+b1_13*x13+b1_14*x14+b1_15*x15
+b1_16*x16+b1_17*x17+b1_18*x18+b1_19*x19+b1_20*x20
+b1_21*x21+b1_22*x22+b1_23*x23+b1_24*x24;
beta2=b2_1*x1+b2_2*x2+b2_3*x3+b2_4*x4+b2_5*x5
+b2_6*x6+b2_7*x7+b2_8*x8+b2_9*x9+b2_10*x10
+b2_11*x11+b2_12*x12+b2_13*x13+b2_14*x14+b2_15*x15
+b2_16*x16+b2_17*x17+b2_18*x18+b2_19*x19+b2_20*x20
+b2_21*x21+b2_22*x22+b2_23*x23+b2_24*x24;
exp1=exp(theta-beta1);
exp2=exp(2*theta-beta1-beta2);
denom=1+exp1+exp2;
if (y=0) then p=1/denom;
else if (y=1) then p=exp1/denom;
else if (y=2) then p=exp2/denom;
if (p>1e-8) then ll=log(p);
else ll=-1e100;
MODEL y ~ general(ll);
RANDOM eps ~ normal(0,sd**2) subject=person;
ESTIMATE 'sd**2' sd**2;
ESTIMATE 'exp(1SD*g1)' exp(4.85*g1);
ESTIMATE 'exp(g2)' exp(g2);
RUN;
```

Comments

1. The statements contain an error trap: Before taking the logarithm of the probability p, it is checked whether p is large enough.

2. In the RANDOM statement sd**2 is used for the variance which yields then an estimate of the σ_θ. In order to obtain an estimate of the variance one can either replace sd**2 with var (or another term such as sd2) or one can formulate an ESTIMATE statement as explained in comment 3.

3. The three ESTIMATE statements at the end are included to find the estimate of the variance and the effect of the person predictors on the odds scale. However, more importantly, the output of these estimates also contains the standard errors of the transformed parameters. For the effect

of Trait Anger, we requested directly the effect of an increase of 1 standard deviation $(SD = 4.85)$.

3.8.2 Graded response model with item and person predictors (verbal aggression data)

Code

```
PROC NLMIXED data=aggression_poly method=gauss
technique=newrap noad qpoints=20;
PARMS a=0 g1-g2=0 d1-d4=0 lambda=.5 sd=1.5;
BOUNDS lambda>0;
theta=eps+g1*anger+g2*male;
beta=a+d1*do+d2*self+d3*curse+d4*scold;
exp1=exp(theta-beta);
exp2=exp(theta-(beta+lambda));
denom1=1+exp1;
denom2=1+exp2;
if (y=0) then p=exp1/denom1;
else if (y=1) then p=exp1/denom1-exp2/denom2;
else if (y=2) then p=exp2/denom2;
if (p>1e-8) then ll=log(p);
else ll=-1e100;
MODEL y ~ general(ll);
RANDOM eps ~ normal(0,sd**2) subject=person;
ESTIMATE 'sd**2' sd**2;
ESTIMATE '1SD*g1' exp(4.85*g1);
ESTIMATE 'exp(g2)' exp(g2);
ESTIMATE 'exp(-d1)' exp(-d1);
ESTIMATE 'exp(-d2)' exp(-d2);
ESTIMATE 'exp(-d3)' exp(-d3);
ESTIMATE 'exp(-d4)' exp(-d4);
RUN;
```

Comments

In the ESTIMATE statements we request an estimate of the variance, and of the person predictor and item predictor effects on the odds scale. The BOUNDS statement was included in order to restrict lambda to be positive.

3.9 Exercises

1. Show that the columns of the fixed-effects predictor matrix of a rating scale model form a subset of the columns of the transformed fixed-effects

predictor matrix of a partial credit model. How many fixed-effects regression coefficients does the PCM have and how many does the RSM have?

2. The following data are given: The responses of P persons to 2 items with each four ordered response categories ("never," "rarely," "often," and "always"). Suppose you suspect that men have the tendency to avoid the extreme categories (never, always), more than women. Set up a predictor matrix for an adjacent-categories logit model that can test this hypothesis. What kind of predictor do you need to test the hypothesis? (Stack two predictor matrices below one another: one for a woman and one for a man.)

3. Assume that in the verbal aggression data there is a cost associated with responding in a higher category due to social desirability. The cost of a 0-response ("no") is 0, of a 1-response ("perhaps") is 1 and of a 2-response ("yes") is 2. Construct the predictor matrices for a full item-by-logit and item and logit main-effects adjacent-categories logit model and discuss both predictor matrices.

4. Define the probit version of the GRM.

5. When the person predictors Trait Anger and Gender are included in the PCM, the relative differences among category crossing parameters both within and between items are preserved. However, their absolute values increase by approximately 1.2; hence, the whole scale seems to be shifted to the right compared to the PCM without person predictors. How can you explain this finding?

6. Which test would you use to evaluate whether the item property Behavior Type contributes to the explanation of the responses in the PCM with person and item predictors, the PCM (person, item) in Table 3.3?

7. Can you improve the goodness of fit of a PCM with person predictors and logit-specific item predictors by including two-way interactions between item predictors? Start from Figure 3.4 to make a choice of candidate interactions. Try to find a parsimonious model by dropping nonsignificant interaction terms. Discuss the interpretation of the remaining interaction parameters and relate the effects back to Figure 3.4.

8. Estimate a RSM with the person predictors Trait Anger and Gender and with the three item properties (Behavior Mode, Situation Type, and Behavior Type) as item predictors. Assess the fit of the model and interpret the regression coefficients on the odds scale (the scale with exponential instead of logarithmic parameters).

3.10 References

Adams, R.J., & Wilson, M. (1996). Formulating the Rasch model as a mixed coefficients multinomial logit. In G. Engelhard & M. Wilson (Eds), *Objective Measurement: Theory and Practice. Vol. 3* (pp. 143–166). Norwood, NJ: Ablex.

Adams, R.J., Wilson, M., & Wang, W.C. (1997). The multidimensional random coefficients multinomial logit model. *Applied Psychological Measurement, 21*, 1–23.

Agresti, A. (1999). Modeling ordered categorical data: Recent advances and future challenges. *Statistics in Medicine, 18*, 2191–2207.

Agresti, A. (2002). *Categorical Data Analysis (2nd ed.)*. New York: Wiley.

Agresti, A., & Liu, I. (2001). Strategies for modelling a categorical variable allowing multiple category choices. *Sociological Methods & Research, 29*, 403–434.

Andersen, E.B. (1995). Polytomous Rasch models and their estimation. In G.H. Fischer & I.W. Molenaar (Eds), *Rasch Models: Foundations, Recent Developments, and Applications* (pp. 271–291). New York: Springer.

Andrich, D. (1978). A rating formulation for ordered response categories. *Psychometrika, 43*, 561–573.

Andrich, D. (1982). An extension of the Rasch model to ratings providing both location and dispersion parameters. *Psychometrika, 47*, 105–113.

Bartholomew, D.J., Steel, F., Moustaki, I., & Galbraith, J.I. (2002). *The Analysis and Interpretation of Multivariate Data for Social Scientists*. London: CRC Press.

Bock, R.D. (1972). Estimating item parameters and latent ability when responses are scored in two or more nominal categories. *Psychometrika, 37*, 29–51.

Boyd, J., & Mellman, J. (1980). The effect of fuel economy standards on the U.S. automotive market: A hedonic demand analysis. *Transportation Research A, 14*, 367–378.

Cardell, S., & Dunbar, F. (1980). Measuring the societal impacts of automobile downsizing. *Transportation Research A, 14*, 423–434.

Ezzet, F., & Whitehead, J. (1991). A random effects model for ordinal responses from a crossover trial. *Statistics in Medicine, 10*, 901–907.

Fahrmeir, L., & Tutz, G. (2001). *Multivariate Statistical Modelling Based on Generalized Linear Models (2nd ed.)*. New York: Springer.

Fischer, G.H., & Parzer, P. (1991). An extension of the rating scale model with an application to the measurement of treatment effects. *Psychometrika, 56*, 637–651.

Fischer, G.H., & Ponocny, I. (1994). An extension of the partial credit model with an application to the measurement of change. *Psychometrika,*

59, 177–192.

Glas, C.A.W., & Verhelst, N.D. (1989). Extensions of the partial credit model. *Psychometrika, 54*, 635–659.

Hartzel, J., Agresti, A., & Caffo, B. (2001). Multinomial logit random effects. *Statistical Modelling, 1*, 81–102.

Harville, D.A., & Mee, R.W. (1984). A mixed-model procedure for analysing ordered categorical data. *Biometrics, 40*, 393–408.

Hedeker, D., & Gibbons, R.D. (1994). A random-effects ordinal regression model for multilevel analysis. *Biometrics, 50*, 933–944.

Jansen, J. (1990). On the statistical analysis of ordinal data when extravariation is present. *Applied Statistics, 39*, 74–85.

Jansen, P.G.W., & Roskam, E.E. (1986). Latent trait models and dichotomization of graded responses. *Psychometrika, 51*, 69–91.

Linacre, J.M. (1989). *Many-faceted Rasch Measurement*. Chicago: MESA Press.

Luce, R.D. (1959). *Individual Choice Behavior*. New York: Wiley.

Masters, G.N. (1982). A Rasch model for partial credit scoring. *Psychometrika, 47*, 149–174.

McCullagh, P. (1980). Regression models for ordinal data (with discussion). *Journal of the Royal Statistical Society, Series B, 42*, 109–142.

McCullagh, P., & Nelder, J.A. (1989). *Generalized Linear Models (2nd ed.)*. London: Chapman & Hall.

McCulloch, C.E., & Searle, S. (2001). *Generalized, Linear, and Mixed Models*. New York: Wiley.

McFadden, D. (1974). Conditional logit analysis of qualitative choice behavior. In P. Zarembka (Ed.), *Frontiers in Econometrics* (pp. 105–142). New York: Academic Press.

Molenaar, I.W. (1983). *Item steps* (Heymans Bulletin 83-630-EX). Groningen, The Netherlands: Heymans Bulletins Psychologische Instituten, R.U. Groningen.

Muraki, E. (1992). A generalized partial credit model: Application of an EM algorithm. *Applied Psychological Measurement, 16*, 159–176.

Ramsey, F.L. & Schafer, D.W. (2001). *The Statistical Sleuth: A Course in Methods of Data Analysis*. Pacific Grove, CA: Duxbury Press.

Rasch, G. (1961). On the general laws and the meaning of measurement in psychology. In J. Neyman (Ed.), *Proceedings of the IV Berkeley Symposium on Mathematical Statistics and Probability, Vol. IV* (pp. 321–333). Berkeley: University of California Press.

Samejima, F. (1969). Estimation of ability using a response pattern of graded scores. *Psychometrika Monograph*, No. 17.

Thissen, D., & Steinberg, L. (1986). A taxonomy of item response models.

Psychometrika, 51, 567–577.

Thurstone, L. (1927). A law of comparative judgment. *Psychological Review, 34*, 273–286.

Train, K.E. (2003). *Discrete Choice Models with Simulation*. Cambridge: Cambridge University Press.

Tutz, G. (1990). Sequential item response models with an ordered response. *British Journal of Mathematical and Statistical Psychology, 43*, 39–55.

Tutz, G. (1997). Sequential models for ordered responses. In W.J. van der Linden & R.K. Hambleton (Eds), *Handbook of Modern Item Response Theory* (pp. 139–152). New York: Springer.

Tutz, G., & Hennevogl, W. (1996). Random effects in ordinal regression models. *Computational Statistics & Data Analysis, 22*, 537–557.

Wilson, M., & Adams, R.J. (1993). Marginal maximum likelihood estimation for the ordered partition model. *Journal of Educational Statistics, 18*, 69–90.

Wilson, M., & Masters, G.N. (1993). The partial credit model and null categories. *Psychometrika, 58*, 87–99.

Wu, M.L., Adams, R.J., & Wilson, M. (1998). *ACERConquest*. Hawthorn, Australia: ACER Press.

Chapter 4

An Introduction to (Generalized (Non)Linear Mixed Models

Geert Molenberghs
Geert Verbeke

4.1 Introduction

In applied sciences, one is often confronted with the collection of *correlated data* or otherwise hierarchical data. This generic term embraces a multitude of data structures, such as multivariate observations, clustered data, repeated measurements (called 'repeated observations' in this volume), longitudinal data, and spatially correlated data. In particular, studies are often designed to investigate changes in a specific parameter which is measured repeatedly over time in the participating persons. This is in contrast to cross-sectional studies where the response of interest is measured only once for each individual. Longitudinal studies are conceived for the investigation of such changes, together with the evolution of relevant covariates.

A very important characteristic of data to be analyzed is the type of outcome. Methods for continuous longitudinal data form no doubt the best developed and most advanced body of research (Verbeke & Molenberghs, 1997, 2000); the same is true for software implementation. This is natural, since the special status and the elegant properties of the normal distribution simplify model building and ease software development. A number of software tools, such as the SAS procedure MIXED, the S-PLUS function lme, HLM, and MLwiN have been developed in this area. However, categorical (nominal, ordinal, and binary) and discrete outcomes are also very prominent in statistical practice. For example, in many surveys regarding educational testing or quality of life, as well as in behavioral observations, responses are often scored on binary or ordinal scales.

Two fairly different views can be adopted. The first one, supported by large-sample results, states that normal theory should be applied as much as possible, even to non-normal data such as ordinal scores and counts. A different view is that each type of outcome should be analyzed using instruments that exploit the nature of the data, giving categorical data, counts, etc. their proper methods for analysis. Extensions of generalized linear models to the longitudinal case are discussed in Diggle, Heagerty, Liang, and Zeger (2002), where a lot of emphasis is on generalized estimating equations (Liang & Zeger 1986). Generalized linear mixed models have been proposed and/or studied by, for example, Stiratelli, Laird, and Ware (1984), Wolfinger and O'Connell (1993), and Breslow and Clayton (1993). Fahrmeir and Tutz (2001) devote an entire book to generalized linear models for multivariate settings. Subscribing to the second point of view, this review will present, discuss, and illustrate methodology specific to the case of non-continuous data.

In correlated settings, each unit (respondent, cluster, person, patient,...) typically has a *vector* Y of responses (here, we will use the terms 'person' or 'individual' to indicate study units). This leads to several, generally non-equivalent, extensions of univariate models. In a *marginal model*, marginal distributions for each component of Y are modeled based on a set X of predictor variables. The correlation among the components of Y can then be captured either by adopting a fully parametric approach or by means of working assumptions, such as in the semiparametric approach of Liang and Zeger (1986). Alternatively, in a *random-effects model*, the predictor variables X are supplemented with a vector θ of random effects, conditional upon which the components of Y are usually assumed to be independent. This does not preclude that more elaborate models are possible if residual dependence is detected (Longford, 1993). Finally, a *conditional model* describes the distribution of the components of Y, conditional on X but also conditional on (a subset of) the other components of Y. Well-known members of this class of models are loglinear models (Gilula & Haberman, 1994). See also Chapters 7 and 10 for applications of conditional models.

A more elaborate sketch of the different model families is provided in Section 4.2. Random-effects models, and in particular the generalized linear mixed model, are discussed in Section 4.3. Specific attention is devoted to fitting algorithms (Section 4.5), as well as to inference (Section 4.6). These ideas are exemplified using a case study from a medical context in Section 4.7. Issues arising when data are incomplete are reviewed in Section 4.8, while a brief overview of possible extensions is given in Section 4.9.

4.2   Model families

In the case that responses are of a continuous nature, a number of marginal, conditional, and random-effects models fit, to a large extent, within the framework of the linear mixed model. This convenient property is due to the elegant properties of the normal distribution, the fact that the identity link function can be used, implying a high degree of linearity, and a separation between the mean vector and the covariance matrix within the normal context. These properties of normal models do not extend to the general case of non-normally distributed repeated observations, which are the focus of this volume. In conditionally-specified models the probability of a positive response for one member of the cluster is modeled conditionally upon other outcomes for the same person, while marginal models relate the covariates directly to the marginal probabilities. Random-effects models differ from the two previous models by the inclusion of parameters which are specific to the cluster.

Let us illustrate the three modeling families in the context of a survey with two items $i = 1, 2$ recorded for a number of persons $p = 1, \ldots, P$, with outcomes Y_{p1} and Y_{p2}. Covariate information is assumed to be present but suppressed from notation. A marginal model is built from univariate models for each of the outcomes Y_{pi} separately such as, for example, two logistic regressions $(i = 1, 2)$. Such logistic regressions may or may not have parameters in common. This approach does not fully specify the joint distribution of the outcomes. In some settings, this does not pose problems as the scientific question of interest may be phrased completely in terms of such univariate distributions. In other settings, for example, when the association between the outcomes is of direct interest, or when one has an interest in so-called joint probabilities (e.g., the probability of scoring a certain level on both responses simultaneouly), one has to specify the joint distribution. In this case, this is achieved by considering a measure of association between the two outcomes (e.g., correlation, odds ratio, Cohen's kappa coefficient, Kendall's tau). A conditional model starts from, for example, a specification of the distribution of Y_{p1} given $Y_{p2} = y_{p2}$, and, at the same time Y_{p2} given $Y_{p1} = y_{p1}$. Not every pair of specifications is valid since one has to ensure that the model specification corresponds to exactly one joint distribution. In the loglinear model specification, this correspondence is always satisfied. In a random-effects model, one assumes person-specific unobserved random effects (e.g., θ_p in the scalar version), such that the Y_{pi} $(i = 1, 2)$, are independent, conditional upon θ_p. This so-called conditional independence model is the simplest instance of a random-effects model. Formulating a model is relatively easy since, due to the conditional independence, one merely has to consider a univariate model for each $Y_{pi}|\theta_p$, in conjunction with a distribution for the random effects.

Marginal models are appropriate to investigate the effect of covariates on the univariate marginal probabilities at the level of the population. If of scientific interest, the effect of covariates on the associations can be studied as well. Conditional models are especially suited for inferences on conditional probabilities, for example, on transition probabilities. Finally, random-effects models are the preferred choice to model differences and heterogeneity and sources of random variation in general, and if one wants to make inferences on the effect of covariates at the individual level.

All of this implies that each model family requires its own specific analysis and, consequently, software tools. In many cases, standard maximum likelihood analyses are prohibitive in terms of computational requirements.

Therefore, specific methods such as generalized estimating equations (Liang & Zeger 1986) and pseudo-likelihood (Aerts, Geys, Molenberghs, & Ryan 2002) have been developed. Both apply to marginal models, whereas pseudo-likelihood methodology can be used in the context of conditional models as well. In situations where random-effects models are used, the likelihood function involves integration over the random-effects distribution for which generally no closed forms are available. Estimation methods then either employ approximations to the likelihood or score functions, or resort to numerical integration techniques (see Section 4.5).

These considerations imply that it is important to reflect on which model family to select for analysis. The proper process is to reflect on the scientific question, in terms of which the most appropriate model formulation is then chosen.

For example, opting for a marginal model for repeated binary data precludes the researcher from answering conditional and transitional questions in terms of simple model parameters, because the joint distribution is not of primary interest. Based on the model formulations, parameter estimation and inferential methods then need to be chosen. Finally, the appropriate software tool needs to be determined. Of course, from a pragmatic point of view, the method that is used to fit the model, depends not only on the assumptions the investigator is willing to make, but also (to some extent) on the availability of computational algorithms. In the remainder of this chapter, we will briefly describe the marginal and conditional families. Subsequent chapters are devoted to random-effects models.

Throughout this chapter, Y_{pi} will denote the ith observation for person p, $p = 1, \ldots, P$, $i = 1, \ldots, I$. In many applications, the different observations within persons will refer to responses to a series of items in a testing situation. In other examples, the different observations refer to a single response measured repeatedly over time within all persons. In the latter case, the data are called longitudinal. A key aspect of longitudinal data is the fact that the 'time' dimension is usually of interest. This means that one wishes to study how the response of interest evolves over time in the participating persons. It should be emphasized that most models that will be discussed here do not explicitly assume the number of observations to be the same for all persons. However, we do not include that possibility in our notation, in order to keep the notation as simple as possible. Finally, let $\boldsymbol{Y_p} = (Y_{p1}, \ldots, Y_{pI})'$ denote the vector of all measurements available for person p.

4.2.1   Marginal models

In marginal models, the parameters characterize the marginal probabilities of a subset of the outcomes, without conditioning on the other outcomes or on random effects. Advantages and disadvantages of marginal modeling have been discussed in Diggle et al. (2002), and Fahrmeir and Tutz (2001).

The classical route is to specify the full joint distribution for the set of measurements $Y_{p1}, \ldots, Y_{pI}$ per individual. Clearly, this implies the need to specify all moments up to order I. Especially for longer sequences, not only specifying such a distribution, but also making inferences about its parameters, traditionally done using maximum likelihood principles, can become cumbersome. Therefore, a number of simplifying alternative inferential methods have been proposed, necessitating the specification of a small number of moments only. In a large number of cases, one is primarily interested in the mean structure, hence only the first moments need to be specified. Sometimes, there is also interest in the association structure, quantified, for example using odds ratios or correlations. As will be discussed further, a popular non-likelihood framework is that of generalized estimating equations.

Bahadur (1961) proposed a fully specified marginal model for binary data, accounting for the association via marginal correlations, and enabling likelihood inference. This model has also been studied by Cox (1972), Kupper and Haseman (1978), and Altham (1978). The general form of the Bahadur model requires the specification of a number of parameters, exponential in the number of measurements per person, often prohibiting its use.

Let

$$\epsilon_{pi} = \frac{Y_{pi} - \mu_{pi}}{\sqrt{\mu_{pi}(1 - \mu_{pi})}} \quad \text{and} \quad e_{pi} = \frac{y_{pi} - \mu_{pi}}{\sqrt{\mu_{pi}(1 - \mu_{pi})}},$$

where y_{pi} is an actual value of the binary response variable Y_{pi}. Further, let $\rho_{pii'} = E(\epsilon_{pi}\epsilon_{pi'})$, $\rho_{pii'i''} = E(\epsilon_{pi}\epsilon_{pi'}\epsilon_{pi''})$, ..., $\rho_{p12\ldots I} = E(\epsilon_{p1}\epsilon_{p2}\ldots\epsilon_{pI})$. The parameters $\rho_{pii'}$ are classical Pearson type correlation coefficients.

The general Bahadur model can be represented by the expression $f(\boldsymbol{y}_p) = f_1(\boldsymbol{y}_p)c(\boldsymbol{y}_p)$, where

$$f_1(\boldsymbol{y}_p) = \prod_{i=1}^{I} \pi_{pi}^{y_{pi}}(1 - \pi_{pi})^{1-y_{pi}},$$

and

$$c(\boldsymbol{y}_p) =$$
$$1 + \sum_{i<i'} \rho_{pii'} e_{pi} e_{pi'} \tag{4.1}$$
$$+ \sum_{i<i'<i''} \rho_{pii'i''} e_{pi} e_{pi'} e_{pi''} + \ldots + \rho_{p12\ldots I} e_{p1} e_{p2} \ldots e_{pI}.$$

Thus, the probability mass function is the product of the independence model $f_1(\boldsymbol{y}_p)$ (combining I logistic regressions) and the correction factor $c(\boldsymbol{y}_p)$. The factor $c(\boldsymbol{y}_p)$ can be viewed as a model for overdispersion.

A drawback of the Bahadur approach is the existence of severe constraints on the correlation parameter space, specified by Equation 4.1. A general study of this phenomenon is given in Declerck, Aerts and Molenberghs (1998).

Molenberghs and Lesaffre (1994) and Lang and Agresti (1994) have proposed models which parametrize the association in terms of marginal odds ratios. Dale (1986) defined the bivariate global odds ratio model, based on a bivariate Plackett distribution (Plackett, 1965). Molenberghs and Lesaffre (1994, 1999) extended this model to multivariate ordinal outcomes. Alternative marginal models include the correlated binomial models of Altham (1978) and the double binomial model of Efron (1986).

The main issue with full likelihood approaches is the computational complexity they entail. When we are mainly interested in first-order marginal mean parameters and pairwise interactions, a full likelihood procedure can be replaced by quasi-likelihood methods (McCullagh & Nelder, 1989). In quasi-likelihood, the mean response is expressed as a parametric function of covariates; the variance is assumed to be a function of the mean up to possibly unknown scale parameters. Wedderburn (1974) first noted that likelihood and quasi-likelihood theories coincide for exponential families and that the quasi-likelihood 'estimating equations' provide consistent estimates of the regression parameters β in any generalized linear model, even for choices of link and variance functions that do not correspond to exponential families.

Liang and Zeger (1986) proposed so-called *generalized estimating equations* (GEE, later denoted as GEE1) which require only the correct specification of the univariate marginal distributions provided one is willing to adopt 'working' assumptions about the association structure. They estimate the parameters associated with the marginal expected value of an individual's vector of binary responses and express the working assumptions about the association between pairs of outcomes in terms of marginal correlations. The method combines estimating equations for the regression parameters β with moment-based estimation for the correlation parameters entering the working assumptions.

Prentice (1988) extended their results to allow joint estimation of probabilities and pairwise correlations. Lipsitz, Laird and Harrington (1991) modified the estimating equations of Prentice (1988) to allow modeling of the association through marginal odds ratios rather than marginal correlations. When adopting GEE1, one does not use information about the association structure to estimate the main effect parameters. As a result, it can be shown that GEE1 yields consistent main effect estimators, even when the association structure is misspecified. However, severe misspecification may seriously affect the efficiency of the GEE1 estimators. In addition, GEE1 should be avoided when some scientific interest is placed on the association parameters.

A second order extension of these estimating equations (GEE2) that include the marginal pairwise association as well has been studied by Liang, Zeger and Qaqish (1992). They note that GEE2 is nearly fully efficient though bias may occur in the estimation of the main effect parameters when the association structure is misspecified.

Ample technical detail can be found in Diggle et al. (2002), and Aerts et al. (2002).

4.2.2 Conditional models

In a conditional model the parameters describe a feature (probability, odds, logit, etc.) of (a set of) outcomes, given values for the other outcomes (Cox, 1972). The best known example is undoubtedly the loglinear model. Rosner (1984) described a conditional logistic model. Owing to the popularity of marginal (especially generalized estimating equations) and random-effects models for correlated binary data, conditional models have received relatively little attention, especially in the context of multivariate clustered data. Diggle et al. (2002) criticized the conditional approach because the interpretation of the covariate effects on the probability of one outcome is conditional on the responses of other outcomes for the same individual, outcomes of other individuals and the cluster size. Many conditional models, in particular the loglinear model, fall within the framework of the exponential family.

One proposal is the model by Cox (1972). Specific choices for its parameters lead to specific forms of the loglinear model. The probability mass function is given by

$$f_p(\boldsymbol{y}_p \mid \boldsymbol{\theta}_p) = \exp\left(\sum_{i=1}^{I} \theta_{pi} y_{pi} + \sum_{i<i'} \omega_{pii'} y_{pi} y_{pi'} + \dots \right.$$
$$\left. + \omega_{p1\dots I} y_{p1} \dots y_{pI} - A(\boldsymbol{\theta}_p)\right).$$

The θ parameters can be thought of as 'main effects,' whereas the ω parameters are association parameters or interactions.

Models that do not include all interactions are derived by replacing the vector of ω parameters by one of its subvectors. A useful special case is found by setting all third- and higher-order parameters equal to zero, which is a member of the quadratic exponential family discussed by Zhao and Prentice (1990). Thélot (1985) studied the case where $I = 2$. If $I = 1$, the model reduces to ordinary logistic regression. The parameters $\omega_{pii'}$ can be interpreted as conditional odds ratios, i.e., the odds ratio between responses to items i and i', conditional upon all other outcomes being zero.

In the very specific case of ordered items within persons, it is natural to model later item responses Y_{pi}, not only in terms of covariates, but also in terms of earlier item responses $Y_{p1}, \dots, Y_{p,i-1}$, i.e., its history. This class of models is usually referred to as transition or autoregressive models. The joint density $f(y_{p1}, \dots, y_{pI})$ can then be decomposed as

$$f(y_{p1}, \dots, y_{pI}) = f(y_{p1})f(y_{p2}|y_{p1})f(y_{p3}|y_{p1}, y_{p2}) \dots f(y_{pI}|y_{p1}, \dots, y_{p,I-1}),$$

naturally leading to maximum likelihood inference. Often, dependence on the history is restricted to a fixed and small number of recent responses.

4.3   Mixed-effects models

Models with person-specific parameters are differentiated from population-averaged models by the inclusion of parameters which are specific to the cluster. Unlike the case for correlated Gaussian outcomes, the parameters of the random-effects and population-averaged models for correlated binary data describe different types of effects of the covariates on the response probabilities (Neuhaus, 1992).

The choice between population-averaged and random-effects strategies may heavily depend on the scientific goals. Population-averaged models evaluate the overall risk as a function of covariates. With a random-effects approach, the response rates are modeled as a function of covariates and parameters, specific to a person. In such models, interpretation of fixed-effect parameters is conditional on a constant level of the random-effects parameter. As such the effect of a change in a covariate can be studied both at the population-averaged level and at the level of the individual (Neuhaus, Kalbfleisch, & Hauck, 1991).

Person-specific parameters can be dealt with in essentially three ways: (1) as fixed effects, (2) as random effects, and (3) by conditioning upon their sufficient statistics. The first approach is seemingly simplest but in many cases flawed since the number of parameters then increases with a rate proportional to the sample size, thereby invalidating most standard inferential results. This first approach corresponds to what is called joint maximum likelihood (JML) in psychometrics. The second approach is very popular. There are two routes to introduce randomness into the model parameters. Stiratelli et al. (1984) assume the parameter vector to be normally distributed. This idea has been carried further in the work on so-called *generalized linear mixed models* (Breslow & Clayton, 1993) which is closely related to linear and nonlinear mixed models. This corresponds to what is called marginal maximum likelihood (MML) in psychometrics. Alternatively, Skellam (1948) introduced the beta-binomial model, in which the adverse event probability of any response of a particular person comes from a beta distribution. Hence, this model can also be viewed as a random-effects model. The third approach is well known in epidemiology, more precisely in the context of matched case-control studies. In particular, conditional logistic regression is then often considered (Breslow & Day, 1987; Agresti, 1990). In general, with so-called conditional likelihood methods, one conditions on the sufficient statistics for the random effects (Conaway, 1989; Ten Have, Landis, & Weaver, 1995). This corresponds to what is called conditional maximum likelihood (CML) in psychometrics. Note that the conditioning considered here is different from the one considered in Section 4.2.2, since here we condition on sufficient statistics within a random-effects model rather than formulating the model directly in conditional terms. In the remainder of this section we will consider very briefly the beta-binomial model and more extensively the classical mixed-effects models.

4.3.1   The beta-binomial model

Rather than modeling marginal functions directly, a popular approach is to assume a random-effects model in which each unit has a random parameter (vector). Skellam (1948) and Kleinman (1973) assume the success probability π_p of any response in unit p to come from a beta distribution with parameters α_p and β_p:

$$\frac{\pi^{\alpha_p-1}(1-\pi)^{\beta_p-1}}{B(\alpha_p,\beta_p)},\qquad 0\leq \pi \leq 1,$$

where $B(.,.)$ denotes the beta function. Conditional on π_p, the number of correct responses $S_p = \sum_{i=1}^{I} Y_{pi}$ in the pth unit follows a binomial distribution. This leads to the well-known beta-binomial model. The mean of this distribution is $\mu_p = I\pi_p = I\alpha_p/(\alpha_p + \beta_p)$, and the variance is $\sigma_p^2 = I\pi_p(1 - \pi_p)(1 + I\theta_p)/(1 + \theta_p)$ with $\theta_p = 1/(\alpha_p + \beta_p)$. It can be shown that the intraclass correlation is given by $\rho_p = (\alpha_p + \beta_p + 1)^{-1}$.

Generalized linear model ideas can be applied to model the mean parameter π_p (e.g., using a logit link) and the correlation parameter ρ_p (e.g., using Fisher's z transform). Kupper and Haseman (1978) compare the Bahadur model to the beta-binomial model. They conclude that the models perform similarly in three clustered data experiments, whereas they both outperform the (naive) binomial model. This model is of interest if there are no covariates for the repeated observations. It would not be relevant if there are systematic differences between items.

4.3.2   Mixed models

Perhaps the most commonly encountered person-specific (or random-effects) model is the generalized linear mixed model. It is best to first introduce linear mixed models and nonlinear mixed models as a basis for the introduction of generalized linear mixed models. To emphasize they fit within a single common framework, we first give a general formulation.

General formulation

As before, let Y_{pi} denote the ith measurement available for the pth person, and let $\boldsymbol{Y}_p$ denote the corresponding vector of all measurements. Our general model assumes that $\boldsymbol{Y}_p$ (possibly appropriately transformed) satisfies

$$\boldsymbol{Y}_p|\boldsymbol{\theta}_p \ \sim \ F_p(\boldsymbol{\xi},\boldsymbol{\theta}_p), \tag{4.2}$$

meaning that conditional on $\boldsymbol{\theta}_p$, $\boldsymbol{Y}_p$ follows a pre-specified distribution F_p, possibly depending on covariates, and parametrized through a vector $\boldsymbol{\xi}$ of unknown parameters, common to all persons. Further, $\boldsymbol{\theta}_p$ is a R-dimensional vector of person-specific parameters, called random effects, assumed to follow a so-called mixing distribution G which may depend on a vector ψ of unknown parameters, i.e., $\theta_p \sim G(\psi)$. The θ_p reflect the between-person heterogeneity in the population with respect to the distribution of Y_p. Different specifications of F_p will lead to different models. For example, considering the factors made up of the outcomes Y_{pi} given its predecessors $(Y_{p1}, \ldots, Y_{p,i-1})'$ leads to a so-called transitional model. Note also that omission of the random effects θ_p results in a marginal model, discussed earlier in Section 4.2.1, for the response vector Y_p. In the presence of random effects, conditional independence is often assumed, under which the components Y_{pi} in Y_p are independent, conditional on θ_p. The distribution function F_p in Equation 4.2 then becomes a product over the I independent elements in Y_p.

Specific choices for the distributions F_p and G lead to specific models. One approach is to leave G completely unspecified and to use non-parametric maximum likelihood (NPML; Böhning, 1999) estimation, which maximizes the likelihood over all possible distributions G. The resulting estimate $\hat{G}$ is then always discrete with finite support. Depending on the context, this may or may not be a realistic reflection of the true heterogeneity between units. One therefore often assumes G to be of a specific parametric form. Most models used in this volume will assume the random-effects distribution G to be normal, leading to the classical mixed model (utilized up to Chapter 10), or to be a finite mixture of normals, as in Chapter 11. If G is discrete with fixed support size, the classical latent class models are obtained. See also Chapter 12 for a discussion on choices for G.

The linear mixed model as discussed in Section 4.3.2 is the most special case, due to its convenient normality and linearity properties. All other models exhibit nonlinearity in one or another sense. Note that nonlinearity of a model can arise due to the choice of model form (the link function in generalized linear model terms) as well as due to the nonlinearity of the systematic component. Hence, normal response variables and normal random effects, combined with a nonlinear predictor, still produces a nonlinear mixed model.

Linear mixed models

When continuous (normally distributed) hierarchical data are considered (repeated observations, clustered data, geographical data, longitudinal data, etc.), a general, and very flexible, class of parametric models is obtained from introducing random effects $\tilde{\theta}_p$ in the multivariate linear regression model. Suppose that a specific outcome Y is observed repeatedly over time for a set of persons, and suppose that the individual trajectories are of the type as shown in Figure 4.1 (the term 'evolution' will be used for such trajectories). Obviously, a linear regression model with intercept and linear time effect seems plausible to describe the data. However, different persons tend to have different intercepts and different slopes. One can therefore assume that the outcome Y_{pi}, measured at time t_{pi}, satisfies

Individual profiles with random intercepts and slopes

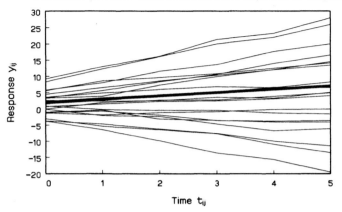

FIGURE 4.1. Hypothetical example of continuous longitudinal data which can be well described by a linear mixed model with random intercepts and random slopes. The thin lines represent the observed subject-specific evolutions. The bold line represents the population-averaged evolution.

$Y_{pi} = \tilde{\theta}_{p0} + \tilde{\theta}_{p1}t_{pi} + \varepsilon_{pi}$. Assuming the vector $\tilde{\boldsymbol{\theta}}_p = (\tilde{\theta}_{p0}, \tilde{\theta}_{p1})'$ of person-specific parameters to be bivariate normal with mean $(\beta_0, \beta_1)'$ and 2×2 covariance matrix $\boldsymbol{\Sigma}$ (to be distinguished from $\boldsymbol{\Omega}$, see Equations 4.3 and 4.4), and assuming the error terms ε_{pi} to be normal as well, this leads to a so-called linear mixed model. In practice, one will often formulate the model as

$$Y_{pi} = (\beta_0 + \theta_{p0}) + (\beta_1 + \theta_{p1})t_{pi} + \varepsilon_{pi},$$

with $\tilde{\theta}_{p0} = \beta_0 + \theta_{p0}$ and $\tilde{\theta}_{p1} = \beta_1 + \theta_{p1}$, and the new random effects $\boldsymbol{\theta}_p = (\theta_{p0}, \theta_{p1})'$ are now assumed to have mean zero.

In order to present the model, a notation will be used which is slightly different from the notation used in most chapters of this volume. $\boldsymbol{X}$ will be used for the item by item covariate matrix for item covariates with fixed effects denoted by $\boldsymbol{\beta}$; and $\boldsymbol{Z}$ will be used for the item by item covariate matrix for item covariates with random effects, denoted by $\boldsymbol{\theta}_p$. Since, in principle, these matrices can differ depending on the person, they are given a person subscript. In fact, in this way, one can also define person covariates, with columns in $\boldsymbol{X}_p$ and $\boldsymbol{Z}_p$, that do not differ depending on the item but only on the person.

The above model can be viewed as a special case of the general linear mixed model which assumes that the outcome vector $\boldsymbol{Y}_p$ follows a multivariate normal distribution, with mean vector $\boldsymbol{X}_p\boldsymbol{\beta} + \boldsymbol{Z}_p\boldsymbol{\theta}_p$ and some covariance matrix $\boldsymbol{\Omega}$, and assumed that the random effects $\boldsymbol{\theta}_p$ also follow a (multivariate) normal distribution, meaning that the I-dimensional vector $\boldsymbol{Y}_p$ satisfies

$$\boldsymbol{Y}_p|\boldsymbol{\theta}_p \sim N(\boldsymbol{X}_p\boldsymbol{\beta} + \boldsymbol{Z}_p\boldsymbol{\theta}_p, \boldsymbol{\Omega}), \tag{4.3}$$

$$\boldsymbol{\theta}_p \quad \sim \quad N(\mathbf{0}, \boldsymbol{\Sigma}), \tag{4.4}$$

where $\boldsymbol{X}_p$ and $\boldsymbol{Z}_p$ are $(I \times K)$ and $(I \times J)$ dimensional matrices of known covariates, $\boldsymbol{\beta}$ is a K-dimensional vector of regression parameters, called the fixed effects, $\boldsymbol{\Sigma}$ is a general $(J \times J)$ covariance matrix, and $\boldsymbol{\Omega}$ is a $(I \times I)$ covariance matrix. This so-called hierarchical formulation corresponds to making Gaussian assumptions about F_p (in Equation 4.3) and about G (in Equation 4.4), both introduced in Section 4.3.2.

Nonlinear mixed models

An extension of the model in Equation 4.3 which allows for nonlinear relationships between the responses in $\boldsymbol{Y}_p$ and the covariates in $\boldsymbol{X}_p$ and/or $\boldsymbol{Z}_p$ is

$$\boldsymbol{Y}_p | \boldsymbol{\theta}_p \quad \sim \quad N(f_{\text{link}}^{-1}(\boldsymbol{X}_p, \boldsymbol{Z}_p, \boldsymbol{\beta}, \boldsymbol{\theta}_p), \boldsymbol{\Omega}) \tag{4.5}$$

for some known inverse link function f_{link}^{-1}. The definition of $\boldsymbol{X}_p$, $\boldsymbol{Z}_p$, $\boldsymbol{\beta}$, and $\boldsymbol{\theta}_p$ remains unchanged, the random effects $\boldsymbol{\theta}_p$ are again assumed to be normally distributed with mean vector $\mathbf{0}$ and covariance matrix $\boldsymbol{\Sigma}$.

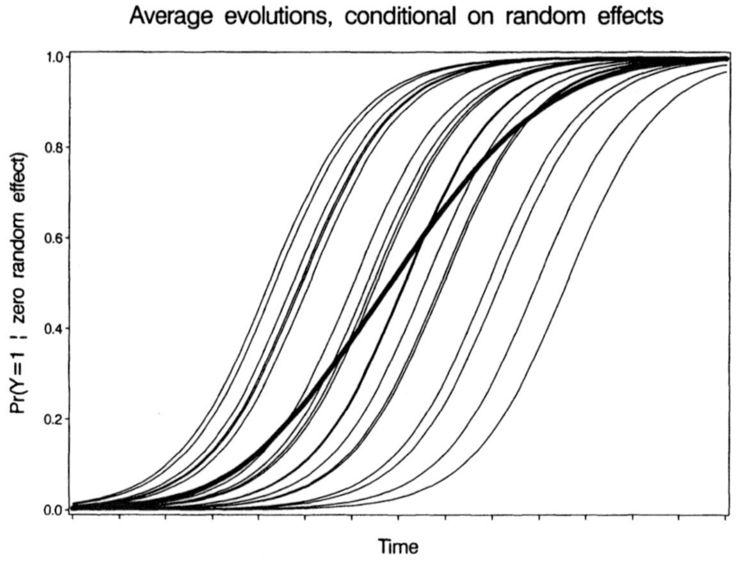

FIGURE 4.2. Graphical representation of a random-intercepts logistic model. The thin lines represent the person-specific logistic regression models. The bold line represents the population-averaged evolution.

The generalized linear mixed model

The generalized linear mixed model is the most frequently used random-effects model for discrete outcomes. As an example, consider a study in which a specific test is taken repeatedly over time, on a set of children. The outcome Y_{pi} taken at time (age) t_{pi} is of the binary type, i.e., pass/fail. Continuing the use of person-specific regression models, a logistic model could be proposed in this case, i.e., one could assume Y_{pi} to be Bernoulli distributed with success probability π_{pi} satisfying

$$\text{logit}(\pi_{pi}) = (\beta_1 + \theta_p) + \beta_2 t_{pi}.$$

Hence, we have a logistic regression model for each person separately. Through the person-specific intercepts θ_p, the model allows all persons to be different with respect to their ability to pass the tests. As before, the θ_p will be called random effects, and will be assumed to be normaly distributed with mean zero. A graphical representation of this model is given in Figure 4.2. As for the linear model, person-specific slopes could have been included as well.

A general formulation is as follows. Conditionally on random effects $\boldsymbol{\theta}_p$, it is assumed that the elements Y_{pi} of $\boldsymbol{Y}_p$ are independent, with density function of an exponential family form

$$f_p(y_{pi}|\boldsymbol{\theta}_p) = \exp\left((y_{pi}\eta_{pi} - a(\eta_{pi}))/\phi + c(y_{pi}, \phi)\right), \qquad (4.6)$$

with a and c functions and ϕ an overdispersion parameter, with η_{pi} as the canonical or natural parameter and further with mean $E(Y_{pi}|\boldsymbol{\theta}_p) = a'(\eta_{pi}) = \mu_{pi}(\boldsymbol{\theta}_p)$ and variance $\text{Var}(Y_{pi}|\boldsymbol{\theta}_p) = \phi a''(\eta_{pi})$. If

$$\boldsymbol{\eta}_p = \boldsymbol{X}_p \boldsymbol{\beta} + \boldsymbol{Z}_p \boldsymbol{\theta}_p, \qquad (4.7)$$

then a'^{-1} is the *canonical link function*. The link function f_{link} is canonical if it maps the mean into a parameter that is both the canonical parameter and a linear function of the covariates as in Equation 4.7.

The random effects $\boldsymbol{\theta}_p$ are assumed to follow

$$\boldsymbol{\theta}_p \sim N(\boldsymbol{0}, \boldsymbol{\Sigma}). \qquad (4.8)$$

Usually, the canonical link function is used, i.e., $f_{\text{link}} = a'^{-1}$. For binomial data, the logit link is canonical, but the probit link is not. For Poisson data, the log link is canonical. Note that the linear mixed model is a special case, with an identity link function. The advantage of a canonical link is that it results in a simplified form for the score equations for which, in many cases, fast and stable fitting algorithms can be constructed.

4.4 Interpretation of regression parameters in mixed models

The common aspect in the mixed models introduced in Section 4.3.2 is the fact that all these models can be interpreted as person-specific statistical models for the outcome Y which contain person-specific parameters, and therefore require an interpretation conditionally on the person. More specifically, the vector β of regression parameters needs to be interpreted conditionally on the random effect θ_p. This can be indicated explicitly using the notation β^{RE}. In many practical situations however, one is interested in studying 'average outcomes,' such as average success probabilities, and how these averages depend on known covariates. In general, such population-averaged profiles can be obtained from fitting marginal models such as the ones described in Section 4.2.1. These models could, in principle, contain the same covariates X_p, and the corresponding vector β^M of regression parameters would have a marginal interpretation. It should be strongly emphasized that, except in very specific cases, β^{RE} and β^M are not identical, and have a different interpretation. This will be further explained in the following sections, for linear, nonlinear, and generalized linear mixed models, respectively.

4.4.1 Linear mixed models

As discussed before, the linear mixed model can be interpreted as a linear regression model for the vector Y_p of repeated observations for each unit separately, where some of the regression parameters are specific to the individual (random effects, θ_p), while others are not (fixed effects, β). Note that the assumption $E(\theta_p) = 0$ implies that the mean of Y_p still equals $X_p\beta$, such that the fixed effects in the random-effects model of Equation 4.3 can also be interpreted marginally. Hence, in this case, $\beta^{RE} = \beta^M$. This is a very important and useful property in the linear mixed model setting, that does not carry over to more general, nonlinear settings. Thus, in this context, not only do the fixed effects reflect the effect of changing covariates within specific units (within individuals), they also measure the marginal effect in the population of changing the same covariates.

4.4.2 Nonlinear mixed models

While general nonlinear models (including models for continuous outcomes) are somewhat outside of the scope of this volume, we believe it is useful to briefly sketch a general nonlinear framework for mixed models, from which generalized linear mixed models can be derived as a special but important case (Section 4.4.3).

Thus, let us consider the marginal ('average') evolution of a continuous outcome Y, modeled through a nonlinear mixed model. Let $f_p(y_p|\theta_p)$ and $g(\theta_p)$ denote the density functions corresponding to the distributions F_p and G, respectively; then we have that the average response is given by

$$\mathrm{E}(Y_p) = \int y_p \int f_p(y_p|\theta_p)g(\theta_p)d\theta_p dy_p,$$

which, in general, is not of the form $f_{\text{link}}^{-1}(X_p, Z_p, \beta, 0)$, but rather integrates the random effects from $f_{\text{link}}^{-1}(X_p, Z_p, \beta, \theta_p)$. Hence, the vector β^{RE} of regression parameters in the nonlinear mixed model will, in general, not have a marginal interpretation, and thus will be different from β^M.

4.4.3   Generalized linear mixed models

Because most generalized linear mixed models involve nonlinear link functions f_{link}, we have that, in general, the regression parameters cannot be marginally interpreted. We will illustrate this for the case of the logistic GLMM. We again refer to Figure 4.2 for the graphical representation. Using the logit link, the average conditional on the random effects, equals

$$E(Y_{pi}|\theta_p) = Pr(Y_{pi} = 1|X_p, Z_p, \beta, \theta_p) = \frac{\exp(X_p\beta + Z_p\theta_p)}{1 + \exp(X_p\beta + Z_p\theta_p)}.$$

The population averaged mean, implied by the above generalized linear mixed model, is obtained from integrating over the random effects:

$$
\begin{aligned}
E(Y_{pi}) = E(Pr(Y_{pi} = 1|X_p, Z_p, \beta, \theta_p)) &= E\left(\frac{\exp(X_p\beta + Z_p\theta_p)}{1 + \exp(X_p\beta + Z_p\theta_p)}\right) \\
&\neq \frac{\exp(X_p\beta)}{1 + \exp(X_p\beta)}.
\end{aligned}
$$

Note that the implied population average is *not* of a logistic form any more. In general,

$$f_{\text{link}}^{-1}(X_p\beta) \neq E\left(f_{\text{link}}^{-1}(X_p\beta + Z_p\theta_p)\right),$$

for an arbitrary link function $f_{\text{link}}(\cdot)$, except for specific cases such as the identity link, the population-averaged (β^M) and person-specific (β^{RE}) fixed effects are not identical. As discussed by Neuhaus, Kalbfleisch, and Hauck (1991), the parameter estimates obtained from fitting the logistic mixed model are typically larger in absolute value than their marginal counterparts that would be obtained from fitting a marginal model with mean model

$$E(Y_{pi}) = \frac{\exp(X_p\beta)}{1 + \exp(X_p\beta)}.$$

However, one should not refer to this phenomenon as *bias* since the two sets of parameters target different scientific questions. Nevertheless, in some cases an approximate relationship can be derived between the marginal and random-effects model parameters.

Consider the specific case of the binomial model for binary data, with the logit canonical link function, and where the only random effects are intercepts θ_p. As before, let β^{RE} represent the vector of regression parameters in the mixed model. It can then be shown that the *implied* marginal mean

$\mu_p = E(Y_p)$ (Y_p is the vector of Y_{p1} to Y_{PI}) satisfies $f_{\text{link}}(\mu_p) \approx X_p \beta^M$ with

$$\beta^M = (c^2 \text{Var}(\theta_p) + 1)^{-1/2} \beta^{RE}, \qquad (4.9)$$

in which c equals $16\sqrt{3}/15\pi$. Hence, although the parameters β in the generalized linear mixed model have no marginal interpretation, they do show a strong relation to their marginal counterparts. Note that indeed, we obtain marginal parameters which are smaller in absolute value than the mixed model counterparts, with larger differences for larger random-intercepts variances. In Figure 4.2, this is reflected in the less steep increase in the population-averaged evolution when compared to all person-specific evolutions.

This discussion points to the need to carefully reflect on the choice of (a) the model for the responses and (b) the distribution of the random effects. It is perhaps fair to say that the choice for a logistic model with normally distributed random effects is based, to a large extent, on the combination of the familiar logistic model with elements of the linear mixed-effects model. However, some of the nice properties of the logistic model do not carry over to the random-effects setting. Indeed, it is important to understand the main differences between the linear mixed model and the nonlinear or generalized linear mixed models, particularly in the case of the logistic type. In the first case, all properties of the normal distribution can be invoked, while in the second case one typically resorts to the exponential family. In the normal distribution, there is no mean-variance link, while such a link plays a prominent role in most exponential family models. In addition, the link function is linear in the first case and usually nonlinear in the second case. In the linear mixed model case, the sources of variability all enter the same linear predictor as additive terms. However, there is no additive relationship between them in other settings. To see this, consider the logistic model. An outcome can be written, with obvious notation, as $Y_{pi} = \mu_{pi} + \varepsilon_{pi}$. Thus, while the measurement error is connected linearly to the outcome, the random-effects variability enters nonlinearly since the linear predictor is coupled to the mean μ_{pi} via the link function. Thus, not only is model fitting different, but also a number of interpretational differences follow, including a different meaning for the regression parameters in both types of models. Note that, unlike the univariate case, there are important qualitative differences between mixed models with a logit link on the one hand and with a probit link on the other hand. Indeed, integrating a probit mixed model over normally distributed random effects still leads to a (often high-dimensional) probit model. Thus, choosing a probit link renders the connection between the hierarchical and marginal form more transparent.

4.5 Fitting mixed models

In general, unless a fully Bayesian approach is followed (see, e.g., Gelman, Carlin, Stern, & Rubin, 1995), inference is based on the marginalized model for Y_p which is obtained from integrating out the random effects, over their distribution $G(\psi)$. Then we have that the marginal density function of Y_p equals

$$f_p(y_p) \;=\; \int f_p(y_p|\theta_p)g(\theta_p)d\theta_p, \qquad (4.10)$$

which depends on the unknown parameters ξ (in F_p) and ψ (in G). Assuming independence of the units, estimates $\widehat{\xi}$ and $\widehat{\psi}$ can be obtained from maximizing the likelihood function built from Equation 4.10, and inferences immediately follow from classical maximum likelihood theory.

Depending on F_p and G, the integration in Equation 4.10 may or may not be possible analytically. Proposed solutions are based on Taylor series expansions of $f_p(y_p|\theta_p)$, or on numerical approximations of the integral, such as (adaptive) Gaussian quadrature, or on the EM algorithm (Dempster, Laird, & Rubin, 1977). Some of these techniques will be discussed further in this section.

Even when one would usually be primarily interested in estimating the parameters in the marginal model, it is often useful to calculate estimates for the random effects θ_p as well. They reflect between-person variability, which makes them helpful for detecting special profiles (i.e., outlying individuals) or groups of individuals showing extraordinary behavior. They are especially meaningful in the measurement context of psychometrics. Also, estimates for the random effects are needed whenever interest is in person-specific predictions. Inference for the random effects is often based on their so-called posterior distribution $f_p(\theta_p|y_p)$, given by

$$f_p(\theta_p|y_p) \;=\; \frac{f_p(y_p|\theta_p)\,g(\theta_p)}{\int f_p(y_p|\theta_p)\,g(\theta_p)\,d\theta_p}, \qquad (4.11)$$

in which the unknown parameters ξ and ψ are replaced by their estimates obtained earlier from maximizing the marginal likelihood. The mean or mode corresponding to Equation 4.11 can be used as point estimates for θ_p, yielding the so-called empirical Bayes (EB) estimate.

It should be emphasized that, although the likelihood corresponding to the implied marginal distribution in Equation 4.10 is maximized, no marginal model, as introduced in Section 4.2.1, is fitted, since the model is still formulated in terms of parameters that have a hierarchical interpretation. Hence the resulting estimates for the regression parameters have no population-averaged interpretation. The parameters in the marginal model are still those from the original mixed model, and hence can only be interpreted conditionally on the random effects in the model.

In the remainder of this chapter, we will discuss how the marginal likelihood constructed from Equation 4.10 is maximized in practice, for linear mixed models and for nonlinear and generalized linear mixed models, respectively. Note that a wide number of different algorithms have been proposed, many of which are based on approximations. Consequently, sometimes substantial differences can be observed when the same model is fitted to the same data, but by way of a different maximization approach. We will hereby restrict ourselves to the case of normally distributed random effects θ_p with mean zero and covariance matrix Σ. The parameters in Equation 4.10 are then the regression parameters β on one hand, and the scale parameter ϕ as in Equation 4.6 and the elements in Σ on the other hand. This last set of parameters will be combined into the vector λ of so-called variance components.

4.5.1 Linear mixed models

From a computational point of view, the main difference between the linear mixed model and the nonlinear or the generalized linear mixed model is that the marginal distribution Equation 4.10 can easily be derived analytically. Indeed, it immediately follows from Equation 4.3 and Equation 4.4 that, marginally, Y_p follows the normal distribution

$$Y_p \sim N(X_p\beta, V_p = Z_p\Sigma Z'_p + \Omega). \tag{4.12}$$

Hence, another multivariate linear regression model is obtained. The mean vector equals $X_p\beta$, which again shows that the regression parameters in the mixed model also have a marginal interpretation. The covariance matrix V_p has a very simple parametrization, with the parameters in Σ and Ω as unknown parameters.

Conditionally on λ, the maximum likelihood (ML) estimate for β equals

$$\widehat{\beta}(\lambda) = \left(\sum_p X'_p V_p^{-1} X_p\right)^{-1} \sum_p X'_p V_p^{-1} Y_p,$$

which is normally distributed with mean β and covariance matrix $(\sum_p X'_p V_p^{-1} X_p)^{-1}$. This can be used to construct Wald-type tests. In practice, however, λ is not known and has to be replaced by an estimate. In order to take into account the variability introduced by estimating the variance components, the chi-squared reference distribution is often replaced by an approximate F-distribution, with the usual numerator degrees of freedom. The denominator degrees of freedom need to be estimated from the data. This is often based on so-called Satterthwaite-type approximations (Satterthwaite, 1941). We refer to Verbeke and Molenberghs (1997; Section 3.5.2 and Appendix A) for a detailed discussion on this. Kenward and Roger (1997) proposed a scaled Wald statistic, based on an adjusted covariance estimate which accounts for the extra variability introduced by estimating λ, and they show that its small sample distribution can be well approximated by an F-distribution with denominator degrees of freedom also obtained via a Satterthwaite-type approximation. In general, the different methods usually lead to different results. However, unless in models with crossed random effects (with random person as well as random item parameters), the data consist of independent blocks of information, resulting in numbers of denominator degrees of freedom which are typically large enough, whatever estimation method is used, to lead to very similar p-values. Only for very small samples, or when linear mixed models are used with random person parameters as well as random item parameters, different estimation methods for degrees of freedom may lead to severe differences in the resulting p-values.

Estimation of λ can be based on the maximum likelihood principle as well. In practice, however, one usually uses restricted maximum likelihood (REML) estimation (Harville, 1974), which allows one to estimate the covariance parameters without having to estimate the mean $X\beta$ first. The rationale for using REML is a reduction and in some cases removal of finite-sample bias, present in the estimation of variance components when using maximum likelihood, due to the fact that degrees of freedom are spent on the estimation of mean parameters. The basic idea is that the vector Y of all responses Y_{pi} is transformed to a vector $U = A'Y$ of so-called error contrasts, where A is chosen such that its columns are orthogonal to the design space construced from the design matrices X_p. The distribution of U no longer depends on β, while the variance components in λ can now be estimated maximizing the likelihood of these error contrasts. This yields the so-called REML estimate for λ. It is known from simpler models, such as linear regression models, that this provides better estimates than the classical maximum likelihood method. We refer to Verbeke and Molenberghs (2000; Section 5.3) for more details on REML estimation and for a comparison between REML and ML estimation. Inference about the variance components in λ is usually based on the asymptotic properties of maximum likelihood estimates, or more specifically on asymptotic Wald tests, likelihood-ratio tests, or score tests. We refer to Verbeke and Molenberghs (2000; Chapter 6, 2003) for a detailed discussion on issues for testing variance components.

4.5.2 Nonlinear and generalized linear mixed models

In contrast to the case of the linear mixed model, the marginal distribution in Equation 4.10 can no longer be derived analytically, in this general situation. In this section, we will briefly discuss ways to handle this issue. A more extensive discussion can be found in Chapter 12. First, a brief summary will be given of how Bayesian methods apply in this context. Afterwards, alternative methods will be discussed, distinguishing between approximations to the integrand, and methods based on approximations to the integral. A useful reference on estimation methods is Lavergne and Trottier (2000). Pinheiro and Bates (1995) discuss connections between both families to deal with the integral. In contrast to the linear mixed model, inference under nonlinear or generalized linear mixed models has been worked out in much less detail in the statistical literature. It is usually based on the asymptotic properties of maximum likelihood estimates, leading to asymptotic Wald-type tests.

Bayesian methods

The need for numerical integration can be avoided by casting the generalized linear random-effects model into a Bayesian framework and by resorting to the Gibbs sampler (Zeger & Karim, 1991).

In Bayesian generalized linear mixed models one also starts from Equations 4.6 to 4.8. In addition, there is the need to select prior distributions for β and λ. For β, one commonly chooses either normal distributions or flat, noninformative priors. Standard noninformative priors for elements in λ are Jeffreys priors (Zeger & Karim, 1991). Fahrmeir and Tutz (2001) report that such choices can lead to improper posteriors (see also Hobert & Casella 1996). Besag, Green, Higdon, and Mengersen (1995) proposed the use of proper but highly dispersed inverted Wishart priors for the random-effects covariance matrix Σ, i.e., $\Sigma \sim IW_r(\Xi, \Psi)$, where the hyperparameters Ξ and Ψ have to be selected very carefully. Under conditional independence, and assuming prior independence of β and λ, the posterior distribution can be expressed as

$$f(\beta, \lambda, \theta_1, \ldots, \theta_P | Y) \propto \prod_{p=1}^{P} \prod_{i=1}^{I} f(y_{pi}|\beta, \lambda, \theta_p) \prod_{p=1}^{P} f(\theta_p|\lambda) f(\lambda) f(\beta).$$

Full conditionals for the fixed effects β, the random effects θ_p, and the variance components λ often take simple forms and standard algorithms can be used for drawing samples from the posterior distribution (Ripley, 1987). Zeger and Karim (1991) used Gibbs sampling with rejection sampling for the fixed and random effects. Gamerman (1997) proposed a more efficient algorithm, exploiting the computational advantage of one-step Fisher scoring. A number of authors have considered alternatives to Gaussian random effects for a Bayesian approach such as, for example, scale mixtures of normals (Besag, et al., 1995; Knorr-Held, 1997). An introduction to Bayesian methods and an application for probit item response models can be found in Chapter 6.

Approximation of the integrand

Breslow and Clayton (1993) exploit the penalized quasi-likelihood (PQL) estimator by applying Laplace's method for integral approximation. They also consider marginal quasi-likelihood (MQL), a name they give to a procedure previously proposed by Goldstein (1991). These two approaches entail iterative fitting of linear models based on first-order Taylor expansions of the mean function about the current estimated fixed part predictor (MQL) or the current predicted value (PQL). The method proposed by Gilmour, Anderson, and Rae (1985) has seen some use as well. Wolfinger and O'Connell (1993) proposed a variation on this theme based on iteratively fitting linear mixed models to an approximately chosen working variate. They termed their procedures pseudo-likelihood and restricted pseudo-likelihood.

As Rodríguez and Goldman (1995) demonstrate, the approximate procedures PQL and MQL, proposed by Breslow and Clayton (1993), may be seriously biased when applied to binary response data. Their simulations reveal that both fixed effects and variance components may suffer from substantial, if not severe, attenuation bias in certain situations which we will discuss at the end of this section. Goldstein and Rasbash (1996) show that including a second-order term in the PQL expansion (yielding PQL2) greatly reduces the bias described by Rodríguez and Goldman. Other authors have advised the introduction of bias-correction terms (Lin & Breslow, 1996) or the use of iterative bootstrap (Kuk, 1995).

Goldstein (1986) proposed *iterative generalized least squares* (IGLS). His algorithm simply iterates between the estimation of the fixed and random parameters obtained by standard generalized least squares formulae, hence its name. The attraction of IGLS lies in its efficiency with large data sets. Note that the IGLS algorithm can be slightly modified (RIGLS) to perform similarly to residual (or restricted) maximum likelihood estimation, which yields unbiased estimates for variance components in random-effects models (Verbeke & Molenberghs, 2000). It should be noted that the properties of RIGLS, in contrast to REML, are not well understood.

The approach proposed by Wolfinger and O'Connell (1993) is based on an extension of the method of Nelder and Wedderburn (1972) (see also McCullagh & Nelder, 1989) to fit fixed-effects generalized linear models. Let us briefly recall this procedure. Dropping the person-specific index p, the basic form of a generalized linear model is $\eta = X\beta$, where $\eta = f_{\text{link}}(\mu)$, $\mu = E(Y)$ and f_{link} is an appropriate link function. Nelder and Wedderburn (1972) showed that maximum likelihood estimates for β can be obtained using 'working' dependent variables y^*, which are linearized versions of the y (McCullagh & Nelder, 1989). Wolfinger and O'Connell's method (see also Schall, 1991; and Breslow & Clayton, 1993) is implemented in the SAS macro GLIMMIX.

The approach is known to have some drawbacks such as, for example, downward biases in fixed-effects and covariance parameters. This issue will be taken up in the next section. The estimation procedure is based on iterating between the computation of working dependent variables on the one hand and fitting a *linear* mixed model to it on the other hand. The explicit steps of the algorithm can be found in, for example, Aerts et al. (2002).

Roughly speaking, the methods discussed so far are based on the approximation of the integrand $\prod_i f_p(y_{pi}|\boldsymbol{\theta}_p)$ by a normal density such that the integral can be calculated analytically, as in the normal linear model. As an example, consider the generalized linear mixed models with canonical link, where this integrand is

$$\prod_i f_p(y_{pi}|\boldsymbol{\theta}_p)$$

$$= \exp\left(\sum_i \phi^{-1}(y_{pi}\eta_{pi} - a(\eta_{pi})) + \sum_i c(y_{pi}, \phi)\right)$$

$$= \exp\left(\phi^{-1}\left(\boldsymbol{\beta}'\sum_i \boldsymbol{x}_{pi}y_{pi} + \boldsymbol{\theta}_p'\sum_i \boldsymbol{z}_{pi}y_{pi} - a(\eta_{pi})\right) + \sum_i c(y_{pi}, \phi)\right).$$

The sufficient statistics for $\boldsymbol{\beta}$ and $\boldsymbol{\theta}_p$ are $\sum_i \boldsymbol{x}_{pi}y_{pi}$ and $\sum_i \boldsymbol{z}_{pi}y_{pi}$, respectively. Hence, the approximation will be accurate whenever these sufficient statistics are approximately normally distributed, which means that responses y_{pi} are 'sufficiently continuous' and/or if I is sufficiently large. This explains why the approximation methods perform poorly in cases with binary repeated observations, with a relatively small number of repeated observations available for all persons (Wolfinger, 1998).

Approximation of the integral

Especially in cases where the above approximation methods for the integrand will fail, approximations to the integral (i.e., numerical integration) prove to be very useful. Of course, a wide toolkit of numerical integration tools, available from the optimization literature, can be applied. Several of those have been used in such software tools as the NLMIXED procedure in SAS and the MIXOR program. A general class of quadrature rules selects a set of abscissas and constructs a weighted sum of function evaluations over those. In the particular context of random-effects distributions, so-called *adaptive* quadrature rules can be used (Pinheiro & Bates, 2000), where the numerical integration is centered around the EB estimates of the random effects, and the number of quadrature points is then selected in terms of the desired accuracy.

To illustrate the main ideas, we consider Gaussian and adaptive Gaussian quadrature, as implemented in the SAS procedure NLMIXED. For ease of notation, it is also assumed that the model has been reparametrized such that the random effects $\boldsymbol{\theta}_p$ have a unit covariance matrix. The likelihood contribution for person p then is given in Equation 4.13, with the density of the (multivariate) standard normal distribution denoted by $\varphi(\cdot)$. Note that one integral evaluation per independent unit is necessary, since not only the common function φ but also the person-specific functions f_p are used in the integration.

Gaussian as well as adaptive Gaussian quadrature are based on the replacement of the integral by a weighted sum

$$\int f(z)\varphi(z)dz \;\approx\; \sum_{m=1}^{M} w_m f(z_m). \qquad (4.13)$$

M is the order of the approximation. The higher M the more accurate the approximation will be. Further, the so-called nodes (or quadrature points) z_m are solutions to the Mth-order Hermite polynomial, while the w_m are well-chosen weights. The nodes z_m and weights w_m are reported in tables. Alternatively, an algorithm is available for calculating all z_m and w_m for any value M (Press, Teukolsky, Vetterling, & Flannery, 1992).

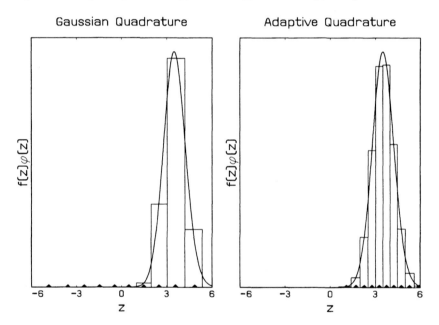

FIGURE 4.3. Graphical illustration of Gaussian (left window) and adaptive Gaussian (right window) quadrature of order $M = 10$. The black triangles indicate the position of the quadrature points, while the rectangles indicate the contribution of each point to the integral.

In the case of univariate integration, the approximation consists of subdividing the integration region into intervals, and approximating the surface under the integrand by the sum of surfaces of the so-obtained approximating rectangles. An example is given in the left-hand window of Figure 4.3, for the case of $M = 10$ quadrature points. A similar interpretation is possible for the approximation of multivariate integrals.

Note that the figure immediately highlights one of the main disadvantages of (nonadaptive) Gaussian quadrature, which is that the quadrature points z_m are chosen based on $\varphi(z)$, independent of the function $f(z)$ in the integrand. Depending on the support of $f(z)$, the z_m will or will not lie in the region of interest. Indeed, the quadrature points are selected to perform well in case $f(z)\varphi(z)$ approximately behaves like $\varphi(z)$, and thus, like a standard normal density function. This will be the case, for example, if $f(z)$ is a polynomial of a sufficiently low order. In our applications however, the function $f(z)$ will take the form of a density from the exponential family, hence an exponential function. It may then be helpful to rescale and shift the quadrature points such that more quadrature points lie in the region of interest. This is shown in the right hand window of Figure 4.3, and is thus called *adaptive* Gaussian quadrature.

With adaptive Gaussian quadrature, the quadrature points are centered and scaled based on $f(z)\varphi(z)$ as if it were a normal distribution (see the right window in Figure 4.3), and not based on $\varphi(z)$ (as in the left window in Figure 4.3). The mean of this normal distribution would be the mode $\hat{z}$ of $\ln(f(z)\varphi(z))$, while the variance would equal $\left(-\frac{\partial^2}{\partial z^2}\ln(f(z)\varphi(z))\big|_{z=\hat{z}}\right)^{-1}$.

Note that, when Gaussian or adaptive Gaussian quadrature is used in the fitting of generalized linear mixed models, an approximation as in Equation 4.13 is applied to the likelihood contribution of each of the P units in the data set. In general, the higher the order M, the better the approximation will be of the P integrals in the likelihood. Typically, adaptive Gaussian quadrature needs (much) fewer quadrature points than classical Gaussian quadrature. On the other hand, adaptive Gaussian quadrature requires for each unit the numerical maximization of a function of the form $\ln(f(z)\varphi(z))$ for the calculation of $\hat{z}$. This implies that adaptive Gaussian quadrature is much more time consuming. Moreover, as these functions $\ln(f(z)\varphi(z))$ depend on the unknown parameters β, Σ and ϕ, the quadrature points, as well as weights used in adaptive Gaussian quadrature, depend on those parameters, such that maximizing the approximate likelihood

$$L(\beta, \Sigma, \phi) \approx \prod_{p=1}^{P}\left(\sum_{m=1}^{M} w_m^+(\boldsymbol{y_p}, \beta, \Sigma, \phi)\prod_{i=1}^{I} f_p(y_{pi}|z_m^+(\boldsymbol{y_p}, \beta, \Sigma, \phi), \beta, \Sigma, \phi)\right)$$

also requires calculation of first-order and second-order derivatives of the quadrature points and weights. This again may increase the calculation times considerably.

4.6   Inference in generalized linear mixed models

Since fitting of generalized linear mixed models is based on maximum likelihood principles, inferences for the parameters are readily obtained from classical maximum likelihood theory. Indeed, assuming the fitted model is appropriate, the obtained estimators are asymptotically normally distributed with the correct values as means, and with the inverse Fisher information matrix as covariance matrix. Hence, Wald-type tests, comparing standardized estimates to the standard normal distribution can be easily performed. Composite hypotheses can be tested using the more general formulation of the Wald statistic which is a standardized quadratic form, to be compared to the chi-squared distribution.

4.6.1   Inference for fixed effects

In many software packages, standard errors for the regression coefficients in β are obtained from inverting only that part of the Hessian matrix that refers to β, omitting the part corresponding to λ. This is especially the case for linear mixed models where analytic expressions are available for $\widehat{\beta}$ as well as for the associated standard errors, but not for the estimates or standard errors of λ. This way, the standard errors used in the Wald tests for elements in β are typically too small, since they ignore the variability introduced in the estimation of β that results from replacing the unknown variance components in λ by their estimates. Therefore, the standard normal reference distribution is often replaced by a t distribution, in an attempt to reflect the additional uncertainty in the estimates. In case of composite hypotheses, the chi-squared reference distribution is then replaced by an F-distribution, with the same numerator degrees of freedom as the original chi-squared distribution. The denominator degrees of freedom need to be estimated from the data. This is often based on so-called Satterthwaite-type approximations (Satterthwaite, 1941), and is only fully developed for the case of linear mixed models. We refer to Verbeke and Molenberghs (2000, Section 6.2) for more information on this aspect. However, in most applications considered in this volume, different persons contribute independent information, which results in numbers of denominator degrees of freedom which are typically large enough, whatever estimation method is used, to lead to very similar p-values. Only for very small samples, or when mixed models would be used with crossed random effects (random effects for persons as well as for items) different estimation methods for degrees of freedom may lead to severe differences in the resulting p-values.

Further, apart from the Wald-type inferential procedures, one can also apply likelihood ratio (LR) tests or score tests for the comparison of nested generalized linear mixed models.

4.6.2   Inference for variance components

If one wishes to interpret Σ as the covariance matrix of the underlying random effects, it should be estimated under the restriction of non-negative definiteness. Many of the null hypotheses about the variance components, of interest in practice, are then on the boundary of the parameter space. This implies that the classical maximum likelihood theory no longer applies, and that none of the above described classical testing procedures remain valid. A typical example is the test for the need of a specific random effect. Consider a model as in Section 4.3.2 with random intercepts and slopes, and the hypothesis of interest is that no random slopes are needed. Under the alternative hypothesis, Σ is a two by two non-negative definite matrix, which reduces to a non-negative scalar under the null hypothesis. Clearly, the null hypothesis is on the boundary of the alternative parameter space as it requires the random-slopes variance to be zero. Stram and Lee (1994, 1995) have shown that, in this case, the asymptotic null distribution for the likelihood-ratio test statistic is a mixture of a χ_1^2 and a χ_2^2, with equal probability $1/2$, rather than the standard χ_2^2 one would expect under the classical likelihood theory. In general, the asymptotic null distribution for the likelihood-ratio test statistic for testing a null hypothesis which allows for J correlated random effects versus an alternative of $J + 1$ correlated random effects, is a mixture of a χ_J^2 and a χ_{J+1}^2, with equal probability $1/2$. For more general settings, e.g., comparing models with J and $J+q'$ $(q' > 1)$ random effects, the null distribution is a mixture of χ^2 random variables (Shapiro, 1988; Raubertas, Lee, & Nordheim, 1986), the weights of which can only be calculated analytically in a number of special cases. Similar results can be derived for the score test. Building upon Silvapulle and Silvapulle (1995) and Shapiro (1988), Verbeke and Molenberghs (2003) have shown that the score test is asymptotically equivalent to the likelihood-ratio test, and that the same mixtures of chi-squared distributions appear as asymptotic null distributions.

4.6.3   Marginal/hierarchical models versus marginal/hierarchical inference

A graphical overview of the available modeling and inferential options is given in Figure 4.4. As extensively discussed before, item response data can be modeled using marginal models, as well as hierarchical (random-effects) models, leading to regression parameters β^M and β^{RE}, respectively, with a different interpretation. This corresponds to the left and right branch in Figure 4.4, respectively. It should be emphasized that, although estimation and inference for generalized linear mixed models is based on the marginal likelihood obtained from integrating over the person-specific parameters, the obtained parameter estimates for the regression coefficients retain their hierarchical interpretation and therefore are estimates of β^{RE}, rather than of β^M.

Where a marginal model is considered, as in the left-hand branch of Figure 4.4, the inference can be based on full likelihood methods as well

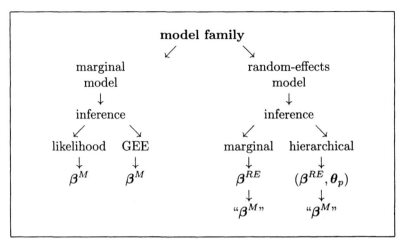

FIGURE 4.4. Representation of model families and corresponding inference. A superscript 'M' stands for marginal, 'RE' for random effects. A parameter between quotes indicates that marginal functions but no direct marginal parameters are obtained, since they result from integrating out the random effects from the fitted hierarchical model.

as on generalized estimating equations. Of course, GEE only models and estimates first-order marginal parameters, while full likelihood methods specify all higher-order marginal parameters as well.

When a random-effects model is considered, as in the right-hand branch of Figure 4.4, the most natural inference to make is a hierarchical one (based on the random effects), but one can still also make marginal inferences. The marginal mean profile can be derived from $E(\boldsymbol{Y}_p) = E(E(\boldsymbol{Y}_p|\boldsymbol{\theta}_p))$, where the inner expectation immediately follows from the posited hierarchical model. In practice, the outer expectation can be obtained, for example, by numerical integration (i.e., Gaussian quadrature) or by simulation methods. Note however that it will generally not produce a simple parametric form. In Figure 4.4 this is indicated by putting the corresponding parameter between quotes. In general, the matrix $\boldsymbol{\Sigma}$ does not need to be positive definite in order to obtain a valid marginal model. For example, in the linear mixed model case, a valid model as in Equation 4.12 is obtained whenever the marginal covariance $\boldsymbol{\mathcal{V}}_p$ is positive definite. Of course, in the case of non-positive definite $\boldsymbol{\Sigma}$, the marginal model can no longer be believed to be derived from an underlying hierarchical random-effects structure. In principle, similar arguments hold in mixed models in general. This implies that, even within the random-effects model, inference can be drawn with or without giving the model a hierarchical interpretation, and thus, with or without the additional restrictions on the variance components.

4.6.4   Model comparison

Comparing non-nested models is often done based on so-called information criteria, the main idea behind which is to compare models based on their maximized log-likelihood value, but to penalize for the use of too many parameters. More specifically, let ℓ be the maximized log-likelihood and let $\mathcal{F}(\#\boldsymbol{\beta}, \#\boldsymbol{\lambda})$ be any monotone function of the number of fixed weight parameters and the number of variance components, then $\ell - \mathcal{F}(\#\boldsymbol{\beta}, \#\boldsymbol{\lambda})$ defines an information criterion which can be used to discriminate between different statistical models. The model with the largest penalized log-likelihood value is then deemed best. Depending on the exact form of $\mathcal{F}$, different criteria are obtained. The most frequently used ones are the Akaike (AIC; Akaike, 1974) and the Schwarz (BIC; Schwarz, 1978) criterion, defined by $\mathcal{F}(\#\boldsymbol{\beta}, \#\boldsymbol{\lambda}) = \#\boldsymbol{\beta} + \#\boldsymbol{\lambda}$ and $\mathcal{F}(\#\boldsymbol{\beta}, \#\boldsymbol{\lambda}) = (\#\boldsymbol{\beta} + \#\boldsymbol{\lambda})(\log n)/2$ in which n is the number of observations. In an item response context often the number of persons is used as the effective number of observations. In the multilevel literature the number of higher level units is commonly used for n (Goldstein, 2003), which is in line with the previous. This interpretation is followed for example in the SAS procedure NLMIXED. For a discussion, see Raftery (1995). Note that, in contrast to AIC, BIC involves the sample size, implying that differences in likelihood need to be viewed, not only relative to the differences in numbers of parameters but also relative to the number of observations included in the analysis. As the sample size increases, more drastic increases in likelihood are required before a complex model will be preferred over a simple model. This means that, when compared to BIC, AIC tends to favor more complex models.

4.7   Case study: onychomycosis data

In this section, we will focus (a) on differences between a marginal and a random-effects model and (b) on the comparison of Gaussian and adaptive Gaussian quadrature, with special attention to the selection of the number of quadrature points in the approximation. The context is a randomized, double-blind, parallel group, multicenter study, for the comparison of two oral treatments for toenail dermatophyte onychomycosis. Patients with a clinical diagnosis of toe onychomycosis confirmed by a positive direct microscopy and a positive culture for dermatophytes at a central laboratory were randomly assigned to treatment A or treatment B. After a treatment period of 12 weeks, there was a follow-up period of 36 weeks. Patients returned to the hospital at months 0 (baseline), 1, 2, 3, 6, 9, and 12. More details can be found in De Backer et al., (1998). One of the outcomes observed at each occasion was the severity of the infection, coded as 0 (not severe) or 1 (severe). The question of interest was whether the rate of severe infections decreased over time, and whether that evolution was different for

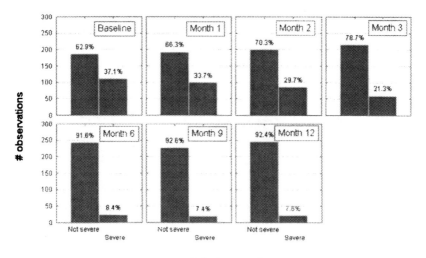

FIGURE 4.5. Frequencies of patients with severe and non-severe onychomycosis, at 7 occasions (onychomycosis data).

the two treatment groups. The overall (both treatments together) evolution of severity is shown in Figure 4.5. Although 189 patients were initially included in each group, only 118 patients from group A and 108 patients from group B completed the study. However, we will for now ignore this dropout problem, and we refer to Verbeke and Molenberghs (2000) for an extensive discussion on dropout, and on missing data in general. As before, let Y_{pi} denote the outcome for person p, measured at time $t_{pi} = t_i$. Note that the items refer here to different visits over time. The seven observations made over time have a status similar to seven items.

4.7.1   Random-effects model versus marginal model

Table 4.1 displays parameter estimates (standard errors) for a random-effects model and a marginal model. The marginal model parameters are obtained using generalized estimating equations, where a marginal logit function is combined with unstructured working assumptions. The working correlation matrix is seven by seven, and not assumed to be of any specific parametric form. We assume a random-intercepts model of the logistic type, with normally distributed random effects:

$$Pr(Y_{pi} = 1 | T_p, t_{pi}, \theta_p) = \frac{\exp(\beta_0 + \theta_p + \beta_1 T_p + \beta_2 t_{pi} + \beta_3 T_p t_{pi})}{1 + \exp(\beta_0 + \theta_p + \beta_1 T_p + \beta_2 t_{pi} + \beta_3 T_p t_{pi})}, \tag{4.14}$$

where t_{pi} is the time at which measurement i on person p is taken, T_p

TABLE 4.1. Parameter estimates (standard errors) for a generalized linear mixed model (GLMM) and a marginal model (GEE), as well as the ratio between both sets of parameters (onychomycosis data).

Parameter	GLMM Estimate (SE)	GEE Estimate (SE)	Ratio
Intercept group A	-1.63 (.44)	-.72 (.17)	2.26
Intercept group B	-1.75 (.45)	-.65 (.17)	2.69
Slope group A	-.40 (.05)	-.14 (.03)	2.87
Slope group B	-.57 (.06)	-.25 (.04)	2.22
SD random intercept	4.02		

equals zero for a person with treatment A and one for a person with treatment B. The random intercepts θ_p are assumed normal with mean 0 and variance σ_θ^2. The results reported in Table 4.1 have been obtained using adaptive Gaussian quadrature with 50 quadrature points. The marginal model has the same form as Equation 4.14, except there is, of course, no random intercept. More specifically, the following marginal logistic model is assumed:

$$Pr(Y_{pi} = 1 | T_p, t_{pi}, \theta_p) = E\left(\frac{\exp(\beta_0 + \theta_p + \beta_1 T_p + \beta_2 t_{pi} + \beta_3 T_p t_{pi})}{1 + \exp(\beta_0 + \theta_p + \beta_1 T_p + \beta_2 t_{pi} + \beta_3 T_p t_{pi})}\right),$$

where the expectation is taken over the random intercept θ_p.

There is a huge difference between the parameter estimates for both model families. However, the ratio between both sets, indicated in the last column of Table 4.1 is well in line with what we should expect from Equation 4.9. In this case, the random effects variance estimate equals 16.16, yielding $[c^2 \text{Var}(\theta_p) + 1]^{1/2} = 2.56$. In Figure 4.6 the marginal evolutions (obtained with GEE) are contrasted with the evolutions following from the random-effects model, given $\theta_p = 0$. While such evolutions would be exactly the same in the linear mixed model case, they are clearly different in our current setting.

4.7.2   The impact of the quadrature method

In order to investigate the accuracy of the numerical integration method, the model was refitted, for varying numbers of quadrature points, and for adaptive as well as nonadaptive Gaussian quadrature. All calculations were performed using the SAS procedure NLMIXED. The results have been summarized in Table 4.2. First, it should be emphasized that each reported log-likelihood value equals the maximum of the approximation to the model

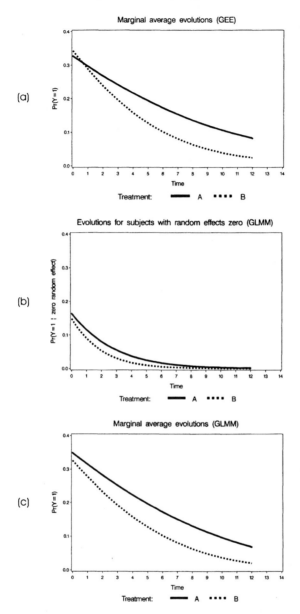

FIGURE 4.6. Treatment-specific evolutions: (a) marginal evolutions as obtained from a marginal (GEE) model, (b) evolutions for an average person, i.e., with $\theta_p = 0$, and (c) average evolution as obtained from marginalizing the GLMM (onychomycosis data).

log-likelihood, which implies that log-likelihoods corresponding to different estimation methods and/or different numbers of quadrature points are not

TABLE 4.2. Summary of parameter estimates and associated standard errors obtained from fitting the model of Equation 4.14, for varying numbers M of quadrature points, and for adaptive as well as nonadaptive Gaussian quadrature. For each model the deviance (-2ℓ) is given (onychomycosis data).

| | Gaussian quadrature | | | | |
	$M = 3$	$M = 5$	$M = 10$	$M = 20$	$M = 50$
β_0	-1.52 (.31)	-2.49 (.39)	-.99 (.32)	-1.54 (.69)	-1.65 (.43)
β_1	-.39 (.38)	.19 (.36)	.47 (.36)	-.43 (.80)	-.09 (.57)
β_2	-.32 (.03)	-.38 (.04)	-.38 (.05)	-.40 (.05)	-.40 (.05)
β_3	-.09 (.05)	-.12 (.07)	-.15 (.07)	-.14 (.07)	-.16 (.07)
σ	2.26 (.12)	3.09 (.21)	4.53 (.39)	3.86 (.33)	4.04 (.39)
-2ℓ	1344.1	1259.6	1254.4	1249.6	1247.7

| | Adaptive Gaussian quadrature | | | | |
	$M = 3$	$M = 5$	$M = 10$	$M = 20$	$M = 50$
β_0	-2.05 (.59)	-1.47 (.40)	-1.65 (.45)	-1.63 (.43)	-1.63 (.44)
β_1	-.16 (.64)	-.09 (.54)	-.12 (.59)	-.11 (.59)	-.11 (.59)
β_2	-.42 (.05)	-.40 (.04)	-.41 (.05)	-.40 (.05)	-.40 (.05)
β_3	-.17 (.07)	-.16 (.07)	-.16 (.07)	-.16 (.07)	-.16 (.07)
σ	4.51 (.62)	3.70 (.34)	4.07 (.43)	4.01 (.38)	4.02 (.38)
-2ℓ	1259.1	1257.1	1248.2	1247.8	1247.8

necessarily comparable. Indeed, differences in log-likelihood values reflect differences in the quality of the numerical approximations, and thus higher log-likelihood values do not necessarily correspond to better approximations. Further, we find that different values for the number of quadrature points can lead to considerable differences in estimates as well as standard errors. For example, using nonadaptive quadrature, with $M = 3$, and looking at β_3, we found no difference in time effect between both treatment groups ($t = -.09/.05, p > .05$). Using adaptive quadrature, with $M = 50$, this interaction between the time effect and the treatment was found to be statistically significant ($t = -.16/.07, p < .05$). Finally, assuming that $M = 50$ is sufficient, the 'final' results are well approximated with smaller M under adaptive quadrature, but not under nonadaptive quadrature. With a small number of items, the risk is higher that nonadaptive quadrature performs less well than adaptive quadrature.

4.8   Missing data

Whenever units are observed repeatedly, it is not unusual for some profiles to be incomplete. More often than not, it is necessary to address this problem in an explicit way. Early work on missing values was largely concerned with algorithmic and computational solutions to the induced lack of balance or deviations from the intended study design (Afifi & Elashoff, 1966; Hartley & Hocking, 1971). More recently, general algorithms such as expectation-maximization (EM) (Dempster, et al., 1977), and data imputation and augmentation procedures (Rubin, 1987), combined with powerful computing resources, have largely provided a solution to this aspect of the problem. There remains the very difficult and important question of assessing the impact of missing data on subsequent statistical inference.

When referring to the missing-value, or non-response, process, we will use the terminology of Little and Rubin (1987, Chapter 6). A non-response process is said to be *missing completely at random* (MCAR) if the missingness is independent of both observed and unobserved data. For example, dropout of patients may be related to factors that are unrelated to the observations. The non-response process is said to be *missing at random* (MAR) if, conditional on the observed data, the missingness is independent of the unobserved data. For example, a patient's partially observed severity profile might be sufficient information to predict dropout. In other words, the unobserved portion of this patient's profile would not convey any additional information with respect to dropout. A process that is neither MCAR nor MAR is termed *non-random* (MNAR). For example, the missingness of income data may depend on the level of the income. In the context of likelihood inference, and when the parameters describing the observation process are functionally independent of the parameters describing the missingness process, MCAR and MAR are *ignorable,* while MNAR is non-ignorable.

In many situations, missingness is dealt with by such simple techniques as *complete case analysis* (i.e., all patients with incomplete data are dropped from analysis) or simple forms of *imputation* (i.e., missing observations are filled in following a certain set of prescribed rules). Such methods are seemingly simple but suffer from major drawbacks. In particular, even the strong MCAR assumption will not guarantee that inference from simple imputation methods is valid. Under MAR, and hence *a fortiori* under MCAR, valid inference can be obtained through a likelihood-based analysis, without the need for modeling the dropout process. As a consequence, one can simply use, for example, linear or generalized linear mixed models, without additional complication or effort. We will argue that such an analysis not only enjoys much wider validity than the simple techniques such as complete case analysis and imputation but in addition is easy to conduct, *without additional data manipulation.* Hence, we only need software tools, such as the SAS procedure NLMIXED, which allow for units with unequal numbers of observations.

In realistic settings, the reasons for dropout are varied and it is therefore difficult to fully justify on *a priori* grounds the assumption of MAR. At first sight, this calls for a further shift towards MNAR models. However, some careful considerations have to be made, the most important one of which is that no modeling approach, whether MAR or MNAR, can recover the lack of information that occurs due to incompleteness of the data. First, although it is only rarely that MAR is known to hold (Murray & Findlay, 1988), ignorable analyses may provide reasonably stable results also when the assumption of MAR is violated, in the sense that such analyses constrain the behavior of the unseen data to be similar to that of the observed data. A discussion of this phenomenon in the survey context has been given in Rubin, Stern, and Vehovar (1995). These authors argue that, in well conducted experiments (such as surveys and confirmatory clinical trials), the assumption of MAR is often to be regarded as a realistic one. Second, while MNAR models are more general and explicitly incorporate the missingness mechanism, the inferences they produce are typically highly dependent on the untestable and often implicit assumptions built in regarding the distribution of the unobserved measurements given the observed ones. The quality of the fit to the observed data need not reflect at all the appropriateness of the implied structure governing the unobserved data. This point is irrespective of the MNAR route taken, whether a parametric model of the type of Diggle and Kenward (1994) is chosen, or a semiparametric approach such as in Robins, Rotnitzky, and Zhao (1995).

Rubin (1976) and Little and Rubin (1987) have shown that, under MAR and mild regularity conditions, likelihood-based inference is valid when the missing data mechanism is ignored (see also Verbeke & Molenberghs, 2000). Practically speaking, the likelihood of interest is then based upon the factor $f(y_p^o|\theta)$, where y_p^o is the vector of observed components for person p. This is called *ignorability*.

The practical implication is that a software module with likelihood estimation facilities and with the ability to handle incompletely observed persons manipulates the correct likelihood, providing valid parameter estimates and likelihood ratio values. Of course, when at least part of the scientific interest is directed towards the non-response process, obviously both processes need to be considered.

Even though the assumption of likelihood ignorability encompasses the MAR and not only the more stringent and often implausible MCAR mechanisms, it is difficult to exclude the option of a more general nonrandom dropout mechanism. Based on these considerations, we recommend, for primary analysis purposes, the use of ignorable likelihood-based methods. An alternative solution is to fit an MNAR model as proposed by Diggle and Kenward (1994). However, it has been reported repeatedly that such an approach is surrounded with difficulty (Verbeke & Molenberghs 2000, Chapter 18). A sensible compromise between blindly shifting to MNAR models or ignoring them altogether is to make them a component of a sensitivity analysis (Verbeke & Molenberghs 2000, Chapter 18 to 20). In that sense, it is important to consider the effect on key parameters such as treatment effect.

4.9   Framework extensions

Among the clustered data settings, longitudinal data perhaps require the most elaborate modeling of the random variability, because they often show serial dependence. On the other hand, serial dependence of longitudinal data is but one instance of dependencies. Diggle et al. (2002) and Verbeke and Molenberghs (2000) distinguish among three types of variability which may play a role in longitudinal data. The first one groups traditional random effects (as in a random-effects ANOVA model) and random coefficients (Longford, 1993) reflecting interindividual variability (i.e., heterogeneity between individual profiles). The second type, serial association, is present when residuals close to each other in space or time are more similar than residuals further apart. This notion is well known in the spatial and time-series literature (Cressie, 1991; Diggle, 1983, 1990; Ripley, 1981). Finally, in addition to the other two types, there is potentially also measurement error.

Formulating models that incorporate at the same time the random effects and serial association is not straightforward for non-normal outcomes. This follows from the rather strict separation between random-effects models and conditional models, as discussed in Section 4.2. For binary outcomes, a few proposals are available. Wolfinger and O'Connell's (1993) method, described in Section 4.5.2, allows for a serial component in the model for the working dependent variate y^*. Renard, Molenberghs, and Geys (2002) construct a mixed model for binary outcomes using a probit rather than a logit link function. This choice allows for an easy inclusion of a serial component through inclusion of such a component in the linear mixed model for the latent Gaussian random vector. The corresponding marginal model is of the multivariate probit type. Within the multilevel modeling framework (Goldstein, 1995) extensions have been formulated that also include serial correlation.

As discussed before, most models considered here heavily rely on the normality assumption for the random effects. Lee and Nelder (1996) have argued that, especially for non-normal outcomes, it can be of interest to entertain other than normal random effects. Situations have been described where the choice of random-effects distributions can have important consequences on the inferences (Spiessens, Lesaffre, Verbeke, & Kim, 2002, 2003; Verbeke & Lesaffre, 1996). One possible model extension is obtained from replacing the normal distribution by a finite mixture of normals. This is a very flexible class of models, not only allowing for symmetric as well as skewed distributions, but also for multi-modality in the mixing distribution. This will be discussed and illustrated at length in Chapter 11.

4.10   Concluding remarks

In this chapter, a general framework for modeling repeated categorical data has been sketched, with three main model families: marginal, conditional, and person-specific (random effects). We have focused mainly on person-specific or random-effects models, with some emphasis on the generalized linear mixed models. Interpretation, estimation, and optimization algorithms have been discussed. These tools have been exemplified using a simple but illustrative analysis. While the similarities between linear and generalized linear mixed models are often pointed out, perhaps rightly so, one should be very aware of the differences.

First, there is a close connection between parameter estimates from all model families when the responses are normally distributed. But this is not true in the generalized linear case. Indeed, in marginal modeling, the regression parameters are unequivocally population parameters; they determine the effect of explanatory variables on the population mean response. In conditional (e.g., transition) and random-effects modeling, the regression parameters are still population parameters, in the sense that they operate on all persons, but they determine the effects of explanatory variables on the mean response of an individual person, *conditional* on that person's measurement history (transition model), or on the person's own random characteristics (random-effects model). As discussed in Section 4.6.3, a conversion is possible in some contexts, but additional computations are required.

Second, the random effects and the measurement error interact completely differently in linear and generalized linear mixed models. In a linear mixed model, the random effects are part of the linear predictor, and this is shared with the generalized linear mixed model case. However, the measurement error (residual error) term is *also* within the linear predictor in the linear mixed model. The measurement error or the corresponding element in the generalized case determines the distribution of the data given the linear predictor value. The transformed linear predictor value based on the inverse link function is the expected value of the distribution. In principle, the measurement error cannot be incorporated into the linear predictor because of the transformation implied by the link function. Hence, both components of variability are not part of the same linear function in the generalized case.

Third, the presence of a link function generally prohibits the existence of a closed form expression for the score-equation contributions, so that integrals cannot be avoided. This renders parameter estimation more complicated and a wide class of algorithms have been proposed, with an associated class of software tools (see Chapter 12). Arguably, knowledge of several (software) tools with a good understanding of the approximations on which they are based can greatly enhance insight.

4.11   Exercises

1. Formulate the Rasch model as a generalized linear mixed model using the notation of this chapter.

2. Describe two studies with item responses as the dependent variables: (1) with fixed item effects and (2) with random item effects.

3. Consider two groups of items (e.g., language and science oriented). It is of interest to determine differences in difficulty between the types of items (language, science). Formulate appropriate models, thereby reflecting carefully on the model family that is appropriate to answer the question.

4. Among scientists, it is believed that respondents are either science-oriented or humanities-oriented. Formulate a model that reflects this assumption. This question could in principle be tackled using the general model formulation. However, you may find it helpful to first consider Chapter 8.

5. Persons and items are being followed over time. Formulate a candidate generalized linear mixed model to incorporate this structure.

4.12   References

Aerts, M., Geys, H., Molenberghs, G., & Ryan, L.M. (2002). *Topics in Modeling of Clustered Binary Data*. London: Chapman & Hall.

Afifi, A., & Elashoff, R. (1966). Missing observations in multivariate statistics I: Review of the literature. *Journal of the American Statistical Association, 61*, 595–604.

Agresti, A. (1990) *Categorical Data Analysis*. New York: John Wiley & Sons.

Akaike, H. (1974) A new look at the statistical model identification. *IEEE Transactions on Automatic Control, 19*, 716–723.

Altham, P.M.E. (1978). Two generalizations of the binomial distribution. *Applied Statistics, 27*, 162-167.

Bahadur, R.R. (1961). A representation of the joint distribution of responses of P dichotomous items. In H. Solomon (Ed.), *Studies in Item Analysis and Prediction* (pp. 158–168). Stanford, CA: Stanford University Press.

Besag, J., Green, P.J., Higdon, D., & Mengersen, K. (1995). Bayesian computation and stochastic systems. *Statistical Science, 10*, 3–66.

Böhning, D. (1999). *Computer-Assisted Analysis of Mixtures and Applications : Meta-analysis, Disease Mapping and Others*. London: Chapman & Hall.

Breslow, N.E., & Clayton, D.G. (1993). Approximate inference in generalized linear mixed models. *Journal of the American Statistical Association, 88*, 9–25.

Breslow, N.E., & Day, N.E. (1987). *Statistical Methods in Cancer Research, Volume II*. Oxford: Oxford University Press.

Conaway, M. (1989). Analysis of repeated categorical measurements with conditional likelihood methods. *Journal of the American Statistical Association, 84*, 53–62.

Cox, D.R. (1972). The analysis of multivariate binary data. *Applied Statistics, 21*, 113–120.

Cressie, N.A.C. (1991). *Statistics for Spatial Data*. New York: Wiley.

Dale, J.R. (1986). Global cross-ratio models for bivariate, discrete, ordered responses. *Biometrics, 42*, 909–917.

De Backer, M., De Vroey, C., Lesaffre, E., Scheys, I., & De Keyser, P. (1998). Twelve weeks of continuous oral therapy for toenail onychomycosis caused by dermatophytes: A double-blind comparative trial of terbinafine 250 mg/day versus itraconazole 200 mg/day. *Journal of the American Academy of Dermatology, 38*, S57–63.

Declerck, L., Aerts, M., & Molenberghs, G. (1998). Behaviour of the likelihood-ratio test statistic under a Bahadur model for exchangeable binary data. *Journal of Statistical Computations and Simulations, 61*, 15–38.

Dempster, A.P., Laird, N.M., & Rubin, D. B. (1977). Maximum likelihood from incomplete data via the EM algorithm (with discussion). *Journal of the Royal Statistical Society, Series B, 39*, 1–38.

Diggle, P.J. (1983). *Statistical Analysis of Spatial Point Patterns*. London: Academic Press.

Diggle, P.J. (1990). *Time Series: A Biostatistical Introduction*. Oxford: Oxford University Press.

Diggle, P.J., Heagerty, P., Liang, K-Y., & Zeger, S.L. (2002). *Analysis of Longitudinal Data*. New York: Oxford University Press.

Diggle, P.J., & Kenward, M.G. (1994). Informative drop-out in longitudinal data analysis (with discussion). *Applied Statistics, 43*, 49–93.

Efron, B. (1986). Double exponential families and their use in generalized linear regression. *Journal of the American Statistical Association, 81,* 709–721.

Fahrmeir, L., & Tutz, G. (2001). *Multivariate Statistical Modeling Based on Generalized Linear Models.* Heidelberg: Springer.

Gamerman, D. (1997). Efficient sampling from the posterior distribution in generalized linear mixed models. *Statistics and Computing, 7,* 57–68.

Gelman, A., Carlin, J.B., Stern, H.S., & Rubin, D.B. (2004). *Bayesian Data Analysis.* London: Chapman & Hall.

Gilmour, A.R., Anderson, R.D., & Rae, A.L. (1985). The analysis of binomial data by a generalized linear mixed model. *Biometrika, 72,* 593–599.

Gilula, Z., & Haberman, S. (1994). Conditional log-linear models for analyzing categorical panel data. *Journal of the American Statistical Association, 89,* 645–656.

Goldstein, H. (1986). Multilevel mixed linear model analysis using iterative generalized least squares. *Biometrika, 73,* 43-56.

Goldstein, H. (1991). Nonlinear multilevel models, with an application to discrete response data. *Biometrika, 78,* 45–51.

Goldstein, H. (1995). *Multilevel Statistical Models (2nd ed.).* London: Arnold.

Goldstein, H. (2003). *Multilevel Statistical Models (3rd ed.).* London: Arnold.

Goldstein, H., & Rasbash, J. (1996). Improved approximations for multilevel models with binary responses. *Journal of the Royal Statistical Society A, 159,* 505–513.

Hartley, H.O., & Hocking, R. (1971). The analysis of incomplete data. *Biometrics, 27,* 7783–808.

Harville, D.A. (1974). Bayesian inference for variance components using only error contrasts. *Biometrika, 61,* 383–385.

Hobert, J.P., & Casella, G. (1996). The effect of improper priors on Gibbs sampling in hierarchical linear mixed models. *Journal of the American Statistical Association, 91,* 1461–1473.

Kenward, M.G., & Roger, J.H. (1997). Small sample inference for fixed effects from restricted maximum likelihood. *Biometrics, 53,* 983–997.

Kleinman, J. (1973). Proportions with extraneous variance: single and independent samples. *Journal of the American Statistical Association, 68,* 46–54.

Knorr-Held, L. (1997). *Hierarchical Modeling of Discrete Longitudinal Data; Applications of Markov Chain Monte Carlo.* München: Utz.

Kuk, A.Y.C. (1995). Asymptotically unbiased estimation in generalised linear models with random effects. *Journal of the Royal Statistical Society B,57,* 395–407.

Kupper, L.L., & Haseman, J.K. (1978). The use of a correlated binomial model for the analysis of certain toxicology experiments. *Biometrics, 34,* 69-76.

Lang, J.B., & Agresti, A. (1994). Simultaneously modeling joint and marginal distributions of multivariate categorical responses. *Journal of the American Statistical Association, 89*, 625–632.

Lavergne, C., & Trottier, C. (2000). Sur l'estimation dans les modèles linéaires généralisés à effets aléatoires. *Revue de Statistique Appliquée, 48*, 49–67.

Lee, Y., & Nelder, J.A. (1996). Hierarchical generalized linear models (with discussion). *Journal of the Royal Statistical Society, Series B, 58*, 619–678.

Liang, K.-Y., & Zeger, S.L. (1986). Longitudinal data analysis using generalized linear models. *Biometrika, 73*, 13–22.

Liang, K.Y., Zeger, S.L., & Qaqish, B. (1992). Multivariate regression analyses for categorical data. *Journal of the Royal Statistical Society, Series B, 54*, 3–40.

Lin, X., & Breslow, N.E. (1996). Bias correction in generalized linear mixed models with multiple components of dispersion. *Journal of the American Statistical Association, 91*, 1007–1016.

Lipsitz, S.R., Laird, N.M., & Harrington, D.P. (1991). Generalized estimating equations for correlated binary data: using the odds ratio as a measure of association. *Biometrika, 78*, 153–160.

Little, R.J.A., & Rubin, D.B. (1987). *Statistical Analysis with Missing Data*. New York: Wiley.

Longford, N.T. (1993). *Random Coefficient Models*. London: Oxford University Press.

McCullagh, P., & Nelder, J.A. (1989). *Generalized Linear Models*. London: Chapman & Hall.

Molenberghs, G., & Lesaffre, E. (1994). Marginal modeling of correlated ordinal data using a multivariate Plackett distribution. *Journal of the American Statistical Association, 89*, 633–644.

Molenberghs, G., & Lesaffre, E. (1999). Marginal modeling of multivariate categorical data. *Statistics in Medicine, 18*, 2237–2255.

Murray, G.D., & Findlay, J.G. (1988). Correcting for the bias caused by drop-outs in hypertension trials. *Statististics in Medicine, 7*, 941–946.

Nelder, J.A., & Wedderburn, R.W.M. (1972). Generalized linear models. *Journal of the Royal Statistical Society, Series B, 135*, 370–384.

Neuhaus, J.M. (1992). Statistical methods for longitudinal and clustered designs with binary responses. *Statistical Methods in Medical Research, 1*, 249-273.

Neuhaus, J.M., Kalbfleisch, J.D., & Hauck, W.W. (1991). A comparison of cluster-specific and population-averaged approaches for analyzing correlated binary data. *International Statistical Review, 59*, 25–35.

Pinheiro, J.C., & Bates, D.M. (1995). Approximations to the log-likelihood function in the nonlinear mixed-effects model. *Journal of Computational and Graphical Statistics, 4*, 12–35.

Pinheiro, J.C., & Bates D.M. (2000). *Mixed Effects Models in S and S-PLUS*. New-York: Springer.

Plackett, R.L. (1965). A class of bivariate distributions. *Journal of the American Statistical Association, 60*, 516–522.

Prentice, R.L. (1988). Correlated binary regression with covariates specific to each binary observation. *Biometrics, 44*, 1033–1048.

Press, W.H., Teukolsky, S.A., Vetterling, W.T., & Flannery, B.P. (1992). *Numerical recipes in FORTRAN. (2nd ed.)*. Cambridge, MA: Cambridge University Press.

Raftery, A.E. (1995). Bayesian model selection in social research. *Sociological Methodology, 25*, 111-163.

Raubertas, R.F., Lee, C.I.C., & Nordheim, E.V. (1986). Hypothesis tests for normal means constrained by linear inequalities. *Communications in Statistics–Theory and Methods 15*, 2809–2833.

Renard, D., Molenberghs, G., & Geys, H. (2002). A pairwise likelihood approach to estimation in multilevel probit models. *Computational Statistics and Data Analysis*. Manuscript accepted for publication.

Ripley, B.D. (1981). *Spatial Statistics*. New York: Wiley.

Ripley, B.D. (1987). *Stochastic Simulation*. New York: Wiley.

Robins, J.M., Rotnitzky, A., & Zhao, L.P. (1995). Analysis of semiparametric regression models for repeated outcomes in the presence of missing data. *Journal of the American Statistical Association, 90*, 106–121.

Rodríguez, G., & Goldman, N. (1995). An assessment of estimation procedures for multilevel models with binary responses. *Journal of the Royal Statistical Society A, 158*, 73–89.

Rosner, B. (1984). Multivariate methods in opthalmology with applications to other paired-data. *Biometrics, 40*, 1025–1035.

Rubin, D.B. (1976). Inference and missing data. *Biometrika, 63*, 581–592.

Rubin, D.B. (1987). *Multiple Imputation for Nonresponse in Surveys*. New York: Wiley.

Rubin, D.B., Stern, H.S., & Vehovar V. (1995). Handling "don't know" survey responses: the case of the Slovenian plebiscite. *Journal of the American Statistical Association, 90*, 822–828.

Satterthwaite, F.E. (1941). Synthesis of variance. *Psychometrika, 6*, 309–316.

Schall, R. (1991). Estimation in generalised linear models with random effects. *Biometrika, 78*, 719–727.

Schwarz, G. (1978). Estimating the dimension of a model. *The Annals of Statistics, 6*, 461–464.

Shapiro, A. (1988). Towards a unified theory of inequality constrained testing in multivariate analysis. *International Statistical Review 56*, 49–62.

Silvapulle, M.J., & Silvapulle, P. (1995). A score test against one-sided alternatives. *Journal of the American Statistical Association 90*, 342–349.

Skellam, J.G. (1948). A probability distribution derived from the binomial distribution by regarding the probability of success as variable between the sets of trials. *Journal of the Royal Statistical Society, Series B, 10*, 257–261.

Spiessens, B., Lesaffre, E., Verbeke, G., & Kim, K. (2002). Group sequential methods for an ordinal logistic random-effects model under misspecification. *Biometrics, 58*, 569–575.

Spiessens, B., Lesaffre, E., Verbeke, G., & Kim, K. (2003). The use of mixed models for longitudinal count data when the random-effects distribution is misspecified. Manuscript submitted for publication.

Stiratelli, R., Laird, N., & Ware, J.H. (1984). Random-effects model for serial observations with binary response. *Biometrics, 40*, 961–971.

Stram, D.O., & Lee, J.W. (1994). Variance components testing in the longitudinal mixed-effects model. *Biometrics, 50*, 1171–1177.

Stram, D.A., & Lee, J.W. (1995). Correction to: Variance components testing in the longitudinal mixed-effects model. *Biometrics, 51*, 1196.

Ten Have, T.R., Landis, R., & Weaver, S.L. (1995). Association models for periodontal disease progression: A comparison of methods for clustered binary data. *Statistics in Medicine, 14*, 413–429.

Thélot, C. (1985). Lois logistiques à deux dimensions. *Annales de l'Insée, 58*, 123–149.

Verbeke, G., & Lesaffre, E. (1996). A linear mixed-effects model with heterogeneity in the random-effects population. *Journal of the American Statistical Association, 91*, 217–221.

Verbeke, G., & Molenberghs, G. (1997). *Linear Mixed Models in Practice: A SAS-Oriented Approach*. Lecture Notes in Statistics 126. New York: Springer.

Verbeke, G., & Molenberghs, G. (2000). *Linear Mixed Models for Longitudinal Data*. New York: Springer.

Verbeke, G., & Molenberghs, G. (2003). The use of score tests for inference on variance components. *Biometrics, 59*, 254–262.

Wedderburn, R.W.M. (1974). Quasi-likelihood functions, generalized linear models, and the Gauss-Newton method. *Biometrika, 61*, 439–447.

Wolfinger, R. (1998). Towards practical application of generalized linear mixed models. In B. Marx and H. Friedl (Eds), *Proceedings of the 13th International Workshop on Statistical Modeling* (pp. 388–395). New Orleans, Louisiana.

Wolfinger, R., & O'Connell, M. (1993). Generalized linear mixed models: A pseudo-likelihood approach. *Journal of Statistical Computing and Simulation, 48*, 233–243.

Zeger, S.L., & Karim, M.R. (1991). Generalised linear models with random effects: a Gibbs sampling approach. *Journal of the American Statistical Association, 86*, 79–102.

Zhao, L.P., & Prentice, R.L. (1990). Correlated binary regression using a quadratic exponential model. *Biometrika, 77*, 642–648.

Part II: Models with external factors – predictors and their effects

The aim of this and the following part is to present more complex item response models that build on the framework presented in Part I. We start with a basic scheme: The basic unit of observation is a pair of a person and an item. The observable dependent variable is Y_{pi}, and its expected value, η_{pi} is modeled as a function of a set of predictors, functioning, in Part II, as *external factors* to analyze the data. Two broad kinds of extensions of the four models from Chapter 2 will be introduced here and developed further in this book.

The first and most evident set of extensions concern combinations of:
(1) the nature of the external factors, person predictors, item predictors, person-by-item predictors; and
(2) the nature of the effects: fixed or random effects of the external factors.

Before describing the system, we will briefly comment here also on a second set of extensions, where external factors are replaced with or supplemented with *internal factors*. This will be the focus of Part III. For this second set of extensions we will stretch the meaning of the term 'predictor' to include predictors with latent values (parameters), and predictors that are themselves random variables, such as the responses on other items. We will call such predictors internal factors, because they stem from the data to be analyzed. This extension leads to the two-parameter (logistic and normal-ogive) model, the multidimensional model with item weights, mixture models, and local item dependence models. The chapters related to these extensions are grouped in Part III.

We start the description of the system to build models as in Part II with a discussion of the sources of variation, followed by a discussion of what external factors can explain and how they are connected with random variation.

II.1. Variation

Beyond global means, we need to model variation (and co-variation). We will consider two types of variation: random variation, and variation due to fixed effects of external factors, and we start with a discussion of the first type of variation.

Given that persons as well as items are involved, random variation can occur on either side, persons or items, and the variation can occur separately or in combination. The person side is the most natural one to think about in terms of random variation, as persons are more often drawn at random than items are.

II.1.1 Levels of random variation at the person side

If one considers two or more observations regarding different persons, these observations may differ for several reasons.

(1) The persons may belong to different groups. For example, perhaps neighborhoods differ as to how verbally aggressive people tend to be on the average.

(2) The persons are different individuals within the group they belong to. Continuing the example, it is highly likely that people differ although they live in the same neighborhood.

(3) The observations may differ because people can vary over occasions (i.e., within themselves). People's behavior commonly varies depending on the occasion when the observation is made, so that when the observations differ it may be due to the occasions of observation, even when all other influences are equal. See Figure II.1 for a graphical representation of the levels.

Suppose that at each of these three levels the variation is random variation, because the occasions, the persons, and the groups are all drawn from populations. These populations are hierarchically ordered: a population of occasions within each person, a population of persons within each group, and finally a population of groups. The observed variation at a given level includes variation due to sampling at the lower level (i.e., occasions for a person, persons for a group). Conversely, the observed variation at one level also stems partly from higher levels. In the example above, the variation between persons stems not only from the occasions but also from the neighborhood the persons live in. Models can differ in where they locate random variation. Here, we have assumed that random variation occurs at all levels – a reasonable alternative would be that the variation between groups does not stem from random variation, but from the specific and fixed effects that the groups have.

Where the random variation is located is not without consequences. Suppose one wants to isolate the part of variance that stems from individual differences while assuming that random variation occurs at all three levels. Then the variation among all persons will, in general, be an overestimation of the variation stemming from the persons. This is so, first, because part of the variation stems from the occasions, and second, because part of the variation stems from group differences. One can subtract the variation that stems from the groups, but one should realize that the observed between-group variation is not a pure indication of the group differences because

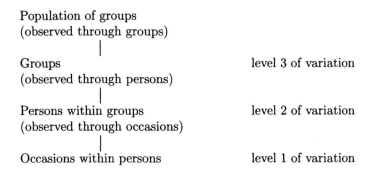

Population of groups
(observed through groups)

Groups   level 3 of variation
(observed through persons)

Persons within groups   level 2 of variation
(observed through occasions)

Occasions within persons   level 1 of variation

FIGURE II.1. Three levels of variation.

these differences include also some random variation due to the sampling of persons, and because the groups themselves are sampled.

To handle these problems one needs a model to isolate the variation from each of these different levels. We will illustrate this with an extension of the random-intercepts model. The corresponding model is presented in Figure II.2. The second row shows the model for π_{pi} (linked to η_{pi} through the link function), and the third row displays the model for the hypothetical underlying continuous variable.

(1) The basic level of random variation corresponds to ε_{pi}. This basic variation concerns the occasion and is indicated as level 1 in Figure II.1 and Figure II.2 (see Figure 1.3b for the distribution; the notation follows from Chapter 2). In its binary form (after dichotomization), this source of variation is reflected in the Bernoulli distribution that defines the random component of a GLMM.

(2) The person level of random variation corresponds to θ_p – the random intercept (or person parameter from the item response model terminology). The random person variation is the variation in η_{pi} given the fixed effects, and it is located within the linear component. As mentioned earlier, the slopes as well as the intercept may show random variation over persons. The person level is the level 2 of random variation in Figure II.1 and Figure II.2.

(3) Variation may occur also at the group level, and although this variation is not included in the models we have seen in earlier chapters, its inclusion is rather simple. One can add group-specific effects of the predictors X as in Figure II.2. We have used the same Xs for person predictors and group predictors, but they can of course also be different. We will use g as a group index, $g = (1, \ldots, G)$. The group level is the level 3 of random variation in Figure II.1 and Figure II.2.

(4) Besides the three random parts, the model also contains a fixed part: the fixed effects of item predictors and person predictors. This part is presented to the left of the three random parts in Figure II.2.

Following the above, the equation in Figure II.2 has four parts on the right hand side: A fixed part, a random group variation part, a random person part, and a random occasion part. The first three parts constitute the linear predictor η_{pi}, including the variation at levels 2 and 3. The fourth part constitutes the random component or the variation at level 1. The last three parts constitute different levels of random variation, while the first reflects variation attributed to the fixed effects of external factors.

When random variation is defined, a distribution must also be specified. In the normal-ogive models a normal distribution is assumed for ε_{pi}, with mean zero, and variance σ_ε^2 independent of the pair (p, i). In the corresponding logistic models, a logistic distribution is assumed. In all models of this volume, except for the chapter on mixture models, θ_{pk} is normally distributed with mean zero, and variance $\sigma_{k(p)}^2$. In a similar way, θ_{gk} is normally distributed with mean zero, and variance $\sigma_{k(g)}^2$.

Model for	Fixed effects	Random groups Level 3	Random persons Level 2	Random occasions Level 1
π_{pi}	η_{pi}: Linear component			Random component
$V_{pi} =$	$\Sigma\beta_k X_{ik} + \Sigma\vartheta_j Z_{pj} +$	$\Sigma\theta_{gk} X_{ik} +$	$\Sigma\theta_{pk} X_{ik} +$	ε_{pi}

FIGURE II.2. Schematic presentation of different levels of random person variation.

The alternative to random variation is *fixed variation*. This means that the variation would stem from fixed occasions, fixed persons, or fixed groups. The concept of 'occasions' is introduced in this volume to deal with the uncertainty that remains when everything else of relevance is known about the pair of a person and an item. Therefore it does not make sense to define occasions as fixed. However, persons and groups may indeed be considered as fixed. One may be interested in persons not so much as members of a group they are sampled from, but as persons in their own right. Or one may be interested in groups not so much as members of a larger set of groups (e.g., neighborhoods as members of a town), but as groups in their own right. For example, one may want to know what the differences are between two specific neighborhoods. Models differ as to where they locate random variation: at all three levels, at the occasion level and the person level, or only at the occasion level. In general, fixed variation can take the place of random variation, except for level 1, where, as noted above, the variation is always random. This means that in Figure II.2 the random variation may be replaced by fixed variation in the middle cells (levels 2 and 3).

II.1.2 Levels of random variation at the item side

The levels we have just described for persons may also be considered for items. The basic level would be the same, but the next two levels would be for items and groups of items. Suppose an inventory were constructed with 24 frustrating situations: 12 other-to-blame situations and 12 self-to-blame situations. The specific situations could have been selected at random from two much larger sets, one of each type, gathered through a survey in which people were asked to list common frustrating situations. It is somewhat harder to think of item groups as also being selected at random from a set of item groups. Although possible in principle, we will not discuss it further, as we do not have an interesting application for this concept.

Continuing the example above, when one is interested in the two types of frustrating situations, it makes sense to sample more specific situations within each of these types, in order to infer from the two samples what the difference is between the types of frustrating situations. But the two types themselves are studied for their fixed effect, as one is interested in them as two specific types and not as representatives of categories of situation types. Therefore, a reasonable model for the variation at the item side would be one with fixed effects for item groups (level 3 for items), and random variation at the item level (level 2 for items), and random occasion variation (level 1) (see Chapter 6).

II.1.3 Hierarchical and crossed random variation

When random variation is taken into account at *both* the item side and the person side, and at levels higher than the level of occasions (level 1), for example for items and persons, then there is no longer a strict hierarchy of random variation. The observation concerning a pair (p, i) belongs to both a person and an item. The classification of the pairs is a cross-classification according to the persons and the items. Random variation is then associated simultaneously with categories that are crossed in the observations, hence, the random variations may be called *crossed random variation*. This is contrasted with random variation that is associated with strictly hierarchical categories (occasions, persons, person groups), in which case the random variations may be called *hierarchical random variation*.

Crossed random variation may concern persons and items, as obviously persons and items are crossed, but may also concern categories of items. For example, one could see the Behavior Type levels (Curse, Scold, Shout) as sampled from a larger framework of verbally aggressive behaviors. And one could see the situations from the two Situation Types as being sampled from a larger framework of situations. Since Behavior Type and Situation Type are crossed in the items, a crossing of random variation would need to be considered.

Chapter 5 describes hierarchical random variation on the side of the persons (persons and groups of persons), as in the more common applications of multilevel modeling. Chapter 6 describes hierarchical random variation on the side of the items, and also discusses crossed random variation: random person variation combined with random item variation within item groups.

II.1.4 Variation based on fixed effects

One common way to account for variation in the data is to assign the variation to fixed effects of external factors; see the first right-hand part of the equation presented in Figure II.2. As illustrated in Chapter 2, properties of items and properties of persons can be included in the model to explain variation in the data of different items and persons. For example, whether someone else or oneself is to blame for a frustrating situation can make a difference for the verbal aggression tendency. Other-to-blame versus Self-to-blame is an item property, and also Behavior Type (Curse, Scold, Shout), and Behavior Mode (Do versus Want) are item properties. In a similar way, Gender and Trait Anger are person properties that can be external factors influencing the response data. They can all function as external factors or predictors of the variation in the responses. When they turn out to have an effect on the observations, then this contributes to our understanding of the responses.

Another, less explanatory and more descriptive way of analyzing variation is the use of indicators. For example, in the Rasch model, item indicators with fixed effects are used to describe the variation between the data from different items.

II.2 External factors

The sources of variation we have discussed thus far are of two types. The variation either stems from a random sampling process for persons, groups, or items, independent of any external factors; or it stems from the fixed effects external factors have. There is a third possibility in that external factors may have random effects and not just fixed effects.

We have seen in Chapter 2 that people tend to actually act less than they want when it comes to verbal aggression. However, it might be that not all persons show the same discrepancy between wanting and doing. Some may have almost no discrepancy, while others tend to inhibit themselves quite a bit (see Figure 1.2). In this case, the effect of doing versus wanting would be no longer fixed (the same for all persons), but heterogeneous over persons. Thus, the effect an external factor may also show *random variation*. In sum, external factors may have fixed effects or random effects.

Except for the constant predictor, there are no models formulated in earlier chapters that have predictors with a random effect. We have mentioned this possibility in general, but we have not looked at such models in more detail. When these models are discussed later in the book, we will focus on random variation over persons, but also random variation over items is possible.

External factors can be of different types independent of whether they concern items or persons (properties, indicators, constant predictors), and depending on the types that are included, the model is of a different type as well. Together with the kind of effect (fixed or random), the kind of external factors included also defines differences between models.

II.2.1 Properties

External factors may be item properties, person properties, or person-by-item properties. For example, Gender is a person property, Behavior Mode is an item property. Person properties and item properties are features of persons and items, respectively, which have the following characteristics: (1) they differentiate between persons and items (the constant predictor is excluded) and (2) they do more than indicate a person or an item (indicators are excluded).

A special type of person and item property is a group: the group a person or an item belongs to. Models including such properties are extensively discussed in Chapters 5 and 6. These groups can in turn have properties, so-called *group properties*: properties of person groups or of item groups. For example, the population density of a neighborhood is a person group property. Formally they can be treated as person properties and item properties, respectively, with all persons (or items) of the group being assigned the same value.

Thus far only person properties and item properties have been used in the item response models we have touched upon. However, *person-by-item properties* can also be very meaningful to incorporate in a model. For example, it turns out that in the example study, the inhibition (discrepancy between wanting and doing) is larger for women than for men (see Chapter 7). In order to obtain a person-by-item property one can simply multiply the corresponding coding for person and item properties. We have introduced the symbols X and Z for item predictors and person predictors, respectively, so that it seems appropriate to introduce a separate symbol for person-by-item properties as well: W, with an index $h, h = 1, \ldots, H$. An example of a person-by-item property would be $W_{pi\ gender \times do}$, with $W_{pi\ gender \times do} = 1$ if $Z_{p\ gender} = 1$ and $W_{i\ do-want} = 1$, and $W_{pi\ gender \times do} = 0$ otherwise. The fixed effects are denoted by $\delta_{gender \times do}$. The corresponding random effects of interaction parameters would be denoted by γ.

This third kind of property is an important one to model differential item functioning (DIF), since DIF basically is group-by-item interaction. Another application is the use of responses to one item as a predictor for the responses on another item, for example to study local item dependence. Since this kind of predictor is not used for all items (has a zero value for other items), and since people would differ in their response to the predictor item, it too is a person-by-item predictor. Because responses to other items are in fact internal factors, these models are discussed in Part III. Chapter 7 gives a description of how person-by-item predictors can be used in a GLMM context for item response models.

II.2.2 Indicators

Formally speaking, indicators are external factors, but they differ from properties in that they do not assign a characteristic to a person or an item, but only an identification label instead. In the models we have seen so far, the fixed effects of item indicators are the item parameters. They are the effect of individual items. Just as for item indicators, person indicators may be defined, each with its own fixed effect. This would correspond to seeing the persons not as representatives of a group, but as individual persons that each come with their own individual fixed effect. The inference to be made would then be about these individual persons, and not about the group they belong to.

There is a model that is based on the logic of fixed persons: the joint maximum likelihood (JML) equivalent of the Rasch model. The *JML model* is a model with both item indicators and person indicators, each with its own fixed effect. The effects are known not to have consistent estimations, because the number of parameters increases with both the number of persons and the number of items. Another good reason for not using this model is that it makes sense to think of persons as sampled from a larger group, rather than as being selected because of who they each are individually.

A special type of indicator is the *group indicator*. An example would be the specific schools that students came from, or the specific neighborhood that specific survey responses came from. A group indicator indicates the group a person belongs to, and therefore they are also person properties, and can be treated as such. However, although they are properties they do not have much explanatory value. Only when group properties are also included can one explore and test factors underlying group differences.

II.2.3 Constant predictors

The constant predictor is a predictor with only one value for all elements, the value one, either for all items (X_0) or for all persons (Z_0). The fixed effect of the constant predictor is the intercept in the linear component. If for all other predictors the coding is centered on the overall mean of the predictors, the effect of the constant predictor reflects the overall mean. It does not make sense to use a constant predictor for both the items and the persons simultaneously if their effect is fixed. The two intercepts can simply be added into one $(\beta_0 X_{i0} + \vartheta_0 Z_{p0})$, which can either be assigned to the constant item predictor (the new β_0 = the old β_0 + the old ϑ_0) while the fixed effect of the person constant predictor is set equal to zero (the new $\vartheta_0 = 0$), or vice versa.

When the effect of a constant predictor is a random effect, a random intercept is obtained. For example, the random intercept θ_{p0} (or ε_p) is the normally distributed effect of the constant item response predictor X_{i0}. One may exchange X_0 for Z_0, so that θ_{p0} is the random effect of Z_0, which should be denoted by ζ_{p0}, since the symbol ζ will be used for random effects of person predictors Z, but since one could have used X_0 instead of Z_0, in practice θ_p or θ_{p0} are preferred. The two formulations of the random intercept we gave are equivalent. In both formulations, the variation is random over persons. What matters is the mode (the persons or items) over which the random variation is defined: over persons or over items. As will be shown in Chapter 6, the intercept can also be random over items.

II.3 Random variation and external factors as building blocks for models

External factors (the properties, indicators, the constant predictors discussed above) may have fixed effects or random effects, and the effects may vary over persons, over items, over groups of persons, or over groups of items. Predictors and their effects are the building blocks of modeling. They can be combined in various ways in order to build a model according to one's needs for description and explanation. As will be explained, the type of coding of the predictor also plays a role. In the next five sections (II.3.1 to II.3.5) we provide a sample of meaningful combinations of these building blocks to illustrate the variety that is possible.

A general observation is that when more than one random person effect is defined, the model is multidimensional and also the elements of the variance-covariance matrix are parameters. This applies in an analogous way to models with more than one random item effect, although these models would commonly not be called multidimensional. The term 'multidimensional' is usually reserved for the dimensionality of person variation. Multidimensional models are not a topic of Part II of this book, but of Part III instead. However, as we will describe here a general system, some examples of multidimensional models will also be given.

II.3.1 Effects of item properties

Let us consider the *item property* Do vs Want as an example, and assume a dummy coding, so that for do-items the value is 1 and for want-items it is 0. The following effects may be considered as meaningful effects:

(1) *Fixed effect.* The fixed effect of the item property reflects the mean difference between doing and wanting. This difference is to be interpreted as an item independent and person independent inhibition effect $\beta_{do-want}$.

(2) *Random person effect.* This would mean that people vary in how much they inhibit their verbal aggression, which would be expressed through the random effect $\theta_{p\ do-want}$ (with index p for persons).

(3) *Random item effect.* This would mean that the 12 do-items differ with respect to how much people inhibit their verbal aggression. Given that for want-items the property has a value of zero, the random do-effect tells us how large the inhibition is for each of the 4×3 combinations of a situation and a behavior (i.e., for each of the do-items). The symbol for this random effect would be $\theta_{i\ do-want}$ (with index i for items).

(4) *Random group effect.* The effect would reflect the random variation of groups, for example neighborhoods, with respect to how much they inhibit verbal aggression. This effect $\theta_{g\ do-want}$ (with index g for groups) is a hierarchically higher effect in comparison with $\theta_{p\ do-want}$.

The effects (2) and (4) are hierarchically related random effects, while the effects (2) and (3) are crossed random effects when included into the same model. All these effects come on top of the basic random variation as expressed in the random component (the Bernoulli distribution) at the level of the occasions.

II.3.2 Effects of person properties

Let us consider Gender as a *person property*, first with a dummy coding so that for males the value is 1 and for females it is 0. A second coding will be used for illustrative reasons, with a double dummy coding: the first with 1 and 0 (as before), and the second with 0 and 1, for males and females, respectively. The following effects may be considered.

(1) *Fixed effect.* The fixed effect of the single-coded Gender is simply the effect of being male, ϑ_{male}. This fixed effect is included in models from Chapters 2 and 3 that use person properties. Remember that the difference was not statistically significant when analyzing binary data, but this was different when the three response categories were taken into account.

(2) *Random item effect.* This effect implies that depending on the item, the difference between males and females with respect to verbal aggression depends on the item; this random effect is denoted with $\zeta_{i\ male}$ (with index i for items). The effect may be interpreted as differential item functioning with the degree of differential functioning varying at random depending on the item. Note that the interaction of Gender with one or more items can be studied also as a fixed effect; see Section II.3.4.

(3) *Random group effect.* Suppose that there is variation over neighborhoods in how different are males and females. This would be reflected in an effect $\zeta_{g\ male}$ (with index g for groups).

Given the dummy coding, a random person effect does not make much sense, although possible in principle. It would imply that males differ while females do not. A more elegant way to model variation within the two genders is to use a double dummy coding.

(4) *Random person effect.* Instead of using one random intercept, one may define random effects for two gender properties Z_{female} (= 1 if female, = 0 if male) and Z_{male} (= $1 - Z_{female}$): $\zeta_{p\ female}$ and $\zeta_{p\ male}$ (with index p for persons). They can each be seen as gender-specific intercepts. If the variances of the two normal distributions are not fixed to be equal, then this is also a way to allow for a different variance for the two genders (i.e., heteroscedasticity).

II.3.3 Effects of group properties

Let us consider neighborhoods as groups, and the density of the population as a group property. The following meaningful effects can be considered.

(1) *Fixed effect.* For example, perhaps it is socially more stressful to live in a densely populated neighborhood, so that the tendency to be verbally aggressive is higher. This would be reflected in a fixed effect ϑ_{dense} of a binary (or continuous) density property.

(2) *Random person effect.* Perhaps some people are affected more than others by the density of their neighborhood. This can be expressed in a random effect parameter $\zeta_{p\ dense}$ (with index p for persons) of a binary density property.

II.3.4 Effects of item indicators

Let us consider the *item indicator* 1 in Table 1.1 (for cursing when a bus fails to stop), one among the 24. Three effects can be considered.

(1) *Fixed effect.* The fixed effect of the indicator is simply the item parameter β_1.

(2) *Random person effect.* The indicator may have an effect that is random over persons, θ_{p1} (with index p for persons), so that a specific dimension is introduced for cursing when buses fail to stop.[1] Note that item indicators cannot have an effect that is random over items, because by definition an item indicator concerns only one item.

(3) *Random group effect.* If the indicator in question had a random group effect θ_{g1} (with index g for groups), it would mean, for example, that the neighborhoods differ in how easily people curse when a bus fails to stop. This might make sense if bus drivers are more negligent with respect to stopping in some neighborhoods than in others. Random group effects for

---

[1]Note that when an item indicator effect has a random effect in one group, this will translate into a smaller degree of discrimination of the item for the group in question. Consequently, this will be a case of nonuniform DIF (see Chapter 7). Conversely, a random item indicator effect is a possible interpretation for nonuniform DIF.

item indicators are a way to test for differential item functioning. For example, one may try out each of the items in turn, to find out whether they show a random group effect. If an item does, this is a clear indication of DIF. Note that as an alternative – fixed interaction effects can be also formulated – this would make sense, for example, if Gender interacted with one or more items.

As explained earlier, the use of person indicators is much less common because one is normally not so much interested in the behavior of individual persons. An exception might be when one wants to find out about person fit, but even so it would be cumbersome to work with as many indicators as there are persons (see Chapter 6).

II.3.5 Effects of constant predictors

Suppose a *constant item predictor* is included in the model. The following meaningful effects may be considered. (Note that a constant person predictor can fulfill an equivalent role, because just like a constant item response predictor it has a value of 1 in the expression for all Y_{pi}.)

(1) *Fixed effect.* The fixed effect of the constant predictor is an intercept β_0, as in the LLTM. This intercept reflects the mean level of the responses if the mean of the person parameter is zero and the other predictors are included with a coding that is centered on the overall mean. When in addition a plus parametrization $(\theta_p + \ldots + \beta_0)$ is used, a positive β_0 indicates that the verbal aggression tendency is high enough to yield response probabilities that are on the average higher than .50.

(2) *Random person effect.* The random person effect θ_{p0} or θ_p (with index p for persons) of the constant predictor is simply a random person intercept, as in the models from Chapter 2.

(3) *Random item effect.* When the effect is random over items, it is assumed that the item difficulties differ at random, with an effect θ_{i0} (with index i for items). This may be a meaningful assumption if one considers the items as being sampled from a broader set, without being interested in the individual items as such (as explained in Chapter 6).

The following chapters, from Chapter 5 to 7, illustrate how person predictors, item predictors, and person-by-item predictors can lead to various item response models, depending on the kind of predictor and the kind of effect they are assumed to have.

Chapter 5

Person regression models

Wim Van den Noortgate
Insu Paek

5.1 Introduction

In this chapter, we focus on the person side of the logistic mixed model. As described in Chapter 2, the simple Rasch model can be extended by including person characteristics as predictors. The resulting models can be called latent regression models, since the latent person abilities (the θs) are regressed on person characteristics. A special kind of a person characteristic is a person group: for instance, pupils can be grouped in schools. Then there are two possibilities for modeling, either we can define random school effects, or we can utilize school indicators with fixed effects.

In the following, person regression models will be discussed within the framework of multilevel analysis. We start with a presentation of multilevel data and models. Next, we show how data in item response modeling applications are often hierarchically structured, with measurement occasions nested within persons, and how the simple Rasch model can be regarded as a *descriptive 2-level model*. We will describe how this model can be extended by including person characteristics as predictors, resulting in a *latent regression 2-level model*. We furthermore discuss the extension of the descriptive or latent regression models with one or more additional levels, to model the nesting of persons in groups of persons, e.g., schools. This extension results in a *descriptive* or a *latent regression multilevel model with three or more levels*. We close the chapter with some further model extensions, a set of exercises, and a section containing software commands that will allow the reader to carry out some of the analyses.

5.2 Multilevel models

The reality investigated in social and behavioral research is usually multilayered. For instance, individuals generally belong to specific groups, or are observed in specific social contexts. An example of a multilevel structure in education is the grouping of pupils in classes or in schools (Figure 5.1).

Often data are gathered about the units at different levels. Table 5.1 shows a representation of a multilevel data set (with data from pupils nested

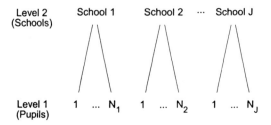

FIGURE 5.1. A multilevel data structure.

in schools). Note that the school variable is constant over pupils from the same school, and that the number of observed pupils (level-1 units) per school (level-2 unit) varies over schools.

TABLE 5.1. A multilevel data set.

School	Pupil	School Size	Gender	Math
1	1	156	M	78
1	2	156	F	91
...	...	...	...	...
1	N_1	156	F	84
2	1	177	M	62
2	2	177	M	77
...	...	...	...	...
2	N_2	177	M	80
...				
J	1	212	F	72
J	2	212	M	81
...	...	...	...	...
J	N_J	212	F	76

Often there are different sources of variability associated with these levels. For instance, besides variation between math-scores from pupils within the same school, there may be systematic differences between schools in the performance of the pupils. Variation between higher level units induces dependence in the lower level scores: if schools differ in their performance, this means that in general pupils from the same school are more similar than pupils from different schools. Traditional analyses (e.g., linear regression with fixed effects) often ignore the different sources of variation from different levels and therefore may result in wrong conclusions. In multilevel models, these different sources of variation are explicitly taken into account. Moreover, multilevel models allow characteristics of the units at different levels to act as predictors, as we shall see later.

During the last two decades, hierarchical linear and hierarchical generalized linear models were developed in order to analyze such 'multilevel' data (Goldstein, 1987a; Raudenbush, 1988; Longford, 1993). A simple example is a hierarchical linear model with two levels and a predictor on each level, which reads as follows:

$$
\begin{aligned}
\text{Level 1} \quad & Y_{ij} = \beta_{0j} + \beta_{1j} X_{ij} + e_{ij}, \\
\text{Level 2} \quad & \beta_{0j} = \gamma_{00} + \gamma_{01} Z_j + u_{0j}, \\
& \beta_{1j} = \gamma_{10} + \gamma_{11} Z_j + u_{1j},
\end{aligned}
\tag{5.1}
$$

with $i = 1, 2, \ldots, N_j$ indicating the level-1 units (e.g., pupils) 'nested' within the level-2 units (e.g., schools), indicated by index $j = 1, 2, \ldots, J$.

For Equation 5.1, we used the model formulation and notation that are typical in multilevel literature, but deviate from those used in the following sections and in the rest of the volume. The first line of Equation 5.1 describes the scores of the level-1 units using characteristics of the level-1 units as predictors. It differs from an ordinary regression equation in that the regression coefficients (including the intercept) can depend on the level-2 unit. The variation of the coefficients is described by new regression equations on the second level. The coefficients of these level-2 equations may in turn be regressed on a third level, and so on. Substituting the level-1 coefficients with the right hand sides of the level-2 equations results in the following equation, after reordering the terms:

$$
Y_{ij} = (\gamma_{00} + \gamma_{10} X_{ij} + \gamma_{01} Z_j + \gamma_{11} X_{ij} Z_j) + (u_{0j} + u_{1j} X_{ij} + e_{ij}). \tag{5.2}
$$

Equation 5.2 includes four kinds of predictors: a constant predictor (equal to 1 for all units), a level-1 predictor X, a level-2 predictor Z, and the product of the level-1 and level-2 predictor. In the first part of the right hand side of the equation, the coefficients of the predictors do not vary but are fixed instead. Therefore, this part of the equation is called the fixed part. In the second part, the coefficients vary randomly. The constant predictor has a coefficient (e_{ij}) that varies randomly over level-1 units and a coefficient (u_{0j}) that varies randomly over level-2 units. The level-1 predictor has a coefficient (u_{1j}) that varies randomly over the level-2 units. A hierarchical linear model thus includes predictors with fixed and/or random effects, and therefore is often called a mixed model.

In case the dependent variable Y_{ij} is a dichotomous (or categorical) variable, the hierarchical linear model as described above must be adapted to a hierarchical generalized linear model. This is done in much the same way as the linear regression model is adapted to a generalized linear regression model (McCullagh & Nelder, 1989). A probit or logit link function is defined, as described in Chapter 1. Adapting the hierarchical linear 2-level model given in Equation 5.1, by defining a logit link function, results in the following hierarchical logistic 2-level model, again using the notation typical to multilevel modeling:

$$
\begin{aligned}
\text{Level 1} \quad & V_{ij} = \beta_{0j} + \beta_{1j}X_{ij} + e_{ij}, \\
\text{Level 2} \quad & \beta_{0j} = \gamma_{00} + \gamma_{01}Z_j + u_{0j}, \\
& \beta_{1j} = \gamma_{10} + \gamma_{11}Z_j + u_{1j},
\end{aligned}
\tag{5.3}
$$

with V_{ij} the covert continuous variable from which Y_{ij} is a dichotomization, e_{ij} logistically distributed (see Chapter 1), $Y_{ij}\sim$Bernoulli(π_{ij}), π_{ij} equal to the probability that $Y_{ij} = 1$, and logit(π_{ij}) $= \beta_{0j} + \beta_{1j}X_{ij}$.

Parameters of multilevel models are commonly estimated using maximum likelihood procedures. To obtain the likelihood function, the random effects are integrated out. Unfortunately, for the hierarchical logistic model, unlike for the hierarchical linear model, this likelihood cannot be written in a closed form. One solution for solving the integral in the likelihood is numerical integration, for example using the Gaussian quadrature, as implemented in the procedure NLMIXED from SAS. A second solution is to approximate it with linearization techniques. This is done in the iterative quasi-likelihood procedures for generalized linear mixed models (Breslow & Clayton, 1993), which are typically used in specialized software for hierarchical (generalized) linear models, such as HLM (Bryk, Raudenbush, & Congdon, 1996) and MLwiN (Goldstein et al., 1998). More details about the estimation procedures are given in Chapters 4 and 12, and about software in Chapter 12.

It has been shown before that several popular item response models can be formulated as hierarchical generalized linear models (Adams, Wilson, & Wu, 1997; Kamata, 2001; Raudenbush & Sampson, 1999, Rijmen et al., 2003). In the following section, we will illustrate the hierarchical structure of typical item response data, and reformulate the basic Rasch model as a descriptive hierarchical 2-level logistic model. Further, the extension of the model by including person characteristics, resulting in a 2-level model with latent regression on the second level, will be described.

5.3   The Rasch model and the latent regression model as 2-level models

In item response modeling applications, each person responds to a set of items. Each person therefore is repeatedly observed. One way of dealing with the repeated observations in item response modeling applications is by regarding this situation as a multilevel problem, with observation occasions ($u = 1, 2, \ldots, U_p$) nested within persons ($p = 1, 2, \ldots, P$), as shown in Figure 5.2 . Note that typically each person responds to each item, such that the number of measurement occasions per person equals the number of items ($U_p = I$ for all p), but the same framework could also be used if some persons do not respond to all items or respond to specific items on several occasions. As a result of this multilevel structure, the data sets in item response modeling applications often look very similar to typical multilevel data sets, such as the one given in Table 5.1.

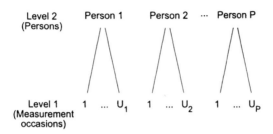

FIGURE 5.2. The multilevel data structure in regular item response modeling applications.

In the MML formulation of the Rasch model (Bock & Aitkin, 1981), the response of person p to an item i, Y_{pi}, is regarded as a function of the person ability (θ_p) and the item difficulty (β_i); persons are regarded as a random sample from a population in which the person abilities are identically and independently normally distributed (Equation 5.4 below). Note that in order to make the model identified, a constraint needs to be added, say make the mean of the population distribution zero. The Rasch model is given by:

$$\eta_{pi} = \theta_p - \beta_i, \qquad (5.4)$$

with $i = 1, \ldots, I$ indicating the item, $p = 1, \ldots, P$ indicating the person, $Y_{pi} \sim \text{Bernoulli}(\pi_{pi})$, $\eta_{pi} = \text{logit}(\pi_{pi})$ given θ_p, and $\theta_p \sim N(0, \sigma_\theta^2)$.

The Rasch model can be reformulated as a 2-level logistic model, with measurement occasions (level 1) nested in persons (level 2). On the different occasions, persons respond to different items. Since items usually differ in difficulty, it can be expected that part of the variation within persons can be explained by the items. Since one is interested in the variation of the scores within persons as far as they can be explained by the items, item indicators are included in the model as characteristics of the measurement occasions, resulting in the following level-1 model:

$$V_{piu} = \theta_{p0} + \sum_{k=1}^{K} \beta_k X_{iuk} + \varepsilon_{piu}, \qquad (5.5)$$

with index u for occasions, $X_{iuk} = 1$ if $k = i$, $X_{iuk} = 0$ otherwise, $K = I$, and ε_{piu} logistically distributed.

In item response modeling applications, persons typically respond only once to the items, hence, from now on we will use V_{pi} and ε_{pi} instead of V_{piu} and ε_{piu}. The distribution of the intercept in the population of persons forms the between-person or level-2 model:

$$\theta_{p0} \sim N(0, \sigma^2_{\theta_{(p)}}), \tag{5.6}$$

with $\sigma^2_{\theta_{(p)}}$ as the variance over persons (the alternative is the variance over groups; see further).

An alternative way to formulate the model, which is common in the multilevel literature, is to use the formulation

$$V_{piu} = \theta_{p0} + \sum_{k=1}^{K} \theta_{pk} X_{iuk} + \varepsilon_{piu}, \tag{5.7}$$

with

$$\theta_{p0} \sim N(\theta, \sigma^2_{\theta_{(p)}}),$$
$$\theta_{p1} = \beta_1,$$
$$\ldots$$
$$\theta_{pK} = \beta_K.$$

We will not pursue this way of formulating models in the following.

Equations 5.4 and 5.5 are equivalent if one defines $Y_{pi} = 1$ iff $V_{pi} > 0$, and $Y_{pi} = 0$ otherwise, with the fixed effects of the item indicators in the multilevel logistic model (Equation 5.5) corresponding to minus the item difficulty parameters ($-\beta$) of Equation 5.4. From now on, we will no longer use the model formulation with the continuous underlying variable as in Equations 5.5, but instead the logit formulation as in Equation 5.4 will be used.

The Rasch model is a *descriptive 2-level model*, since the person abilities and the item difficulties are not related to properties of persons or items. The only predictors that are included in the model are the item indicators and the level-independent constant predictor. In *latent regression models*, on the contrary, the latent person abilities are described as a linear combination of one or more person properties and an error term. While in the descriptive 2-level model described above, the intercept varies completely randomly over persons, in the latent regression 2-level model, the intercept varies partly randomly, partly according to person properties. A latent regression model therefore is a specific instantiation of what in the multilevel literature is often called an *intercepts-as-outcomes model*. The first level model remains unchanged (see Equation 5.5), but on the second level the intercept is regressed on person properties, the Zs. To ease the interpretation, predictors can be centered (Snijders & Bosker, 1999). Note that the meaning of the intercept differs depending upon which kind of centering is used. The second level model for θ_{p0} now reads as:

$$\theta_{p0} = \sum_{j=1}^{J} \vartheta_j Z_{pj} + \varepsilon_p, \tag{5.8}$$

with ϑ_j as the fixed effect of person predictor, and with $\varepsilon_p \sim N(0, \sigma^2_{\varepsilon_{(p)}})$.

5.4 Application of the descriptive and the latent regression 2-level model to the verbal aggression data

To illustrate the 2-level models, we reanalyze the verbal aggression example described in Chapter 1. In Chapter 2, the parameters of the Rasch model and of the latent regression model were estimated using the procedure NLMIXED from SAS. Since these models are in fact hierarchical generalized linear models, specialized software for multilevel models can also be used, such as MLwiN and HLM.

In the second column of Table 5.4, the parameter estimates and corresponding standard errors of estimation are presented for the unknown parameters of the descriptive 2-level model with binary item indicators. The same results are reported in Table 12.3 of Chapter 12. The estimates were obtained by means of the PQL2 procedure of MLwiN, calling in each step the RIGLS algorithm to obtain the restricted maximum likelihood estimates of the linearized model (see also Chapter 12). The estimates are quite close to those of the procedure NLMIXED from SAS (see Chapter 2). Using PQL2 should reduce the downward bias inherent to PQL, as explained in Chapters 4 and 12.

For each item, there is one estimated regression coefficient, to be interpreted as minus the item difficulties, and indicating how the average person tends to react in a specific verbally aggressive way and in a specific situation. Besides the fixed item parameters, MLwiN also returns the variance estimates for the residuals. The estimate of the between persons variance (this is $\sigma^2_{\theta_{(p)}}$ from Equation 5.6) given by MLwiN equals 1.87, with a SE of .17. Comparing the ratio of the estimate and the SE to a standard normal distribution, reveals that the differences between participants are highly significant ($z = 10.90$, $p < .001$). Note that because 0 is the boundary for variances the p-values are conservative (see Section 4.6.2 of Chapter 4).

That the propensity to react in a verbally aggressive way differs from person to person raises the question of how to explain this variance. Therefore, we extend the model to a latent regression model, by regressing the level-1 intercepts on the person properties Gender and Trait Anger (see Section 5.9.1 for the MLwiN model formulation). The results are given in

TABLE 5.2. Parameter estimates and standard errors for the 2-level models using MLwiN (verbal aggression data).

			Estimate (SE)	
			Descriptive model	Latent regression
Fixed effects of				
Bus	Want	Curse	1.22 (.16)	.01 (.38)
Bus	Want	Scold	.56 (.15)	-.65 (.37)
Bus	Want	Shout	.08 (.15)	-1.14 (.37)
Train	Want	Curse	1.74 (.17)	.53 (.38)
Train	Want	Scold	.71 (.15)	-.51 (.37)
Train	Want	Shout	.01 (.15)	-1.20 (.37)
Store	Want	Curse	.53 (.15)	-.69 (.37)
Store	Want	Scold	-.69 (.16)	-1.90 (.38)
Store	Want	Shout	-1.53 (.17)	-2.74 (.38)
Call	Want	Curse	1.08 (.16)	-.13 (.38)
Call	Want	Scold	-.35 (.15)	-1.57 (.37)
Call	Want	Shout	-1.04 (.16)	-2.26 (.38)
Bus	Do	Curse	1.22 (.16)	.01 (.38)
Bus	Do	Scold	.39 (.15)	-.83 (.37)
Bus	Do	Shout	-.87 (.16)	-2.09 (.38)
Train	Do	Curse	.87 (.16)	-.34 (.37)
Train	Do	Scold	-.06 (.15)	-1.27 (.37)
Train	Do	Shout	-1.48 (.17)	-2.70 (.38)
Store	Do	Curse	-.21 (.15)	-1.43 (.37)
Store	Do	Scold	-1.50 (.17)	-2.72 (.38)
Store	Do	Shout	-2.96 (.23)	-4.18 (.42)
Call	Do	Curse	.71 (.15)	-.51 (.37)
Call	Do	Scold	-.38 (.15)	-1.60 (.37)
Call	Do	Shout	-1.99 (.18)	-3.21 (.39)
Gender				.32 (.19)
Trait Anger				.06 (.02)
Variance components				
Level 2 (persons)			1.87 (.17)	1.81 (.17)

the last column of Table 5.4. The coefficient of Gender (.32) is not statistically significant ($z = 1.68$, $p > .05$). The effect of Trait Anger (.06) on the contrary is statistically highly significant ($z = 3.00$, $p < .001$): Persons with a higher score on the Trait Anger scale of the STAXI questionnaire

(Spielberger, 1988) generally react in a more verbally aggressive way.

Table 5.4 further reveals that adding the person properties affects the item parameter estimates. The parameters however have a different meaning in the two models. In the descriptive model, an item parameter refers to the expected logit of the probability of a 1-response from an average person. In the latent regression model, the expected logit of the probability of a 1-response for an average person is calculated by filling in the average values of the person properties into the regression equation. According to the latent regression model, the expected logit for an average person and for the first item is .007 + .317*.231 + .057*20.003=1.220, which is also the value of the item parameter of the descriptive model. To ease the interpretation of the item parameters, one could center the person properties around their means. The resulting item parameters are comparable with the item parameters from the descriptive model.

The estimate of the (residual) variance between persons is 1.81. Comparing this estimate with the estimate of the descriptive 2-level model (1.87) reveals that a (small) part of the differences in person abilities is explained by the person properties Gender and Trait Anger. Note that we did not use any fit statistics based on the likelihood to evaluate the absolute or relative model fit, because PQL2 uses only an approximate likelihood, not the 'real' likelihood. As a result, fit statistics based on the likelihood are also only very approximate and should not be used for testing the model fit (Hox, 2002). Therefore, MLwiN does not report the likelihood statistic for generalized multilevel models. Instead, it is recommended to use the Wald test, although the results of this test also should be used with care, especially for testing the variance components (Goldstein et al., 1998).

5.5   Models with three or more levels

In many applications, persons belong to groups. It is important to model group memberships or hierarchical structures in the data because they may induce dependencies in the data (between responses from different persons). For instance, pupils from the same class are usually more alike than pupils from different classes, because of selection effects or because of a common social and didactic context. Sometimes, the groups are regarded as unique and the researcher wants to draw conclusions regarding each of these particular groups. The researcher for instance may want to compare males and females, as in the previous application. For that purpose, binary indicators can be used to indicate the group the person belongs to, and these variables can be included in the second level model as person properties with fixed effects. The resulting model is thus another latent regression 2-level model, as illustrated for Gender in the previous application.

Sometimes however, groups can be considered to be merely a sample from a population of groups. For instance, classes or schools pupils belong to may be considered as elements of a population of classes or schools. While researchers are typically not primarily interested in the specific classes or schools in the sample, it is interesting to obtain an overall idea of the influence of the class or school on the individual scores. When the groups are seen as randomly drawn from a population of groups, the group effects are modeled as random rather than as fixed effects. This can again be done by using binary group indicators as person predictors. This time, however, the weights of the group indicators are defined to vary randomly over groups, with a common population variance. However, a more economical way to model the random group effects is to define a random group weight for the constant predictor, a weight that varies randomly over groups. This means that the models that were presented in the preceding sections are extended by defining an additional level of units, resulting in a 3-level model: measurement occasions (1st level) can be grouped according to the person (2nd level) they stem from, while the persons in turn are nested in groups of persons (3rd level). The model on the *first level* remains unchanged except for an additional index g, indicating the level-3 units:

$$\eta_{gpi} = \theta_{gp0} + \sum_{k=1}^{K} \beta_k X_{ik}, \tag{5.9}$$

with index g referring to person group g. The use of an index g, in addition to the p index, allows persons to be numbered within each person group separately, as is common in multilevel research.

On the *second level*, the level of persons, the person abilities θ_{gp0} are defined to vary randomly over persons around a group-specific mean θ_{g0}, with a variance equal to $\sigma^2_{\varepsilon_{(p)}}$:

$$\theta_{gp0} = \theta_{g0} + \varepsilon_{gp}, \tag{5.10}$$

with $\varepsilon_{gp} \sim N(0, \sigma^2_{\varepsilon_{(p)}})$. Equation 5.10 assumes that the variance between persons $(\sigma^2_{\varepsilon_{(p)}})$ is the same for all person groups. The model can easily be extended to allow heteroscedasticity, by defining the εs as the random effects of group indicators, instead of as the effects of an overall constant predictor, as will be discussed below.

On the *third level*, the mean person ability varies randomly over groups, with a variance equal to $\sigma^2_{\theta_{(g)}}$. To identify the model, the overall mean of the person abilities is assumed to be zero:

$$\theta_{g0} \sim N(0, \sigma^2_{\theta_{(g)}}). \tag{5.11}$$

Combining Equations 5.9 and 5.10 in a single equation, results in:

$$\eta_{gpi} = \theta_{g0} + \sum_{k=1}^{K} \beta_k X_{ik} + \varepsilon_{gp}. \tag{5.12}$$

Because in the model neither the item difficulties nor the person abilities are explained, this model can be called a *descriptive 3-level model*. In Figure 5.3, the systematic component of the descriptive 3-level model is presented, with random effects on the person level and on the level of groups of persons. Note that, for simplicity, the random component and the logit link are omitted from Figure 5.3, and this will also be the case in the following.

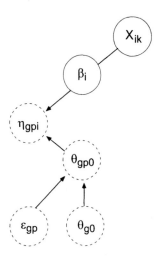

FIGURE 5.3. Graphical representation of a descriptive 3-level model.

It is possible to combine person properties with fixed or random effects and person groups with random effects. Pupils can be grouped according to the class they belong to (random effect), while the researcher is possibly also interested in differences between male and female pupils (fixed effect). In this case, one may extend the descriptive 3-level model by including person properties as predictors on the second level (as in the 2-level latent regression model described above). Because in such a 3-level model, the latent person abilities are regressed on person predictors, this model could be called a *3-level model with latent regression on level 2*. On the second level, the level of persons, Equation 5.10 must be adapted in order to describe the variation in person abilities around the group means as partly random, partly as a function of an external person predictor:

$$\theta_{gp0} = \theta_{g0} + \sum_{j=1}^{J} \zeta_{gj} Z_{gpj} + \varepsilon_{gp}, \tag{5.13}$$

with $\varepsilon_{gp} \sim N(0, \sigma^2_{\varepsilon_{(p)}})$. The effects of the external person predictors (the Zs) possibly depend on the group. Therefore, ζ_{gj} with subscript g is used for the weights of the person properties with ζ_{gj} possibly being random over groups. If the effects of the person properties are fixed and the same for each group, the $\zeta_{gj} = \vartheta_j$ for all j. The model with fixed effects for the person properties is presented graphically in Figure 5.4.

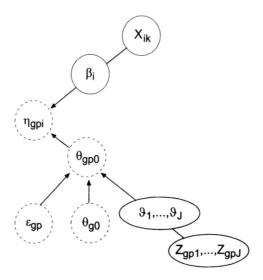

FIGURE 5.4. Graphical representation of a 3-level model with latent regression on level 2.

Note that the data analyst usually will not be satisfied when finding random effects on the level of groups, but rather will be challenged to explain the variation. This can be done in a similar way as we did for investigating the variance between the person abilities on level 2. Higher level predictors can be included in the model, resulting in a *3-level model with latent regression on level 3*. For instance, random school effects could be further described using school predictors with fixed effects (e.g., school size).

Also, higher-order grouping variables may be defined (e.g., the region or state the school is situated in), yielding a 4-level model, with measurement occasions, persons, schools and regions being the units on the respective levels. Also on this fourth level a latent regression may be defined. Note that an aggregated predictor of a lower level can be used as a higher level predictor. A variable therefore can have effects on different levels. It is for instance possible that the performance of an individual pupil depends not only on the individual gender, but also on the proportion of girls in the school the pupil belongs to (this is the school mean of a dichotomous pupil variable, e.g., with female coded 1, male coded 0).

5.6   Application of 3-level models to the mathematics and science data

To illustrate models with three or more levels, we use a data set from CTB - McGraw Hill. The mathematics and science data set includes the results of 1500 grade 8 students from 35 schools. Each of the students responded to 76 items, measuring different objectives and subskills related to mathematics and science. Since in this chapter the discussion is restricted to models with a dichotomous outcome variable, we use only the responses on the 56 multiple-choice items (among the 76 items, item 1 to 31, and item 42 to 66), which are coded 0 (wrong response) or 1 (correct response).

TABLE 5.3. Parameter estimates and standard errors for 3-level models with and without latent regression on level 2 and 3 (mathematics and science data).

	Estimate (SE)	
	Descriptive model	Latent regression
Fixed effects of		
Item1	1.02 (.11)	1.07 (.12)
Item2	1.11 (.11)	1.16 (.12)
. . .		
Item65	-.22 (.11)	-.16 (.12)
Item66	-.30 (.11)	-.25 (.12)
Gender		-.09 (.04)
Catholic		.35 (.29)
Other private		-.34 (.26)
Public		.00 (-)
Bachelor		.23 (.09)
Variance components		
Level 3 (schools)	.29 (.08)	.22 (.07)
Level 2 (students)	.63 (.03)	.63 (.03)

In the procedure NLMIXED from SAS, the effects may be random over only one kind of unit. In other words, the NLMIXED procedure does not allow one to define more than two levels and, thus, cannot be used for the example. Therefore, we use the SAS macro GLIMMIX (Wolfinger & O'Connell, 1993), in which both marginal and penalized quasi-likelihood procedures (MQL and PQL, respectively) for fitting generalized linear mixed models are implemented (see Chapter 12). We start with a descriptive 3-level model, with measurement occasions, students and schools. This is a random intercept model in which (only) the intercept varies completely randomly on each level. The SAS code for the example (using GLIMMIX) is described in Section 5.9.2. The results are given in Table 5.3.

In the first part of the table, the estimates of the fixed coefficients are given, which can be interpreted as minus the item difficulties. These parameter estimates (which are not all reported here) vary from -1.58 to 2.59 (items 29 and 15 respectively). Standard errors are given as well. Furthermore, it is clear that the success rate (probability of a 1-response) does not depend on the items only, but on the students and schools as well. There are substantial differences between students within the same school (the variance is $.63$, $z = 21.00$, $p < .001$). To obtain an idea of the size of this between-student variance, we can calculate the probability of a 1-response for a student with an ability that is one SD lower and for a student with an ability of one SD higher than the ability of a student with a $.50$ probability of a 1-response on a specific item. These probabilities are $.31$ and $.69$, or $\exp(-\sqrt{.63})/(1+\exp(-\sqrt{.63}))$ and $\exp(\sqrt{.63})/(1+\exp(\sqrt{.63}))$, respectively. There is also evidence for differences between schools (the variance is $.29$, $z = 3.63$, $p < .001$), though these differences are smaller. If for a specific school the probability of a 1-response is $.50$, the probability is $.37$ and $.63$ for a school with an ability of one SD lower or higher, respectively.

In the next step, we introduced student and school characteristics as predictors in the model, in an attempt to explain the differences in the performance levels of students and of schools. On the second level, the student level, the intercept is regressed on Gender (female = 1, male = 0). On the third level, the school level, School Type and the Educational Level of the region the school is located in were included to explain the intercept. Three types of schools are involved: Catholic schools, other private schools, and public schools. For the Educational Level, a transformed and standardized variable indicating the percentage of adult residents with at least a Bachelor's degree was determined for each school zip code. This group predictor is called Bachelor in Table 5.3. The SAS-code to estimate the parameters of this 3-level model with latent regression on the second and third level using the GLIMMIX macro is given in Section 5.9.2. The results are given in the last column of Table 5.3. Note that SAS uses the last category of a categorical variable (in this case the category 'Public' for School Type) as the reference category.

Comparing the variance estimates for the previous random intercept model and this latent regression model, we conclude that the inclusion of the school and student predictors results hardly at all in a reduction of the unexplained variance between students. The estimate of the between-school variance is reduced from $.29$ to $.22$, but it remains relatively large ($z = 3.14$, $p < .001$). The results further indicate that female students performed slightly worse, a difference that is statistically significant ($z = -2.25$, $p < .05$): If for male students the probability of a 1-response on a specific item is $.50$, the predicted probability for female students from a comparable school is $.48$ corresponding to $\exp(0)/(1+\exp(0))$ and $\exp(-.09)/(1+\exp(-.09))$, respectively. The evidence for the effect of the percentage adults with at least a Bachelor's degree is more convincing. The effect is .23, $z = 2.26$, $p < .05$. Finally, the predicted probability of a 1-response is highest in Catholic schools, and lowest in other private schools. If in a public school the expected probability is .50, it is .59 in Catholic schools and .42 in other kinds of private schools. To evaluate the effect of categorical predictors (e.g., School Type), modeled with two or more binary indicators, one can look at the results of the F-tests that are automatically performed for each predictor with fixed effects when running GLIMMIX, and found in the output under the heading 'Type 3 tests for fixed effects.' The F-values are based on the so-called Type III SS, which are the reduction in error SS due to adding the term after all other terms have been added to the model except terms that contain the effect being tested. According to this test, the effect of the School Type is not significant ($F(2, 82407) = 1.98$, $p > .10$).

5.7   Model extensions

The use of the framework of multilevel modeling suggests several extensions for the descriptive and latent regression models we discussed so far. We will explore briefly some of these extensions.

First, the discussion in this chapter was restricted to models that are descriptive on the item side. In the multilevel model, item indicators with fixed effects were included as characteristics of the level-1 units, the measurement occasions. Instead of the item indicators, externally observed item properties can be included in the model as level-1 predictors, resulting in explanatory models for the item side. The model looks the same as the descriptive and the latent regression models described above, but this time the level-1 predictors are not item indicators but rather item properties, whose number is typically smaller than the number of items, $K < I$ (see Chapter 6).

Second, in this chapter we focused on multilevel models in which only the intercept of the level-1 equation varies on higher levels. It is also possible that one or more other regression coefficients of the level-1 equation varies over persons. Equation 5.14 extends the 2-level latent regression model, by allowing that besides the intercept, the weight of the first item property varies over persons, partly randomly, and partly according to person properties:

$$\eta_{pi} = \theta_{p0} + \theta_{p1} X_{i1} + \sum_{k=2}^{K} \beta_k X_{ik},$$

$$\theta_{p0} = \sum_{j=1}^{J} \vartheta_{j0} Z_{pj} + \varepsilon_{p0},$$

$$\theta_{p1} = \sum_{j=1}^{J} \vartheta_{j1} Z_{pj} + \varepsilon_{p1},$$

(5.14)

with ϑ_{j0} and ϑ_{j1} as the fixed effects of predictor j on the random intercept and the effect of the first item property, respectively; with $\varepsilon_p = \begin{pmatrix} \varepsilon_{p0} \\ \varepsilon_{p1} \end{pmatrix} \sim$ $N(\mathbf{0}, \boldsymbol{\Sigma})$, where $\mathbf{0}$ is a vector of zero means and $\boldsymbol{\Sigma}$ is the variance-covariance matrix of the random effects. As for the preceding models, if one finds that the effect of the constant predictor varies over persons, this means that persons differ in their overall performance. In the model of Equation 5.14, however, persons also can differ in the effect of an item property. Thus, instead of one, two kinds of abilities are modeled; see Chapter 8 for a discussion of such models. Note that ϑ_{j1} indicates how large the effect is of the jth person predictor on the random effect of the first item predictor.

Third, the items were assumed to be fixed. Item indicators were used as level-1 predictors with fixed effects. Sometimes however, it is plausible to consider the items to be a random set. If both items and persons are considered to be random, the model includes random item effects and random person effects. Items and persons therefore are not modeled with binary indicators, but rather define two sources of random variation. The data structure is not hierarchical anymore, since items are not nested within persons, and persons are not nested within items. Rather we have a model with observation occasions (1st level) nested within items and within persons (2nd level). Since we can distinguish two kinds of classification on the same level which are crossed in the design, the model is often called a cross-classification model or a crossed random-effects model (Goldstein, 1987a; Raudenbush, 1993). For an application of crossed random-effects models in psychometrics, see Van den Noortgate, De Boeck and Meulders (2003). Models with randomly varying item effects are discussed in Chapter 6.

Finally, the models can be adapted to allow for heteroscedasticity from the second level on. Heteroscedasticity refers to the phenomenon that the residual variance depends on the level of a predictor. To model heteroscedasticity, a property is assumed to have random effects for the units it describes. For instance, let us look back at the descriptive 2-level model (Equations 5.5 and 5.6). Suppose that on the second level a person property Z_1, such as age, is added to explain the random intercept, and that the effect of this person property is defined to be random over persons. Then, it follows that

$$\theta_{p0} = \zeta_{p1} Z_{p1} + \varepsilon_{p0}, \tag{5.15}$$

with $\varepsilon_p = \begin{pmatrix} \varepsilon_{p0} \\ \zeta_{p1} \end{pmatrix} \sim N(\mathbf{0}, \boldsymbol{\Sigma})$. As a result, the variance between persons is not constant anymore, but is a quadratic function of the age:

$$\sigma^2_{\theta_{(p)}} = \sigma^2_{\varepsilon_{(p)0}} + 2\mathrm{cov}(\varepsilon_{p0}, \zeta_{p1}) Z_{p1} + \sigma^2_{\zeta_{(p)1}} Z^2_{p1}. \tag{5.16}$$

In case the variance depends on the person group, groups can be dummy coded with as many indicators as there are groups, and the effect of the indicators is defined to be random over persons. For example, to estimate the within-group variance for males and females separately, two binary indicators are used (Z_p Male and Z_p Female), each with an effect that varies at random over persons (ζ_p Male and ζ_p Female, respectively):

$$\theta_{p0} = \zeta_p \text{ Male} Z_p \text{ Male} + \zeta_p \text{ Female} Z_p \text{ Female}. \qquad (5.17)$$

It is necessary to fix the covariance of θ_p Male and θ_p Female to zero, since there is no information available on their correlation.

5.8   Concluding remarks

Since their appearance in the literature during the 1980s (Goldstein, 1987b; Raudenbush, 1988), hierarchical (generalized) linear models have become more and more popular in an increasing number of research domains. One of the main reasons for the success of the models is their flexibility. In this chapter, we showed that hierarchical generalized linear models can be useful in item response modeling applications. In fact, the commonly used item response models can be reformulated as hierarchical generalized linear models, as shown before (e.g., Adams, et al., 1997; Kamata, 2001; Raudenbush & Sampson, 1999). For example, the simple Rasch model and the latent regression model are a descriptive and a latent regression 2-level model respectively. We showed how these models can be extended by including one or more additional levels, in order to model random person group effects, thereby extending the traditional item response models. For the latest developments of hierarchical (generalized) linear models, including the parameter estimation and testing, see for example, Raudenbush and Bryk (2002), Goldstein (2003), Hox (2002), and Snijders and Bosker (1999).

5.9   Software

5.9.1   2-level models (verbal aggression data)

For the latent regression model from Section 5.4, with two person predictors (TA and Gender), the model formulation using MLwiN reads as follows:

Code

$$
\begin{aligned}
\text{logit}(\pi_{ij}) = \ & \beta_2 \text{item1}_{ij} + \beta_3 \text{item2}_{ij} + \beta_4 \text{item3}_{ij} + \beta_5 \text{item4}_{ij} + \\
& \beta_6 \text{item5}_{ij} + \beta_7 \text{item6}_{ij} + \beta_8 \text{item7}_{ij} + \beta_9 \text{item8}_{ij} + \\
& \beta_{10} \text{item9}_{ij} + \beta_{11} \text{item10}_{ij} + \beta_{12} \text{item11}_{ij} + \beta_{13} \text{item12}_{ij} + \\
& \beta_{14} \text{item13}_{ij} + \beta_{15} \text{item14}_{ij} + \beta_{16} \text{item15}_{ij} + \beta_{17} \text{item16}_{ij} +
\end{aligned}
$$

$$\beta_{18}\text{item17}_{ij} + \beta_{19}\text{item18}_{ij} + \beta_{20}\text{item19}_{ij} + \beta_{21}\text{item20}_{ij} +$$
$$\beta_{22}\text{item21}_{ij} + \beta_{23}\text{item22}_{ij} + \beta_{24}\text{item23}_{ij} + \beta_{25}\text{item24}_{ij} +$$
$$\beta_{26}\text{Gender}_j + \beta_{27}\text{TA}_j + u_{1j}\text{cons}$$

Comments

1. For the descriptive 2-level model, the terms $\beta_{26}\text{Gender}_j$ and $\beta_{27}\text{TA}_j$ are omitted.

2. Other aspects of the model setup and parameter estimation with MLwiN are explained in Chapter 12 and on the website indicated in the Preface.

5.9.2   3-level models (mathematics and science data)

Code for the descriptive 3-level model

```
%glimmix(data=MASC, procopt = covtest,
 stmts=%str(class school student;
 model score=item1 item2 item3 item4 item5 item6 item7
 item8 item9 item10 item11 item12 item13 item14 item15
 item16 item17 item18 item19 item20 item21 item22 item23
 item24 item25 item26 item27 item28 item29 item30 item31
 item42 item43 item44 item45 item46 item47 item48 item49
 item50 item51 item52 item53 item54 item55 item56 item57
 item58 item59item60 item61 item62 item63 item64 item65
 item66 /solution noint;
 random intercept/sub=student(school);
 random intercept / sub = school;
 parms .5 .5 1 /eqcons = 3;), error = binomial); run;
```

Code for the latent regression 3-level model

```
%glimmix(data=MASC, procopt = covtest,
 stmts=%str(class school student gender type;
 model score=item1 item2 item3 item4 item5 item6 item7
 item8 item9 item10 item11 item12 item13 item14 item15
 item16 item17 item18 item19 item20 item21 item22 item23
 item24 item25 item26 item27 item28 item29 item30 item31
 item42 item43 item44 item45 item46 item47 item48 item49
 item50 item51 item52 item53 item54 item55 item56 item57
 item58 item59item60 item61 item62 item63 item64 item65
 item66 gender type bachelor /solution noint;
 random intercept/sub=student(school);
 random intercept / sub = school;
 parms .5 .5 1 /eqcons = 3;), error = binomial); run;
```

Comments

1. Because for the latent regression 3-level model of the second example, only the fixed part of the model has changed, the `random` statements of the second example are the same as those of the first.

2. The `model` statement is adapted in the second example by including three more independent variables: `gender, type, bachelor`. Because Gender and School Type are categorical variables, they are included in the `class` statement as well (as `gender` and `type`, respectively).

5.10   Exercises

1. The item indicators used in the Rasch model can be seen as observation occasion properties. Explain why that is so and where the error term of the level-1 units can be found.

2. Use MLwiN to reanalyze the verbal aggression data using the latent regression 2-level model (see Chapter 2), but now with PQL. The difference between PQL and PQL2 is explained in Chapter 12.

3. In Section 5.6, the mathematics and science data have been analyzed using a descriptive 3-level model. In traditional item response modeling, levels above the person level (e.g., the level of schools) are usually ignored. Use GLIMMIX to explore the consequences of ignoring a higher level for the results of the analysis, by comparing the parameter estimates of the example with those obtained using a 2-level model.

4. Adapt the descriptive model for the mathematics and science data to check if the within-school variance depends on the school type (i.e., a case of heteroscedasticity). Use GLIMMIX or MLwiN to estimate and test the parameters.

5. Check to what extent mathematics is a separate source of individual differences in the mathematics and science data. See the last extention in Section 5.7. It is recommended to read Chapter 8 first, but use MLwiN for the estimation.

5.11   References

Adams, R.J., Wilson, M., & Wu, M. (1997). Multilevel item response models: An approach to errors in variables regression. *Journal of Educational and Behavioral Statistics, 22,* 47–76.

Bock, R.D., & Aitkin, M. (1981). Marginal maximum likelihood estimation of item parameters: Application of an EM algorithm. *Psychometrika, 46,* 443–459.

Breslow, N.E., & Clayton, D.G. (1993). Approximate inference in generalized linear mixed models. *Journal of the American Statistical Association, 88,* 9–25.

Bryk, A.S., Raudenbush, S.W., & Congdon, R.T. (1996). *HLM: Hierarchical Linear and Non-linear Modeling with the HLM/2L and HLM/3L Programs.* Chicago, IL: Scientific Software.

Goldstein, H. (1987a). Multilevel covariance components models. *Biometrika, 74,* 430–431.

Goldstein, H. (1987b). *Multilevel Models in Educational and Social Research.* London: Griffin.

Goldstein, H. (2003). *Multilevel Statistical Models (3rd ed.).* London: Arnold.

Goldstein, H., Rasbash, J., Plewis, I., Draper, D., Browne, W., Yang, M., Woodhouse, G., & Healy, M. (1998). *A User's Guide to MLwiN.* Multilevel Project, University of London.

Hox, J. (2002). *Multilevel Analysis. Techniques and Applications.* Mahwah, NJ: Lawrence Erlbaum.

Kamata, A. (2001). Item analysis by the hierarchical generalized linear model. *Journal of Educational Measurement, 38,* 79–93.

Longford, N.T. (1993). *Random Coefficient Models.* Oxford: Clarendon Press.

McCullagh, P., & Nelder, J. A. (1989). *Generalized Linear Models (2nd ed.).* London: Chapman & Hall.

Raudenbush, S.W. (1988). Educational applications of hierarchical linear models: A review. *Journal of Educational Statistics, 13,* 85–116.

Raudenbush, S.W. (1993). A crossed random effects models for unbalanced data with applications in cross-sectional and longitudinal research. *Journal of Educational Statistics, 18,* 321–349.

Raudenbush, S.W., & Bryk, A.S. (2002). *Hierarchical Linear Models: Applications and Data Analysis Methods (2nd ed.).* London: Sage.

Raudenbush, S.W., & Sampson, R. (1999). Assessing direct and indirect effects in multilevel designs with latent variables. *Sociological Methods & Research, 28,* 123–153.

Rijmen, F., Tuerlinkx, F., De Boeck, P., & Kuppens (2003). A nonlinear mixed model framework for item response theory. *Psychological Methods, 8,* 185–205.

Snijders, T.A.B., & Bosker, R.J. (1999). *Multilevel Analysis. An Introduction to Basic and Advanced Multilevel Modeling.* London: Sage.

Spielberger, C.D. (1988). *State-Trait Anger Expression Inventory Research Edition. Professional Manual.* Odessa, FL: Psychological Assessment Resources.

Van den Noortgate, W., De Boeck, P., Meulders, M. (2003). Cross-classification multilevel logistic models in psychometrics. *Journal of Educational and Behavioral Statistics*. Manuscript accepted for publication.

Wolfinger, R., & O'Connell, M. (1993). Generalized linear mixed models: A pseudo-likelihood approach. *Journal of Statistical Computation and Simulation, 48*, 233–243.

Chapter 6

Models with item and item group predictors

Rianne Janssen
Jan Schepers
Deborah Peres

6.1 Introduction

In the present chapter, the focus is on extending item response models on the item side. Item and item group predictors are included as external factors *and* the item parameters β_i are considered as random effects. When the items are modeled to come from one common distribution, the models are descriptive on the item side. When item predictors of the property type are included, the models are explanatory on the item side. Item groups are a special case of item properties. They refer to binary, non-overlapping properties indicating group membership. The resulting models with item properties can all be described as linear logistic test models (LLTM; Fischer, 1995) with an error term in the prediction of item difficulty. When this random item variation is combined with random person variation, models with *crossed random effects* are obtained. All models in this chapter are of that kind.

The idea of random item variation is relatively uncommon in item response modeling. Traditionally, item effects are treated as fixed. There are a few exceptions to the fixed-item approach. For example, in the Bayesian estimation of standard item response models like the Rasch model (e.g., Swaminathan & Gifford, 1982) one assumes that the items come from a particular prior distribution. This can be seen as a random-effects model for the items with only one item group. One can have several reasons for considering such a model. For example, perhaps the test is seen as a rather homogeneous set of items without a design and with the single purpose of measuring the latent dimension. As another example, the test may be inspired by the theory of domain-referenced testing. A domain represents the knowledge and skills required for mastery of a specific content area. It refers to a universe of items. Test items are considered to be a random sample from this universe. The domain score is the probability of success on a randomly selected item of the domain.

Recently, there has been a renewed interest in Bayesian data analysis (e.g., Gelman, Carlin, Stern & Rubin, 1995). In particular Gibbs sampling techniques gave new possibilities for the estimation of item response models (see e.g., Béguin & Glas, 2001; Maris & Maris, 2002; Patz & Junker, 1999). Using this approach, models with random item effects have also been proposed. Bradlow, Wainer and Wang (1999) extended the basic two- and three-parameter item response model with a random person-by-item effect to account for the effect of testlets. Glas, Wainer, and Bradlow (2000) showed that this model is a special case of bi-factor analysis with one general ability dimension and a specific ability dimension for each testlet. However, this is not what we mean by random item effects. Janssen, Tuerlinckx, Meulders, and De Boeck (2000) included item group predictors into the two-parameter item response model and Glas and Van der Linden (2002) did the same for the three-parameter model. In these hierarchical item response models, items are nested within item groups. Within each item group, the item parameters are modeled as random and the item group parameters are treated as fixed. Mislevy (1988) had already extended the LLTM with an error term using item properties other than item groups. For this model, Janssen, De Boeck, and Schepers (2003) proposed a Gibbs sampling scheme.

In the following, the item side of models with random item variation is described, for (a) the general case where item properties are used, and (b) for the more particular case where item groups are used as predictors. Next, the full model is presented including the person side as well. It will be explained how a Bayesian approach with the Gibbs sampler can be used for such a model. Finally, two applications are described.

6.2   The model on the item side

6.2.1   Item predictors

The LLTM as a starting point

In the verbal aggression data set, the items were constructed according to an orthogonal design with the Situation Type, Behavior Type, and Behavior Mode as factors of the design (see Table 1.1). In Chapter 2, these item predictors were used in a LLTM. The LLTM assumes that item difficulty is equal to a linear combination of the X_{ik}:

$$\beta'_i = \sum_{k=0}^{K} \beta_k X_{ik},$$

so that $\beta'_i = \beta_i$. However, this is a strong assumption. It implies that item difficulty can be perfectly predicted by the item properties. For the verbal aggression data, a high correlation was found between β'_i and β_i, but the correlation was not perfect, implying that the Rasch item difficulty parameters β_i deviated from the item effects β_i' predicted by the linear combination of item properties. In fact, such deviations are a common finding in applications of the LLTM. As a result, the goodness of fit of the model is almost invariably inferior to that of the Rasch model, resulting in a significant likelihood ratio test. This is not surprising: In the LLTM the I item indicators of the Rasch model are replaced with $K < I$ item predictors.

Adding random item variation

As a relaxation of the LLTM, suppose that the Rasch item difficulties β_i can be described by a regression model with item predictors X_{ik}:

$$
\begin{aligned}
\beta_i &= \sum_{k=0}^{K} \beta_k X_{ik} + \varepsilon_i, \\
&= \beta_i' + \varepsilon_i,
\end{aligned}
\tag{6.1}
$$

with $\varepsilon_i \sim N(0, \sigma_\varepsilon^2)$ or, equivalently,

$$
\beta_i \sim N(\beta_i', \sigma_\varepsilon^2).
\tag{6.2}
$$

Interpretation of the random item variation

Equations 6.1 and 6.2 describe a model with item predictors as external factors *and* with random item variation. The model in Equation 6.1 stresses a *random error* interpretation of the random item effect. Items have a structural part, which is described by the linear combination of the item predictors, and an item-specific deviation part, which is described by the ε_i. As in regression analysis, σ_ε^2 refers to the residual variance in the regression of the β_i on the item predictors X_{ik}. The smaller σ_ε^2 in comparison with the total variance of the β_i, the better the explanatory power of the item predictors.

Another interpretation is that the item parameters β_i are *randomly sampled*. This is stressed in the formulation of the model in Equation 6.2. Items that share the same values on the item predictors belong to the same item population. Given these values, the items in the test are considered as exchangeable. Each item population is characterized by an expected difficulty β_i' and a within-population variance σ_ε^2 of item difficulty. Individual items in the test are seen as a random sample from this population and their difficulty β_i may therefore differ from β_i'.

Literature and type of applications

In a sense, Fischer (1995) hinted at the possibility of a random-effects version of the LLTM with both of the above interpretations. He stated that

"... if the formal model of item difficulty specified by an LLTM
for a given item universe is at least approximately true, it should
be possible to predict item difficulty for new items of the same
universe in new samples of persons" (p. 148).

The fact that a model for item difficulty can be approximately true refers
to a random error interpretation. The prediction of item difficulty for new
items refers to a random sampling interpretation.

Mislevy (1988) proposed the model in Equation 6.1 to show that one
can gain information, and, hence, increase the precision of estimation of
the item difficulty parameters of a Rasch model by exploiting the auxiliary
information about the items as described by the item properties. Sheehan
and Mislevy (1990) illustrated that in this way one can integrate a cognitive
theory about the items with the psychometric information as found in a
calibration study. Janssen et al. (2003) further discussed the LLTM and
the random-effects extension of the LLTM as in Equation 6.1.

6.2.2   Item groups as predictors

The model

The random sampling interpretation is especially apt when the items are
partitioned in item groups (item populations). In that case, Equation 6.2
can be rewritten to describe the item difficulty β_{ig} of item i belonging to
group g:

$$\beta_{ig} \sim N\left(\beta_g, \sigma_\varepsilon^2\right), \tag{6.3}$$

where β_g indicates the item group effect and σ_ε^2 the within-group variance.
In Equation 6.3, β_g represents the linear combination of G item group
indicators X_{ig}:

$$\beta_{ig} \sim N\left(\sum_{g=1}^{G} \beta_g X_{ig}, \sigma_\varepsilon^2\right), \tag{6.4}$$

where $G \geq 1$. Equation 6.4 shows that models with (non-overlapping) item
groups as predictors and models with item predictors differ only in the kind
of predictors.

Equations 6.3 and 6.4 describe a simple *multilevel model* for the items.
There are only two levels: Individual items and item groups. The group
weight β_g is fixed. Further extensions are possible. First, one may consider
a three-level structure where the groups of items are themselves sampled
from a larger population of item groups. The item groups may refer to different subdomains (or subtests) that belong to one general, unidimensional
domain (or test). For example, for reading comprehension as a general domain, a sample of reading texts of varying general difficulty can be drawn,
and for each text a sample of items can be presented. Second, in Equation
6.3 or 6.4 it is also assumed that all item groups have the same within-group

variance. Models with group-specific variances are possible. Of course, such heteroscedastic models require data sets with a sufficiently large number of items in each item group to estimate the variances in a reliable way.

Literature and type of applications

The two-level model on the item side can be applied in test designs where the items in the test are considered to be a random sample from a larger population of items. In such cases, sets of items in the test can be considered as exchangeable given group membership. Consequently, the (fixed) group effects become the focus of interest rather than the individual item effects.

As a first example of application, Janssen et al. (2000) applied their multilevel item model to a test design for domain-referenced measurement. They analyzed a test where the items were partitioned according to several curriculum standards in reading comprehension for primary education in Flanders. Each curriculum standard specified a required level of processing (describing, structuring, or evaluating) and a type of text (e.g., school texts, stories, or advertisements). All curriculum standards referred to one common, underlying dimension of reading comprehension, but their average difficulty differed. Every student received a domain score on each curriculum standard. The domain score was estimated by calculating the success probability on a typical, fictitious item of the domain, namely an item with difficulty equal to the mean of the item distribution of the domain. The domain score was calculated as

$$\frac{\exp\left(\theta_p - \beta_g\right)}{1 + \exp\left(\theta_p - \beta_g\right)}.$$

Using cut-off points on the domain score scale, examinees were classified in different levels of mastery for each domain.

As a second example, Glas and Van der Linden (2002) referred to the area of automated item generation as a field of application of their multilevel model on the item side. In automated item generation (e.g., Bejar, 2002; Embretson, 1999), items are considered to be clones from a parent, but the cloning is not perfect, making individual item variation possible. Hence, each parent characterizes a distribution of items. The expected value of the parent distribution is the item parameter of a typical or 'average' item of the parent. The variance of the parent distribution indicates how strongly individual item parameters deviate from the typical item. In some testing situations, a person's ability parameter θ_p can then be estimated by using the fixed (hyper)parameters that describe the parents' distribution, and by treating the item parameters as random. Note that in their two-level item response model, Glas and Van der Linden (2002) only described the parents as item groups without a design (Equation 6.3). Another way of modeling automatically generated items is to describe them as being generated from a parent that is defined by a set of item design variables, and, hence, use a model with item properties (Equation 6.1).

6.3   The full model

6.3.1   Fixed person effects

Equations 6.1 to 6.4 describe only the systematic component of the item response model for the item mode. Hence, they should be complemented with a model for the person mode. In principle, the person effects can be considered either as fixed or as random. As noted in the Introduction to Part II and in Chapter 12, fixed person effects are equivalent to a joint maximum likelihood formulation of the model. Modeling the persons' main effects with fixed rather than random effects is generally not the best choice. First, it is not in line with the standard statistical formulation for the person side. It is common to consider persons as sampled from a population of persons. Second, models with fixed person weights require a large number of person predictors (one indicator per person) and consequently also a large number of parameters. Third, when combined with fixed item effects, inconsistent estimates are obtained (Haberman, 1997). Some software packages for GLMM such as the NLMIXED procedure from SAS do not allow for crossed random variation. A possible way out would be to use fixed person effects. However, it is unclear what the quality of the estimated predictor weights would be in such a model. For example, using NLMIXED for the verbal aggression data, the estimates were quite different for the regular LLTM with fixed versus with random effects for the persons. These practical estimation problems and the earlier mentioned more theoretical problems have discouraged us from pursuing models with fixed person effects.

6.3.2   Random person effects

Complementing Equations 6.1 to 6.4 with random person weights leads to a two-mode random-effects model or crossed random-effects model. When the random person effects concern the intercept, the conditional formulation of the full model reads as:

$$\eta_{pi} = \theta_p Z_{p0} - \sum_{k=0}^{K} \beta_k X_{ik} + \varepsilon_i, \qquad (6.5)$$

with $\theta_p \sim N(0, \sigma_\theta^2)$ and $\varepsilon_i \sim N(0, \sigma_\varepsilon^2)$ (remember that η_{pi} is conditional on θ_p and in this case it is also conditional on ε_i).

6.3.3   Graphical representation

Figure 6.1 gives a graphical representation of the model in Equation 6.5. Note that the random component and the link function are omitted. The item parameter β_i is explained in terms of the item predictors X_{ik} and their effects β_k, and the unexplained part is ε_i. The person parameter θ_p can be seen as the random effect of the constant person predictor. Note that elsewhere θ_p is sometimes seen as the random effect of the constant item predictor, but our formulation is equivalent and leaves the constant item predictor for the random item effect.

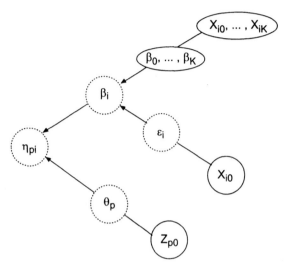

FIGURE 6.1. Graphical representation of a model with item properties, random item effects, and random person effects.

6.4   Bayesian estimation

6.4.1   Estimating crossed random-effects models in general

The estimation of crossed random-effects models is complicated when using a maximum likelihood approach because there is an integral for each pair of a person and an item (see Chapter 12). The alternatives are an approximative method based on a linearization of the integrand, as in the SAS macro GLIMMIX, and a Bayesian method. For an application of GLIMMIX to a crossed random-effects model see Van den Noortgate, De Boeck, and Meulders (2003). For crossed random-effects models with item predictors, Janssen et al. (2003) showed that Bayesian estimation and GLIMMIX gave a comparable goodness of recovery. In the following, we will briefly summarize the main features of Bayesian data analysis.

6.4.2   A short review of Bayesian data analysis

Posterior-based inferences

An essential feature of Bayesian data analysis is that all unknowns are treated as random variables. Consequently, when fitting a model to a data set, the model includes both a likelihood function, $g(y|\theta)$, and a prior distribution for the parameters, $g(\theta)$, where $g(\cdot)$ is a general notation for a density function. Bayesian inference is based on the posterior distribution, which is a probability function on the parameters of the model, $g(\theta|y)$. Using Bayes' theorem, one can derive that the posterior distribution is proportional to the product of the likelihood and the prior distribution:

$$g(\theta|y) \propto g(y|\theta)g(\theta).$$

The influence of the prior distributions on the posterior can be kept small by using uninformative priors. The posterior distribution of a parameter is usually summarized by its mean, which is called the expected *a posteriori* estimator (EAP). Its standard deviation is used to describe the posterior uncertainty for the parameter at hand.

Markov chain Monte Carlo methods

For a long time, the applicability of Bayesian data analysis depended heavily on the mathematical tractability of the posterior. This changed with the advent of Markov chain Monte Carlo (MCMC) techniques (Gelman et al., 1995; Gilks, Richardson & Spiegelhalter, 1996; Tanner, 1996). MCMC refers to methods of simulating random samples from any theoretical multivariate distribution. Features of the theoretical distribution can then be estimated by corresponding features of the random samples. The sampling scheme is based on a Markov chain, which after a burn-in period converges to the theoretical distribution. When using MCMC to describe the posterior distribution of a model, successive samples of parameter values are drawn from that distribution. For each model parameter, the mean and standard deviation of these samples are used as summary measures. There exist various versions of MCMC methods, such as the Gibbs sampling or the Metropolis-Hastings sampling techniques. Patz and Junker (1999) described the implementation of several of these for item response models. In the present chapter, we will only describe data augmented Gibbs sampling (see Section 6.4.3). This method was originally developed for item response models with the probit link function, but results can be obtained on an approximate logit scale using the scale transformation discussed in Section 1.7.3.

Model checking

According to Gelman et al. (1995), the usual Bayesian prior-to-posterior analysis cannot proceed without model checking. Given the two components of the posterior distribution, one can check the sensitivity of the model inferences to the choice of a particular prior distribution and one can check the plausibility of the model (likelihood) for the data. For the latter aspect of model checking, Meng (1994) and Gelman, Meng, and Stern (1996) developed the technique of posterior predictive checks (PPC). The basic idea of a PPC is that "if the model fits, then replicated data generated under the model should look similar to observed data" (Gelman et al., 1995, p. 165). Model fit is assessed by defining a test quantity for an aspect of the data that is relevant to the validity of the model. Variation of the test quantity for the replicated data denotes the random fluctuation of the test quantity under the model's own assumptions. If the model does not fit the data, and when the test quantity is defined in the appropriate direction, the test quantity should be systematically higher when calculated on the observed data, than when calculated on the replicated data generated under the model. A PPC p-value for assessing the model fit is defined as

$$\text{PPC } p\text{-value} = 1 - \Pr(T_{obs} > T_{rep} \mid \boldsymbol{Y}),$$

where T_{obs} denotes a test quantity $T(.)$ that is calculated on the data, and T_{rep} denotes the same test quantity calculated on the replicated data. $T(.)$ is either a statistic of the data (i.e., a function of the data only), denoted by $T(\boldsymbol{Y})$ and $T(\boldsymbol{Y}_{rep})$, or it is also a function of the parameters, and it is then called a 'discrepancy measure,' denoted by $T(\boldsymbol{Y}, \Theta)$ and $T(\boldsymbol{Y}_{rep}, \Theta)$, where Θ is the parameter space. Small values of the PPC p-value indicate bad fit. Note that when using a PPC, researchers can develop their own test quantities, depending on the aspects of the model one is interested in. In contrast with classical test statistics, Bayesian test quantities (1) are not restricted to test quantities with theoretically derived sampling distributions, and (2) allow for dependence of the test quantities on parameter estimates (which are not a function of the data in a Bayesian analysis). Using samples from the posterior, one can also calculate descriptive measures of fit. For the model with item predictors, one could for example use the proportion of variance accounted for by the linear combination of item predictors.

6.4.3 Data augmented Gibbs sampling for models with item (group) predictors

Posterior distribution

Suppose the following crossed random-effects item response model is estimated:

$$\begin{aligned}
\eta_{pi} &= \theta_p - \beta_i, \\
\theta_p &\sim N\left(0, \sigma_\theta^2\right), \\
\beta_i &\sim N\left(\beta_i', \sigma_\varepsilon^2\right), \\
\beta_i' &= \sum_{k=0}^{K} \beta_k X_{ik}.
\end{aligned} \tag{6.6}$$

As before, β_i' denotes the structural, fixed part of item difficulty, which is determined by the item predictor matrix X. Depending on X, Equation 6.6 can refer to a model with item properties, to a model with item group predictors, or to the null model where all items come from one population.

In our applications, an uninformative, flat prior was chosen for each fixed parameter β_k. As is convenient for variance parameters, a scaled inverse-χ^2 distribution was chosen with scale parameter s^2 and ν degrees of freedom for both variance parameters σ_θ^2 and σ_ε^2 (with $\nu = 1$). For the parameters θ_p and β_i no prior distribution is needed, as the model already specifies a distribution for them. Given these prior distributions, the posterior distribution of the model equals

$$g(\boldsymbol{\theta}, \boldsymbol{\beta}, \sigma_\varepsilon^2, \sigma_\theta^2 | \boldsymbol{Y}, \boldsymbol{X}) \propto$$
$$g(\sigma_\theta^2)g(\sigma_\varepsilon^2) \times \left(\prod_{p=1}^{P} N(\theta_p; 0, \sigma_\theta^2)\right) \left(\prod_{i=1}^{I} N\left(\beta_i; \beta_i', \sigma_\varepsilon^2\right)\right)$$
$$\times \left(\prod_{p=1}^{P} \prod_{i=1}^{I} \Pr(Y_{pi} = 1 | \theta_p, \beta_i)^{y_{pi}} (1 - \Pr(Y_{pi} = 1 | \theta_p, \beta_i))^{1 - y_{pi}}\right),$$

where $N(\beta_i; \beta_i', \sigma_\varepsilon^2)$ and $N(\theta_p; 0, \sigma_\theta^2)$ represent the normal density for β_i and for θ_p, respectively. The posterior consists of three parts: (a) the prior distributions with densities $g(\sigma_\theta^2)$ and $g(\sigma_\varepsilon^2)$, (b) the random-effects distribution for the persons and for the items, and (c) the likelihood of the data given the person and item parameters. Independence assumptions are made in all three parts: (a) independence of the priors, (b) independence of the person and item parameters, and (c) independence of the observations across persons (i.e., experimental independence) and of the observations within persons given θ_p (i.e., local independence).

Data augmented Gibbs sampling

For the estimation of the model based on a MCMC approach, we use the Gibbs sampler with data augmentation. The Gibbs sampler takes a modular approach to sampling from the posterior distribution. It creates a Markov chain by successively sampling from a set of full conditional distributions. The Gibbs sampler is therefore also called alternating conditional sampling (Gelman et al., 1995). Each full conditional distribution describes the conditional posterior distribution of a parameter (or parameter vector) given the previously sampled value of all the other parameters.

A crucial step in the Gibbs sampler is the derivation of the conditional distributions. Albert (1992) showed that for normal-ogive item response models these conditional distributions can be derived analytically if the posterior distribution of the model is augmented with latent data (Tanner, 1996). See Maris and Maris (2002) for the logistic model. The latent data were already introduced in Chapter 1 and consist of the continuous, covert variable V_{pi} for each corresponding pair of person p and item i. As was explained, it is assumed that

$$V_{pi} \sim N(\eta_{pi}, 1) \text{ with } \begin{cases} V_{pi} \leq 0 & \text{when} \quad Y_{pi} = 0, \\ V_{pi} > 0 & \text{when} \quad Y_{pi} = 1. \end{cases} \tag{6.7}$$

Hence, the probability that $V_{pi} > 0$ equals the probability of a 1-response. By including the latent data, the posterior distribution changes into a joint posterior density of all model parameters (latent data and the other parameters):

$$g(\boldsymbol{V}, \boldsymbol{\theta}, \boldsymbol{\beta}, \sigma_\varepsilon^2, \sigma_\theta^2 | \boldsymbol{Y}, \boldsymbol{X}) \propto$$
$$g(\sigma_\theta^2)g(\sigma_\varepsilon^2) \times \left(\prod_{p=1}^{P} N(\theta_p; 0, \sigma_\theta^2) \right) \left(\prod_{i=1}^{I} N(\beta_i; \beta_i', \sigma_\varepsilon^2) \right) \times$$
$$\left(\prod_{p=1}^{P} \prod_{i=1}^{I} N(V_{pi}; \theta_p - \beta_i, 1) \left(I(V_{pi} > 0)I(Y_{pi} = 1) + I(V_{pi} \leq 0)I(Y_{pi} = 0) \right) \right),$$

where $I(.)$ is the indicator function. Intuitively speaking, one could say that by introducing the latent data variables V_{pi}, the observed data are projected on the same continuous scale as the parameters of the model. Indeed, one could rewrite Equation 6.7 as

$$V_{pi} = \eta_{pi} + \varepsilon_{pi},$$

with $\varepsilon_{pi} \sim N(0, 1)$. Consequently, a sampled value of V_{pi} implies that for the pair of person p and item i, θ_p can be approximated by $V_{pi} + \beta_i$, and, vice versa, β_i can be approximated by $\theta_p - V_{pi}$. These latent residuals for θ_p and β_i, respectively, play a major role in the full conditional distributions for θ_p and β_i.

Full conditional distributions

Table 6.1 presents the full conditional distributions for all the parameters in the augmented posterior, for the case of the normal-ogive model. The constant c in Table 6.1 equals 1 if the normal-ogive model is used and 1.7 if one wants to approximate a logistic model (see Section 1.7.3). This is the inverse of the operation that is used to approximate the normal-ogive model from the logistic model. When calculating the full conditional posterior distribution for a particular parameter from the augmented posterior, a lot of parameters cancel out due to the independence assumptions made. The mathematical tractability of the conditional distributions is not only due to the data augmentation step, but also to the distributional form of the priors and of the random-effects model. As an example, the derivations of the full conditional distribution for θ_p and σ_θ^2 are presented in Section 6.10.

TABLE 6.1. Full conditional distributions of the data augmented Gibbs sampler for an item response model with random item effects.

$$V_{pi}|\theta_p, \beta_i, Y_{pi} \sim \begin{cases} N\left(\theta_p - \beta_i, c^2\right) \text{ truncated at 0 to the right if } Y_{pi} = 0 \\ N\left(\theta_p - \beta_i, c^2\right) \text{ truncated at 0 to the left if } Y_{pi} = 1 \end{cases}$$

$$\theta_p|\boldsymbol{\beta}, \boldsymbol{V}_p, \sigma_\varepsilon^2 \sim N\left(\sum_{i=1}^{I}(V_{pi} + \beta_i)\Big/\left(I + \frac{c^2}{\sigma_\theta^2}\right), \quad c^2\Big/\left(I + \frac{c^2}{\sigma_\theta^2}\right)\right)$$

$$\beta_i|\boldsymbol{\beta}, \boldsymbol{V}_i, \sigma_\varepsilon^2, \beta_i' \sim N\left(\left(\sum_{p=1}^{P}(\theta_p - V_{pi}) + \frac{c^2\beta_i'}{\sigma_\varepsilon^2}\right)\Big/\left(P + \frac{c^2}{\sigma_\varepsilon^2}\right),\right.$$

$$\left. c^2\Big/\left(P + \frac{c^2}{\sigma_\varepsilon^2}\right)\right)$$

$$(\beta_0, \beta_1, \ldots, \beta_k, \ldots, \beta_K)|\boldsymbol{\beta}, \sigma_\varepsilon^2, \boldsymbol{X} \sim N\left((\boldsymbol{X}'\boldsymbol{X})^{-1}\boldsymbol{X}'\boldsymbol{\beta}, (\boldsymbol{X}'\boldsymbol{X})^{-1}\sigma_\varepsilon^2\right)$$

$$\sigma_\theta^2|\theta, \mu_\theta \sim \text{Inv-}\chi^2\left(P + \nu, \left(\sum_{p=1}^{P}(\theta_p - \mu_\theta)^2 + s^2\right)\Big/(P + \nu)\right)$$

$$\sigma_\varepsilon^2|\boldsymbol{\beta}, \beta_i' \sim \text{Inv-}\chi^2\left(I + \nu, \left(\sum_{i=1}^{I}(\beta_i - \beta_i')^2 + s^2\right)\Big/(I + \nu)\right)$$

where $\boldsymbol{V}_p = (V_{p1}, \ldots, V_{pi}, \ldots, V_{pI})'$
$\boldsymbol{V}_i = (V_{1i}, \ldots, V_{pi}, \ldots, V_{Pi})'$
$\boldsymbol{\beta} = (\beta_1, \ldots, \beta_i, \ldots, \beta_I)'$

When taking a closer look at Table 6.1, one can see that the full conditional distribution for V_{pi} is an equivalent expression to Equation 6.7. For θ_p and β_i, the mean of the conditional posterior distribution is determined by the sum of their latent residuals and by the mean of their random-effects distribution (0 for θ_p, β_i' for β_i). For β_i, one can see that the larger the variance is of the random effect, the smaller the impact of the mean random effect is on the mean of the conditional posterior distribution and the smaller the gain is in the precision of the obtained estimate by the inclusion of the item predictor matrix X. For the item predictor weights β_k, a multivariate normal distribution is defined. The mean and variance of this distribution are obtained from a standard linear regression of the item difficulties β_i on the item predictor matrix X. For example, when the items are modeled to come just from one distribution (i.e., $\beta_i \sim \mathrm{N}(\mu_\beta, \sigma_\varepsilon^2)$), the full condition distribution is

$$\mu_\beta | \boldsymbol{\beta}, \sigma_\varepsilon^2 \sim N \left(\sum_{i=1}^{I} \beta_i / I, \sigma_\varepsilon^2 / I \right).$$

Finally, the variance parameters σ_θ^2 and σ_ε^2 are determined both by the sum of squared differences of the parameters at hand and by the scale parameter s^2 of the prior. It can be seen that the information in the prior with ν degrees of freedom is equivalent with the information of ν additional observations, for σ_θ^2 and σ_ε^2, respectively.

All full conditional posterior distributions are standard statistical distributions: the (truncated) normal, the multivariate normal, and the scaled inverse-χ^2. One can sample directly from these distributions using standard routines. Hence, given Table 6.1, estimating the item response model with item predictors using the data augmented Gibbs sampler implies successively sampling from these distributions. At each iteration, the previously sampled parameter values are taken as constant values. After the sampling process is finished, summary measures are calculated for each sample of parameter values. This is not only done for the fixed effects of the model (β_k, σ_θ^2 and σ_ε^2), but also for the random effects θ_p and β_i. Hence, in contrast with a likelihood-based approach, no empirical Bayes procedure is needed to estimate individual random effects.

We will now report on two applications. In Section 6.5 a model with item properties as predictors is used for the verbal aggression data, and a Bayesian approach is followed. In Section 6.6 a model with item groups as predictors is used for the mathematics and science data, using GLIMMIX for the estimation.

6.5 Application of the crossed-random effects model with item predictors to the verbal aggression data

6.5.1 Method of model estimation and model checking

Method of model estimation

The model with item predictors was estimated for the verbal aggression data using the data augmented Gibbs sampler. Details about the estimation are given in Section 6.8.1. The same item design and the same coding scheme for the item predictors (see Figure 2.7) were used as in Chapter 2 for the LLTM. The results were compared with those obtained for the LLTM, when estimated with a Bayesian method (Janssen et al., 2003) or with the NLMIXED procedure from SAS.

Method of model checking

Three important aspects of the model were checked. First, the general goodness of fit of the model was evaluated. Replicated data were obtained by comparing the probability of a correct response for each pair of θ_p and β_i with a random draw from a uniform distribution on the unit interval. The χ^2- statistic was used as a discrepancy measure (see also Janssen et al., 2000). For each draw from the posterior, the sorted vector θ was partitioned in five adjacent ability groups. The χ^2- statistic compared the observed and expected number of 1- and 0-responses for each item in the different ability groups. It was calculated for each Gibbs iteration for both the observed and for the replicated data. The resulting values of the χ^2-statistics were summed over items for the general test. The degree of deviance of the model for the data was expressed by a Bayesian p-value, which was estimated as 1 minus the proportion of iterations for which the discrepancy measure was larger for the data than for the replicated data. Small Bayesian p-values indicate bad fit. Second, the goodness of fit was also evaluated in the same way for each item separately.

Third, the goodness of fit of the item explanatory part of the model was assessed. The correlation over items between β_i and β_i' was calculated for each draw from the posterior. The squared correlation was used as a measure of the proportion of explained variance in the β_i by the item predictors in X. Also, the residual $\beta_i - \beta_i'$ was calculated for each item separately for each draw from the posterior. The residual values were summarized using a 90% and 95% central posterior interval. Items for which the interval did not contain the value zero were not in line with the item explanatory part of the model.

6.5.2 Results

Model checking

The model for the data fitted well using the general test. For the total data set, the χ^2- based PPC led to a Bayesian p-value of .24. For the individual items, the Bayesian p-value varied between .16 and .62. As an illustration, Figure 6.2 gives a plot of the posterior mean of the observed proportion of correct answers against the posterior mean of θ_p in the five ability groups for the worst fitting item (Store - Want - Curse, $p = .16$) and for the best fitting item (Bus - Do - Curse, $p = .48$). Both plots are compared with the theoretical item response curve obtained using the value of the posterior mean of β_i as item difficulty. Although not deviant at the 5%-level, the worst fitting item had a lower slope than the other items in the data set.

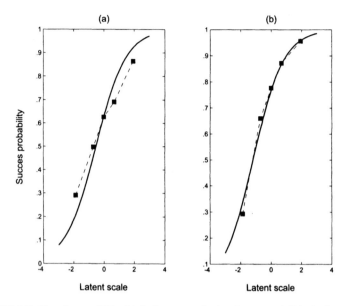

FIGURE 6.2. Goodness of fit of (a) the worst fitting item, and (b) the best fitting item on the χ^2-based PPC.

Also the model for the item parameters fitted well. The posterior mean of the squared correlation between β_i and β_i' was .89 with a posterior standard deviation of .02. This is comparable to the correlation of .94 mentioned in Section 2.5.3, which was calculated between the item parameter estimates from the Rasch model and the reconstructed item parameters from the LLTM. A correlation of .94 corresponds to a proportion of explained variance of .89. Hence, the item design variables predicted item difficulty very well. Nevertheless, for some items the main effects of Behavior Mode, Behavior Type, and Situation Type were not sufficient to explain item difficulty. Four items were deviant according to the 95% central posterior interval and eight items according to the 90% central posterior interval. As an illustration, the posterior mean of β_i is plotted against the posterior mean of β_i' for the three types of behavior (Curse, Scold, Shout) in two situations. Figure 6.3a displays the results for Want when missing the train. All three items showed good fit, as evidenced by the almost parallel and flat lines between β_i and β_i'. Figure 6.3b displays the results for Do when being disconnected while calling. In this situation, the threshold for cursing and for scolding is higher than predicted by the model. Hence, in comparison with model predictions, cursing and scolding are less likely when being disconnected. Maybe this reflects the fact that this situation is the only one where the actor is most likely alone.

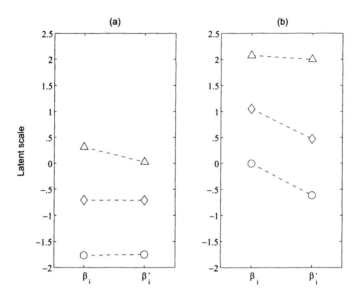

FIGURE 6.3. The posterior mean of β_i and of β_i' for Curse (O), Scold ($\diamond$) and Shout ($\triangle$) for (a) Want when missing the train, and (b) Do when being disconnected from a phone call.

Parameter estimates

Table 6.2 gives the estimates of the item predictor weights and of the variance parameters. The estimates for the LLTM were very similar for the NLMIXED and the Bayesian analysis. However, in comparison with the model with random item effects, the item parameter estimates of the LLTM were smaller in absolute value and their standard error was much smaller. Also the estimated person variance in the LLTM was smaller. The differences between the LLTM and the model with random item effects can be explained by how the model is scaled. As explained in Chapter 1, the larger the unexplained variance is, the smaller the value of the parameter estimates. Adding random effects to a model to describe the data in a better way, results in larger estimates of the other effects. In the present example, the differences between the estimates of the two models are small. This is because the item predictors explained item difficulty very well, so that there is not so much error variance. The difference in standard errors of the two approaches is much larger than the difference in parameter estimates, so that the difference in standard errors can be explained only to a small extent by a scaling effect. For an interpretation of the obtained weight estimates in Table 6.2, we refer to Chapter 2.

TABLE 6.2. Estimates of the item predictor weights and of the variance parameters (with their standard errors) for the LLTM and the model with random item effects (verbal aggression data).

Item predictor	$\beta_i' = \beta_i$		$\beta_i = \beta_i' + \varepsilon_i$
	NLMIXED	Bayesian	Bayesian
Fixed effects			
Do vs Want	.67 (.06)	.68 (.06)	.71 (.17)
Other-to-blame	-1.03 (.06)	-1.03 (.06)	-1.05 (.17)
Blaming*	-1.36 (.05)	-1.35 (.05)	-1.39 (.14)
Expressing**	-.70 (.05)	-.70 (.05)	-.70 (.14)
Intercept	.31 (.09)	.31 (.09)	.33 (.17)
Random effects			
σ_ε^2	--	--	.16 (.06)
σ_θ^2	1.86 (.20)	1.80 (.18)	1.89 (.19)

*Curse & Scold vs Shout
**Curse & Shout vs Scold

6.6 Application of the crossed random-effects model with item groups to the mathematics and science data

6.6.1 Analyses

As an illustration of a model with item groups, the 56 multiple-choice items of the mathematics and science data were analyzed. The data are described in Section 5.6. Remember that the items were partitioned in two domains: mathematics and science. Therefore, the item design matrix consisted of two predictors: the constant predictor and a dummy variable to indicate the mathematics items. This is equivalent with using no constant predictor and two dummy variables: one for the mathematics items and one for the science items. Two models were estimated using the item predictor matrix X: the LLTM, and the model with crossed random item effects. Both models were estimated with GLIMMIX using a logit link (see Section 6.8.2).

6.6.2 Results

The estimation results are displayed in Table 6.3. The items turned out to be relatively easy for the respondents. For the model with random item effects, the average difficulty was $-.72$ for the science items and $-.42 (= -.72 + .30)$ for the mathematics items. On the average, the mean student (with $\theta_p = 0$) had an expected success probability of .67 on the science items and .60 for the mathematics items. The estimated effect of item group predictor (mathematics) was not significant ($p > .10$) so that one may not conclude that the math items were more difficult than the science items. The within-group item variance σ_ε^2 was almost as large as the person variance σ_θ^2. The standard error of the latter variance was much smaller, as it is based on a much larger number of observations (1500 students versus 56 items).

The results of the LLTM differed in three ways from those of the model with random item effects. First, the fixed-effect estimates in the LLTM were slightly smaller in absolute value. Second, the estimated standard errors of the estimates were much smaller in the LLTM. As a consequence, on the basis of the LLTM one would conclude that the mathematics items differ significantly in difficulty from the science items ($p < .001$), whereas the difference is not significant in the model with random item effects. Finally, the estimated person variance was smaller in the LLTM.

TABLE 6.3. GLIMMIX estimates of the fixed effects and of the variance parameters (with their standard errors) for the LLTM and the model with random item effects (mathematics and science data).

Effect	$\beta_i' = \beta$	$\beta_i = \beta_i' + \varepsilon_i$
Fixed Effects		
Intercept	-.66 (.02)	-.72 (.16)
Mathematics	.30 (.01)	.30 (.22)
Random Effects		
σ_ε^2	--	.74 (.14)
σ_θ^2	.65 (.03)	.87 (.04)

The observed differences between the LLTM and the model with random item effects parallel those of the first application, the much larger standard errors included. However, in this second application, this has serious consequences for the inference regarding the effect of the item groups (significant difference between item groups or not). The two models represent different views on the data. One either takes the inter-item variance into account for the statistical test (in the model with random item effects) or not (in the LLTM).

6.7   Concluding remarks

In item response modeling, items are traditionally modeled as fixed effects. It was shown in the present chapter that models with random item effects offer a viable alternative when using item properties or item groups as predictors. These models can be applied in the case where one is not interested in the particular effects of the individual items (models with a single item group), when one has a multilevel model on the item side (models with multiple item groups), or when one is interested in the effects of item properties (models with item properties as predictors). All three models can be defined on the basis of random item effects. Using a model with random item effects seems a useful option given that it is less restrictive than the LLTM.

The application of item response models with random item effects is somewhat hampered by the difficulty of estimating a GLMM with crossed random effects. However, it was shown in the present chapter that a Bayesian approach or GLIMMIX can be used. The Bayesian approach has the advantage that estimates of the individual item effects β_i can also be obtained, giving extra possibilities for model checking. As was indicated in Chapter 2, models with item properties and item group properties as predictors can be combined with models with person properties and person groups as predictors leading to doubly explanatory models with crossed random effects. In such models, the item side and the person side are treated in the same way, using random effects to describe the unexplained variation.

6.8   Software

6.8.1   Model with item predictors (verbal aggression data)

The model with item predictors was estimated using the data augmented Gibbs sampler. For the analysis of the verbal aggression data, a scaled inverse-χ^2 distribution with $s^2 = .0001$ and $\nu = 1$ was used to give an uninformative prior. Five Markov chains of length 4000 were used. The first 1000 iterations were used as burn-in. The maximum value of the convergence measure $\hat{R}$ (Gelman, 1995) equaled $(1.0034)^2$, indicating convergence of the Markov chains. The Gibbs sampling procedure was programmed in Matlab. The code is given on the website indicated in the Preface.

6.8.2   Model with item group predictors (mathematics and science data)

The macro GLIMMIX from SAS was used for all analyses of the mathematics and science data. General information on this macro is given in

Chapters 5 and 12. In all analyses, a random intercept was included on the person side. The origin of the scale was the mean of the random-effects distribution.

Code for crossed-effects model

```
%glimmix(data=MASC,
procopt = covtest, stmts=%str(
class pupil item;
model score = constant mathematics/solution noint;
random intercept / sub = pupil;
random intercept / sub = item;
),
link = logit
error = binomial
);
run;
```

Comments

1. Two item predictors were used: a constant predictor (**constant**) and a dummy variable to indicate mathematics items (**mathematics**). In order to obtain estimates of item difficulty, the item predictors (dummy variables and constant) were first multiplied with -1.
2. In order to estimate the LLTM, the statement **random intercept/sub= item;** is omitted.

6.9   Exercises

1. Derive the full conditional posterior distributions for β_i and σ_ε^2.

2. In Section 2.6 of Chapter 2 a doubly explanatory model was proposed, which was called the latent regression LLTM. Reformulate that model by including a random error component on the item side.

3. Explain why σ_ε^2 is so much smaller than σ_θ^2 in Table 6.2 compared to Table 6.3. Is a near equality of σ_ε^2 and σ_θ^2 (such as in Table 6.3) a good feature of a test?

4. Compare the results of the Bayesian analysis of the verbal aggression data as reported in Table 6.2 with the results you obtain with GLIMMIX. Can you calculate the percentage of explained variance in the β_i from the GLIMMIX output?

5. For the mathematics and science data, estimate a crossed random-effects

model using GLIMMIX (a) where all items are assumed to come from one distribution, and (b) where the mathematics and science items come from a different distribution, each with their own mean and variance. Compare the obtained results with an estimate of the item effects from the output of a Rasch model, also estimated with GLIMMIX.

6.10   Appendix: Derivation of the full conditional distributions for θ_p and σ_θ^2

In the following, the derivation of the full conditional posterior distribution is given for θ_p and σ_θ^2 given the model and the choice of the priors discussed in Section 6.4.3. An important feature of the derivation is that constant values can be freely dropped or added as the full conditional distribution is calculated only up to a proportionality constant. The derivation itself consists in successively expanding the exponents, collecting terms and then completing the wanted distributional form (e.g., the so-called 'completing the square' in θ_p).

$$\theta_p | \boldsymbol{\beta}, \boldsymbol{V}, \sigma_\theta^2$$

$$\propto N(\theta_p; 0, \sigma_\theta^2) \prod_{i=1}^{I} N(V_{pi}; \theta_p - \beta_i, c^2)$$

$$\propto \exp\left(-\frac{1}{2\sigma_\theta^2}\theta_p^2\right) \prod_{i=1}^{I} \exp\left(-\frac{1}{2c^2}(V_{pi} - (\theta_p - \beta_i))^2\right)$$

$$\propto \exp\left(-\frac{1}{2\sigma_\theta^2}\theta_p^2\right) \prod_{i=1}^{I} \exp\left(-\frac{1}{2c^2}\left(\theta_p^2 - 2\theta_p(V_{pi} + \beta_i)\right)\right)$$

$$\propto \exp\left(-\frac{1}{2\sigma_\theta^2}\theta_p^2\right) \exp\left(-\frac{1}{2c^2}\left(I\theta_p^2 - 2\theta_p \sum_{i=1}^{I}(V_{pi} + \beta_i)\right)\right)$$

$$\propto \exp\left(-\frac{1}{2}\left(\left(\frac{I}{c^2} + \frac{1}{\sigma_\theta^2}\right)\theta_p^2 - \frac{2\theta_p}{c^2}\sum_{i=1}^{I}(V_{pi} + \beta_i)\right)\right)$$

$$\propto \exp\left(-\frac{1}{2}\left(\frac{I}{c^2} + \frac{1}{\sigma_\theta^2}\right)\left(\theta_p^2 - \frac{2\theta_p \sum_{i=1}^{I}(V_{pi} + \beta_i)}{c^2(\frac{I}{c^2} + \frac{1}{\sigma_\theta^2})}\right)\right)$$

$$\propto N\left(\theta_p; \frac{\sum_{i=1}^{I}(V_{pi}+\beta_i)}{c^2(\frac{I}{c^2}+\frac{1}{\sigma_\theta^2})}, \frac{1}{\frac{I}{c^2}+\frac{1}{\sigma_\theta^2}}\right)$$

$$\propto N\left(\theta_p; \frac{\sum_{i=1}^{I}(V_{pi}+\beta_i)}{I+\frac{c^2}{\sigma_\theta^2}}, \frac{c^2}{I+\frac{c^2}{\sigma_\theta^2}}\right)\sigma_\theta^2|\theta,\mu_\theta$$

$$\propto g\left(\sigma_\theta^2\right)\exp\prod_{p=1}^{P}\left(\theta_p;\mu_\theta,\sigma_\theta^2\right)$$

$$\propto \left(\sigma_\theta^2\right)^{-\left(\frac{\nu}{2}+1\right)}\exp\left(-\frac{s^2}{2\sigma_\theta^2}\right)\prod_{p=1}^{P}\left(\left(\frac{1}{\sigma_\theta^2}\right)^{\frac{1}{2}}\exp\left(-\frac{1}{2\sigma_\theta^2}(\theta_p-\mu_\theta)^2\right)\right)$$

$$\propto \left(\sigma_\theta^2\right)^{\left(-\frac{\nu}{2}+1\right)}\exp\left(-\frac{s^2}{2\sigma_\theta^2}\right)\left(\sigma_\theta^2\right)^{-\frac{P}{2}}\exp\left(-\frac{1}{2\sigma_\theta^2}\sum_{p=1}^{P}(\theta_p-\mu_\theta)^2\right)$$

$$\propto \left(\sigma_\theta^2\right)^{\left(-\frac{\nu}{2}+1\right)}\left(\sigma_\theta^2\right)^{-\frac{P}{2}}\exp\left(-\frac{1}{2\sigma_\theta^2}\left(s^2+\sum_{p=1}^{P}(\theta_p-\mu_\theta)^2\right)\right)$$

$$\propto \left(\sigma_\theta^2\right)^{\left(-\frac{P+\nu}{2}+1\right)}\exp\left(-\frac{1}{2\sigma_\theta^2}\frac{(P+\nu)}{(P+\nu)}\left(s^2+\sum_{p=1}^{P}(\theta_p-\mu_\theta)^2\right)\right)$$

$$\propto \text{Inv-}\chi^2\left(P+\nu, \left(\sum_{p=1}^{P}(\theta_p-\mu_\theta)^2+s^2\right)/(P+\nu)\right)$$

6.11   References

Albert, J.H. (1992). Bayesian estimation of normal ogive item response curves using Gibbs sampling. *Journal of Educational Statistics, 17*, 251–269.

Béguin, A.A. & Glas, C.A.W. (2001). MCMC estimation and some model-fit analyses of multidimensional IRT models. *Psychometrika, 66*, 541–561.

Bejar, I.I. (2002). Generative testing: From conception to implementation. In S.H. Irvine & P.C. Kyllonen (Eds), *Generating Items from Cognitive Tests: Theory and Practice* (pp. 199–217). Mahwah, NJ: Lawrence

Erlbaum.

Bradlow, E.T., Wainer, H. & Wang, X. (1999). A Bayesian random effects model for testlets. *Psychometrika*, *64*, 153–168.

Embretson, S.E. (1999). Generating items during testing: Psychometric issues and models. *Psychometrika*, *64*, 407–433.

Fischer, G.H. (1995). The linear logistic test model. In G.H. Fischer & I.W. Molenaar (Eds), *Rasch Models: Foundations, Recent Developments, and Applications* (pp. 131–155). New York: Springer.

Gelman, A. (1995). Inference and monitoring convergence. In W.R. Gilks, S.Richardson & D.J. Spiegelhalter (Eds), *Markov Chain Monte Carlo in Practice* (pp. 131–143). New York: Chapman & Hall.

Gelman, A., Carlin, J.B., Stern, H.S. & Rubin, D.B. (1995). *Bayesian Data Analysis*. New York: Chapman & Hall.

Gelman, A., Meng, X.L. & Stern, H.S. (1996). Posterior predictive assessment of model fitness via realized discrepancies (with discussion). *Statistica Sinica*, *6*, 733–807.

Gilks, W.R., Richardson, S. & Spiegelhalter, D.J.E. (1996). *Markov Chain Monte Carlo in Practice*. New York: Chapman & Hall.

Glas, C.A.W. & Van der Linden, W. (2002). Modeling variability in item response models. (Research Report.) University of Twente, Faculty of Educational Science and Technology, Department of Educational Measurement and Data Analysis.

Glas, C.A.W., Wainer, H. & Bradlow, E.T. (2000). MML and EAP estimates for the testlet response model. In W.J. Van der Linden & C.A.W. Glas (Eds), *Computerized Adaptive Testing: Theory into Practice* (pp. 271–287). Boston, MA: Kluwer-Nijhoff.

Haberman, S.J. (1997). Maximum likelihood estimates in exponential response models. *Annals of Statistics*, *5*, 815–841.

Janssen, R., De Boeck, P. & Schepers, J. (2003). The random-effects version of the linear logistic test model. Manuscript submitted for publication.

Janssen, R., Tuerlinckx, F., Meulders, M. & De Boeck, P. (2000). A hierarchical IRT model for criterion-referenced measurement. *Journal of Educational and Behavioral Statistics*, *25*, 285–306.

Maris, G. & Maris, E. (2002). A MCMC-method for models with continuous latent responses. *Psychometrika*, *67*, 335–350.

Meng, X.L. (1994). Posterior predictive p-values. *Annals of Statistics*, *22*, 1142–1160.

Mislevy, R.J. (1988). Exploiting auxiliary information about items in the estimation of Rasch item difficulty parameters. *Applied Psychological Measurement*, *12*, 725–737.

Patz, R.J. & Junker, B.W. (1999). A straightforward approach to Markov Chain Monte Carlo methods for item response models. *Journal of Edu-*

cational and Behavioral Statistics, 24, 146–178.

Sheehan, K. & Mislevy, R.J. (1990). Integrating cognitive and psychometric models to measure document literacy. *Journal of Educational Measurement, 27*, 255–277.

Swaminathan, H. & Gifford, J. (1982). Bayesian estimation in the Rasch model. *Journal of Educational Statistics, 7*, 175–191.

Tanner, M.A. (1996). *Tools for statistical inference: Methods for the exploration of posterior distributions and likelihood functions (3rd ed.).* New York: Springer.

Van den Noortgate, W., De Boeck, P. & Meulders, M. (2003). Cross-classification multilevel logistic models in psychometrics. *Journal of Educational and Behavioral Statistics.* Manuscript accepted for publication.

Chapter 7

Person-by-item predictors

Michel Meulders
Yiyu Xie

7.1 Introduction

In this chapter we consider the inclusion of person-by-item predictors into
the model. Unlike person predictors or item predictors, person-by-item predictors vary both within and between persons. The inclusion of person-by-
item predictors besides person predictors or item predictors is relevant for
modeling various phenomena such as differential item functioning (DIF)
and local item dependencies (LID) (see Zwinderman, 1997). To describe
models with person-by-item predictors we will distinguish between static
and dynamic interaction models. We concentrate here on models for DIF
and LID, but the interaction concept is of course more general.

Static interaction models include person-by-item predictors that are not
directly based on the responses that are modeled, but that are independently supplied, or that are constructed on the basis of person and item
predictors. The inclusion of a person-by-item predictor which is derived as
the product of an item indicator and a person predictor indicating group
membership can be used to investigate DIF. Studies on DIF – also called
item bias – are generally concerned with the question whether an item
is 'fair' for members of some focal group compared to members of a reference group. An item is said to be unbiased if it is equally difficult for
persons of the focal and the reference group who are matched with respect
to the underlying dimension that the test purportedly measures. Some authors reserve the term 'bias' for the case in which the matching criterion
is judged to be construct-valid in the sense that it is matching persons
on the basis of the underlying dimension the test is designed to measure
without contamination from other unintended-to-be-measured dimensions
(Shealy & Stout, 1993a,b). However, in this chapter we will use the terms
DIF and item bias as synonyms to indicate the statistical phenomenon of
item-by-group interaction.

Currently there are many procedures available for detecting DIF (for an
overview see: Millsap & Everson, 1993). Widely-used classical approaches
are the Mantel-Haenszel procedure as modified by Holland and Thayer
(1988) and the standardized p-difference index of Dorans and Kulick (1986).
In item response modeling several procedures have been developed to de-

tect item bias, for instance, using loglinear item response models (Mellenbergh, 1982; Kelderman, 1989), logistic regression models (Swaminathan & Rogers, 1990), area measures (Raju, 1988), Wald statistics (Lord, 1980) and likelihood-ratio tests (Thissen, Steinberg & Wainer, 1988). Besides differential item functioning it may be of interest to investigate differential test functioning, that is, how DIF in individual items affects the distribution of the test scores in different groups. Shealy and Stout (1993a,b) present a nonparametric multidimensional method, called SIBTEST, that can be used to assess DIF. Wainer, Sireci, and Thissen (1991) present a parametric item response modeling approach to model DIF in testlet scores.

In the section on static interaction models we will mainly focus on item response modeling for DIF detection that can be implemented using the procedure NLMIXED from SAS. Furthermore, we will extend the concept of DIF in two ways: (1) we will indicate how DIF in individual items can sometimes be modeled in a more parsimonious way as differential facet functioning (DFF), and (2) we will show how to model individual differences in DIF or DFF by making item-by-group or facet-by-group interaction parameters random over persons.

In *dynamic* interaction models, item responses are modeled on the basis of other item responses. Fahrmeir and Tutz (2001) label these models *conditional models* because they are built by specifying the probability of a response given predictors and other responses. For instance, when the components of the response vector may be considered as ordered (e.g., longitudinal data), one can use transition models (for an overview, see Diggle, Heagerty, Liang & Zeger, 2002) in order to model responses on the basis of previous responses. In the context of cognitive and educational testing, dynamic models are typically used to assess learning during test taking (Klauer & Sydow, 2001; Verguts & De Boeck, 2000; Verhelst & Glas, 1993, 1995). Another application is to model responses to one item on the basis of responses to another item that shares (up to a certain point) the same stimulus content. For instance, in the verbal aggression data, one could dynamically model the responses to a want-item on the basis of responses to the corresponding do-item.

The inclusion of dynamic person-by-item predictors can also be regarded as one particular approach to model local item dependencies (LID) or correlations between responses beyond those from the random intercept (Verhelst & Glas, 1993). Hunt and Jorgensen (1999) discuss this type of LID modeling in the context of latent-class clustering. Other approaches consider responses to sets of possibly interdependent items as the basic unit of the analysis. Such sets have been labeled testlets (Wainer & Kiely, 1987) or item bundles (Rosenbaum, 1988; Wilson & Adams, 1995). Different ways of handling item dependencies between items within a testlet are available, as explained in Chapter 10. The way to model LID we will follow here is to parametrize the joint distribution of the item responses in the testlet in terms of single-item effects and second-order or higher-order interactions. Examples of this approach are given by Kelderman (1984), Jannarone (1986), and Hoskens and De Boeck (1995, 1997). This approach can easily be formulated in a loglinear-model framework.

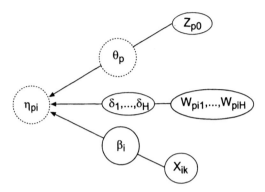

FIGURE 7.1. Graphical representation of an extended Rasch model that includes person-by-item predictors.

For both types of models (static and dynamic) with person-by-item predictors, Figure 7.1 shows a graphical representation of a Rasch model that is extended with such predictors. The random component and the logit link are omitted. This model explains the logit of the success probability of person p for item i (i.e., η_{pi}) on the basis of one (constant) person predictor Z_0 with a weight θ_p that is random over persons, I item indicators, X_{i1} to X_{iK} (with $K = I$), with corresponding fixed weights, β_1 to β_I, and H person-by-item predictors W_{pi1} to W_{piH}, with fixed weights, δ_1 to δ_H. The W predictors can be properties with values that depend on the person and the item or they can be responses to another item. In the following two sections we further describe how static and dynamic models can be specified by including person-by-item predictors, and models of each type are applied to the verbal aggression data.

7.2   Static interaction models

In this section we will mainly focus on person-by-item predictors that are computed as the product of a person predictor (representing a person group) and an item indicator (representing an item indicator or item property). This type of predictor can be used to investigate *differential item functioning (DIF)* as well as *differential facet functioning* (DFF; Engelhard, 1992), which concerns differential effects of item properties.

7.2.1   Differential item functioning

Differential item functioning (for an overview, see Holland & Wainer, 1993) refers to differences among groups in the functioning of items where the groups are matched on the underlying dimension measured by the test (Dorans & Holland, 1993; Scheuneman, 1979). More specifically, we have to make a distinction between *differential impact*, which refers to a difference in performance between groups, and *DIF*, which refers to a difference in performance between groups after groups have been matched with respect to the dimension that the test purportedly measures. Defining the latent variable θ as the underlying dimension for which the observed item Y is an indicator, and Z as the person predictor which indicates group membership, the absence of DIF can be formally defined in a very general way (see Millsap & Everson, 1993):

$$\Pr(Y = y | \theta, Z = z) = \Pr(Y = y | \theta), \qquad (7.1)$$

for all values of θ and Z (and omitting subscripts). Note that θ in Equation 7.1 can be discrete or continuous, and univariate or multivariate. In the special case that θ is continuous and univariate, Equation 7.1 reduces to Lord's (1980) definition of the absence of DIF, which is commonly used in item response modeling. Note that the definition of DIF based on a violation of Equation 7.1 implies the existence of a suitable measurement model that holds across groups.

In order to describe the formal modeling of DIF we consider the analysis of a test of I items which has been administered to two groups defined by a variable Z ($= 0, 1$). The groups are commonly referred to as the reference group ($Z = 0$) and the focal group ($Z = 1$). It is assumed that the I items consist of two sets: the first set of I_a items ($i = 1, \dots, I_a$) can be considered an anchor set of unbiased items with item response functions that can be adequately described by the 2PL model (for a discussion of the 2PL model, see Chapter 8), whereas for the second set of $I - I_a$ items ($i = I_a + 1, \dots, I$), we wish to investigate whether DIF occurs. Table 7.1 displays the logit of the success probability for persons of each group on anchor items and on items that are suspected of DIF.

As will be explained, the parametrization ($\alpha_i \theta_p - \beta_i$) is used because it is convenient to describe different types of DIF and because it yields simple effect size measures of DIF (that do not involve other parameters than those where the DIF is concentrated). Note that the consequence of this parametrization is that β_i indicates the value $\alpha_i \theta_p$ where the success probability is .5 (when $\beta_i = \alpha_i \theta_p$), and that the ratio β_i / α_i indicates the value of θ_p where the success probability is .5 (when $\beta_i / \alpha_i = \theta_p$). However, we will still use the term 'item location' for β_i, but now the location applies to the $\alpha_i \theta_p$-scale.

In Table 7.1, for each group (i.e., for each value z of Z) the random intercept is assumed to be normally distributed with group-specific mean and variance. In order to identify the model it is necessary to fix the mean and the variance of one of the groups. In particular, we may assume that $\theta \sim N(0,1)$ for the reference group and that $\theta \sim N(\mu, \sigma^2)$ for the focal group. In case one uses the Rasch model (i.e., $\alpha_i = 1$ for all values of i up to I, and $\delta_i^{(\alpha)} = 0$ for all values of i, from $I_a + 1$ to I) only the mean of one of the groups needs to be fixed (and no other distribution parameters).

As can be seen in Table 7.1 the logits of the success probabilities for anchor items are equivalent across groups because the item parameters for locations and slopes are constrained to be equivalent across groups. For items suspected of DIF, the logits for both groups may differ in two respects: the item locations and the slopes. In particular, the item location of the focal group is obtained by adding a parameter $\delta^{(\beta)}$ to the location parameter of the reference group and, in the same way, the slope of the focal group is obtained by adding a parameter $\delta^{(\alpha)}$ to the slope parameter of the reference group.

TABLE 7.1. Logit of the success probability of persons of different groups on anchor items and items suspected of DIF.

Group	Z	Anchor items	Item suspected of DIF
Reference	0	$\alpha_i \theta_p - \beta_i$	$\alpha_i \theta_p - \beta_i$
Focal	1	$\alpha_i \theta_p - \beta_i$	$[\alpha_i + \delta_i^{(\alpha)}]\theta_p - [\beta_i + \delta_i^{(\beta)}]$

The parameters $\delta^{(\beta)}$ and $\delta^{(\alpha)}$ are actually group-by-item interaction effects. This can easily be seen by writing the logit of the success probability on items suspected of DIF ($i = I_a + 1, \ldots, I$) in the following way:

$$\eta_{pi} = \left(\sum_{k=I_a+1}^{I} \left(\alpha_k X_{ik} + \delta_k^{(\alpha)} W_{pik} \right) \right) \theta_p - \sum_{k=I_a+1}^{I} \left(\beta_k X_{ik} + \delta_k^{(\beta)} W_{pik} \right),$$

with X_{ik} being item indicators that equal 1 if $i = k$ and 0 otherwise, and with W_{pik} being static predictors that equal the product of a binary group indicator Z_p and an item indicator, so that $W_{pik} = X_{ik}Z_p$.

Mellenbergh (1982) distinguished between different types of DIF: when DIF involves the slope ($\delta^{(\alpha)} \neq 0$) and possibly also item location, it is labeled as *non-uniform* and when it involves only item location ($\delta^{(\beta)} \neq 0, \delta^{(\alpha)} = 0$), it is labeled as *uniform*. Finally, the absence of DIF implies equality of item locations and slopes across groups ($\delta^{(\alpha)} = \delta^{(\beta)} = 0$).

As the interaction parameters $\delta^{(\beta)}$ and $\delta^{(\alpha)}$ actually reflect the difference between group-specific item locations and slopes, respectively, DIF in individual items can be detected with a Wald test for the null hypothesis that the interaction parameters equal zero. Furthermore, the null hypothesis of jointly having no DIF in a set of items can be tested using a likelihood ratio (LR test) that compares a restricted model without interactions and an unrestricted model which includes interactions for the set of items under investigation. We will not rely on LR tests to assess static interaction models but we will for the dynamic interaction models.

A useful effect-size measure for DIF can be obtained by subtracting the logits in the right-hand column of Table 7.1. In particular we can derive that

$$\delta_i^{(\alpha)}\theta_p - \delta_i^{(\beta)} = \eta_{pi|Z=1} - \eta_{pi|Z=0}.$$

Hence, $\exp(\delta_i^{(\alpha)}\theta_p - \delta_i^{(\beta)})$ can be interpreted as the odds ratio $\Pr(Y_{pi} = 1|\theta, Z)/\Pr(Y_{pi} = 0|\theta, Z)$ for members of the second group ($Z = 1$) versus members of the first group ($Z = 0$) after correcting for the group effect on θ_p. Figure 7.2 illustrates $\exp(\delta_i^{(\alpha)}\theta_p - \delta_i^{(\beta)})$ as a function of θ for different types of DIF. When there is no DIF ($\delta_i^{(\alpha)} = \delta_i^{(\beta)} = 0$), the odds equal 1 for all values of the random intercept. When the item shows uniform DIF in favor of the focal group ($\delta_i^{(\alpha)} = 0, \delta_i^{(\beta)} < 0$), the odds are always a constant value higher than 1 and they are equal for all values of the random intercept (i.e., $\exp(-\delta_i^{(\beta)})$). Finally, when an item shows non-uniform DIF ($\delta_i^{(\alpha)} > 0$), the odds exponentially rise as a function of θ. Depending on the value of θ, non-uniform DIF can be in favor of the reference group ($\delta_i^{(\alpha)}\theta_p < \delta_i^{(\beta)}$) or in favor of the focal group ($\delta_i^{(\alpha)}\theta_p > \delta_i^{(\beta)}$).

7.2.2 Differential facet functioning

As explained in the previous section, DIF can formally be regarded as an interaction between an item indicator and a qualitative person predictor that indicates group membership. In an analogous way we can define *differential facet functioning* (DFF) as the interaction between an item property or item facet and a group indicator. In other words, DFF implies that the effect of item properties on item difficulty depends on the group. DFF can be of interest for two reasons. First, modeling DFF may be a way to summarize and explain DIF of several items. For instance, in the verbal aggression data it could happen that all items regarding cursing display a particular type of DIF (e.g., positively signed uniform DIF). As a result, it would be meaningful to restrict the corresponding DIF parameters to be equal, which is formally equivalent to including an interaction between the item facet 'cursing' and the group indicator. DFF may be a parsimonious way to summarize and explain DIF. For example to model DIF in item locations on the basis of item facets we model the interaction parameters $\delta^{(\beta)}$ in Table 7.1 as a linear function of the K facets. The logit of the success

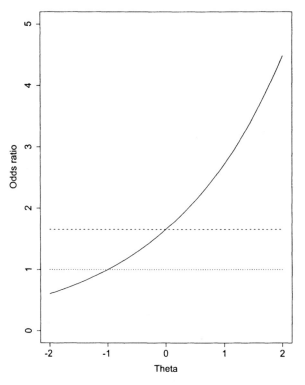

FIGURE 7.2. Odds ratio $\Pr(1 \mid \theta, z)/\Pr(0 \mid \theta, z)$ for $Z = 1$ versus $Z = 0$ as a function of θ in case of no DIF (....), uniform DIF (- - - -), and non-uniform DIF (——) assuming $\delta^{(\alpha)} = -\delta^{(\beta)} = .5$.

probability on items that are suspected of DIF then becomes

$$\eta_{pi} = \left(\alpha_i + \delta_i^{(\alpha)} Z_p\right) \theta_p - \left(\beta_i + \sum_{k=1}^{K} \delta_k X_{ik} Z_p\right).$$

In the same way, one may model DIF in the slopes by specifying the parameters $\delta^{(\alpha)}$ to be a linear function of item properties.

Second, modeling DFF may be a way to investigate the effects of a facet: its main effect and interaction effect. More specifically, in the example in Table 7.1 we may model item locations for both groups by specifying the following model for the logit of the success probability:

$$\eta_{pi} = \left(\alpha_i + \delta_i^{(\alpha)} Z_p\right) \theta_p - \left(\sum_{k=0}^{K} \beta_k X_{ik} + \sum_{k=1}^{K} \delta_k X_{ik} Z_p\right).$$

In a similar way, slopes in both groups can be modeled on the basis of item properties.

7.2.3   Random-weights DIF/DFF

A natural extension of models that include DIF- or DFF-interaction parameters is to make some of these interaction parameters random over
persons. The resulting models are denoted as random-weights differential
item functioning (RW-DIF) models and random-weights differential facet
functioning (RW-DFF) models. In this section, we will discuss some topics
that are important for modeling RW-DIF but that also hold for modeling
RW-DFF. First, note that each random DIF effect effectively adds an extra
person dimension to the model. Therefore, in practice, one can often only
consider a limited number of random interaction parameters (i.e., 2 or 3)
as models including several random effects are highly multidimensional and
therefore hard to estimate (within a maximum likelihood framework).

Second, an important issue in modeling RW-DIF is that the heterogeneity
that can be captured by a certain random DIF parameter depends on
whether one uses dummy coding or contrast coding for the group variable
Z. In order to illustrate this we will describe different types of RW-DIF
models for a set of I items that includes $I - 1$ anchor items which fit
the Rasch model and one item i that is to be checked for uniform DIF.
Modeling the heterogeneity in DIF in more complex situations (e.g., non-
uniform DIF in several items) is a straightforward extension. However, one
should realize that the information included in one item is a poor basis for
the estimation of a random effect. This is less of a problem when the same
effect (i.e., a facet effect) relates to more than one item.

For the above described situation, the logit of the success probability for
person p on item i equals

$$\eta_{pi} = \theta_p - \beta_i - \gamma_p X_{ik} Z_p, \tag{7.2}$$

with X_{ik} an item indicator variable that equals 1 if $k = i$ and 0 otherwise.
For each group (i.e., each value z of Z) one may assume a bivariate normal
distribution for the random effects θ_p and γ_p with a group-specific vector
of means and a group-specific variance-covariance matrix (allowing for het-
eroscedasticity), that is, $(\theta, \gamma \mid z) \sim N(\boldsymbol{\mu}_z, \boldsymbol{\Sigma}_z)$ with $\boldsymbol{\mu}_z = (\mu_{\theta_z}, \mu_{\gamma_z})$ and
$\boldsymbol{\Sigma}_z = (\sigma^2_{\theta_z}, \sigma_{\theta\gamma_z}, \sigma^2_{\gamma_z})$. Note that, to save space, we do not write the entire
matrix $\boldsymbol{\Sigma}$ but only list its lower diagonal elements in subsequent rows as a
vector. It is necessary to fix $\boldsymbol{\mu}_z$ for one of the groups in order to identify
the model. It is most natural to do this for the reference group, so that
$\boldsymbol{\mu}_{ref} = (0, 0)$. When the 2PL is used, it is also necessary to fix the variance
of θ_p in one of the groups, so that $\boldsymbol{\Sigma}_{ref} = (1, \sigma_{\theta\gamma_{ref}}, \sigma^2_{\gamma_{ref}})$. Finally, as can
be seen from the logits in Table 7.2 a model that uses dummy coding for
the group variable only allows one to model individual differences in DIF
among the persons of the focal group. As a result, when using a dummy
coding scheme one should specify $\boldsymbol{\Sigma}_{ref} = (\sigma^2_{\theta_{ref}}, 0, 0)$ when using the Rasch
model and $\boldsymbol{\Sigma}_{ref} = (1, 0, 0)$ when using the 2PL as it is not meaningful to
estimate the variance of the γ-dimension for the reference group. On the

other hand, when using contrast coding for Z, the γ-dimension can be used to model individual differences in DIF among members of both groups.[1]

TABLE 7.2. Logit of the success probability for RW-DIF models using dummy coding or contrast coding for the group indicator Z.

Coding scheme	Group	Z	Anchor items	Item suspected of DIF
Dummy coding	reference	0	$\theta_p - \beta_i$	$\theta_p - \beta_i$
	focal	1	$\theta_p - \beta_i$	$\theta_p - \beta_i - \gamma_p$
Contrast coding	reference	-1	$\theta_p - \beta_i$	$\theta_p - \beta_i + \gamma_p$
	focal	1	$\theta_p - \beta_i$	$\theta_p - \beta_i - \gamma_p$

7.3   Application of static interaction models

In order to illustrate static interaction models, the verbal aggression data are analyzed in three steps. In a first step, we investigate DIF for Gender. In a second step, we aim at a more parsimonious model by constraining similar DIF effects that occur systematically in certain situation-behavior combinations to be equal. This actually leads to a DFF model. Finally, in a third step, we make the DFF parameter random over persons to see whether there is evidence for individual differences on the DFF dimension within groups (i.e., among men and among women). All the models are estimated with the NLMIXED procedure of SAS. The options that are used are described in Section 7.7.

Differential item functioning

A general problem with DIF detection is that, under many approaches (e.g., SIBTEST; Shealy & Stout, 1993a,b), one needs a valid subset or an anchor set of unbiased items in order to link the scales of the two groups. When such an *a priori* set of unbiased items is not available (as is the case for the verbal aggression data), one can follow an exploratory approach to detect DIF. In particular, we can distinguish between a forward and a backward approach. In a forward approach, DIF is first estimated for single items and afterwards all significant DIFs are included in one model.

---

[1]When dummy coding is used for Z_p, and both Z_p and $1 - Z_p$ are used as predictors to define the interaction, so that two interaction predictors are obtained ($X_{ik}Z_p$ and $X_{ik}(1 - Z_p)$), then the two γ_ps can be defined, one for each group (with zero correlation between them). This is an alternative way to model heteroscedasticity.

In a backward approach, DIF is allowed simultaneously for all items and subsequently nonsignificant interactions are dropped from the model. Note that, in the first step of the backward approach, item-by-group interactions can only be estimated for $I - 1$ items because otherwise the model would not be identified. To solve this problem we did not include an item-by-group interaction for the last item. We can investigate the soundness of starting with this assumption by carrying out a second DIF detection procedure that starts with another item. In this paper we present the results of the backward approach. The results of the forward approach were similar.

The following four models are compared: (1) a Rasch model without DIF for the entire data set, (2) a 2PL without DIF for the entire data set, (3) a Rasch model with group-specific location parameters for all items (except the last), (4) a 2PL with group-specific location and slope parameters for all items (except the last), each time using dummy coding for Gender ($Z = 1$ for males and $Z = 0$ for females).

TABLE 7.3. Number of parameters (N_{par}) and AIC and BIC values for eight models (verbal aggression data).

Model		N_{par}	AIC	BIC
1.	Rasch model, no DIF	27	8124	8225
2.	2PL, no DIF	50	8127	8315
3.	Rasch model, uniform DIF all items	50	8099	8287
4.	2PL, non-uniform DIF all items	96	8134	8495
5.	Rasch model, uniform DIF do-items	39	8092	8238
6.	Rasch model, DFF actually scolding or cursing	28	8078	8183
7.	Rasch model, RW-DFF actually scolding or cursing dummy coding for Gender	30	8055	8167
8.	Rasch model, RW-DFF actually scolding or cursing contrast coding for Gender	32	7982	8102

Note: Parameters that are used to model the distribution of the random effects are included in N_{par}.

Table 7.3 shows AIC and BIC values for each of the four models (first four lines in the table). As AIC and BIC values are smaller for the Rasch model than for the 2PL (i.e., $8124 < 8127$ and $8225 < 8315$), we can conclude that different slope parameters are not needed, and in fact, are detrimental to optimum fit. Further, the AIC indicates that there is evidence for uniform DIF ($8099 < 8124$) whereas, according to the BIC, models with no DIF are better (i.e., $8225 < 8287$ and $8315 < 8495$). Inspection of the interaction parameters of the uniform-DIF model (i.e., parameter $\delta^{(\beta)}$ in Table 7.1) indicates that none of the want-items shows significant uniform DIF and that significant uniform (and negative) DIF occurs for actually cursing or scolding in each of the situations. This means that thresholds for actually cursing or scolding are lower for men than for women, and hence that men have a higher probability to display these behaviors than women (or more strictly interpreted, to report that they would display these behaviors). When the nonsignificant interactions between Gender and want-items are excluded from the analysis, DIF for Gender in actually cursing and scolding is even more pronounced (see Table 7.4). As can be seen from line 5 in Table 7.3, the AIC and BIC (8092 and 8238, respectively) for this model are lower than for the model that includes uniform DIF for all but the last item (8099 and 8287, respectively).

As discussed before, the effect-size measure of an interaction parameter (i.e., $\exp(-\delta_i)$) can be interpreted as the odds ratio of displaying the behavior in the situation rather than not doing so for men versus women after correcting for differences in mean tendencies of showing aggression between men and women. These effect-size measures are shown in Table 7.4. For Shout the estimated odds ratios vary between 1.00 and 2.14 and they do not significantly differ from 1. For Curse and Scold the estimated odds ratio's vary between 1.90 and 3.80 and they are always significantly higher than 1 except for Curse in the first situation.

TABLE 7.4. DIF parameter estimates, standard errors, effect-size measures and corresponding 95% confidence intervals in a model that assumes uniform DIF with respect to Gender for do-items (verbal aggression data).

Situation	Behavior	δ	$SE(\delta)$	$\exp(-\delta)$	95% CI
Bus	Curse	-.64	.37	1.90	[.92,3.91]
	Scold	-1.03	.34	2.79	[1.43,5.43]
	Shout	-.15	.34	1.16	[.60,2.25]
Train	Curse	-1.34	.38	3.80	[1.81,7.97]
	Scold	-1.30	.33	3.69	[1.92,7.08]
	Shout	-.52	.36	1.69	[.84,3.40]
Store	Curse	-1.21	.33	3.37	[1.77,6.41]
	Scold	-1.12	.35	3.07	[1.55,6.07]
	Shout	-.76	.49	2.14	[.82,5.60]
Call	Curse	-.83	.35	2.29	[1.16,4.53]
	Scold	-.87	.32	2.38	[1.26,4.50]
	Shout	.00	.42	1.00	[.44,2.27]

Differential facet functioning

As DIF for Gender occurs only for certain types of items and consistently has the same sign, we can attempt to model DIF in a more parsimonious way by constraining these similar DIF effects to be equal. This leads to a DFF model with one facet variable for actually cursing or scolding in a situation versus all other items. Note that this item property corresponds to the earlier defined 'blaming' property of a behavior (see Chapter 2), but is now restricted to do-items. For this DFF model (on line 6 in Table 7.3) the AIC and BIC equal 8078 and 8183, respectively, which is lower than for the model that includes uniform DIF for all do-items (i.e., 8092 and 8238, respectively, as shown on line 5 in Table 7.3). Hence, the proposed DFF model can indeed be used to summarize DIF in a more parsimonious way. We may conclude that women show less blaming behavior than men, although their blaming tendency (wanting to blame) is equally high in the same situations.

Random-weights differential facet functioning

In a last step of the analysis, we can investigate the consistency of the DFF effect over persons by making the DFF parameter random over persons. As explained in the section on RW-DFF, adopting a different coding scheme for the group variable (i.e., contrast coding or dummy coding) has important consequences for the kind of individual differences that are included by the model (see Table 7.2). In particular, dummy coding ($Z = 1$ for males and $Z = 0$ for females) would only allow individual differences on the DFF dimension for men, whereas contrast coding ($Z = 1$ for males and $Z = -1$ for females) would allow individual differences on this dimension for both men and women. RW-DFF models using both dummy coding and contrast coding for Gender were estimated. The results are shown on lines 7 and 8 in Table 7.3. The RW-DFF model with contrast coding for Gender (the AIC and BIC equal 7982 and 8102, respectively) fits better than the RW-DFF model with dummy coding for Gender (the AIC and BIC equal 8055 and 8167, respectively), and both RW-DFF models fit better than a model with a fixed DFF effect (the AIC and BIC equal 8078 and 8183, respectively).

For the best fitting RW-DFF model (i.e., with contrast coding for Gender) the logit of the probability of a 1-response for person p on item i equals

$$\eta_{pi} = \theta_p - \beta_i - \gamma_p X_i Z_p, \qquad (7.3)$$

with X a facet variable which equals 1 for items that involve actually scolding or cursing. Table 7.5 shows the parameter estimates (not including the item location parameters) that were obtained with the NLMIXED procedure of SAS.

The estimated mean of the overall underlying dimension θ for males (i.e., $\mu_\theta = -.04$, $p > .10$) is not significantly different from the mean for females which was fixed at 0. On the other hand, the estimated mean of the DFF dimension γ for males (i.e., $\mu_\gamma = -1.12$, $p < .001$) differs significantly from the mean for females which was fixed at 0. More specifically, it follows from Equation 7.3 that, for persons with the same value of θ, on average, the

TABLE 7.5. Estimates and standard errors for parameters of the RW-DFF model with contrast coding for Gender (verbal aggression data).

Group	Parameter	Estimate	SE
Female	σ_θ^2	2.05	.25
	$\sigma_{\theta\gamma}$	.05	.21
	σ_γ^2	1.47	.30
Male	μ_θ	-.04	.21
	μ_γ	-1.12	.23
	σ_θ^2	1.91	.43
	$\sigma_{\theta\gamma}$	.29	.37
	σ_γ^2	1.60	.54

Note: Item location parameters are not included.

odds to actually scold or curse rather than not to display these behaviors are $\exp(E(\eta_{pi|Z=1} - \eta_{pi|Z=-1})) = \exp((\mu_{\theta\ male} - \beta_i - \mu_{\gamma\ male}) - (\mu_{\theta\ fem} - \beta_i + \mu_{\gamma\ fem})) \approx 2.9$ times higher for males than for females and most of this effect is explained by DFF since the difference is very small between $\mu_{\theta\ male}$ and $\mu_{\theta\ female}$ (μ_θ in Table 7.5). Furthermore, the results indicate that the estimated variance-covariance matrix is similar for males and females: the variance of the DFF-dimension is about the same for females and males (1.47 and 1.60, respectively) and is almost as large as the variance of the overall underlying dimension in these groups (2.05 and 1.91, for females and males, respectively). Table 7.5 does not present p-values to test whether there is significant variation within each of the groups on the θ or γ-dimension because there is no asymptotic theory available for the nonlinear mixed case. However, the fact that the estimates are at least three times as large as their standard errors suggest that the variation among persons on each dimension is substantial. Finally, Table 7.5 shows that the covariance between the overall underlying dimension and the DFF-dimension is nonsignificant for both females ($\sigma_{\theta\gamma} = .05, p > .10$) and males ($\sigma_{\theta\gamma} = .29, p > .10$).

As a further illustration of the difference between males and females in actually cursing or scolding, Figure 7.3 displays the probability to actually curse or scold as a function of θ (i.e., the overall individual aggression effect) for males and females with a mean score in their own Gender group (i.e., μ_{γ_z}), a low score (i.e., $\mu_{\gamma_z} - 2\sigma_\gamma$), and a high score (i.e., $\mu_{\gamma_z} + 2\sigma_\gamma$) on the DFF-dimension. Note that (because of the contrast coding with $+1$ and -1) females with a higher γ-score have generally a higher probability to curse or scold whereas males with a higher γ-score have a lower probability to curse or scold. In other words, for females the γ-dimension reflects a tendency to actually blame other persons whereas for males it indicates the tendency

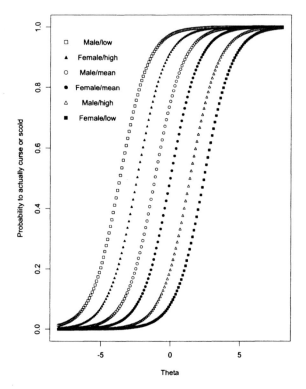

FIGURE 7.3. Probability to actually curse or scold as a function of θ for males and females with a mean score (i.e., μ_γ), a low score (i.e., $\mu_{\gamma z} - 2\sigma_{\gamma z}$) and a high score (i.e., $\mu_{\gamma z} + 2\sigma_{\gamma z}$) in their own Gender group on the γ-dimension.

to inhibit this type of behavior. As can be seen in Figure 7.3 males have on average a higher probability to curse or scold than females. However, we also see that there is substantial variation on the DFF-dimension within each Gender group and that the scores of males and females on the DFF-dimension show considerable overlap.

7.4 Dynamic interaction models

In dynamic interaction models, item responses are modeled on the basis of other responses possibly in addition to static predictors. The models are sometimes denoted as conditional models (Fahrmeir & Tutz, 2001) because they are built by specifying the distribution of a response conditional on other responses rather than by specifying the joint distribution of all the item responses. In this chapter we will only provide a brief description of conditional models and afterwards focus on the application of the models to the verbal aggression data. However, a more fully theoretical treatment of the models is given in Chapter 10 where they are also denoted as 'recursive' models.

Depending on the nature of the responses, different types of dynamic models can be of interest. First, when the components of the vector of responses can be considered as ordered (e.g., longitudinal data), it can be interesting to use transition models for modeling responses on the basis of previous outcomes (see Chapter 4, and Diggle et al., 2002). In this case, the joint distribution of the item responses is decomposed in the following way:

$$\Pr(Y_{p1} = y_{p1}, \ldots, Y_{pI} = y_{pI} | X) =$$
$$\Pr(Y_{p1} = y_{p1} | X)\Pr(Y_{p2} = y_{p2} | y_{p1}, X) \ldots \Pr(Y_{pI} = y_{pI} | y_{p1}, \ldots, y_{p,I-1}, X),$$
$$(7.4)$$

with X a set of static predictors. An example of a transition model is the first-order Markov model which assumes that responses to subsequent test items depend on a random intercept, a fixed item location and on the response to the previous item. When this kind of dependence is added to the Rasch model, the logit of the success probability of person p on item i $(i = 2, .., I)$ reads

$$\eta_{pi} = \theta_p - \beta_i + \delta w_{pi},$$

with $w_{pi} = y_{p,i-1}$. Another example is the dynamic Rasch model which assumes that the success probability is determined by a random intercept, a fixed item location and the sum of successes on previous items. This model can be useful to investigate learning effects in achievement testing. The logit of the success probability equals

$$\eta_{pi} = \theta_p - \beta_i + \delta w_{pi},$$

with $w_{pi} = \sum_{h=1}^{i-1} y_{ph}$.

Second, when some components of the response vector can be viewed as dependent – for instance because they share the same stimulus content – dynamic models can be useful to capture the dependence between these components that goes beyond the overall underlying dimension. For example, in the context of the verbal aggression data it can be interesting to dynamically model responses to items of one mode on the basis of responses to items of the other mode (e.g., Do vs Want). As such, two types of dependence models can be considered: (1) a model that explains doing on the basis of wanting, and (2) a model that explains wanting on the basis of doing.

We will formally describe the model that explains doing on the basis of wanting. This model is further denoted as the Want-Do model. Models in which wanting is explained on the basis of doing, further denoted as Do-Want models, are analogous.

Consider the items of Table 1.1 of Chapter 1. For a Want-Do model with situation-behavior specific dynamic weights, the joint distribution

$\Pr(y_h, y_{(h+12)} | \theta, \beta_h, \beta_{(h+12)}, \delta_h)$ of the want and do behavior for a particular situation-behavior pair h $(h = 1, \ldots, 12)$ equals

$$\Pr(y_h | \theta, \beta_h) \Pr(y_{(h+12)} | y_h, \theta, \beta_{(h+12)}, \delta_h)$$

$$= \frac{\exp(y_h(\theta - \beta_h))}{1 + \exp(\theta - \beta_h)} \times \frac{\exp(y_{(h+12)}(\theta - \beta_{(h+12)} + \delta_h y_h))}{1 + \exp(\theta - \beta_{(h+12)} + \delta_h y_h)}$$

$$= \frac{\exp(y_h(\theta - \beta_h) + y_{(h+12)}(\theta - \beta_{(h+12)}) + \delta_h y_h y_{(h+12)})}{1 + \exp(\theta - \beta_h) + \exp(\theta - \beta_{(h+12)} + \delta_h y_h) + \exp(2\theta - \beta_h - \beta_{(h+12)} + \delta_h y_h)}$$

(7.5)

To estimate this model with the NLMIXED procedure of SAS, in addition to a random intercept and item indicators, we include, for each situation-behavior pair h, a dynamic predictor W_{pih} that equals 1 for the do-item if the corresponding want-item equals 1, and 0 otherwise. The logit of the probability of a 1-response for person p on item i $(i = 1, \ldots, 24)$ can be expressed as follows:

$$\eta_{pi} = \theta_p - \beta_i + \sum_{h=1}^{12} \delta_h w_{pih}.$$

(7.6)

The model in Equation 7.6 assumes that the weights of the dynamic predictors are specific to the situation-behavior pair. If needed, one can constrain some of the dynamic weights to be equal, for instance, $\delta_1 = \delta_2$. Formally, this can be done by replacing W_{pi1} and W_{pi2} by their sum $W_{pi1} + W_{pi2}$.

Note that models based on the decomposition in Equation 7.4 are asymmetric in the sense that responses have an influence on subsequent responses and not vice versa. If the components of the vector of responses are not ordered, it may be of interest to include mutual dynamic predictors. For example, one might try to explain doing on the basis of wanting and vice versa. Here one is positing no psychological order but only a mutual consistency. Such a model would be characterized by two families of conditional distributions for each situation-behavior pair h $(h = 1, \ldots, 12)$:

$$
\begin{cases}
\Pr(y_{(h+12)} | y_h, \theta, \beta_{(h+12)}, \delta_{1h}) &= \dfrac{\exp(y_{(h+12)}(\theta - \beta_{(h+12)} + \delta_{1h} y_h))}{1 + \exp(\theta - \beta_{(h+12)} + \delta_{1h} y_h)}, \\[3mm]
\Pr(y_h | y_{(h+12)}, \theta, \beta_h, \delta_{2h}) &= \dfrac{\exp(y_h(\theta - \beta_h + \delta_{2h} y_{(h+12)}))}{1 + \exp(\theta - \beta_h + \delta_{2h} y_{(h+12)})}.
\end{cases}
$$

(7.7)

However, it is important to note that there is no guarantee that the families in Equation 7.7 are compatible in the sense that there exists a joint distribution for (Y_h, Y_{h+12}) with the given families as its conditional distributions (Arnold & Press, 1989; Gelman & Speed, 1993). In fact, it is easy to show that the densities in Equation 7.7 are only compatible if the dynamic weights δ_{1h} and δ_{2h} are equal (see Theorem 3.1, in Arnold & Press, 1989). The resulting joint distribution then turns out to be the same as for the *constant combination dependence model—((CCDM), a term used by Hoskens and De Boeck (1997), namely:

$$\Pr(y_h, y_{(h+12)} | \theta, \beta_h, \beta_{(h+12)}, \delta_h) =$$

$$\frac{\exp(y_h(\theta - \beta_h) + y_{(h+12)}(\theta - \beta_{(h+12)}) + y_h y_{(h+12)} \delta_h)}{1 + \exp(\theta - \beta_h) + \exp(\theta - \beta_{(h+12)}) + \exp(2\theta - \beta_h - \beta_{(h+12)} + \delta_h)}.$$

$$(7.8)$$

Hence, the model that includes equal dynamic weights in both directions turns out to be the equivalent of a symmetric local item dependence model. On the other hand, the joint densities of the CCDM (Equation 7.8) and of the asymmetric Want-Do model (Equation 7.5) clearly differ. The relationship between dynamic and symmetric models is discussed in more detail in Chapter 10 where they are referred to as recursive and nonrecursive models, respectively.

With respect to the interpretation of the weights of the dynamic predictors, we note that, for the Want-Do model

$$\delta_h = \begin{array}{c} \text{logit} \left(\Pr(Y_{(h+12)} = 1 | Y_h = 1, \theta) \right) \\ -\text{logit} \left(\Pr(Y_{(h+12)} = 1 | Y_h = 0, \theta) \right), \end{array} \qquad (7.9)$$

which implies that the exponent of the interaction parameter δ_h can be interpreted as the ratio of (1) the odds of actually displaying an aggressive behavior rather than not doing so, given that one also wanted to display the behavior, and (2) the odds of actually displaying an aggressive behavior rather than not doing so, given that one did *not* want to display the behavior. For the CCDM, the exponent of the interaction parameter δ_h can be interpreted as the local odds ratio of having a 1 on both components (want and do) or a 0 on both components rather than having different scores on both components, that is,

$$\delta_h = \log \left(\frac{\Pr(Y_h = 1, Y_{(h+12)} = 1 | \theta) \Pr(Y_h = 0, Y_{(h+12)} = 0 | \theta)}{\Pr(Y_h = 1, Y_{(h+12)} = 0 | \theta) \Pr(Y_h = 0, Y_{(h+12)} = 1 | \theta)} \right). \quad (7.10)$$

7.5   Application of dynamic interaction models

As an illustration of dynamic interaction models, we model local item dependencies between want and do items in the verbal aggression data. Three types of models are compared: (1) a dynamic model that explains doing on the basis of wanting (Want-Do model), (2) a dynamic model that explains wanting on the basis of doing (Do-Want model), and (3) a constant combination dependence model (CCDM) which actually assigns equal weights to both directions. Furthermore, in order to investigate whether dependencies between want-items and do-items depend on specific situations or behaviors, for each model, the dynamic weights are (1) either not constrained (i.e., situation-behavior specific dynamic weights), or constrained in different ways, yielding (2) weights that are constrained to be equal among situations (behavior-specific dynamic weights), (3) weights that are constrained to be equal among behaviors (situation-specific dynamic weights), (4) weights that are constrained to be equal across both situations and behaviors (i.e., one general dynamic weight). These four types of dependence will be denoted SB-specific, B-specific, S-specific and non-specific, respectively. All the models were estimated with the NLMIXED procedure of SAS using the options described in Section 7.7 for the DIF models.

TABLE 7.6. Deviance, AIC, BIC and number of parameters (N_{par}) for the Rasch model and various dynamic extensions (verbal aggression data).

Model	Equality constraints	Deviance	AIC	BIC	N_{par}
Rasch		8073	8123	8216	25
Want-Do	none (SB)	7904	7978	8117	37
	situations (B)	7919	7975	8080	28
	behaviors (S)	7939	7997	8106	29
	sit. and beh. (non)	7949	8000	8098	26
Do-Want	none (SB)	7908	7982	8121	37
	situations (B)	7926	7982	8088	28
	behaviors (S)	7953	8011	8119	29
	sit. and beh. (non)	7964	8016	8114	26
CCDM	none (SB)	7907	7981	8120	37
	situations (B)	7920	7976	8081	28
	behaviors (S)	7944	8002	8111	29
	sit. and beh. (non)	7951	8003	8101	26

Table 7.6 presents a summary of fit measures (Deviance, AIC, BIC) and complexity (number of parameters) for the estimated models. For reasons of comparison, an independence model which assumes responses to want-items and do-items to be independent given θ (i.e., the Rasch model) is also included in Table 7.6. We will first discuss models with SB-specific dynamic weights and afterwards investigate whether the dynamic weights can be constrained to be equal across situations or behaviors.

Models with SB-specific dynamic weights

As can be seen in Table 7.6, the inclusion of SB-specific dynamic weights yields a better fit to the data than the Rasch model: For the Want-Do model, the Do-Want model, and the CCDM, AIC values (7978, 7982 and 7981, respectively) and BIC values (8117, 8121, 8120, respectively) are lower than for the Rasch model (i.e., AIC=8123 and BIC=8216). Also, for each dynamic model, a LR test in which the deviance of a dynamic model is compared to that of the Rasch model favors the dynamic model ($\chi^2(12) = 169$, $p < .001$; $\chi^2(12) = 165$, $p < .001$; $\chi^2(12) = 166$, $p < .001$, for the Want-Do model, the Do-Want model, and the CCDM, respectively). The three proposed models offer a rather similar description of the data: AIC, BIC and Deviance values are about the same, and the estimated dynamic weights and standard errors of estimated dynamic weights are very similar (i.e., correlations higher than .99).

TABLE 7.7. Dynamic weights, standard errors, effect size measures, and corresponding 95% confidence intervals for the Want-Do model with SB-specificity (verbal aggression data).

Situation	Behavior	δ	$SE(\delta)$	$\exp(\delta)$	95% CI
Bus	Curse	.12	.30	1.13	[.63,2.04]
	Scold	.82	.28	2.27	[1.31,3.93]
	Shout	1.17	.31	3.22	[1.75,5.93]
Train	Curse	.17	.32	1.19	[.63,2.23]
	Scold	1.12	.30	3.06	[1.69,5.51]
	Shout	1.95	.42	7.03	[3.07,15.98]
Store	Curse	.30	.27	1.35	[.79,2.31]
	Scold	1.57	.34	4.81	[2.47,9.44]
	Shout	1.62	.48	5.05	[1.97,12.87]
Call	Curse	1.04	.30	2.83	[1.57,5.06]
	Scold	1.41	.29	4.10	[2.31,7.28]
	Shout	2.21	.40	9.12	[4.16,20.01]

Table 7.7 presents estimated dynamic weights and corresponding standard errors for the best fitting model with SB-specific dynamic weights, which is the Want-Do model. To aid interpretation of the dynamic weights, Table 7.7 also displays the exponent of the dynamic weights and the associated 95% confidence interval for the exponent of the dynamic weight. The results in Table 7.7 indicate that persons who want to scold or shout have a higher probability to also actually display these behaviors than can be expected from the underlying dimension and the item parameters. For cursing this is only true for one of the four situations. For shouting, the

dynamic weights are rather large (odds ranging from 3.22 to 9.12), for scolding, the weights are moderately large (odds ranging from 2.27 to 4.81) and for cursing, the weights are rather small and sometimes not significantly larger than 0 (odds ranging from 1.13 to 2.83).

Models with constrained dynamic weights

As can be seen in Table 7.6, models with B-specificity yield the best balance between fit and complexity according to the AIC and BIC: Their AIC and BIC values are lower than those for models with SB-specificity, with S-specificity, or with non-specificity. Also, LR tests indicate that for neither of the three types of models (Want-Do, Do-Want, CCDM) strong evidence exists against the dynamic weights being equal across situations (two p's > .05, one $p = .04$). Furthermore, models with S-specificity or non-specificity do less well than the model with SB-specificity on the basis of LR tests (all p's < .001)

TABLE 7.8. Dynamic weights, standard errors, effect-size measures, and corresponding 95% confidence interval for the Want-Do Model with B-specific dynamic weights (verbal aggression data).

Behavior	δ	$SE(\delta)$	$\exp(\delta)$	95% CI
Curse	.42	.15	1.52	[1.13,2.05]
Scold	1.21	.15	3.35	[2.49,4.53]
Shout	1.68	.19	5.37	[3.66,7.87]

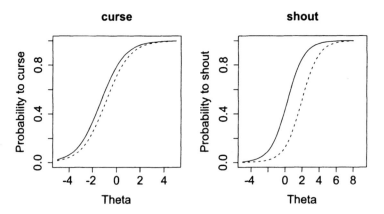

FIGURE 7.4. Probability to curse (left panel) or shout (right panel) for persons who also want (——), or do not want (- - -) to curse or shout in a specific situation (Bus).

Table 7.8 presents the estimated dynamic weights, measures of effect size and the corresponding 95% confidence intervals for the Want-Do Model with B-specificity. Persons who want to curse, scold, or shout have a higher probability to also actually display these behaviors than can be expected on the basis of item parameters and the underlying dimension. For cursing, scolding and shouting the odds of actually displaying the behavior rather than not doing so given that one wanted to act in that way are, respectively, 1.52, 3.35 and 5.37 times larger than the odds of actually displaying the behavior rather than not doing so given that one did *not* want to display the behavior. The odds are significantly larger than 1 for each of the three behaviors, but they can be regarded as large for shouting, of intermediate size for scolding and rather small for cursing. For cursing and shouting the size of the dynamic weight is also visualized in Figure 7.4 which displays the probability to actually curse or shout for persons who say they want or do not want to curse/shout in a specific situation.

A possible explanation for the stronger association between doing and wanting for shouting than for scolding or cursing is that the former kind of aggressive behavior is typically not directed towards others, which means that aggression is unlikely to be inhibited by, for instance, the presence of other persons. 'Shouting' in Dutch ('het uitschreeuwen') does not have a blaming nature, but primarily an expressive nature instead. Wanting and doing may be correlated more highly because individual differences in inhibition play less of a role.

7.6 Concluding remarks

In this chapter it was explained how different phenomena such as DIF and LID can be modeled by adding person-by-item predictors to standard item response models. It was demonstrated that the NLMIXED procedure of SAS can be used to estimate all the presented models. In the following paragraphs we will list some advantages and drawbacks of our approach for modeling DIF or local item dependence as well as describe some further extensions that could be handled with the NLMIXED procedure and other similar software for generalized linear and nonlinear models.

Regarding DIF, an advantage of using general software is that it allows us to build and estimate a wide variety of models. For instance, it allows us to use DFF models for modeling DIF in a set of items on the basis of item properties or to use RW-DIF (or RW-DFF) models for modeling individual differences in DIF (or DFF) among persons of a particular group. Paradoxically, this generality is also an important drawback as the estimation is slower than with specialized software for standard item response models such as the Rasch model, (e.g., BIMAIN 2; Zimowski, Muraki, Mislevy & Bock, 1994).

Another advantage of our approach is that it allows us to jointly test for both uniform and non-uniform DIF in a set of items. We do not know of any other software package that fully supports this type of analysis. For instance, BIMAIN 2 uses the 3 PL to model item responses in each group but only allows one to check for DIF in the item locations. Nonparametric approaches such as SIBTEST (Shealy & Stout, 1993a,b) or crossing SIBTEST (Li & Stout, 1996) allow checking for unidirectional DIF or crossing DIF, respectively, in an item, a set of items or the test as a whole, but they do not allow checking for both of these DIF types simultaneously. Unidirectional DIF is related to uniform DIF as it implies that the DIF is in favor of the same group for all values of the underlying dimension, but is more general because the size of the DIF can be different depending on the value of the latent trait that it is conditioned upon. Crossing DIF is related to non-uniform DIF in that it implies nonparallel item response functions but it is somewhat more specific because it also requires that item response functions intersect. Finally, the logistic regression procedure (Swaminathan & Rogers, 1990) can be used to jointly check for uniform and non-uniform DIF. However, this procedure uses the total test score as a proxy for the random intercept.

Our discussion of DIF was restricted to the modeling of binary data that stem from two populations. However, it is rather straightforward to model DIF for polytomous items (Moore, 1996; Muraki, 1999). Such analyses could be handled with general GLMM and NLMM software as well. Symmetric dependence models for polytomous data are described by Ip, Wang, De Boeck and Meulders (2003) who applied the models to the verbal aggression data and listed the code for estimating the models with the NLMIXED procedure of SAS. For dynamic models, an extension to the case of polytomous data is also straightforward as it simply boils down to modeling the category-specific probabilities for a particular item on the basis of previous responses. For instance, when using the partial credit model for totally ordered responses, one could include dynamic predictors to model the probability of responding in a particular category for a particular item on the basis of the observed number of responses in each of the categories on foregoing items.

A second straightforward extension of the local dependence models that have been discussed in this chapter consists of making the dependence parameters (CCDM) or the effects of dynamic predictors (dynamic interaction models) random over persons. Such random-weights models can easily be formulated along the lines of the RW-DIF or RW-DFF models that were presented in this chapter. Random-weights symmetric dependency models have recently been discussed by Hoskens and De Boeck (1997) and by Ip et al. (2003).

7.7   Software

The NLMIXED procedure of SAS V8 was used for all analyses reported in this section. A nonadaptive Gaussian quadrature method with 20 quadrature points was used to approximate the likelihood and the Newton-Raphson technique was used for optimization.

7.7.1   Uniform DIF for actually cursing or scolding (verbal aggression data)

Code

```
PROC NLMIXED data=aggression_dich method=gauss
technique=newrap noad qpoints=20;
PARMS b1-b24=0 d1-d8=0 mu=0 sd0=0.5 sd1=0.5;
beta=b1*x1+b2*x2+b3*x3+b4*x4+b5*x5+b6*x6+b7*x7
+b8*x8+b9*x9+b10*x10+b11*x11+b12*x12+b13*x13+b14*x14
+b15*x15+b16*x16+b17*x17+b18*x18+b19*x19+b20*x20
+b21*x21+b22*x22+b23*x23+b24*x24;
delta=d1*x13+d2*x14+d3*x16+d4*x17+d5*x19+d6*x20+d7*x22+d8*x23;
ex=exp(theta-beta-delta*male);
p=ex/(1+ex);

MODEL y ~ binary(p);
RANDOM theta ~ normal(male*mu,(1-male)*(sd0**2)+male*(sd1**2))

subject=person;
ESTIMATE 'sd0**2' sd0**2;
ESTIMATE 'sd1**2' sd1**2;
RUN;
```

Comments

1. The data set **aggression_dich** contains a column of binary responses y, a column of person identification labeled **person**, a column of Gender coding, named as **male** (male=0 for females and male=1 for males), and 24 columns of 24 item indicator variables named from x1 to x24.
2. sd0 is the standard deviation of the random intercept for females; mu and sd1 are the mean and standard deviation of the random intercept for males, respectively; b1 to b24 are 24 item location parameters. d1 to d8 are eight DIF parameters for actually cursing or scolding.
3. θ is assumed to follow a $N(0,sd0^2)$ distribution for females and a $N(mu, sd1^2)$ distribution for males.
4. The two **ESTIMATE** statements are used to obtain estimates of the variance of the underlying dimension for males and females.

7.7.2 RW-DFF for actually scolding or cursing using contrast coding for Gender (verbal aggression data)

Code

```
PROC NLMIXED data=aggression_dich method=gauss
technique=newrap noad qpoints=20;
PARMS b1-b24=0 muth1=0 muga1=0 sdth0=0.5 sdth1=0.5
sdga0=0.5 sdga1=0.5 cothga0=0 cothga1=0.5;
beta=b1*x1+b2*x2+b3*x3+b4*x4+b5*x5+b6*x6+b7*x7
+b8*x8+b9*x9+b10*x10+b11*x11+b12*x12+b13*x13+b14*x14
+b15*x15+b16*x16+b17*x17+b18*x18+b19*x19+b20*x20
+b21*x21+b22*x22+b23*x23+b24*x24;
ex=exp(theta-beta-gamma*x25*gender);
p=ex/(1+ex);
MODEL y ~ binary(p);
RANDOM theta gamma ~ normal([male*muth1,male*muga1],
[(1-male)*(sdth0**2)+male*(sdth1**2),
(1-male)*cothga0+male*cothga1,
(1-male)*(sdga0**2)+male*(sdga1**2)]) subject=person;
RUN;
```

Comments

1. The data set `aggression_dich` contains an additional column of facet coding for actually cursing or scolding, namely x25 (x25=1 for do-items regarding cursing or scolding x25=0 otherwise).

2. gamma is the random DFF parameter for actually cursing or scolding; muth1 and muga1 are the means of θ and γ for males; sdth0, cothga0, and sdga0 are the parameters of the variance-covariance matrix for females; sdth1, cothga1, and sdga1 are the parameters of the variance-covariance matrix for males.

3. $(\theta, \gamma) \sim N([0, 0], [(sdth0)^2, cothga0, (sdga0)^2])$ for females and $(\theta, \gamma) \sim N([muth1, muga1], [(sdth1)^2, cothga1, (sdga1)^2])$ for males.

7.8 Exercises

1. Suppose we have a test data set which consists of the responses of 900 students to 20 items (450 students from each of two countries of interest), and we are interested in finding out whether items 11 to 20 function in the same way for different countries. Explain how models that include uniform or non-uniform DIF can be formally specified and how they can be estimated with NLMIXED. When building the model, assume that the 2PL can be used to adequately describe the item responses in each group. Suppose that you find uniform DIF in item 12. Explain how a model in

which this interaction effect is random over persons can be formally specified and how this model can be estimated with NLMIXED. Formulate and characterize models that make use of dummy coding and contrast coding. Explain how the coding scheme of the group variable affects the kind of individual differences that are introduced by the model.

2. Suppose a test for deductive reasoning with 15 items is administered to samples from three populations indicated by a grouping variable Z ($Z = 1, 2, 3$ for populations A, B and C, respectively). Furthermore, suppose that item response functions can be adequately described by the 2PL and that it is reasonable to assume that the first five items have equivalent item response functions across groups. Formulate a model to simultaneously test for differences in location and slope parameters between (1) groups A and C and (2) B and C. It helps to use two dummy variables D_1 and D_2 to code the information in Z. Assume $D_1 = D_2 = 0$ for $Z = 3$; $D_1 = 1$ and $D_2 = 0$ for $Z = 1$; $D_1 = 0$ and $D_2 = 1$ for $Z = 2$. Elaborate on how you could model individual differences within different populations.

3. Suppose you analyze the original trichotomous verbal aggression data in which subjects were asked to what extent they would display a particular behavior in a particular situation (0=no, 1=perhaps, 2=yes). Specify and estimate a partial credit model for these data (see also Chapter 3) that includes behavior-specific dynamic predictors to model actual behavior on the basis of intended behavior.

4. In the section on dynamic models of this chapter, a Want-Do model with behavior-specific dynamic predictors is selected (see Table 7.8) to model the verbal aggression data. Specify and estimate the model that also includes a random weight for the dynamic predictor associated to 'shouting.' Compute the empirical Bayes estimates for the overall underlying dimension and for the random effect of the dynamic predictor.

5. Specify and estimate a model to test whether the dynamic effects included in the Want-Do model of Table 7.8 in this chapter are different for males and females. For dynamic effects that differ across groups, estimate a model that captures the differences among males and females as well.

7.9   References

Arnold, B.C. & Press, S.J. (1989). Compatible conditional distributions. *Journal of the American Statistical Association, 84*, 152–156.

Diggle, P.J., Heagerty, P., Liang, K. & Zeger, S.L. (2002). *Analysis of Longitudinal Data (2nd ed.)*. New York: Oxford University Press.

Dorans, N.J. & Holland, P.W. (1993). DIF detection and description: Mantel-Haenszel and standardization. In P.W. Holland & W. Howard (Eds), *Differential Item Functioning* (pp. 35–66). Hillsdale, NJ: Lawrence Erlbaum.

Dorans, N.J. & Kulick, E. (1986). Demonstrating the utility of the standardization approach to assessing unexpected differential item performance on the scholastic aptitude test. *Journal of Educational Measurement, 23,* 355–368.

Engelhard, G. (1992). The measurement of writing ability with a many-faceted Rasch model. *Applied Measurement in Education, 5,* 171–191.

Fahrmeir, L. & Tutz, G. (2001). *Multivariate Statistical Modeling Based on Generalized Linear Models (2nd ed.).* New York: Springer.

Gelman, A. & Speed, T.P. (1993). Characterizing a joint probability distribution by conditionals. *Journal of the Royal Statistical Society. Series B, 55,* 185–188.

Holland, P.W. & Thayer, D.T. (1988). Differential item functioning and the Mantel-Haenszel procedure. In H. Wainer & H.I. Braun (Eds), *Test Validity* (pp. 129–145). Hillsdale, NJ: Lawrence Erlbaum.

Holland, P.W. & Wainer, H. (1993). *Differential Item Functioning.* Hillsdale, NJ: Lawrence Erlbaum.

Hoskens, M. & De Boeck, P. (1995). Componential IRT models for polytomous items. *Journal of Educational Measurement, 32,* 364–384.

Hoskens, M. & De Boeck, P. (1997). A parametric model for local dependence among test items. *Psychological Methods, 2,* 261–277.

Hunt, L.A. & Jorgensen, M.A. (1999). Mixture model clustering: A brief introduction to the MULTIMIX program. *Australian and New Zealand Journal of Statistics, 41,* 153–171.

Ip, E.H., Wang, J.W., De Boeck, P. & Meulders, M. (2003). Locally dependent latent trait models for polytomous responses. *Psychometrika.* Manuscript accepted for publication.

Jannarone, R.J. (1986). Conjunctive item response theory kernels. *Psychometrika, 51,* 357–373.

Kelderman, H. (1984). Loglinear Rasch model tests. *Psychometrika, 49,* 223–245.

Kelderman, H. (1989). Item bias detection using loglinear IRT. *Psychometrika, 54,* 681–697.

Klauer, K.C. & Sydow, H. (2001). Dynamic IRT models. In A.Boomsma, M.A.J. van Duijn & T.A.B. Snijders (Eds), *Essays on Item Response Theory* (pp. 69–87). New York: Springer.

Li, H. & Stout, W. (1996). A new procedure for detection of crossing DIF. *Psychometrika, 61,* 647–677.

Lord, F.M. (1980). *Applications of Item Response Theory to Practical Test-*

ing Problems. Hillsdale, NJ: Lawrence Erlbaum.

Mellenbergh, G.J. (1982). Contingency table models for assessing item bias. *Journal of Educational Statistics, 7*, 105–118.

Millsap, R.E. & Everson, H.T. (1993). Methodology review: Statistical approaches for assessing measurement bias. *Applied Psychological Measurement, 17*, 297–334.

Moore, S.M. (1996). Estimating differential item functioning in the polytomous case with the RCML model. In G. Engelhard & M. Wilson (Eds), *Objective Measurement: Theory into Practice (Vol.3)* (pp. 219–240). Norwoord, NJ: Ablex.

Muraki, E. (1999). Stepwise analysis of differential item functioning based on multiple-group partial credit model. *Journal of Educational Measurement, 36*, 217–232.

Raju, N.S. (1988). The area between two item characteristic curves. *Psychometrika, 53*, 495–502.

Rosenbaum, P.R. (1988). Item bundles. *Psychometrika, 53*, 349–359.

Scheuneman, J.D. (1979). A method of assessing bias in test items. *Journal of Educational Measurement, 16*, 143–152.

Shealy, R. & Stout, W. (1993a). An item response theory model for test bias and differential item functioning. In P.W. Holland & W. Howard (Eds), *Differential Item Functioning* (pp. 197–239). Hillsdale, NJ: Lawrence Erlbaum.

Shealy, R. & Stout, W. (1993b). A model-based standardization approach that separates true bias/DIF from group ability differences and detects test bias/DTF as well as item bias/DIF. *Psychometrika, 58*, 159–194.

Swaminathan, H. & Rogers, H.J. (1990). Detecting differential item functioning using logistic regression procedures. *Journal of Educational Measurement, 27*, 361–370.

Thissen, D., Steinberg, L. & Wainer, H. (1988). Use of item-response theory in the study of group differences in trace lines. In H. Wainer & H.I. Braun (Eds), *Test Validity* (pp. 147–169). Hillsdale, NJ: Lawrence Erlbaum.

Verguts, T. & De Boeck, P. (2000). A Rasch model for learning while solving an intelligence test. *Applied Psychological Measurement, 24*, 151–162.

Verhelst, N.D. & Glas, C.A.W. (1993). A dynamic generalization of the Rasch model. *Psychometrika, 58*, 395–415.

Verhelst, N.D. & Glas, C.A.W. (1995). Dynamic generalizations of the Rasch model. In G.H. Fischer & I.W. Molenaar (Eds), *Rasch Models: Foundations, Recent Developments, and Applications* (pp. 181–201). New York: Springer.

Wainer, H., Sireci, S.G., & Thissen, D. (1991). Differential testlet functioning: Definitions and detection. *Journal of Educational Measurement, 28*, 197–219.

Wainer, H. & Kiely, G. (1987). Item clusters and computerized adaptive testing: A case for testlets. *Journal of Educational Measurement, 24,* 185–201.

Wilson, M. & Adams, R.A. (1995). Rasch models for item bundles. *Psychometrika, 60,* 181–198.

Zimowski, F., Muraki, E., Mislevy, R.J. & Bock, R.D. (1994). *BIMAIN 2: Multiple group IRT analysis and test maintenance for binary items.* Chicago: Scientific Software International.

Zwinderman, A.H. (1997). Response models with manifest predictors. In W.J. van der Linden & R.K. Hambleton (Eds), *Handbook of Modern Item Response Theory* (pp. 245–256). New York: Springer.

Part III: Models with internal factors

Using external factors to explain variation requires fixed *a priori* knowledge about what might play a role in the variation. Such knowledge is not always available or perhaps not precise enough to be used in a model – in such a situation, one can consider using *internal factors*, where the values of the predictors are derived from the data, instead of being given as external information. In a first type of internal factor, one may have no idea at all of the relevant predictors or one may have some idea without having precise knowledge of the values of these predictors. In such situations it can make sense to consider models that deal with 'unknown' predictors or predictors with values that are 'not known *a priori.*' These are together called *latent properties*, and they can relate to either persons or items. Examples are: (a) the so-called 'item discrimination' parameters (an item predictor) and (b) latent class membership (a person predictor). A second type of internal factor is the *observed random predictor*. This is the case when in the model (some of the) observations are considered as a function of other (modeled) observations, such as responses to other items (thus, a person-by-item predictor).

III.1 Latent item properties

Think of a simple model with four item properties defined as follows. The 24 items from the example study can be divided into four groups: want-items and do-items concerning self-to-blame situations, and want-items and do-items concerning other-to-blame situations. Let us define for each of these a dummy coded item property: X_{i1}, X_{i2}, X_{i3}, and X_{i4}, so that $X_{ik} = 1$ if item i has property k ($k = 1, 2, 3, 4$), and $X_{ik} = 0$ if not. Let us now also define a random person effect for each of these properties, while omitting the random person intercept. The four random effects would be θ_{p1}, θ_{p2}, θ_{p3}, and θ_{p4}. This model is a four-dimensional model, with one dimension for each of the four groups of items. It is an example of between-items multidimensionality or a perfect simple structure. The correlation between the four random effects can be estimated, or it can be fixed to a specific value, most commonly to 0. The corresponding logit formula would read as:

$$\eta_{pi} = \theta_{p1}X_{i1} + \ldots + \theta_{p4}X_{i4} - \beta_i, \qquad (\text{III.1})$$

with β_i as the effect of the item indicator i. This model can be seen as a confirmatory factor analysis model, with the Xs as the fixed loadings and the θs as the factor scores.

One could relax this model so that not all Xs are equal to one, on the basis of the conjecture that not all items within the group are equally sensitive to the meaning of the item group (e.g., wanting to be verbally aggressive in an other-to-blame situation). This would mean that some items have higher values and others have lower values. (We don't restrict the models to have 'loadings' between -1 and $+1$.) In a similar way, items from one group may resemble in a slight way items from another group, so that $X_{ik} > 0$ even if item i does not belong to item group k. A possible solution for these problems is to ask experts to make prototypicallity ratings of all items for each of the four groups. This solution would imply a redefinition of the Xs but they would still be predictors with values that are given *a priori*.

A drastically different approach would be not to use external information to determine the Xs, but to rely exclusively on internal information. In other words, the Xs would become parameters to be estimated from the data. The external factors are then replaced with 'internal factors,' denoted with αs: α_{ir} for the value of item i on internal factor r, $r = 1, \ldots, R$. For the rest the model remains the same. The resulting formula in logit terms reads as follows:

$$\eta_{pi} = \theta_{p1}\alpha_{i1} + \ldots + \theta_{pR}\alpha_{iR} - \beta_i, \tag{III.2}$$

with θ_{pr} as the random effect of latent property α_r.

For $R > 1$, the αs (and the corresponding θs) can be rotated, just as in principal components models and factor analysis models. For the case of $R = 1$, this is the 2PL model: $\eta_{pi} = \alpha_i \theta_p - \beta_i$, or, in other words, a model with an item-weighted random intercept. Multidimensional models with external factors, and similar models with internal factors, including the 2PL model are described in Chapter 8.

Thus far the internal factors were defined as factors with a random person effect, as in Equation III.2. This is not a necessity. An alternative is that the effects are fixed. This leads to a kind of model that allows for an analysis of items in terms of a number of unobserved item properties:

$$\eta_{pi} = \theta_p - \beta_1 \alpha_{i1} + \ldots + \beta_R \alpha_{iR}, \tag{III.3}$$

with β_r as the fixed effect of the latent item properties α_r, and with θ_p as the random intercept.

Suppose these latent item properties are the difficulties of underlying component items, then the item difficulty in question, β_i, can be seen as decomposed into a weighted sum of the difficulties of the underlying R component elements. This idea is applied in Chapter 9.

As a consequence of the latent nature of the properties and the fact that their weight is a parameter (random or fixed), the resulting models are no longer linear models but *nonlinear models*. They contain one or more bilinear terms (a product of two parameters). Therefore the models of Equations III.2 and III.3 are not GLMMs but NLMMs.

What we called latent item properties are properties with values that are parameters to be estimated. One may think of these properties as properties one has forgotten to include or which one was not able to include because no observations were made or could be made. In a similar way one may have omitted person properties, even when they are an important source of variation, which is the topic of the next section.

III.2 Latent person properties

Let us assume a random intercept model and suppose that Gender had a rather large effect on the verbal aggression tendency, but that, due to an oversight, it was not included as a predictor in the model. Given the unaccounted effect of Gender, the actual distribution of the persons would be different from a normal distribution but, because we have no extant predictor, the normal distribution would still be assumed for the random intercept. If a normal distribution applies for each of the two groups, then a mixture of two normal distributions holds for the total group. Note also that, when Gender is not included in the model, one cannot tell with certainty who belongs to which distribution (to which Gender), although it is possible to derive a posterior probability. This is an easy example, because one can simply include Gender in the model in order to obtain again the normal distribution after the effect of Gender is accounted for. In a more realistic case, one is not aware of the person predictors that are omitted, so that this easy remedy does not help.

Sometimes the problem is inherent and cannot be solved by including external factors. For example, the concept of 'personality type' implies that the individual differences are not continuous but discrete. Suppose people differ as to what makes them angry and whether or not they inhibit their verbal aggressive tendency when angry. If these differences are not continuous, the following four types may exist (see Figure III.1):

(1) impulsive other-deprecatory (easily angry because of others' failures, and not inhibited),

(2) restrained other-deprecatory (easily angry because of others' failures, and inhibited),

(3) restrained self-deprecatory (easily angry because of one's own failures, and inhibited),

(4) impulsive self-deprecatory (easily angry because of one's own failures, and not inhibited).

Figure III.1 gives a graphical representation of a hypothetical distribution of the four types in a two-dimensional space of $\theta_{p\ do-want}$ and

$\theta_{p\ other-self}$, given the predictors $X_{i\ do-want}$ and $X_{i\ other-self}$. The ovals denote the 95% contours of the bivariate normal distributions (for the case of independent random effects $\theta_{p\ do-want}$ and $\theta_{p\ other-self}$). As can be seen, the discrepancy between doing and wanting is negative for most people, but for two types (Type 4 and Type 1) it is small in comparison to two other types with strong inhibition effects (Type 3 and Type 2). Looking at it in the other way, there are people who become angry primarily because of their own faults (Type 4 and Type 3), and others who become angry primarily because of other people's faults (Type 1 and Type 2).

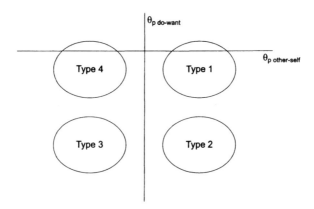

FIGURE III.1. Four verbal aggression types.

In the example in Figure III.1, the global bivariate distribution is a mixture of four different single distributions. Each single bivariate distribution of the four is a component of the mixture for the total group and defines a latent person group, also called a *latent class*. These components are unobserved categorical (discrete) person properties. Given that these types are defined by the data, there is no way to define an external factor that could have captured these types. The latent person properties we just discussed are not forgotten external factors but genuine latent properties. Using this model it is not possible to tell with certainty to which latent group a person belongs, but it is possible to estimate the probability of each latent group, and thus also the estimated size of each group, and it is also possible to derive a posterior probability for each person and each group.

The formula for a model with binary latent person properties reads as follows:

$$\eta_{pi} = \sum_{k=1}^{K} \alpha_{p1}\theta_{pk1}X_{ik} + \ldots + \sum_{k=1}^{K} \alpha_{pR}\theta_{pkR}X_{ik} - \beta_i, \qquad (III.4)$$

with α_{pr} as the binary value of person p on latent binary property r, $\alpha_{pr} = 0$, or 1, so that $\Sigma_{r=1}^{R}\alpha_{pr} = 1$; with θ_{pkr} as the corresponding random effect of item property k (we assume that the multivariate normal distribution of the θs differs depending on r; and with the β_i as the item difficulty). When $R = 1$, Equation III.4 reduces to the general formulation of Equation III.1. The model formulation in Equation III.4 shows the similarity with other models in this volume.

In the example there are two item properties, $X_{i\ do-want}$ and $X_{i\ other-self}$, and four classes of persons. A more complicated version of this model would be one with item difficulties that also depend on the class a person belongs to.

The types in Figure III.1 are heterogeneous types because within a type, people vary on the two random effects: $\theta_{p\ other-self}$ and $\theta_{p\ do-want}$. The implication is that the η_{pi} (and π_{pi}) differ depending on the person within each latent class. In most applications in psychology and education, homogeneous latent classes are used. They would be represented as points in Figure III.1. Homogeneous and heterogeneous mixture models are discussed in Chapter 11, but more attention is given to the latter than to the former.

Note that the mixture models are not linear models, for the same reason as for the models with latent item properties. They imply a multiplication of a latent (discrete) person property and its effect.

III.3 Observed random predictors

The third type of internal factor consists of responses to other items or functions thereof. The responses to an item i (Y_{pi}) are modeled as a function of observed responses on one or more other items, $i', i'', \ldots$ ($Y_{pi'}, Y_{pi''}, \ldots$). Most often this is done in combination with a random effect, such as a random intercept. For example,

$$\eta_{pi} = \theta_p - \beta_i + \delta_h W_{pih}, \tag{III.5}$$

with $W_{pih} = Y_{pi'}$, so that $i \neq i'$, and subscript h denotes the person-by-item predictor that is defined by the responses to item i. The notation for a person-by-item property is used, since the responses on another item define a person-by-item property. The values of the property depend on the person (her response) and the item (the responses matter for item i, but not for all items). This kind of predictor is used in *dynamic interaction models*, as described in Chapter 7. The predictors are not fixed-value predictors but random variables instead (although as predictors they enter the model with their realized and thus fixed value). Both Chapter 7 and Chapter 10 describe such dynamic interaction models, also called *conditional models* in the statistical literature.

As is explained in Chapter 4, apart from conditional modeling, there are two other ways for explaining correlated data: random-effects models and marginal models. In this volume, we chose to concentrate on random-effects modeling, and most commonly random intercept models. However, it might be a good strategy to combine random effects with aspects from the other two modeling approaches: conditional modeling and marginal modeling. This is further explained in Chapter 10 on residual dependence.

Chapter 8

Multiple person dimensions and latent item predictors

Frank Rijmen
Derek Briggs

8.1 Introduction

In this chapter, we discuss two extensions to the item response models presented in the first two parts of this book: *more than one random effect for persons (multidimensionality)* and *latent item predictors*. We only consider models with random person weights (following a normal distribution), and with no inclusion of person predictors (except for the constant). The extensions can be applied in much the same way to the other models that were discussed in the first two parts of this book.

The notion that a data matrix can be characterized by multiple dimensions has its roots in classical factor analysis. When the data matrix consists of continuous variables, classical factor analysis may be applied as the linear regression of observed variables on latent dimensions. For dichotomous variables (e.g., items), the classical factor analytic model must be adjusted such that the expected values of the observed variables are a nonlinear function of the latent dimensions. Traditionally, this nonlinear response function has been the normal-ogive cumulative distribution function (cdf; i.e., a probit link). The nonlinear factor analysis model is based on the matrix of tetrachoric correlations, and proceeds by assuming that the values of each observed dichotomous variable are determined by whether or not a threshold on an unobserved continuous variable is exceeded. When a normal-ogive response function is specified, the parameters can be estimated by generalized least squares (Christofferson, 1975; McDonald, 1967; Muthén, 1978). It has been shown that the parameters from a factor analysis of dichotomous variables can be readily transformed into the item-specific parameters typical of item response theory (Knol & Berger, 1991).

There are two principle distinctions between traditional factor analysis models for dichotomous items and what we will describe as multidimensional item response models (MIRMs). First, the former model is limited to the information from pairwise (tetrachoric) correlation coefficients, and does not take into account the full information available in each person's response vector. Second, the former models differ philosophically from MIRMs in that they are primarily concerned with data reduction and summation, and less so with describing and interpreting the characteristics of items used to produce responses (Ackerman, 1992; 1994; Reckase, 1997).

Bock, Gibbons and Muraki (1988; based on the work of Bock & Aitkin, 1981) developed an approach they termed 'full-information item factor analysis' because it is based on the frequencies of all distinct item response vectors and not just on pairwise correlations. The approach employs a probit link, and produces item parameter estimates by maximizing the marginal likelihood. The approach has been implemented using an EM algorithm in the software package TESTFACT (Wilson, Wood & Gibbons, 1984). Because full information item factor analysis becomes numerically quite cumbersome when multiple integrals (one for each dimension) need to be evaluated, McDonald (1997) has developed an approximation based on a polynomial expansion of the normal-ogive cdf that is often used as an alternative, and that is implemented in the program NOHARM (Fraser & McDonald, 1986).

Considerable effort has been devoted to the development and interpretation of MIRMs since the late 1980s. A primary focus has been on the consequences of applying unidimensional models in situations where the real or simulated data structure is in fact multidimensional (Embretson, 1991; Folk & Green, 1989; Kupermintz, Ennis, Hamilton, Talbert, & Snow, 1995; Luecht & Miller, 1992; Walker & Beretvas, 2000). Additional work has also been done to extend the model to the multidimensional analysis of polytomous items (Adams, Wilson & Wang, 1997; Kelderman, 1997; Kelderman & Rijkes, 1994; Muraki & Carlson, 1995; Wang, Wilson & Adams, 1997).

In what follows, we first present multidimensional extensions of both the Rasch model and the LLTM. Though the conceptual underpinning for multidimensionality is somewhat different for the two models, the two extensions are equivalent within a generalized linear model framework. Next, latent item predictors are introduced. As we will explain, a discrimination or slope parameter of an item in classical item response models (Birnbaum, 1968; McKinley, 1989; McKinley & Reckase, 1983) corresponds to the unknown value of an item predictor. Hence, we describe the discrimination parameter as a *latent* item predictor. The combination of multidimensionality and latent item predictors results in the full-information item factor analysis model developed by Bock et al. (1988), in our case with a logit instead of a probit link function. We illustrate the use of multiple dimensions and latent item predictors with the verbal aggression data.

8.2   Multiple person dimensions

8.2.1   Multidimensional extension of the Rasch model

Adopting the GLMM framework outlined in Chapter 1, the Rasch model is a mixed logistic regression model that incorporates for each item an item indicator X_i with fixed weight β_i , $i = 1, ..., I$ (see Chapter 2). For each person there is an associated weight θ_p for the constant Z_0 that is random over persons, $\theta_p \sim N(0, \sigma_\theta^2)$. The random weight conceptually represents a single latent variable. In vector notation (throughout the chapter, all vectors are defined to be column vectors), the logit of the probability π_{pi} that a person p gives a 1-response to item i is

$$\eta_{pi} = Z_{p0}\theta_p - \mathbf{X}_i'\beta = \theta_p - \beta_i. \qquad (8.1)$$

According to the Rasch model, all dependencies between the responses of a participant are accounted for by the latent variable (random effect) θ_p. Viewed from the item side, the characterization of the latent person space in terms of a single unidimensional latent variable means that all items are located on the same scale, operationalizing the same construct. However, a test often consists of several subscales measuring different, but potentially related constructs. Alternatively, one single item of a test might be measuring more than one construct. In both cases, the assumption of the Rasch model of one underlying unidimensional latent variable may be too restrictive. Extending the Rasch model with the single latent variable (random weight) θ_p to an R-dimensional vector $\boldsymbol{\theta}_p$ of latent variables (random weights), one for each construct the test is measuring, the logit of the conditional probability of success becomes

$$\eta_{pi} = \mathbf{X}_i'\boldsymbol{\theta}_p - \beta_i, \qquad (8.2)$$

where the vector $\mathbf{X}_i$ now specifies to which extent item i is measuring each of the R dimensions. We assume that the random weights $\boldsymbol{\theta}_p$ have a multivariate normal distribution with mean $\mathbf{0}$ and covariance matrix $\boldsymbol{\Sigma}$.

In a *between-item multidimensional model* (Adams et al., 1997), each item is a measurement of only one dimension. That is, $\mathbf{X}_i$ contains only one nonzero element, indicating the dimension to which the item belongs. When a Rasch model is assumed for each subscale, the nonzero element of $\mathbf{X}_i$ equals one for all i, and the fixed weight β_i corresponds to the location of item i on the dimension to which it belongs. The advantages of using the between-item multidimensional model instead of analyzing the different scales separately with a Rasch model is that the test structure is explicitly taken into account, so that estimates for the correlation between the latent dimensions are provided by estimating the covariance matrix $\boldsymbol{\Sigma}$ of the latent variables, and so that more accurate parameter estimates are obtained by relying on the correlation between the dimensions (Adams et al., 1997).

In a *within-item multidimensional model* (Adams et al., 1997), an item can be an indicator of more than one dimension. Hence, the vector $\mathbf{X}_i$ will contain more than one nonzero element. In the latter case, the fixed weight β_i can be thought of as a weighted sum of the locations of item i on the R dimensions. While this decomposition can be useful conceptually, a model formulated in terms of the individual item locations on the dimensions is in general not identified without imposing further restrictions (see Adams et al., 1997, for conditions on identifiability).

A graphical representation of the multidimensional extension of the Rasch model is given in Figure 8.1. Note that there is an item predictor for each dimension (indicating the items that belong to the dimension) and also one for each item, $K = R + I$. It is assumed that $\beta_i = 0$ if $k \leq R$. The logit link that connects π_{pi} to η_{pi}, and the random component that connects π_{pi} to Y_{pi} are omitted, here, and also in the following figures.

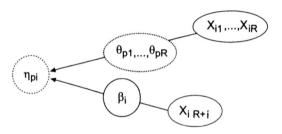

FIGURE 8.1. Graphical representation of the multidimensional extension of the Rasch model.

8.2.2   Multidimensional extension of the LLTM

In this section, an alternative rationale for multiple person dimensions is presented. The starting point this time is the LLTM (Fischer, 1973), a model in which the item parameters are regressed on item properties. As explained in Chapter 2, the LLTM can be conceived of as a logistic regression model with a constant that has a random weight over persons, and with item properties that have fixed weights. Hence, the logit of the conditional probability of success is

$$\eta_{pi} = Z_{p0}\theta_p - \mathbf{X}'_i\boldsymbol{\beta}, \tag{8.3}$$

where $\boldsymbol{\beta}$ is the vector which consists of the K fixed weights. The vector $\mathbf{X}_i$ maps item i onto its respective item properties.

Since only the constant has a random weight, the difference between the logits of the probabilities of success for each pair of participants is constant across items. That is, only person main effects and item property main effects are taken into account by the LLTM, respectively through the person specific weight of the constant θ_p, and the fixed regression weights of the item properties. It is assumed that there are no interactions between item properties and persons. In many situations however, one can expect such interactions, and hence individual differences would be expected in the regression weights of the item properties. For example, consider the cognitive task of solving a linear equation. Completing this task requires two distinct cognitive operations: (a) identifying the variable to be solved, and (b) carrying out algebraic manipulations. It is likely, and often a central issue, that individual differences exist in the degree to which such cognitive operations are mastered. The latter can be accounted for by allowing for person-specific regression weights for (some of) the item properties, leading to the *random-weights linear logistic test model* (RW-LLTM, Rijmen & De Boeck, 2002):

$$\eta_{pi} = Z_{p0}\theta_p + \mathbf{X}'_{ri}\boldsymbol{\theta}_p - \mathbf{X}'_{fi}\boldsymbol{\beta}, \qquad (8.4)$$

where $\mathbf{X}_{ri}$ and $\mathbf{X}_{fi}$ are the vectors that contain the values of item i on the item properties with random and fixed weights, respectively. Throughout the volume, we adopt the convention of defining random weights as the person specific deviations from the mean effect, which is included as a fixed weight, so that $\mathbf{X}_{ri}$ will generally be a subvector of $\mathbf{X}_{fi}$ ($R \leq K$). In terms of the framework of GLMMs, the RW-LLTM is a mixed logistic regression model with random slopes in addition to a random intercept. A graphical representation of the RW-LLTM is given in Figure 8.2.

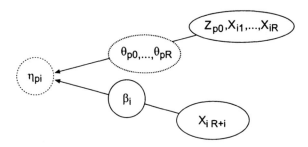

FIGURE 8.2. Graphical representation of the RW-LLTM.

8.2.3   Multidimensionality: two of a kind?

The two rationales we have discussed for arriving at a multidimensional model are, at a first sight, conceptually unrelated. However, both approaches lead to similar models, and are easily translated into each other. The RW-LLTM is a within-item multidimensional model with a decomposition of the fixed weights of the item indicators in terms of item properties. The random weight of the constant represents a dimension that is measured by all items to the same degree. Vice versa, each dimension of a test can be considered to define an item property with a random weight.

8.2.4   Application of a between-item multidimensional model

As an application of a multidimensional model, the verbal aggression data were analyzed with a between-item two-dimensional model. In the study, described in Chapter 1, respondents were presented a frustrating situation and asked whether they would *want* to react in a verbally aggressive manner (want-items), or whether they actually would react in a verbally aggressive manner (do-items). We hypothesized that the want-items and do-items represented two separate dimensions in a between-item model. The model was estimated with the procedure NLMIXED from SAS. A description of the program syntax is given in Section 8.5.1.

The deviance of the resulting model was 7980. The estimates and standard errors of the item parameters are given in Table 8.1. Within each dimension, the items are ordered from easiest (most likely to exhibit the response) to most difficult (least likely to exhibit the response). The results indicate that cursing was the most likely behavior and shouting the least likely, and that wanting was more likely than doing (for the average person, $\theta_{p1} = \theta_{p2} = 0$).

The estimates of the standard deviations for the dimensions corresponding to the want-items and do-items were 1.45 and 1.68 respectively, with SEs of .09 and .10. The estimated correlation between the two dimensions was .78 with a SE of .04. Hence, the two constructs of the questionnaire were highly correlated: respondents who wanted to react in a verbally aggressive way also tended to behave that way.

To test whether the two-dimensional model provides a better fit than the unidimensional Rasch model, a LR test can be used since the Rasch model is nested within the two-dimensional model. The latter becomes clear if we reparametrize the two-dimensional model as follows:

$$X_{i1}^* = \text{Want}_i + \text{Do}_i = 1, \text{and}$$
$$X_{i2}^* = \text{Do}_i,$$

where Want and Do are the item properties with random weights coding for the want-items (Want = 1, Do = 0) and the do-items (Want = 0, Do = 1), respectively. That is, in the reparametrized model, the first predictor with a random weight is the constant, and the second predictor with a random weight is the item property denoting whether or not an item is a do-item. If the variance of the latter is zero, the Rasch model is obtained. Hence, testing the Rasch model (null hypothesis) versus the between-item two-dimensional model (alternative hypothesis) comes down to testing for one versus two random weights. In this case, the asymptotic null distribution of the LR test-statistic is a mixture with equal weights of .5 of two chi-squared distributions, respectively with $df = 2$ and $df = 1$ (Verbeke & Molenberghs, 1997; see also Chapter 4). The LR test statistic amounted to $8072 - 7980 = 92$, $p < .001$, so that one may conclude that the two-dimensional model has a better goodness of fit than the Rasch model. Nevertheless, the estimates for the item parameters were very similar under both models, with a correlation of .99, and the correlation between the dimensions is very high, as mentioned earlier. The estimates of the item parameters for the Rasch model are also given in Table 8.1. Comparing the estimates of the item parameters for both models, it is notable that the estimates for the two-dimensional model are slightly expanded, in comparison with the estimates for the Rasch model.

TABLE 8.1. Estimates and standard errors of the item parameters for the between-item two-dimensional model and the Rasch model (verbal aggression data).

Situation	Behavior Type	Behavior Mode	2-dim β_i	2-dim $SE(\beta_i)$	Rasch β_i	Rasch $SE(\beta_i)$
Train	Curse	Want	-1.79	.18	-1.75	.18
Bus	Curse	Want	-1.25	.17	-1.22	.16
Call	Curse	Want	-1.11	.16	-1.08	.16
Train	Scold	Want	-.73	.16	-.71	.16
Bus	Scold	Want	-.58	.16	-.56	.15
Store	Curse	Want	-.55	.16	-.53	.15
Bus	Shout	Want	-.09	.16	-.08	.15
Train	Shout	Want	-.02	.16	-.01	.15
Call	Scold	Want	.35	.16	.35	.15
Store	Scold	Want	.70	.16	.69	.16
Call	Shout	Want	1.06	.16	1.04	.16
Store	Shout	Want	1.56	.18	1.53	.17
Bus	Curse	Do	-1.32	.18	-1.22	.16
Train	Curse	Do	-.94	.17	-.87	.16
Call	Curse	Do	-.75	.17	-.71	.16
Bus	Scold	Do	-.40	.17	-.39	.15
Train	Scold	Do	.09	.17	.06	.15
Store	Curse	Do	.25	.17	.21	.15
Call	Scold	Do	.44	.17	.38	.15
Bus	Shout	Do	.97	.17	.87	.16
Train	Shout	Do	1.62	.18	1.48	.17
Store	Scold	Do	1.65	.19	1.50	.17
Call	Shout	Do	2.17	.20	2.00	.18
Store	Shout	Do	3.21	.25	2.98	.23

8.3   Latent item predictors

8.3.1   The 2PL and its multidimensional extension

The second extension to be discussed in this chapter is the introduction of
latent item predictors. Again, the starting point is the Rasch model (Equation 8.1). As explained several times throughout this volume, it is assumed
in the Rasch model that there is a person-specific weight (i.e., latent variable) associated with the constant. The extension consists of dropping the
assumption that we know the value of this constant predictor for all items.
The constant, which can be conceived of as an item predictor (X_0) or a
person predictor (Z_0), now becomes a *latent* or unknown *item predictor*
whose values are additional parameters to be estimated from the data.
This extension to the Rasch model is known as the *2PL model* (Birnbaum,
1968):

$$\eta_{pi} = \alpha_i \theta_p - \beta_i. \tag{8.5}$$

In the psychometric literature, α_i is called the *discrimination parameter* of
the item. The larger the discrimination or slope parameter, the steeper the
item response function. In Figure 8.3, the curve is plotted for discrimination
parameters of 1, 2 and 3, and a value of 1 for β_i/α_i. β_i/α_i is the value of θ_p
for which the probability of success equals .5. For the Rasch model, $\alpha_i = 1$
for all i, so that $\beta_i/\alpha_i = \beta_i$.

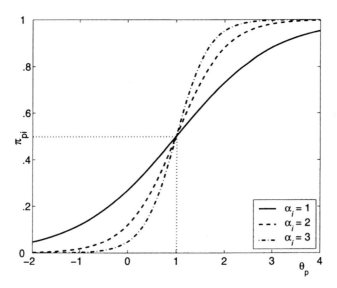

FIGURE 8.3. Item characteristic curves for three different discrimination parameters (one, two, and three) and $\alpha_i/\beta_i = 1$.

Apart from fixing the mean of θ_p to zero (as has been done throughout this volume), an additional constraint is needed to render the 2PL model identifiable, since one can multiply all α_i with a constant, and divide θ_p by the same value. One possible constraint, the one used in our application, is to fix the variance of θ_p to one (or to another value). Note however that a different constraint is implicitly used in the Rasch model: Strictly speaking, the Rasch model is a 2PL model for which all discrimination parameters are equal, but not necessarily equal to one. In the Rasch model the variance of θ_p is not fixed, but instead the (geometric) mean of the discrimination parameters is set to one. All discrimination parameters being equal, the constraint results in $\alpha_i = 1$ for all i, and the common formulation of the Rasch model is obtained.

For multidimensional models, latent item predictors can be introduced in much the same way. In Equation 8.2, the elements of the vector $\mathbf{X}_i$ are now estimated instead of known *a priori*. To distinguish between the known values of an item on manifest item predictors with random weights and the unknown (to be estimated) values of an item on latent item predictors with random weights, we refer to the latter by $\boldsymbol{\alpha}_i$. Hence,

$$\eta_{pi} = \boldsymbol{\alpha}_i' \boldsymbol{\theta}_p - \beta_i. \tag{8.6}$$

One can distinguish between an exploratory model in which all the elements of the vectors $\boldsymbol{\alpha}_i$ are estimated (McKinley & Reckase, 1983), and a confirmatory model in which part of the elements are estimated, and part are fixed to zero (McKinley, 1989). As an example of the latter, consider a situation where it is known *a priori* for each item which single dimension it is measuring (thus we are considering between-item multidimensionality only), but its discriminative power is unknown.

For an exploratory multidimensional model, additional identification restrictions are needed, due to the possibilities of rotation with respect to the dimensions. This can be solved by fixing the correlations between the dimensions, and/or by putting some constraints on the latent item predictors. Alternatively, one can rotate the solution according to some criterion, such as varimax or oblimin. For a confirmatory model, the identification restrictions depend on the specific model that is considered. For example, in a between-item multidimensional model, the constraints are zero loadings on the dimensions other than the one the item belongs to (and if αs are used that the variance has a fixed value). An advantage of considering a between-item multidimensional 2PL model is that the items can be located on the dimension they are measuring, since each item measures only one dimension. Dimension-specific item locations cannot be computed for a within-item multidimensional 2PL model, because a model for which β_i is decomposed as a weighted sum of contributions from the separate dimensions is in general not identified.

In Figure 8.4, the item characteristic curves are presented for a two-dimensional model for $\boldsymbol{\alpha}_i$ equal to $(0,2)', (1,0)'$, and $(1,2)'$. β_i is equal to zero. The value of element r of $\boldsymbol{\alpha}_i$ indicates to what extent item i is discriminating along dimension r.

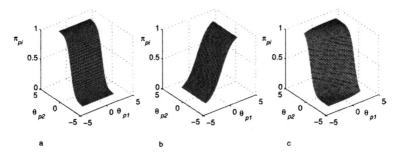

FIGURE 8.4. Item characteristic curves for three sets of discrimination parameters for a two-dimensional 2PL model: (a) $\boldsymbol{\alpha}_i = (0,2)'$, (b) $\boldsymbol{\alpha}_i = (1,0)'$, (c) $\boldsymbol{\alpha}_i = (1,2)'$, with β_i always equal to zero.

The extension towards the inclusion of latent item predictors relates item response modeling to classical factor analysis. As we pointed out in Section 8.1, an item response model equivalent to the multidimensional 2PL model but with a probit instead of a logit link has been called full-information item factor analysis (Bock et al., 1988). Similar to factor loadings in classical factor analysis, the elements of $\boldsymbol{\alpha}_i$ specify the extent to which item i is measuring each of the underlying dimensions or factors (it is the maximum extent when the probability scale, rather than logit scale is used). The α_{ir}'s are sometimes called *item loadings*. However, in contrast with the factor loadings in classical factor analysis with orthogonal factors, they are not the correlation between the item and the dimensions. This becomes clear considering the fact that the α_{ir} can be larger than one, even for orthogonal dimensions, whereas correlations are bounded between minus one and one.

A graphical representation of the 2PL model is given in Figure 8.5. For multidimensional models with latent item predictors, the graphical representation is the same, except that θ_p and α_i are vectors in this case.

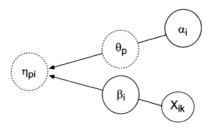

FIGURE 8.5. Graphical representation of the 2PL model.

8.3.2 Application of a multidimensional 2PL model

A confirmatory two-dimensional 2PL model is presented as an illustration. The confirmatory aspect of the model consisted of constraining the want-items and do-items to each measure a single dimension, as in the application discussed in Section 8.2.4. For the want-items, the values of the first latent item predictor with random weights were fixed at zero, and the values of a second latent item predictor with random weights were estimated. For the do-items, the values of the first latent item predictor were estimated, and the values of the second latent item predictor were fixed at zero. Hence, a model quite similar to the application discussed in Section 8.2.4 was estimated. The difference is that now the discrimination parameters of the items on their respective dimensions were also estimated, instead of being set to one.

TABLE 8.2. Estimates and standard errors of the fixed weights, discrimination parameters, and item locations for the confirmatory two-dimensional 2PL model (verbal aggression data).

Situation	Behavior Type	Behavior Mode	β_i	$SE(\beta_i)$	α_{i1}	α_{i2}	$SE(\alpha_i)$
Call	Curse	Want	-1.06	.17	1.29	-	.22
Bus	Curse	Want	-1.45	.23	1.92	-	.32
Train	Curse	Want	-1.05	.15	2.01	-	.36
Store	Curse	Want	-.51	.15	1.20	-	.20
Train	Scold	Want	-.48	.11	2.23	-	.36
Bus	Scold	Want	-.37	.10	2.06	-	.33
Bus	Shout	Want	-.05	.08	1.39	-	.22
Train	Shout	Want	-.03	.15	1.30	-	.21
Call	Scold	Want	.35	.16	1.61	-	.25
Store	Scold	Want	.70	.17	1.57	-	.25
Call	Shout	Want	.93	.15	1.01	-	.18
Store	Shout	Want	1.33	.16	.91	-	.18
Call	Curse	Do	-.76	.17	-	1.64	.25
Bus	Curse	Do	-.75	.12	-	2.09	.33
Train	Curse	Do	-.51	.10	-	1.92	.30
Bus	Scold	Do	-.29	.12	-	2.81	.46
Train	Scold	Do	.07	.20	-	2.37	.37
Store	Curse	Do	.20	.14	-	1.22	.20
Call	Scold	Do	.42	.17	-	1.77	.27
Bus	Shout	Do	.44	.08	-	1.47	.23
Train	Shout	Do	1.59	.22	-	1.66	.28
Store	Scold	Do	1.53	.20	-	1.48	.25
Call	Shout	Do	1.89	.21	-	1.21	.23
Store	Shout	Do	2.81	.30	-	1.20	.26

The model was identified by constraining the means of the two dimensions to zero, and constraining their variances to one. The procedure NL-MIXED from SAS was used to estimate the model. A description of the program syntax is given in Section 8.5.2.

The deviance of the estimated model amounted to 7930. The item parameter estimates are given in Table 8.2. Within each dimension, the items are ordered based on β_i/α_i, the value on the θ-scale where a 1-response on the item has a probability of .50. The estimate of the correlation between the two dimensions was .77, with a standard error of .04.

Since the between-item two-dimensional model without latent item predictors (discrimination parameters) is nested within the between-item two-dimensional model with latent item predictors, a likelihood-ratio test can be used to assess whether latent item predictors should be included. The likelihood ratio statistic amounted to $7980 - 7930 = 50, df = 22, p < .001$. Hence, the model without latent item predictors has poorer goodness of fit to a statistically significant extent. However, the consequences for the parameter estimates may not be large.

The estimates β_i are very similar to the estimates of β_i/α_i for the model with latent item predictors. The correlation amounted to .98. The correlation between the two dimensions was also quite similar under both models: .77 for the model with latent item predictors, and .78 for the model without latent item predictors. At least for some purposes it does not seem to matter much which model is used, but of course, if one is interested in variation in item discrimination parameters, then it does matter.

8.4   Concluding remarks

A psychological test often measures, and is intended to measure, more than one underlying construct. In order to analyze such data properly, MIRMs are called for. Analogous to exploratory factor analysis for continuous responses, MIRMs with latent item predictors can be used to explore the structure of a test. In the case where one is willing to make assumptions regarding the construct(s) an item is measuring, but not regarding to which extent, a confirmatory MIRM with latent item predictors may be appropriate. At the other extreme is a test for which one has knowledge of the relevant item properties (e.g., cognitive processes involved in solving an item). In the latter case, a RW-LLTM, the multidimensional analogon of the LLTM, is the model to be chosen.

A drawback of multidimensional models is that the computation time increases exponentially with the number of dimensions. For example, in a three-dimensional model and with 20 nodes per dimension, the integrals over the random effects are approximated by a summation over $20^3 = 8000$ points. Fortunately, in the context of MIRMs with latent item predictors, Bock et al. (1988) found that the number of nodes per dimension can be reduced with increasing dimensionality without impairing the accuracy of the approximations. It is a point of scientific research to see whether the same result holds for MIRMs in general. Another possibility is to use a Monte Carlo approach (Adams et al., 1997) to approximate the multidimensional integrals.

In this chapter, we have presented latent item predictors as predictors with random weights. In a similar way, it is possible to introduce latent item predictors with fixed weights. The model with internal restrictions on item difficulty (Butter, De Boeck, & Verhelst, 1998), discussed in Chapter 9, is an example of the latter.

8.5   Software

The NLMIXED procedure of SAS V8 was used for both applications discussed in this chapter. The syntax code and comments are given in what follows.

To speed up the estimation, we opted for nonadaptive instead of adaptive Gaussian quadrature to approximate the two-dimensional integral. We specified 20 nodes per dimension, hence $20 \times 20 = 400$ nodes in total.

8.5.1   Between-item two-dimensional model without latent item predictors (verbal aggression data)

The adaptive Gaussian quadrature with the number of nodes to be determined by the NLMIXED procedure did not converge after several days on a PC with a Pentium III processor and 250 Mb RAM. Nonadaptive Gaussian quadrature was used instead. Newton-Raphson was specified for the optimization technique.

Code

```
PROC NLMIXED data=aggression_dich method=gauss
technique=newrap noad qpoints=20;
PARMS b1-b24=0 sd_w=1 co_wd=0 sd_d=1;
theta=theta_w*want+theta_d*do;
beta=b1*x1+b2*x2+b3*x3+b4*x4+b5*x5+b6*x6+b7*x7
+b8*x8+b9*x9+b10*x10+b11*x11+b12*x12+b13*x13+b14*x14
+b15*x15+b16*x16+b17*x17+b18*x18+b19*x19+b20*x20
+b21*x21+b22*x22+b23*x23+b24*x24;
ex=exp(theta-beta);
p=ex/(1+ex);
MODEL y ~ binary(p);
RANDOM theta_w theta_d ~ normal([0,0],[sd_w**2,co_wd,sd_d**2])
subject=person;
ESTIMATE 'var_w' sd_w**2;
ESTIMATE 'var_d' sd_d**2;
ESTIMATE 'cor' co_wd/(sd_w*sd_d);
RUN;
```

Comments

1. The starting value was zero for the fixed weights and for the covariance between the random weights, and one for the standard deviations of the random weights.
2. want and do are the item predictors with random weights coding for the behavior mode (want=1 and do=0 for want-items, and want=0 and do=1 for do-items). The random effects are theta_w and theta_do.

3. The ESTIMATE statement was used to obtain estimates and standard errors for the variances of the random weights, and their intercorrelation.

8.5.2 Confirmatory two-dimensional 2PLM (verbal aggression data)

Since the Newton-Raphson optimization technique did not converge properly, the quasi-Newton optimization technique was used (the default option).

Code

```
PROC NLMIXED data=aggression_dich method=gauss
noad qpoints=20;
PARMS b1-b24=0 a1-a24=1 co_wd=0;
theta=(a1*x1+a2*x2+a3*x3+a4*x4+a5*x5+a6*x6
+a7*x7+a8*x8+a9*x9+a10*x10+a11*x11+a12*it12)*theta_w
+(a13*x13+a14*x14+a15*x15+a16*x16+a17*x17+a18*x18
+a19*x19+a20*x20+a21*x21+a22*x22+a23*x23+ a24*x24)*theta_d;
beta=b1*x1+b2*x2+b3*x3+b4*x4+b5*x5+b6*x6+b7*x7
+b8*x8+b9*x9+b10*x10+b11*x11+b12*x12+b13*x13+b14*x14
+b15*x15+b16*x16+b17*x17+b18*x18+b19*x19+b20*x20
+b21*x21+b22*x22+b23*x23+b24*x24;
ex=exp(theta-beta);
p=ex/(1+ex);
MODEL y ~ binary(p);
RANDOM theta_w theta_d ~ normal([0,0],[1,co_wd,1]) subject=pp;
ESTIMATE   'b1/a1'  b1/a1;
ESTIMATE   'b2/a2'  b2/a2;
ESTIMATE   'b3/a3'  b3/a3;
ESTIMATE   'b4/a4'  b4/a4;
ESTIMATE   'b5/a5'  b5/a5;
ESTIMATE   'b6/a6'  b6/a6;
ESTIMATE   'b7/a7'  b7/a7;
ESTIMATE   'b8/a8'  b8/a8;
ESTIMATE   'b9/a9'  b9/a9;
ESTIMATE   'b10/a10'  b10/a10;
ESTIMATE   'b11/a11'  b11/a11;
ESTIMATE   'b12/a12'  b12/a12;
ESTIMATE   'b13/a13'  b13/a13;
ESTIMATE   'b14/a14'  b14/a14;
ESTIMATE   'b15/a15'  b15/a15;
ESTIMATE   'b16/a16'  b16/a16;
ESTIMATE   'b17/a17'  b17/a17;
```

```
ESTIMATE  'b18/a18' b18/a18;
ESTIMATE  'b19/a19' b19/a19;
ESTIMATE  'b20/a20' b20/a20;
ESTIMATE  'b21/a21' b21/a21;
ESTIMATE  'b22/a22' b22/a22;
ESTIMATE  'b23/a23' b23/a23;
ESTIMATE  'b24/a24' b24/a24;
RUN;
```

Comments

1. The starting value was zero for the fixed weights of the item indicators and the correlation between the random effects, and one for the discrimination parameters.

2. The order of the items in the data set is such that the first 12 items are want-items, and the second 12 do-items. Hence, the terms for the second 12 items can be omitted for the want-dimension (theta_w), and the terms for the first 12 items can be omitted for the do-dimension (theta_d).

3. The ESTIMATE statement was used to obtain estimates and standard errors for the point where the probability of a 1-response is equal to .5.

8.6   Exercises

1. Explain why a within-item two-dimensional model of the form $\eta_{pi} = \theta_{i1} + \theta_{i2} - \beta_i$ does not make sense.

2.(a) The value β_i/α_i indicates the value of θ_p that is required to obtain a probability of .50 for the 1-response (and the 0-response). How would you give meaning to the value of β_i?
(b) Suppose you want to estimate β_i/α_i directly, without an ESTIMATE statement, how would you proceed?

3. Using the verbal aggression data, estimate a within-item two-dimensional model without latent item predictors, with the first dimension common to all items, and a second dimension for the do-items only.

4. Compare the results for the model of Exercise 3 with the results of the between-item two-dimensional model without latent item predictors discussed in Section 8.2.4.

5. Using the example data, estimate a RW-LLTM with the same item predictors as in the LLTM presented in Chapter 2, but with the weight of Other-to-blame vs Self-to-blame being random. Compare the results with the results for the LLTM. Is a random weight for Other-to-blame vs Self-

to-blame needed?

8.7 References

Ackerman, T. (1992). A didactic explanation of item bias, item impact, and item validity from a multidimensional perspective. *Journal of Educational Measurement, 29*, 67–91.

Ackerman, T. (1994). Using multidimensional item response theory to understand what items and tests are measuring. *Applied Measurement in Education, 7*, 255–278.

Adams, R.J., Wilson, M., & Wang, W.-C. (1997). The multidimensional random coefficients multinomial logit model. *Applied Psychological Measurement, 21*, 1–23.

Birnbaum, A. (1968). Some latent trait models and their use in inferring an examinee's ability. In F.M. Lord & M.R. Novick (Eds). *Statistical Theories of Mental Test Scores* (pp. 397–479). Reading, MA: Addison-Wesley.

Bock, R.D., & Aitkin, M. (1981). Marginal maximum likelihood estimation of item parameters: An application of an EM-algorithm. *Psychometrika, 46*, 443–459.

Bock, R.D., Gibbons, R., & Muraki, E. (1988). Full-information item factor analysis. *Applied Psychological Measurement, 12*, 261–280.

Butter, R., De Boeck, P., & Verhelst, N. (1998). An item response model with internal restrictions on item difficulty. *Psychometrika, 63*, 47–63.

Christoffersson, A. (1975). Factor analysis of dichotomized variables. *Psychometrika, 40*, 5–22.

Embretson, S.E. (1991). A multidimensional latent trait model for measuring learning and change. *Psychometrika, 56*, 495–515.

Fischer, G.H. (1973). Linear logistic test model as an instrument in educational research. *Acta Psychologica, 37*, 359–374.

Folk, V.G., & Green, B.F. (1989). Adaptive estimation when the unidimensionality assumption of IRT is violated. *Applied Psychological Measurement, 13*, 373–389.

Fraser, C., & McDonald, R. (1986). *NOHARM II: A FORTRAN program for fitting unidimensional and multidimensional normal ogive models of latent trait theory*. Armidale, NSW, Australia: University of New England.

Kelderman, H. (1997). Loglinear multidimensional item response models for polytomously scored items. In W. van der Linden & R. Hambleton (Eds), *Handbook of Modern Item Response Theory* (pp. 287–304). New York: Springer.

Kelderman, H., & Rijkes, C.P.M. (1994). Loglinear multidimensional IRT models for polytomously scored items. *Psychometrika, 59*, 149–176.

Knol, D. & Berger, M. (1991). Empirical comparison between factor analysis and multidimensional item response models. *Multivariate Behavioral Research, 26*, 457–477.

Kupermintz, H., Ennis, M.M., Hamilton, L.S., Talbert, J.E., & Snow, R.E. (1995). Enhancing the validity and usefulness of large-scale educational assessments .1. Nels-88 Mathematics Achievement. *American Educational Research Journal, 32*, 525–554.

Luecht, R.M., & Miller, R. (1992). Unidimensional calibrations and interpretations of composite traits for multidimensional tests. *Applied Psychological Measurement, 16*, 279–293.

McDonald, R.P. (1967). Nonlinear factor analysis. *Psychometric Monographs*, No. 15.

McDonald, R.P. (1997). Normal-ogive multidimensional model. In W.J. van der Linden & R.K. Hambleton (Eds). *Handbook of Modern Item Response Theory* (pp.257–269). New York: Springer.

McKinley, R.L. (1989). Confirmatory analysis of test structure using multidimensional item response theory. Research Report No. RR-89-31, Princeton, NJ: ETS.

McKinley, R.L., & Reckase, M.D. (1983). MAXLOG: A computer program for the estimation of the parameters of a multidimensional logistic model. *Behavior Research Methods and Instrumentation, 15*, 389–390.

Muraki, E. & Carlson, J.E. (1995). Full-information factor analysis for polytomous item responses. *Applied Psychological Measurement, 19*, 73–90.

Muthén, B.O. (1978). Contributions to factor analysis of dichotomous variables. *Psychometrika, 43*, 551–560.

Reckase, M.D. (1997). A linear logistic multidimensional model for dichotomous item response data. In W. van der Linden & R. Hambleton (Eds), *Handbook of Modern Item Response Theory* (pp. 271–286). New York: Springer.

Rijmen, F., & De Boeck, P. (2002). The random weights linear logistic test model. *Applied Psychological Measurement, 26*, 269–283.

Verbeke, G., & Molenberghs, G. (1997). *Linear Mixed Models in Practice: A SAS-Oriented Approach*. New York: Springer.

Walker, C.M., & Beretvas, S.N. (2000). Using multidimensional versus unidimensional ability estimates to determine student proficiency in mathematics. Paper presented at the 2000 Annual Meeting of the American Educational Research Association, New Orleans, LA.

Wang, W.-C., Wilson, M., & Adams, R.J. (1997). Rasch models for multidimensionality between items and within items. In M. Wilson, K. Draney, & G. Eglehard (Eds), *Objective Measurement (Vol. 4,)*. Norwood, NY:

Ablex.

Wilson, D., Wood, R. & Gibbons, R. (1984). *TESTFACT. Test Scoring, Item Statistics and Item Factor Analysis [Computer software and manual]*. Mooreville, IN: Scientific Software.

Chapter 9

Latent item predictors with fixed effects

Dirk J. M. Smits
Stephen Moore

9.1 Introduction

The Rasch model (Rasch, 1960) and the linear logistic test model (LLTM, Fischer, 1973, 1977) are two commonly used item response models. Both models are discussed in Chapter 2. The Rasch model assumes item indicators as predictors, so that each item has a specific effect, the weight of the corresponding item indicator. The LLTM explains these effects in terms of item properties, or in other words item properties are used as item predictors. Therefore, the LLTM may be considered an item explanatory model, in contrast with the Rasch model which is descriptive.

The requirement that the values of the item properties be known in advance for every item is both a strength and a limitation of the LLTM. The strength is that the model supports a more parsimonious account of item effects, but the limitation is that the values specified for items on the properties imply additional model assumptions. In the current chapter, a model will be introduced with latent item properties: The values of these latent item properties do not have to be known *a priori*, but they may have unknown values that are estimated as model parameters. The model introduced in this chapter is called the *model with internal restriction on item difficulties* (MIRID; Butter, De Boeck, & Verhelst, 1998).

The MIRID was originally published by Butter et al. (1998), based on Butter (1994). In Butter et al. (1998), a conditional maximum likelihood formulation and estimation method was explained, and the results of a simulation study were presented. An application of the MIRID and an extension of the MIRID to the OPLM-MIRID (originally described by Butter, 1994) and the 2PL-MIRID can be found in Smits and De Boeck (2003). A comparison between two estimation methods for the MIRID and the OPLM-MIRID – a conditional maximum likelihood estimation (Smits, De Boeck, Verhelst, & Butter, 2001) and a marginal maximum likelihood estimation, implemented within PROC NLMIXED – can be found in Smits, De Boeck, and Verhelst (2003).

The MIRID in its standard form will be explained in the first part of the chapter. In the standard form, the weights of the latent item predictors are assumed to be fixed. In the second part of the chapter, an extension of the MIRID will be explained in which the weights of some of the latent item predictors are randomly distributed over persons instead of being fixed. This extension is called the *random-weights MIRID* (RW-MIRID). The RW-MIRID parallels the RW-LLTM as an extension of the LLTM (see Chapter 8 for this extension). The graphical representation used in Chapters 1 and 2 and in some other chapters to represent models will not be used here, because the relationship between the items is a complication.

The MIRID assumes a specific relationship among items that the LLTM does not assume. To understand this relationship among items, it is useful to compare the MIRID to the LLTM. In the LLTM, every item reflects or embodies several item properties to some known degree. These item properties are postulated to explain the item effects. In the MIRID, there are two different types of items: *component items*, and *composite items*.

The effect of the composite items is explained on the basis of the effect of component items. The component items are organized in types (components), so that each composite item is associated with one component item from each type. The effects of the component items per type constitute a latent predictor for the composite items. The effects of component items function in the MIRID just as item properties function in the LLTM. For example, Smits and De Boeck (2003), used a questionnaire to test a theory on the components of situational guilt feelings. The data were from 268 persons, 130 males and 138 females between the ages of 17 and 19. Situational guilt feelings were assumed to depend on three latent factors: (1) whether one feels that one has violated a moral, ethic, religious, or personal code in the situation (Norm Violation), (2) whether one worries about what one did or failed to do in the situation (Worrying), and (3) whether one wants to rectify what one did or failed to do in the situation (Tendency to Rectify). The questionnaire contains 10 hypothetical situations (see Section 9.9), and the participants were asked to respond to four questions per situation: a question on each of the three aspects (components), and a fourth question about feeling guilty in the situation. The first three questions are component items and the fourth is a composite item. Since these four questions are repeated for each situation, there are 30 component items and 10 composite items. The effects of the 10 norm violation items define the first latent predictor, the effects of the 10 items about worrying define the second latent predictor, and the effects of the 10 items about wanting to rectify define the third latent predictor. The effect of the composite items is assumed to be a linear function of the effects of the corresponding three component items.

In general, the relations among all items can be expressed in a *relationship matrix* of items by component items (see Figure 9.1). The matrix indicates which component items (columns) are related to each of the items (rows). Note that this matrix relates items, and thus may not be considered

		Component 1 Norm Violation		Component 2 Worrying		Component 3 T. Rectify	
		item 1	item 5	item 2	item 6	item3	item 7
It. fam. 1	item 1	1	0	0	0	0	0
	item 2	0	0	1	0	0	0
	item 3	0	0	0	0	1	0
	item 4	1	0	1	0	1	0
It. fam. 2	item 5	0	1	0	0	0	0
	item 6	0	0	0	1	0	0
	item 7	0	0	0	0	0	1
	item 8	0	1	0	1	0	1

FIGURE 9.1. Example of a relationship matrix for two item families.

a property matrix.

The items shown in the relationship matrix in Figure 9.1 are grouped in two ways: *item families* (sets of rows designated It. fam. 1, It. fam. 2, ...) and *components* (sets of columns). An item family groups the composite item and all the component items that relate to that composite item (i.e., for the guilt example: all component items concerning the same situation). In Figure 9.1, there are two item families: (1) the items 1, 2, 3, and 4 and (2) the items 5, 6, 7, and 8. A component groups all items that embody a particular theoretical factor (in our case, a component or basis for guilt). In Figure 9.1, Component 1 groups the items 1 and 5, Component 2 groups the items 2 and 6, and Component 3 groups the items 3 and 7. All model formulations in this chapter will be based on this item family structure with one component item of each type per composite item. The MIRID can also accommodate a hierarchical family structure in which lower-order composite items in turn function as component items for higher-order composite items.

The latent item predictors in MIRID are the counterparts of the item properties in the LLTM. As in the LLTM, standard MIRID item predictors have fixed weights. In contrast to the item predictors in the LLTM, the values of the latent item predictors are not fixed *a priori*, but are the item parameters of the component items as will be explained in the next paragraph. The effects of the composite items are modeled as a linear function of the item parameters of the corresponding component items.

9.2 The model

9.2.1 The systematic component

Like most item response models including the LLTM, the MIRID has a fixed-effect part and a random-effect part in its systematic component (the one that determines the response probabilities). To explain the formula for the fixed-effect part, two new indices will be used for the items: The index $r(r = 1, \ldots, R)$ denotes the components, and the index $s(s = 1, \ldots, S)$ denotes the item family. For each composite item, the index r will be set equal to $R + 1$. The index $i(i = 1, \ldots, I)$ denotes the item, meaning that each value of i corresponds with a particular combination of the indices r and s. The index $p(p = 1, \ldots, P)$ denotes the person.

In order to formulate the model, two matrices will be introduced: a *latent item predictor matrix* $\mathbf{A}$ and a *componential weight matrix* $\mathbf{\Psi}$. The latent item predictor matrix $\mathbf{A}$ is a matrix of item families by latent item predictors. It contains the values (parameters) of the latent item predictors: the α_{sr}. Each latent item predictor corresponds to a component. See Figure 9.2 for a latent item predictor matrix for the example as presented in Figure 9.1. In addition, a constant predictor is added that will be used to model the composite item responses. In order to see that Figure 9.2 represents the latent item predictor matrix, we have expanded this matrix in Figure 9.3; however, the symbol $\mathbf{A}$ will further be used to denote the collapsed matrix as in Figure 9.2.

	Predictor 1 Component 1	Predictor 2 Component 2	Predictor 3 Component 3	Const. Pred.
Item family 1	α_{11}	α_{12}	α_{13}	1
Item family 2	α_{21}	α_{22}	α_{23}	1

FIGURE 9.2. Example of a latent item predictor matrix $\mathbf{A}$.

		Predictor 1 Comp. 1	Predictor 2 Comp. 2	Predictor 3 Comp. 3	Const. Pred.
It. fam. 1	item 1	α_{11}	α_{12}	α_{13}	1
	item 2	α_{11}	α_{12}	α_{13}	1
	item 3	α_{11}	α_{12}	α_{13}	1
composite	item 4	α_{11}	α_{12}	α_{13}	1
It. fam. 2	item 5	α_{21}	α_{22}	α_{23}	1
	item 6	α_{21}	α_{22}	α_{23}	1
	item 7	α_{21}	α_{22}	α_{23}	1
composite	item 8	α_{21}	α_{22}	α_{23}	1

FIGURE 9.3. Expanded latent item predictor matrix.

The second matrix is the componential weight matrix $\mathbf{\Psi}$, which is a matrix of item type by latent item predictors or components plus a constant predictor for the composite items. The item types are component item type 1 (Component 1), component item type 2 (Component 2), etc., and the composite items. See Figure 9.4 for the example of eight items as presented in Figure 9.1 and 9.2.

The matrix gives the weights of the latent predictors for each of the item types. Component items (rows 1 to 3) have a weight of one for the corresponding component, and zero otherwise. This is reflected in an identity matrix in the upper left part. Composite items have a weight parameter for each of the components and for the constant. The weights are β_1, β_2, β_3, and β_0, respectively.

	Comp. 1	Comp. 2	Comp. 3	Const.Pred.
Comp. item type 1	1	0	0	0
Comp. item type 2	0	1	0	0
Comp. item type 3	0	0	1	0
Composite item	β_1	β_2	β_3	β_0

FIGURE 9.4. Example of a componential weight matrix $\mathbf{\Psi}$.

The product of $\mathbf{A}$ and $\mathbf{\Psi}'$ results in an *item parameter matrix* of item families by item types. The item parameter matrix that corresponds to Figure 9.2 and 9.4 is shown in Figure 9.5. In this matrix, the item parameters for all items can be found, organized by item family.

	Component item type 1	Component item type 2	Component item type 3	Composite item
It. fam. 1	α_{11}	α_{12}	α_{13}	$\sum_{r=1}^{3} \alpha_{1r}\beta_r + \beta_0$
It. fam. 2	α_{21}	α_{22}	α_{23}	$\sum_{r=1}^{3} \alpha_{2r}\beta_r + \beta_0$

FIGURE 9.5. Example of an item parameter matrix.

The *fixed-effect* part of the MIRID can now be formulated as:

$$(\text{fixed-effect part})_{pi} = \beta_i' = \mathbf{A}_s'\mathbf{\Psi}_r, \tag{9.1}$$

with $\mathbf{A}_s' = (\alpha_{s1}, \ldots, \alpha_{s\,R+1})$, and $\mathbf{\Psi}_r$ the transposed row r from $\mathbf{\Psi}$.

The products $\mathbf{A}_s'\mathbf{\Psi}_r$ correspond to the cells in the item parameter matrix. For example, $\mathbf{A}_2'\mathbf{\Psi}_1$ equals $\alpha_{21} = (\alpha_{21}, \alpha_{22}, \alpha_{23}, 1) \times (1, 0, 0, 0)'$, and $\mathbf{A}_2'\mathbf{\Psi}_4$ equals $\alpha_{24} = (\alpha_{21}, \alpha_{22}, \alpha_{23}, 1) \times (\beta_1, \beta_2, \beta_3, \beta_0)'$.

The fixed-effect part for the component item parameters is similar to the fixed-effect part of a Rasch model, as for the component items $\beta_i' = \alpha_{sr}$; see Equation 9.1. This implies that the values of the latent item predictors are also the item parameters of the corresponding component items. The fixed-effect part for the composite items is a linear combination of the component item parameters α_{sr} with weights β_r: $\beta_i' = \sum_{r=1}^{R} \beta_r \alpha_{sr} + \beta_0$. The composite item parameter is decomposed into the item parameters of the component items. In other words, the effect of a composite item is explained in terms of latent item predictors and their weights.

As can be seen in Equation 9.1, the equation for the fixed-effect part is not linear in its parameters, since a product of two parameters is involved. By consequence, the MIRID is not part of the family of generalized linear models, but it is a nonlinear model instead (McCulloch & Searle, 2001). Maris and Bechger (2003) mention that the MIRID is a member of the curved exponential family, which implies among other things that conditional maximum likelihood estimation is possible for α and β. Also in the MIRID, the sum scores are sufficient statistics for the person parameters (θ_{p0}).

The *random-effect part* of the MIRID is the same as for the Rasch model. It consists of θ_{p0}, called the random intercept or person parameter. We assume $\theta_{p0} \sim N\left(0, \sigma_\theta^2\right)$. The subscript 0 is used to differentiate the random intercept from the other types of random effects to be presented later.

The formula for the odds of a 1-response according to the MIRID is analogous to the corresponding formula for the Rasch model or the LLTM:

$$\eta_{pi} = \theta_{p0} - \beta_i', \tag{9.2}$$

with $\theta_{p0} \sim N(0, \sigma_\theta^2)$, for the component items $\beta_i' = \alpha_{sr}$, and for the composite items, $\beta_i' = \sum_{r=1}^{R} \beta_r \alpha_{sr} + \beta_0$, with i as an index for the pairs (s, r).

Equation 9.2 can be rewritten in terms of the previously used matrix notation as follows:

$$\eta_{pi} = \theta_{p0} - \mathbf{A}_s' \mathbf{\Psi}_r. \tag{9.3}$$

9.2.2   Identifiability of the MIRID

The well-known indeterminacy of the Rasch model has implications for the item parameters of the MIRID (Butter et al., 1998). If we rescale so that $\beta_i^* = \beta_i' + c$, then it follows that for the component items $\alpha_{sr}^* = \alpha_{sr} + c$ and for the composite items that $\beta_i^* = \sum_{r=1}^{R} \beta_r \alpha_{sr} + \beta_0 + c$ and also that $\beta_i^* = \sum_{r=1}^{R} \beta_r \alpha_{sr}^* + \beta_0^*$, so that

$$\beta_0^* = \beta_0 + c \left(1 - \sum_{r=1}^{R} \beta_r \right). \tag{9.4}$$

The weights are invariant under translations of the scale, but the constant is not. As for the Rasch model, a restriction is needed to render the model identifiable. If $\sum_{r=1}^{R} \beta_r = 1$, then $\beta_0^* = \beta_0$, so that in this particular case, fixing the constant will not solve the indeterminacy. Fixing the constant will render the model identifiable only if $\sum_{r=1}^{R} \beta_r \neq 1$. In line with the solution for all other models in this volume, we will fix the mean of the distribution of the person parameter to zero.

For a MIRID with other relations between the items than the ones described by the item family structure, more restrictions may be needed to render it identifiable. Bechger, Verhelst, and Verstralen (2001) embedded the MIRID in a more general model called the nonlinear logistic test model (NLTM), and derived the conditions the NLTM has to fulfill in order for the model to be identified. Maris and Bechger (2003) provide more specific conditions for the identifiability of MIRIDs with various kinds of relations, other than the item family structure.

A problem related to the identification is the existence of equivalent MIRIDs. Bechger, Verstralen, and Verhelst (2002) described this problem for the LLTM, and Maris and Bechger (2003) extended it to the MIRID. MIRIDs for different componential theories about an item set may be formally equivalent, so that they cannot be differentiated. For example, if we modify the latent item predictor matrix $\mathbf{A}$ (see Figure 9.2) into $\mathbf{A}^{(1)}$ as shown in Figure 9.6 and the componential weight matrix $\mathbf{\Psi}$ (see Figure 9.4) into $\mathbf{\Psi}^{(1)}$ as shown below in Figure 9.6, an equivalent MIRID is obtained. The resulting item parameter matrix is shown in Figure 9.5. The problem of equivalent MIRIDs is not surprising, since the MIRID is a model with bilinear terms, as in a factor analysis model, so that rotational invariance may come into play. Therefore, we prefer to use the MIRID in a confirmatory way, which is implied when the item family structure is imposed. The item family structure implies that the upper left part of $\mathbf{\Psi}$ is an identity matrix, so that a transformation as from $\mathbf{\Psi}$ to $\mathbf{\Psi}^{(1)}$ is not possible.

$$
\mathbf{A}^{(1)} = \begin{array}{l} \text{Item family 1} \\ \text{Item family 2} \end{array} \left(\begin{array}{cccc} \alpha_{11} - \alpha_{21} & \alpha_{21} & \alpha_{31} & 1 \\ \alpha_{12} - \alpha_{22} & \alpha_{22} & \alpha_{32} & 1 \end{array} \right)
$$

$$
\mathbf{\Psi}^{(1)} = \begin{array}{l} \text{Component item type 1} \\ \text{Component item type 2} \\ \text{Component item type 3} \\ \text{Composite item} \end{array} \left(\begin{array}{cccc} 1 & 1 & 0 & 0 \\ 0 & 1 & 0 & 0 \\ 0 & 0 & 1 & 0 \\ \beta_1 & (\beta_1 + \beta_2) & \beta_3 & \beta_0 \end{array} \right)
$$

FIGURE 9.6. An equivalent MIRID.

9.3   Applications of the MIRID

9.3.1   Application of the MIRID to the guilt data

We will apply the MIRID to the guilt data described above and in Section 9.9. These data are binary. The data are available on the website mentioned in the Preface. For this application, we subtracted θ_{p0} from β_i' (instead of subtracting β_i' from θ_{p0}), so that the probability of feeling guilty is a function of the difference between the guilt inducing power (β_i') of a situation and the personal guilt threshold (θ_{p0}). This parametrization is used for all applications in this chapter, also for applications to the verbal aggression data.

The MIRID was fit with the procedure NLMIXED from SAS. A description of the options and the code is given in Section 9.7.1. Note that based on the study of Smits and De Boeck (2003), we knew that the Rasch model, used as a reference model for the MIRID, did not fit the data in absolute terms. However, for illustrative purposes, we will use it here as if it fits. In the second part of the chapter, a variant of the Rasch model that allows for unequal but fixed discrimination values will be used, called the *one parameter logistic model* (OPLM, Verhelst & Glas, 1995; Verhelst, Glas, & Verstralen, 1994).

The goodness-of-fit values of the MIRID are 10549 (deviance), 10619 (AIC), and 10745 (BIC). These values are similar to the goodness-of-fit values for the Rasch model – 10546 (deviance), 10628 (AIC), 10775 (BIC) – meaning that the MIRID fits the data about as well as the Rasch model. The values for the item parameters of the component items are given in Table 9.1. Each column functions as a latent item predictor for the composite items. High values mean a high situational guilt inducing power. The values of the other parameters are given in Table 9.2. The effect of the composite items can be reconstructed based on the αs from Table 9.1 and the βs from Table 9.2. For example, the reconstruction for the composite item of the third item family is equal to $(-.73 \times .50) + (.13 \times .55) + (-.39 \times .03) + (.20) = -.11$. As could be expected from the goodness of fit, there is a good correspondence between the item parameters of the component items and the composite items as estimated under the Rasch model and as estimated (component items) and reconstructed (composite items) under the MIRID: the correlation between both is .99. The correlation between the item parameters of the 10 composite items as estimated under a Rasch model for all 40 items and the composite item parameters as reconstructed from the parameters of the estimated MIRID is also .99.

Two of the componential weights are significant: the weights of Norm Violation and Worrying.[1] The weight of the second component is the largest, meaning that for our set of situations worrying is the most important component of situational guilt feelings. The weight of the composite item constant (.20) is the extra effect of being a composite item. Since the sum of the weights is close to 1.00, the composite items have a β_i' that is almost a weighted average of the first two plus .20. In general, the interpretation of β_0 is not easy because it depends on the centering of the latent predictors and also on the size of their weights. Finally, it is clear that guilt sensitivity as an underlying latent variable shows substantial individual differences ($\sigma_\theta^2 = 1.12$). The variance is statistically significant ($p < .001$) using the conservative Wald test for variances (see Chapter 2).

---

[1]Using the OPLM-MIRID also the weight of the third component was significant.

TABLE 9.1. Estimates and standard errors for the component item parameters or latent item predictor values (guilt data).

Situation	Norm Violation (SE)	Worry (SE)	T. Rectify (SE)
1. Break-up	-.09 (.14)	1.38 (.17)	.52 (.15)
2. Trumpet	-2.70 (.22)	-1.99 (.18)	-2.14 (.20)
3. Shoes	-.73 (.15)	.13 (.14)	-.39 (.15)
4. Movie	.10 (.14)	.42 (.14)	.36 (.15)
5. Discussion	1.48 (.17)	1.97 (.18)	2.55 (.23)
6. Secret	2.81 (.23)	2.26 (.20)	1.94 (.19)
7. Youth movement	1.32 (.16)	1.98 (.18)	.85 (.16)
8. Pen pal	-.14 (.14)	-.28 (.14)	.08 (.15)
9. Jacket	.06 (.15)	1.90 (.19)	3.16 (.28)
10. Homework	-1.31 (.16)	-1.53 (.16)	-1.02 (.16)

TABLE 9.2. Estimates and standard errors for the componential weight parameters and variance of the person parameter (guilt data).

Parameter	Estimate (SE)
β_1(weight of Norm Violation)	.50 (.10)
β_2(weight of Worrying)	.55 (.13)
β_3(weight of Tendency to Rectify)	.03 (.09)
β_0(composite item intercept)	.20 (.08)
σ_θ^2	1.12 (.12)

9.3.2   Application of the MIRID to the verbal aggression data

In the data set on verbal aggression, we have four situations and three different kinds of verbally aggressive reactions (cursing, scolding, and shouting). Each type of aggressive reaction is measured in two different ways, which were called response modes: (1) whether one wants to display the corresponding reaction in that situation (want-item), and (2) whether one actually would display the reaction (do-item). As we are interested in whether actually displaying an aggressive reaction can be explained by wanting to display that aggressive reaction, the items measuring the want-response mode were considered the component items, whereas the items measuring the do-response mode were considered the composite items. Hence, in this example, there is only one component (i.e., wanting), and each item family consists of two items. We will call the wanting component the 'action tendency.'

In total there are 12 item families (four situations × three behaviors). Each situation is associated with three item families: one for each kind of verbally aggressive reaction. The latent item predictor matrix for two situations and the componential weight matrix are given in Figure 9.7. Note that we again used the parametrization $\beta_i' - \theta_{p0}$, to be in line with the interpretation of β_i' as the inducing power of the situation for a certain behavior and θ_{p0} as the personal threshold.

$$
\mathbf{A} =
\begin{array}{l}
\text{Item family 1: Situation 1, Curse} \\
\text{Item family 2: Situation 1, Scold} \\
\text{Item family 3: Situation 1, Shout} \\
\text{Item family 4: Situation 2, Curse} \\
\text{Item family 5: Situation 2, Scold} \\
\text{Item family 6: Situation 2, Shout}
\end{array}
\left(
\begin{array}{cc}
\alpha_{11} & 1 \\
\alpha_{21} & 1 \\
\alpha_{31} & 1 \\
\alpha_{41} & 1 \\
\alpha_{51} & 1 \\
\alpha_{61} & 1
\end{array}
\right)
$$

$$
\mathbf{\Psi} =
\begin{array}{l}
\text{Component item type 1} \\
\text{Composite item}
\end{array}
\left(
\begin{array}{cc}
1 & 0 \\
\beta_1 & \beta_0
\end{array}
\right)
$$

FIGURE 9.7. Latent item predictor matrix $\mathbf{A}$ and componential weight matrix $\mathbf{\Psi}$ for two situations of the verbal aggression data.

The goodness-of-fit values for this MIRID are 8116 (deviance), 8146 (AIC), and 8203 (BIC). These values approach the goodness-of-fit values for the Rasch model (8074 (deviance), 8124 (AIC), and 8218 (BIC)). Based on these criteria, the MIRID has a relatively good fit. The values for the item parameters of the component items are given in Table 9.3, and the values for the other parameters are given in Table 9.4. There is a good correspondence between the item parameters of the component items and the composite items as estimated under the Rasch model and as estimated (component items) and reconstructed (composite items) under the MIRID: The correlation between the item parameters (estimated or reconstructed) of the two models is equal to .99. The correlation between the item parameters of the 12 composite items as estimated by a Rasch model for all items and as reconstructed by the MIRID is also equal to .99.

The weight of the want-response mode is quite large and highly significant, meaning that it has strong predictive power for the do-response mode ($\beta_1 = 1.33$). It follows from the value of β_1 that the do-items have more variation in terms of their inducing power than the want-items have. The effect of being a composite item (constant item predictor in $\mathbf{A}$) is negative ($\beta_0 = -.77$). Given these results, it can be concluded that the inducing power is lower for doing than for wanting: If a want-item has a negative α, the fact that β_1 is larger than 1, and that β_0 is smaller than zero, nec-

TABLE 9.3. Estimates and standard errors for the component item parameters (verbal aggression data).

Situation	Reaction	Item Parameter Want	Estimate (SE)
1. Bus	Curse	α_{11}	1.40 (.13)
1. Bus	Scold	α_{21}	.76 (.12)
1. Bus	Shout	α_{31}	-.02 (.12)
2. Train	Curse	α_{41}	1.40 (.13)
2. Train	Scold	α_{51}	.60 (.12)
2. Train	Shout	α_{61}	-.31 (.12)
3. Store	Curse	α_{71}	.46 (.12)
3. Store	Scold	α_{81}	-.61 (.13)
3. Store	Shout	α_{91}	-1.58 (.15)
4. Call	Curse	$\alpha_{10\,1}$	1.10 (.12)
4. Call	Scold	$\alpha_{11\,1}$	.06 (.12)
4. Call	Shout	$\alpha_{12\,1}$	-.97 (.13)

TABLE 9.4. Estimates and sandard errors for the componential weight parameters and variance of the person parameter (verbal aggression data).

Parameter	Estimate (SE)
β_1 (weight of want-response mode)	1.33 (.08)
β_0 (constant)	-.77 (.08)
σ_θ^2	1.89 (.19)

essarily leads to a lower inducing power for the corresponding do-items. If a want-item has a positive α, the value of β_0 compensates for a β_1 of 1.33 up to values for α as high as 2.33, a value that is not exceeded in Table 9.3. The α-value of 2.33 is calculated by solving the equation $\alpha\beta_1 + \beta_0 = \alpha$ for α, which results in $\alpha = \beta_0/(1 - \beta_1)$. Filling in the values for β_1 and β_0 (Table 9.4), one obtains the value of 2.33. Thus, with these results, the negative value of β_0 means that for all situations and behaviors one is inclined to do less than what one wants. Finally, the variance of the random intercept is quite large ($\sigma_\theta^2 = 1.89$), and highly significant when relying on the conservative Wald test for variances ($p < .001$). In sum, the verbally aggressive behavior (doing) has a lower inducing power than its action tendency (wanting), and the pairs of the behaviors and situations (items) are better differentiated in the actual expression (do-items) than in the action tendency (want-items).

9.4   Extensions with random weights

The MIRID assumes that the weights of the latent item predictors are the same for all persons. It would be interesting to allow for individual differences in these weights. For example, for some people worrying may be more important, whereas for other people the tendency to rectify may be more important, perhaps because they are more action-oriented. An extension of the MIRID, the *random-weights MIRID* (RW-MIRID), allows for the weights to be random variables. Except for its specific componential structure, the RW-MIRID is very similar to a multidimensional 2PL model, as in both the RW-MIRID and the 2PL model person-specific parameters are the weights of latent item predictors. In the multidimensional 2PL model these person-specific weights are the latent variables, and the item loadings correspond to the latent item predictors.

Each random weight, denoted by β_{pr}, can be split into a mean (the fixed-effect part β_r) and a deviation from that mean (the random-effect part θ_{pr}). In line with the previous chapters, the deviation from the mean will be considered the random weight. To construct the formula for the RW-MIRID, the componential weight matrix is now a person-specific matrix, denoted with $\boldsymbol{\Psi}_p$. In the example of Figure 9.8, only the weight of the first latent item predictor is a random effect, all other weights are fixed effects. Of course in other contexts, the other predictors may also have random weights.

	Comp. 1	Comp. 2	Comp. 3	Const. Pred.
Comp. item type 1	1	0	0	0
Comp. item type 2	0	1	0	0
Comp. item type 3	0	0	1	0
Composite item	β_{p1}	β_2	β_3	β_0

FIGURE 9.8. Example of a componential weight matrix $\boldsymbol{\Psi}_p$ for the RW-MIRID.

The formula for the RW-MIRID is

$$\eta_{pi} = \theta_{p0} - \mathbf{A}'_s \boldsymbol{\Psi}_{pr}, \tag{9.5}$$

where for the component items: $\mathbf{A}'_s \boldsymbol{\Psi}_{pr} = \alpha_{sr}$, and for the composite items: $\mathbf{A}'_s \boldsymbol{\Psi}_{p\ R+1} = \sum_r^R \alpha_{sr} \beta_{pr} + \beta_0$, with i as an index for the pairs (s,r), and

$\beta_{pr} = \theta_{pr} + \beta_r$.

Given that more than one random effect is included in the model, a multivariate normal distribution is assumed for $\boldsymbol{\theta}_p$, the vector of random effects. For the example of Figure 9.8, $\boldsymbol{\theta}_p = (\theta_{p0}, \beta_{p1})$.

Another way to extend the MIRID into a multidimensional model is the following: Until now it has been assumed that the same random intercept (θ_{p0}) applies to the component items and the composite items. This is not necessary. There are cases where, dependent on the component, a different random intercept (a different dimension) applies. Such a model is called the *multidimensional MIRID* (MULTI-MIRID; Butter, 1994), but this extension will not be discussed in this chapter. When the intercept of the composite items (β_{p0}) and the overall random intercept (θ_{p0}) are the only random effects, the individual-differences structure of the model is equivalent with that of the learning model of Embretson (1991), with the component items as the equivalents of the stage(s) before learning and the composite items as the equivalents of the stage after learning.

9.5   Applications of the RW-MIRID

9.5.1   Application of the RW-MIRID to the guilt data

In the example of situational guilt feelings three components were considered: Norm Violation, Worrying, and Tendency to Rectify. Because we have no *a priori* hypotheses about which component should have a random weight, three different models were estimated and compared, each with a different component that has a random weight. As mentioned earlier, the random-weights variant will be implemented in the OPLM-MIRID (yielding the RW-OPLM-MIRID), instead of the previously used original MIRID to deal with differences in discrimination between the items. In contrast to the MIRID, the OPLM-MIRID allows for unequal but fixed discrimination values. To investigate the fit of this OPLM-MIRID, it has to be compared with the OPLM.

The random-weights OPLM-MIRID was estimated with the procedure NLMIXED of SAS; see Section 9.7.2. Note that we again used the parametrization $\beta_i' - \theta_{p0}$, to be in line with the interpretation of β_i' as the inducing power from the situation and θ_{p0} as the personal threshold. The goodness-of-fit values for the OPLM-MIRID, and the three RW-OPLM-MIRIDs with one random component weight are given in Table 9.5. All of the goodness-of-fit values of the RW-OPLM-MIRIDs mentioned in Table 9.5 are similar to the ones of the OPLM-MIRID, meaning that adding a random weight to the model does not enhance the fit. It seems that, for this sample of persons and situations, it was not necessary to assume individual differences in the weights of any of the three components.

TABLE 9.5. Goodness of fit of the OPLM-MIRID and the RW-OPLM- MIRID (guilt data).

Model	Deviance	AIC	BIC
OPLM-MIRID	10451	10521	10647
RW-OPLM-MIRID			
Random weight for			
Norm Violation	10449	10523	10656
Worrying	10451	10525	10658
Tendency to Rectify	10451	10525	10658

9.5.2 Application of the RW-MIRID to the verbal aggression data

In the example of the verbal aggression data, the model had only one component. We assume that for some people what they want has a larger effect on what they do than for other people. The goodness-of-fit values for the RW-MIRID are 8028 (deviance), 8062 (AIC), 8125 (BIC), which are clearly better than those for the original MIRID: 8116 (deviance), 8146 (AIC), and 8203 (BIC), meaning that for some people what they want weights heavier in what they do than for other people.

The parameter estimates of the component items (values of the latent item predictor) are given in Table 9.6, and the values for the other parameters are given in Table 9.7. The variance of the weight is much smaller than the variance of the overall random intercept (1.02 vs 2.03). The correlation between both is .10.

As in the MIRID with fixed component weights, wanting again has a serious effect on doing, and people tend to do less than they want when verbal aggression is concerned. The inducing power for the actual behavior is lower (for the average person) than that for the action tendency, up to α-values of 1.78. This is because the negative β_0 (-1.03) compensates for a β_1 larger than 1 in all combinations of situations and behaviors. To investigate the effect of the individual differences we will consider a person with a β_{p1}-value situated 1.5 SD above the mean β_{p1} and a person with a β_{p1}-value situated 1.5 SD below the mean β_{p1}. Persons with a weight of 1.5 SD below the mean β_{p1} ($\beta_{p1} = .07$) do more than they want in situation-behavior combinations with an α-value below -1.11, which is the case for only one behavior-situation combination ($\alpha_{1,9} = -1.24$). Persons with a weight of 1.5 SD above the mean β_{p1} ($\beta_{p1} = 3.09$) do more than they want in situation-behavior combinations with α-values higher than .49, so that in six of the twelve situation-behavior combinations such a person would do more than he or she wanted, while in six of the twelve situation-behavior combinations, some inhibition is expected. This means that, for individuals with a strong action tendency effect, the inhibition would not apply in half of the situations.

TABLE 9.6. Estimates and standard errors for the component item parameters (verbal aggression data).

Situation	Behavior	Item parameter Want	Estimate (SE)
1. Bus	Curse	α_{11}	1.72 (.13)
1. Bus	Scold	α_{21}	.96 (.10)
1. Bus	Shout	α_{31}	.23 (.09)
2. Train	Curse	α_{41}	1.74 (.14)
2. Train	Scold	α_{51}	.81 (.10)
2. Train	Shout	α_{61}	.02 (.10)
3. Store	Curse	α_{71}	.72 (.10)
3. Store	Scold	α_{81}	-.15 (.10)
3. Store	Shout	α_{91}	-1.24 (.15)
4. Call	Curse	$\alpha_{10\ 1}$	1.34 (.12)
4. Call	Scold	$\alpha_{11\ 1}$	.44 (.09)
4. Call	Shout	$\alpha_{12\ 1}$	-.58 (.12)

TABLE 9.7. Estimates and standard errors for the componential weight parameters and variance/covariance of the person-dependent parameters (verbal aggression data).

Parameter	Estimate (SE)
β_1 (mean weight of Component 1)	1.58 (.12)
$\sigma^2_{\theta_{p1}}$ (variance of component weight)	1.02 (.22)
β_0 (constant)	-1.03 (.09)
$\sigma^2_{\theta_{p0}}$ (variance of overall intercept)	2.03 (.22)
$\text{cov}(\theta_{p0}, \theta_{p1})$	.14 (.15)

In sum, the results of the RW-MIRID confirm those of the MIRID with fixed weights, except for the fact that clear individual differences appear in the effect wanting has on doing.

9.6   Concluding remarks

The main advantage of the MIRID and its variants is that in cases where no exact knowledge is available about the values of the components (latent item predictors), these values can be estimated.

An advantage specific to the RW-MIRID is that one can test whether the assumption of fixed weights is reasonable. A better fit of the RW-MIRID with random weights for one or more components would imply that there are individual differences in how important the components are in explaining the composite items. These composite items may be considered criterion items, since the responses to these items are explained (predicted) by the responses to other items.

Finally, the principle behind the MIRID can easily be generalized to other basic models, like for example the 2PL (Birnbaum, 1968) or the multidimensional Rasch model. Because extending the MIRID by incorporating additional random effects is straightforward, the MIRID is a flexible tool to test the decomposition of general concepts into more elementary aspects.

9.7   Software

9.7.1   MIRID (guilt data)

The MIRID was fit using the NLMIXED procedure of SAS V8. For the numerical integration the adaptive Gaussian quadrature method with 15 nodes was used and for the optimization the Newton-Raphson technique was used. Remember that in this application, we had 10 item families, 3 latent item predictors or components, and one item per component per item family.

Code

```
PROC NLMIXED data=guilt method=gauss
technique=newrap qpoints=15;
PARMS a1-a30=1 b1-b3=1 b0=1 sd=1;
alpha1=a1*x1+a2*x2+a3*x3+a4*x4+a5*x5
+a6*x6+a7*x7+a8*x8+a9*x9+a10*x10;
alpha2=a11*x11+a12*it12+a13*x13+a14*x14+a15*x15
+a16*x16+a17*x17+a18*x18+a19*x19+a20*x20;
alpha3=a21*x21+a22*x22+a23*x23+a24*x24+a25*x25
+a26*x26+a27*x27+a28*x28+a29*x29+a30*x30;
ex=exp(-theta+(1-co)*(alpha1+alpha2+alpha3)
+co*(b0+b1*alpha1+b2*alpha2+b3*alpha3));
p=ex/(1+ex);
MODEL y ~ binary(p);
RANDOM theta ~ normal(0,sd**2) subject=person;
```

```
ESTIMATE 'sd**2' sd**2;
RUN;
```

Comments

In the code, the parameters a1 to a30 are renumbered using one index to simplify the SAS code. They can easily be matched to the α_{sr} as given in the formulas. The terms alpha1, alpha2 and alpha3 refer to the components Norm Violation, Worrying and Tendency to Rectify, respectively. The dummy variables x1 to x30 are used to select the correct weight, and the dummy variable co is used to select the appropriate part of the formula: the component items part or the composite items part.

9.7.2   RW-MIRID (guilt data)

The same options were used as for the estimation of the MIRID (Section 9.7.1).

Code

```
PROC NLMIXED data=guilt method=gauss noad
technique=newrap qpoints=15;
PARMS a1-a30=1 b1-b3=1 b0=1 sdth=1 cothga=1 sdga=1;
alpha1=a1*x1+a2*x2+a3*x3+a4*x4+a5*x5
+a6*x6+a7*x7+a8*x8+a9*x9+a10*x10;
alpha2=a11*x11+a12*it12+a13*x13+a14*x14+a15*x15
+a16*x16+a17*x17+a18*x18+a19*x19+a20*x20;
alpha3=a21*x21+a22*x22+a23*x23+a24*x24+a25*x25
+a26*x26+a27*x27+a28*x28+a29*x29+a30*x30;
ex=exp(-theta+(1-co)*(alpha1+alpha2+alpha3)
+co*(b0+b1*alpha1+(b2+gamma)*alpha2+b3*alpha3));
p=ex/(1+ex);
MODEL y ~ binary(p);
RANDOM theta gamma ~ normal([0,0],[sdth**2,cothga,sdga**2])
subject=person;
ESTIMATE 'sdth**2' sdth**2;
ESTIMATE 'sdga**2' sdga**2;
RUN;
```

Comments

1. In the code it is assumed that the second component has a random weight.
2. Note that the code for a RW-MIRID is given, and not for the RW-OPLM-MIRID. To fit a RW-OPLM-MIRID, the term theta in the code has to be replaced with the term a*theta, with a corresponding to the known discrimination value of the current item.

9.8 Exercises

1. Calculate the item parameters for the composite items under the MIRID for both examples.

2. The MIRID is presented as a unidimensional model. However, the item parameters of the composite items are decomposed into different components. Explain why there is no contradiction between the unidimensionality of the model and the decomposition into different item components. Does the same reasoning apply for the RW-MIRID?

3. Using random weights did not pay off for the guilt data. Perhaps it would pay off better to define a dimension per set of component items (a component-specific random intercept). Formulate such a model and explain how you will treat the composite items, and which alternatives could be considered.

4. Examine gender differences in the guilt data with three different MIRIDs: one in which females can differ from males in their overall proneness to experience guilt, one in which the importance of one of the components differs between males and females, and one in which the values of the latent item predictors differ between males and females (e.g., because the interpretations of the situations differs between males and females). Use the NLMIXED procedure from SAS for the estimation.

5. Write down the formula for a MIRID in which the effect of the constant for the composite items is assumed to be a random effect. Estimate this MIRID for the verbal aggression data using the NLMIXED procedure from SAS.

9.9 Appendix: Guilt data

Situations (Original in Dutch)

1. For some time you have been dating a person you are not really in love with. When you break up, you find out that he/she was in love with you (and was taking the relationship very seriously). The break-up hurts him/her considerably. (Break-up)

2. For some years now you have been a member of a brass band. As a result, you learned to play trumpet for free. Now that you're skilled enough, you leave the band because you don't like the members of the band any more. (Trumpet)

3. During the holidays, you are working as a salesperson in a clothing

and shoestore. One day, a mother with four children enters the store. One of the kids wants Samson-shoes (Samson is a popular doll figuring in a Belgian TV-series for children). The mother leaves the child with you while she goes on to look for clothes for the other children. The child tries on different types and sizes of shoes, but after a while the child gets tired of fitting the shoes and refuses to continue. The mother picks a pair that had not been tried on before and you sell this pair to the mother. The next day, the mother wants to return the shoes because they do not fit. Your boss takes back the shoes and reimburses the mother. The shoes have been worn however, and they are dirty. Because of this, they cannot be sold anymore. Your boss says that it doesn't matter, and that everyone is capable of mistaking the size of shoes. (Shoes)

4. A not so close friend asks you if you want to join him/her to go to the movies. You tell him/her that you don't feel like it, and want to spend a quiet evening at home. That evening you do go out with a closer friend. (Movie)

5. During a discussion, you make a stinging remark toward one of your friends. You notice that it hurts him/her, but you pretend not to see it. (Discussion)

6. A friend tells you something in confidence, and adds that he/she would not like you to spread it around. Later, you do tell it to someone else. (Secret)

7. You are a member of a youth movement. One day the group leaders hang a rope between two trees, so you can glide from one tree to another. Jokingly, some other members make the stop of the pulley unclear. You see them doing it, but you do not help them. The following member, who wants to glide to the other tree, did not see that the stop was made unclear. You do not warn him/her. Halfway he falls from the rope, and he passes out. (Youth movement)

8. You have a pen pal. You get bored with writing to him/her, and suddenly, you stop corresponding with him/her. After one and a half years, he/she writes to you again, and again, but you do not respond. (Pen pal)

9. You borrowed a jacket from a friend to wear when you go out. At the party, you leave the jacket on a chair. When you are about to leave, you notice the jacket has disappeared. In all probability, it has been stolen. (Jacket)

10. One evening, you do not feel like doing your homework. The following day, you copy the assignment of a friend who clearly has gone through

a lot of trouble finishing it. You get a good grade for your assignment, the same grade as your friend. (Homework)

Items

1. Do you feel like having violated a moral, an ethic, a religious and/or a personal code?

2. Do you worry about what you did or failed to do?

3. Do you want to do something to rectify what you did or failed to do?

4. Do you feel guilty about what you did or failed to do?

Respondents

The respondents were 268 high-school students between 17 and 19 years old from three high schools. Each school distributed the inventories to students. The students were given some time during the day to fill in the inventories individually. Within two weeks, 268 completed inventories were returned from 138 female students and from 130 male students.

9.10 References

Bechger, T.M., Verhelst, N.D., & Verstralen, H.H.F.M. (2001). Identifiability of nonlinear logistic test models. *Psychometrika, 66*, 357–371.

Bechger, T.M., Verstralen, H.H.F.M., & Verhelst, N.D. (2002). Equivalent linear logistic test models. *Psychometrika, 67*, 123–136.

Birnbaum, A. (1968). Some latent trait models. In F.M. Ford & M.R. Novick (Eds), *Statistical Theories of Mental Test Scores* (pp. 397–424). Reading: Addison-Wesley.

Butter, R. (1994). Item response models with internal restrictions on item difficulty. Unpublished doctoral dissertation, K.U.Leuven (Belgium).

Butter, R., De Boeck, P., & Verhelst, N.D. (1998). An item response model with internal restrictions on item difficulty. *Psychometrika, 63*, 1–17.

Embretson, S.E. (1991). A multidimensional latent trait model for measuring learning and change. *Psychometrika, 56*, 495–515.

Fischer, G.H. (1973). The linear logistic test model as an instrument in educational research. *Acta Psychologica, 37*, 359–374.

Fischer, G.H. (1977). Linear logistic trait models: Theory and applications. In H. Spada & W.F. Kempf (Eds), *Structural Models of Thinking and Learning* (pp. 203–225). Bern, Switzerland: Huber.

Maris, G., & Bechger, T. (2003). Equivalent MIRID models. Measurement and Research Department Report 2003-2. Arnhem, The Netherlands: CITO.

McCulloch, C.E., & Searle, S.R. (2001). *Generalized Linear, and Mixed Models*. New York: Wiley.

Rasch, G. (1960). *Probabilistic Models for Some Intelligence and Attainment Tests*. Copenhagen, Denmark: Danish Institute for Educational research.

Smits, D.J.M., & De Boeck, P. (2003). A componential model for guilt. *Multivariate Behavioral Research, 38*, 161–188.

Smits, D.J.M., De Boeck, P., Verhelst, N., & Butter, R. (2001). The MIRID program (version 1.0) (Computer program and manual). K.U.Leuven, Belgium.

Smits, D.J.M., De Boeck, P., & Verhelst, N.D. (2003). Estimation of the MIRID: A program and a SAS based approach. *Behavior Research Methods, Instruments, and Computers, 35*, 537–549.

Verhelst, N.D., & Glas, C.A.W. (1995). One parameter logistic model. In G.H. Fischer & I.W. Molenaar (Eds), *Rasch Models: Foundations, Recent Developments and Applications* (pp. 215–238). New York: Springer.

Verhelst, N.D., Glas, C.A.W., & Verstralen, H.H.F.M. (1994). *One Parameter Logistic Model* (Computer program and manual). Arnhem, The Netherlands: CITO.

Chapter 10

Models for residual dependencies

Francis Tuerlinckx
Paul De Boeck

10.1 Introduction

The models discussed in the previous chapters recognize the clustered structure of data one is confronted with most often in psychometrics (i.e., items within persons). The within-person dependencies arising from this clustering are handled through a random effect or latent variable for person p, denoted as θ_p. In some cases, there are several major sources of individual differences, and they have to be accounted for by more than one random effect (see Chapter 8 on multidimensionality). Conditional on these random effects, the responses to the different items in the data set should be independent – this requirement is called *conditional independence* or *local (stochastic) independence*. However, it appears that in many applications, not all dependence between the responses can be explained by the random effects one assumed to underly the responses. In those cases, it is said that there remain some *residual dependencies* not accounted for by the model, a phenomenon also denoted as *local item dependencies* (LIDs). Situations in which residual dependencies may occur are ample. Consider for instance the case where items of a reading test can be subdivided into groups of items each sharing the same reading passage. Data from a test with reading passages may show more dependencies than can be accounted for alone by a single reading ability dimension. The conditional independence assumption may also be violated if outcome-dependent learning occurs while taking the test. The methods we discuss in this chapter are designed for handling such residual dependencies.

In many cases, residual dependencies are regarded as a nuisance because the researcher is not interested in the structure of the remaining dependencies in and of themselves. The researcher wants to model the dependencies in some way in order not to jeopardize the measurement or inference that is the purpose of the research. However, there are situations in which the dependencies are the phenomena of interest because they further an understanding of the data, or because they are the focus of research questions one has (e.g., Smits, De Boeck, & Hoskens, 2003). For instance, looking at dependencies may be a way to investigate learning, or to understand how a person's behavior is based on what is wanted (see Chapter 7 for the latter).

Residual dependencies are often the result of an additional organizing principle in the data (besides the common items-within-persons clustering) that is not taken into account by the model. For instance, in case a test is built around a few pieces of common stimulus material such as reading paragraphs each followed by several questions, these common stimuli form the additional organizing principle in the data. Another organizer can be that the items are ordered along the time dimension. Any group of items that belong together for some reason and are (suspected of) showing residual dependencies is called an *item bundle* (Rosenbaum, 1988; Wilson & Adams, 1995) or in this chapter, a *testlet* (Wainer & Kiely, 1987) (this widens the usual definition of the testlet). Furthermore, it will be assumed that while conditional independence may be violated within a testlet, it still holds for items not belonging to any testlet and it also holds between testlets. However, it is not always the case that partitions of items can be found between which conditional independence holds; if that happens, all items belong to a single testlet.

In this chapter we focus on handling residual dependencies conditionally on the presence of one or more random effects. Random effects are considered in this volume as the basic modeling tool for correlated data. The development of tools for handling residual dependencies is based on the three approaches already described in Chapter 4: marginal models, conditional models, and random-effects models (see also Fahrmeir & Tutz, 2001). The same three approaches are applied here to models in which random effects are already included but where this proved not to be sufficient. For simplicity, we will evaluate the conditional independence assumption only for models with a single random effect, but all presented methods can be readily generalized to higher dimensions.

We start with a short summary of the three approaches described in Chapter 4. First, a *marginal modeling* approach may be pursued in which we require the probability given the random effect to follow an *a priori* specified functional form, while an additional dependence structure is put on top of these marginals to explain residual dependencies. Second, there are the *conditional models* in which the probability of a certain response on an item is modeled conditionally on some or all other responses on the remaining items. Third, additional *random effects* may be included into the model to account for dependencies. Although the order of the approaches is listed here in increasing degree of complexity (the marginal approach being the simplest and the random-effects one the most difficult), we will present the models in a different order in this chapter because we believe that another order fits better the relative importance of the methods in psychometrics.

Throughout the discussion of each of these approaches, it will become clear that the subject of this chapter is related to the chapter on models for polytomous data (Chapter 3), the chapter with the statistical background (Chapter 4), the chapter on person-by-item predictors (Chapter 7) and the chapter on multidimensionality (Chapter 8). For this reason, the treatment of the dependence models will be largely theoretical in this chapter (except for an illustration of a graphical technique to assess residual dependencies) and the reader is referred to other chapters for the relevant software code to estimate the models.

A more traditional psychometric approach for residual dependencies due to testlets is based on computing the sum of 1-responses to the testlet question and modeling it with a model for ordered polytomous data (e.g., the partial credit model; see Keller, Swaminathan, & Sireci, 2003; Wilson & Adams, 1995; Yen, 1993). However, this sum-score method will not be covered in this chapter. Although a practical approach in many cases, it discards much of the information in the data, because different response patterns with the same sum scores may contain different information, a point which is also made by Wilson and Adams (1995). Keller et al. (2003) show that the inferences based on it are not always valid.

In the next paragraphs we give a short historical overview of the developments in methods for residual dependencies, focusing on the three major types of methods introduced earlier and on assessment tools for residual dependencies. Conditional models were introduced and studied in the statistical literature by Bonney (1987), Connolly and Liang (1988), Cox (1972), Prentice (1988) and Qu, Williams, Beck, and Goormastic (1987) and in econometrics by Lee (1981), Nerlove and Press (1973), and Schmidt and Strauss (1975). Within item response modeling these models were considered by Hoskens and De Boeck (1997), Jannerone (1986), Kelderman (1984), Verhelst and Glas (1993), and Wilson and Adams (1995).

References to models assuming independence extended with random effects to account for additional dependencies are already given in the previous chapters. Bradlow, Wainer, and Wang (1999) were among the first to include additional random effects to model residual dependencies due to testlets. However, multidimensional extensions of unidimensional random-effects models are also motivated by the fact that unidimensionality is often a too strict requirement even without testlets.

Most marginal models are not based on a logit model, but are instead multivariate extensions of the probit model (Ashford & Sowden, 1970; Lesaffre & Molenberghs, 1991). Other marginal modeling approaches will not be discussed in this chapter, but they deserve special mention here. A well-known method of estimating marginal models without random effects and at the same time taking into account dependencies is the generalized estimating equation (GEE) approach, developed by Liang and Zeger (1986) and Zeger and Liang (1986). A likelihood-based variant of the GEE-approach is discussed by Fitzmaurice, Laird, and Rotnitzky (1993), and the latter method is transferred by Ip (2002) to the framework of residual dependencies in random-effects models. Yet another marginal modeling approach is the Bahadur model (Bahadur, 1961) and it has also been generalized to an item response modeling framework by Ip (2000, 2001).

Finally, in the psychometric literature, some research has been devoted to the development of tests or indices for the detection of violations of the conditional independence assumption (see Chen & Thissen, 1997; Douglas, Kim, Habing, & Gao, 1998; Rosenbaum, 1984, 1988; van den Wollenberg, 1982; Yen, 1984).

We will first present a graphical technique for assessing residual dependencies. Next, models of each of the three approaches will be discussed, and finally, the three approaches will be compared. Our main focus in this chapter will be on models for binary items and the basic model we will work with in this chapter is the Rasch model.

10.2   Assessment of residual dependencies

Several exploratory techniques for detecting residual dependencies have been developed by psychometricians (see the historical overview in the preceding section) and most of these techniques are based on formal tests, that is, a numerical value for a test statistic is computed following a recipe which is then compared explicitly to a reference distribution leading to a p-value.

In this chapter we propose a more informal and graphical procedure for evaluating residual dependencies, based on the ideas of the parametric bootstrap (Efron & Tibshirani, 1993) and graphical model evaluation tools (Gelman, 2002; Gelman, Goegebeur, Tuerlinckx, & Van Mechelen, 2000). Our method is also related to the difference test for log odds ratios proposed by Chen and Thissen (1997) and the procedure may be extended to other indices for residual dependencies. Fitting the Rasch model to the verbal aggression data and then applying our technique for the evaluation of residual dependencies results in Figure 10.1.

Empirical log odds ratios

The construction[1] and interpretation of Figure 10.1 needs some clarification and we start with the top row of the figure. First, for all possible pairs out of the 24 items, we computed the empirical log odds ratio, defined[2] as $\frac{(n_{11}+.5)(n_{00}+.5)}{(n_{10}+.5)(n_{01}+.5)}$, where n_{11} is the observed frequency of a joint $(1,1)$-response for the item pair under study, and so on. Next, the log odds ratios are converted into gray-scale values and placed in the upper-diagonal part

---

[1] A Matlab program was written to construct Figures 10.1 and 10.2. It can be obtained from the website mentioned in the Preface.

[2] The number .5 is added to all counts to circumvent the problem that zero counts may pose.

of an image consisting of 23 by 23 squares (the first column and the last row can be deleted); this is the left-hand side figure in the top row. A darker value in the gray-scale matrix refers to a higher value for the empirical log odds ratio, while a lighter value is chosen for a lower one. In a second step, we fitted the Rasch model to the observed data set and simulated four new artificial data sets based on the parameter estimates. The four figures on the right-hand side of the top row represent the empirical log odds ratios of these four artificial data sets.

The order in which the items are represented in the matrices is as follows: first all want-items and then all do-items. Within each Behavior Mode, the order of the four situations is: Bus, Train, Store, and Call. Within each situation the order of Behavior Type is Curse, Scold, and Shout.

Rasch model log odds ratios

If the Rasch model can explain the dependencies in the observed data, the observed gray-scale matrix should not differ systematically from the simulated ones (e.g., if the labels for the five matrices were lost, it would be impossible to pick the observed one from it). By comparing the left observed figure with the four replicated ones, it is clear that the Rasch model is not able to capture the dependence structure in the data. The first striking feature is that in general the left figure appears to be darker, indicating that the observed data have higher empirical log odds ratios than the simulated data. Second, there seem to be regularities in the observed log odds ratio matrix (indicated by the somewhat regular patterns of dark and light squares in the figure) that are not present in the replicated matrices. To see an example where the simulated matrices are much more like the original data matrix, turn to Figure 10.2.

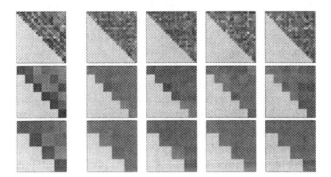

FIGURE 10.1. Log odds ratio plot for the Rasch model. Figures in row 1 contain dependencies between pairs of items; figures in row 2 contain average dependencies based on wanting and doing combined with behaviors; figures in row 3 contain average dependencies based on a common situation. The first figure in each row is derived from the data, the other four stem from data generated from the Rasch model estimates.

Log odds ratios based on item properties

To have a clearer idea where the structure in the observed log odds ratios comes from, we computed average log odds ratios, based on the item properties (Behavior Mode, Situation Type and Behavior Type). The result is shown in the second and third row of Figure 10.1. For the second row, we focused on the six possible combinations of Behavior Mode (Want and Do) with Behavior Type (Curse, Scold, and Shout). All log odds ratios for which both items of the pair refer to the same combination of Behavior Mode and Type are averaged and they are shown on the diagonal of the gray-scale matrix. The off-diagonal elements refer to the average log odds ratios where one item refers to one Behavior Mode-by-Behavior Type combination and the other item to another combination. The ordering of the combinations is as follows: wanting to curse, wanting to scold, wanting to shout, cursing, scolding, and shouting. Again, darker shades represent higher (average) log odds ratios and lighter shades lower values.

It can be seen that the diagonal elements are much darker than most of the off-diagonal ones. This indicates that the items that are based on the same Behavior Mode and Behavior Type have higher dependencies than items based on different Behavior Modes and Behavior Types. We also see that the three off-diagonal elements that correspond to the average log odds ratios of items with the same Behavior Type but a different Behavior Mode are slightly higher than the other off-diagonal elements. There also seems to be a general higher (i.e., darker) dependence between items of the same Behavior Mode but with a different Behavior Type. In comparison, the Rasch-model based simulated log odds ratios show no pattern at all after averaging.

We repeated the averaging procedure, but now on the basis of the four situations (Bus, Train, Store, Call, depicted in that order). Once again, we see that the diagonal elements of the averaged gray-scale matrix tend to have a substantial darker shade, indicating that the items referring to the same situation have a higher dependence. The four frustrating situations can be grouped in two groups according to whether someone else is to blame or one's self is to blame (Situation Type). The two Other-to-blame situations seem to have to a higher interdependence but a similar effect does not show up for the two Self-to-blame situations. Looking at the replicated averaged log-odds ratio matrix, we do not see a pattern that resembles the pattern obtained with the observed data.

These exploratory graphical analyses show that the Rasch model (with the intercept as the only random effect) is unable to explain the pattern of dependencies present in the observed data, so that one may conclude that there will be some residual dependencies. In the following sections, we will supplement the Rasch model with one of the three types of dependence approaches.

10.3   Conditional models for residual dependencies

In a conditional independence model, for example the Rasch model, the probabilities of a response on a certain item can be defined without reference to the responses on other items. In the models discussed in this section, we will condition on the responses on other items to model the probability of a certain response on a given item in order to take into account residual dependencies. Dependent on which responses are conditioned upon, we distinguish between two classes of models: recursive and nonrecursive models.

In *recursive models* (also called transition models in Chapter 4), there exists an *a priori* ordering of the items so that the probability of a response on an item higher in the order can only be influenced by responses on items lower in the order. In such a model, no feedback loops exist between the items. Consequently, at least one of the items should be exogenous, meaning that for modeling its probability distribution no information from the responses on the other items is necessary (the non-exogenous items are endogenous). In *nonrecursive models*, feedback loops are allowed and the possibility exists that all responses influence all others.

Recursive and nonrecursive models will be discussed below. Our labels for distinguishing between these two model classes are borrowed from the domain of structural equations modeling (Bollen, 1989), where a similar distinction exists. However, a different terminology is common in other contexts. For instance, recursive models have also been called autoregressive models (Bonney, 1987), dynamic models (Verhelst & Glas, 1993), asymmetric models (Fahrmeir & Tutz, 2001), and transition models (see Chapter 4 of this volume). Nonrecursive models have been called interaction models (Hoskens & De Boeck, 1997), item bundle models (Wilson & Adams, 1995), simultaneous logit models (Schmidt & Strauss, 1975), and symmetric models (Fahrmeir & Tutz, 2001).

10.3.1   Recursive models

General model

As mentioned above, a requirement for applying recursive models is that an *a priori* ordering of the items exists. The most common example of such an ordering is when the items can be ordered along the time axis and one wants to model outcome-dependent learning while taking the test. Because of the prototypical nature of this example, we will denote items lower in the ordering as 'earlier,' 'previous,' or 'preceding' items and items higher as 'later.' It is assumed here that the indices of the items not only distinguish between the items but also refer to the order of administration. Ordering in time implies a complete order between the items, but that is not necessary to specify recursive models. A partial ordering between items may be sufficient. However, the essential feature is that there are no feedback loops.

In a recursive model, the joint probability of a response vector $\boldsymbol{y}_p$ can be decomposed as follows (for simplicity, we discard in this chapter the conditioning on a predictor vector $\boldsymbol{X}_{pi}$):

$$\Pr(Y_{p1} = y_{p1}, \ldots, Y_{pI} = y_{pI}) \tag{10.1}$$
$$= \Pr(Y_{p1} = y_{p1})\Pr(Y_{p2} = y_{p2}|y_{p1}) \cdots \Pr(Y_{pI} = y_{pI}|y_{p1}, \ldots, y_{p,I-1}).$$

In the full model, the logit of the probability of responding with a 'correct' response on item i ($i > 2$) is defined as

$$\text{logit}(\Pr(Y_{pi} = 1|y_{p1}, \ldots, y_{p,i-1})) = \theta_p - \beta_i + \boldsymbol{W}'_{pi}\boldsymbol{\delta}_i, \tag{10.2}$$

where $\boldsymbol{W}_{pi} = (y_{p1}, \ldots, y_{p,i-1}, y_{p1}y_{p2}, \ldots, y_{p1} \cdots y_{p,i-1})'$ contains all single responses on the preceding items and all possible cross-products of the preceding responses. Item 1 is defined to be the exogenous item, and hence, the vector $\boldsymbol{W}_{p1}$ is empty by definition and for $i = 2$, $\boldsymbol{W}_{p2} = y_{p1}$.

The dependence parameters relevant for item i are contained in the vector $\boldsymbol{\delta}_i$. Note that a single response in the vector $\boldsymbol{W}_{pi}$ introduces a parameter for the effect this earlier item has on the response to item i, a product of two responses in $\boldsymbol{W}_{pi}$ is for modeling the joint effect of two earlier responses and so on. It is straightforward to check that this formulation leads to a fully parametrized model. The full model contains $\binom{I}{1} = I$ β-parameters and $\binom{I}{k}$ k-way dependence parameters ($k = 2, \ldots, I$). The total of all these parameters is $\sum_{i=1}^{I} \binom{I}{i} = 2^I - 1$, which equals the number of free joint probabilities.

Given the responses on the relevant preceding items, the probabilities are independent, which is shown by Equation 10.1. Fitting these recursive models only requires an extension of the predictor matrix to include responses on previous items. To illustrate this adaptation, we first define $\boldsymbol{\delta} = (\boldsymbol{\delta}'_1, \ldots, \boldsymbol{\delta}'_I)'$. Then the predictor submatrix $\boldsymbol{W}_p$ for person p relevant for the dependence parameters is the following:

$$\boldsymbol{W}_p = \begin{pmatrix} \boldsymbol{0}(\boldsymbol{W}'_{p2}) & \boldsymbol{0}(\boldsymbol{W}'_{p3}) & \cdots & \boldsymbol{0}(\boldsymbol{W}'_{pI}) \\ \boldsymbol{W}'_{p2} & \boldsymbol{0}(\boldsymbol{W}'_{p3}) & \cdots & \boldsymbol{0}(\boldsymbol{W}'_{pI}) \\ \boldsymbol{0}(\boldsymbol{W}'_{p2}) & \boldsymbol{W}'_{p3} & \cdots & \boldsymbol{0}(\boldsymbol{W}'_{pI}) \\ \vdots & \vdots & & \vdots \\ \boldsymbol{0}(\boldsymbol{W}'_{p2}) & \boldsymbol{0}(\boldsymbol{W}'_{p3}) & \cdots & \boldsymbol{W}'_{pI} \end{pmatrix},$$

where the notation $\boldsymbol{0}(\boldsymbol{W}'_{p2})$ stands for a matrix of zeros of the same size as $\boldsymbol{W}'_{p2}$. Because $\boldsymbol{W}_p$ may be different for different p, and within the matrix its values differ over items, the predictors in the recursive model are person-by-item predictors (see Chapter 7 in this volume).

Model restrictions

From the general model in Equation 10.2, several interesting models can be derived by putting restrictions on the vector of parameters $\boldsymbol{\delta}$ and the predictor matrices $\boldsymbol{W}_p$ (see also Verhelst & Glas, 1993). A first common model follows by assuming that only the response on the previous item has an effect on the current item. This Markovian assumption is translated into the model by defining the predictor submatrix $\boldsymbol{W}_p$ as follows:

$$\boldsymbol{W}_p = \begin{pmatrix} 0 & 0 & \cdots & 0 \\ y_{p1} & 0 & \cdots & 0 \\ 0 & y_{p2} & \cdots & 0 \\ \vdots & \vdots & & \vdots \\ 0 & 0 & \cdots & y_{p,I-1} \end{pmatrix}, \tag{10.3}$$

and $\boldsymbol{\delta} = (\delta_1, \ldots, \delta_{I-1})'$, where δ_{i-1} is the effect of the response on item $i-1$ on the probability distribution for item i. A further simplification follows by restricting the effect of the previous response to be equal for all items, so that $\boldsymbol{W}_p$ reduces to a single column vector $\boldsymbol{W}_p = (0, y_{p1}, \ldots, y_{p,I-1})'$ and $\boldsymbol{\delta}$ reduces to the scalar δ.

A second well-known model is specified by dropping all cross-products of responses from the $\boldsymbol{W}$-vectors and setting all remaining δ-parameters equal to each other ($\boldsymbol{\delta}$ simplifies to δ). If that is done, then the predictor submatrix $\boldsymbol{W}_p$ reduces to a column vector with only the number of previous 1-responses as a quantitative predictor (see Verhelst & Glas, 1993):

$$\boldsymbol{W}_p = \begin{pmatrix} 0 \\ y_{p1} \\ y_{p1} + y_{p2} \\ \vdots \\ \sum_{i=1}^{I-1} y_{pi} \end{pmatrix}. \tag{10.4}$$

For the combination of the model in Equation 10.4 with item properties as predictors, see Verguts and De Boeck (2000). The model from Equation 10.4 can be relaxed if the number of previous 1-responses is treated as a qualitative predictor such that $I-1$ indicator variables appear in the predictor submatrix $\boldsymbol{W}_p$, each coding for a different sum score ranging from 1 to $I-1$.

As a remark, we add that in the case of only two items, there is no difference between the model in Equation 10.3 and the one in Equation 10.4. The probability of person p for a response y_{p1} on the first item is a simple Rasch model. For illustrative purposes, we present here the model formulation for two items:

$$\Pr(Y_{p1} = y_{p1}) = \frac{\exp\left(y_{p1}(\theta_p - \beta_1)\right)}{1 + \exp\left(\theta_p - \beta_1\right)}, \tag{10.5}$$

and the probability for a response y_{p2} on the second item given the response on the first one equals

$$\Pr(Y_{p2} = y_{p2}|y_{p1}) = \frac{\exp\left(y_{p2}(\theta_p - \beta_2 + y_{p1}\delta)\right)}{1 + \exp\left(\theta_p - \beta_2 + y_{p1}\delta\right)}. \tag{10.6}$$

Note that in the model resulting from Equation 10.4 every preceding correct response has the same effect on the current response. That may be an overly restrictive assumption to make, for instance in long tests, where the responses at the beginning may be forgotten after a while. A possible solution is to construct the following predictor matrix:

$$
W_p = \begin{pmatrix}
0 & 0 & \cdots & 0 \\
y_{p1} & 0 & \cdots & 0 \\
y_{p2} & y_{p1} & \cdots & 0 \\
\vdots & \vdots & & \vdots \\
y_{p,I-1} & y_{p,I-2} & \cdots & y_{p1}
\end{pmatrix},
$$

together with the parameter vector $\delta = (\delta, \delta^2, \ldots, \delta^{I-1})'$ (with $0 \le \delta \le 1$), so that the directly preceding response always has the largest influence and the influence of the other responses decrease if the time lag increases. This model is not a generalized linear mixed model anymore but a nonlinear mixed model instead because the dependence parameter δ enters the logit of the probability in a nonlinear way. However, it can still be estimated with, for example, the procedure NLMIXED from SAS.

Interpretational issues

There are three important interpretation aspects of recursive models we would like to highlight.

First, the interpretation of the δ-parameter(s) deserves some attention. For simplicity, we focus here only on the model that uses the previous number of 1-responses as a quantitative predictor, and in which δ is the *learning parameter*, the effect of one or more previous successes. The log odds of a 1-response on item i given t_a previous successes equal $\theta_p - \beta_i + \delta t_a$ and given t_b previous successes the log odds are $\theta_p - \beta_i + \delta t_b$. Hence the odds of a 1-response change with a factor $e^{\delta(t_a - t_b)}$ if t_a instead of t_b successes are achieved. Now if $\delta > 0$, it is clear that there is a positive effect from positive responses because then the odds of a 1-response to an item increase if a larger number of previous successes was made. If $\delta = 0$, there is no learning and the model simplifies to a product of ordinary Rasch models, therefore the latter is nested within the recursive model.

Second, an interpretational complication arises in the recursive models. In the Rasch model, the functional form of a single item's item characteristic curve is a logistic function and the *item parameter* β_i has the natural and simple interpretation of the difficulty of an item. The latter fact follows because β_i marks the point at which the chances to solve the item are 50% for a person with $\theta_p = \beta_i$. However, except for the first item, these two properties do not hold anymore in the recursive conditional models. Assuming that there are two items, we derive the probability of a correct response on item 2 from Equations 10.5 and 10.6:

$$
\begin{aligned}
\Pr(Y_{p2} = 1) &= \sum_{m=0}^{1} \Pr(Y_{p1} = m, Y_{p2} = 1) \\
&= \sum_{m=0}^{1} \Pr(Y_{p2} = 1 | Y_{p1} = m)\Pr(Y_{p1} = m) \\
&= \frac{\exp(\theta_p - \beta_2)}{(1 + \exp(\theta_p - \beta_2))} \frac{1}{(1 + \exp(\theta_p - \beta_1))} + \\
&\quad \frac{\exp(\theta_p - \beta_2 + \delta)}{(1 + \exp(\theta_p - \beta_2 + \delta))} \frac{\exp(\theta_p - \beta_1)}{(1 + \exp(\theta_p - \beta_1))}. \quad (10.7)
\end{aligned}
$$

Two interesting observations can be made from Equation 10.7. First, the marginal probability is not a logistic function and its shape depends on the dependence structure of the model (in this case, the parameter δ) and on the item parameter β_1 and not just on β_2. Second, the parameter β_2 does not have the natural interpretation of marking the point on the latent scale where the probability of a 1-response is .5. Different values of δ lead to different locations on the latent scale where $\Pr(Y_{p2} = 1) = .5$. Because of these two things (no logistic marginals and item parameters are not the item difficulties), it is said that there is no *reproducibility*[3] in this model (Fahrmeir & Tutz, 2001; Ip, 2002).

A third feature is the so-called *backward learning* (Verhelst & Glas, 1995). Although there is an *a priori* ordering in the items (e.g., time), and although we have modeled the effect of earlier responses on later ones, it seems that later items also have an 'effect' on earlier ones. To explain backward learning, assume we have the responses of person p on two items, Y_{p1} and Y_{p2}. In the recursive model, we specify $\Pr(Y_{p1} = y_{p1})$ and $\Pr(Y_{p2} = y_{p2}|y_{p1})$ and it may seem therefore that the response probability for item 1 is unaffected by the response on item 2. However, when the conditional probability of a response on the first item given the second is derived, some simple but tedious algebra shows that:

$$
\begin{aligned}
\Pr(Y_{p1} = y_{p1}|y_{p2}) &= \frac{\Pr(Y_{p1} = y_{p1}, Y_{p2} = y_{p2})}{\Pr(Y_{p2} = y_{p2})} \quad (10.8) \\
&= \frac{\Pr(Y_{p1} = y_{p1})\Pr(Y_{p2} = y_{p2}|y_{p1})}{\Pr(Y_{p2} = y_{p2})} \\
&= \frac{\exp(y_{p1}(\theta_p - \beta_1 + y_{p2}\delta + f(\theta_p, \beta_2, \delta)))}{1 + \exp(\theta_p - \beta_1 + y_{p2}\delta + f(\theta_p, \beta_2, \delta))},
\end{aligned}
$$

with $f(\theta_p, \beta_2, \delta) = \log\left(\frac{1+e^{\theta_p - \beta_2}}{1+e^{\theta_p - \beta_2 + \delta}}\right)$ and δ as the dependence parameter.

---

[3]We adopt here a pragmatic definition of reproducibility. For a more detailed explanation, see Fitzmaurice, Laird, and Rotnitzky (1993).

From Equation 10.8 we can deduce that, although not specified explicitly and contrary to the ordering in time, the response on item 2 has an 'effect' on item 1 (and more specifically, the effect in both directions actually appears to be the same, see below). The implication of backward learning is unavoidable and it occurs because in the population of persons who give a 1-response to item 2, there is an overrepresentation of persons who also gave a 1-response to item 1 (given that learning occurs, see Verhelst & Glas, 1995).

10.3.2 Nonrecursive models

General model

In nonrecursive models, feedback loops between the different items are allowed and therefore we need to specify for each item which items are directly associated with it. For simplicity, we start with the assumption that all items are endogenous. For the most general model the logit of a 1-response on an item i conditional on the responses on all other items is as follows:

$$
\text{logit}\left(\Pr(Y_{pi} = 1|\boldsymbol{y}_p^{(i)})\right) = \theta_p - \beta_i + \sum_{j \neq i} y_{pj}\delta_{ij} + \sum_{j,k \neq i} y_{pj}y_{pk}\delta_{ijk} + \cdots
$$
$$
+ \sum_{j_1,\ldots,j_{I-1} \neq i} y_{pj_1} \cdots y_{pj_{I-1}}\delta_{ij_1\ldots j_{I-1}}, \quad (10.9)
$$

where the vector $\boldsymbol{y}_p^{(i)}$ contains all responses of person p except the one on item i. As can be seen from Equation 10.9, the conditional distribution of Y_{pi} given all other responses has a logistic form (for all items i).

In Equation 10.9 we have specified all conditional distributions, but we actually need the joint distribution. It turns out that restrictions have to be imposed on the δs to ensure that the conditional probabilities for all items i in Equation 10.9 uniquely determine a joint distribution. If such restrictions are imposed and the conditional distributions lead to a unique joint distribution, it is said that the conditionals are compatible (Arnold, Castillo, & Sarabia, 1999, see also Chapter 7 in this volume). All restrictions are symmetry conditions on the dependence parameters. For two-way associations this means that the parameter representing the association between Y_{pi} and Y_{pj} (i.e., δ_{ij}) should be equal to the parameter representing the association between Y_{pj} and Y_{pi} (i.e., δ_{ji}). Similar symmetry restrictions should also be imposed for higher-order associations.

It can be proven that the symmetry conditions are necessary and sufficient for the existence and uniqueness of a joint distribution (Arnold et al., 1999). We will not present a proof here, but there is an intuitive argument supporting this conclusion. If we start from the most general model in Equation 10.9 with all possible interactions between items included, then it is only after imposing the symmetry restrictions on the parameters that we arrive at a model with as many parameters $(2^I - 1)$ as there are free probabilities.

Moreover, it can be seen from comparing Equations 10.6 and 10.8 that the symmetry condition also holds in the recursive models. In both cases, the parameter δ is the logit difference when the other item has been responded to with a 1 in comparison with a 0. The parameter δ that captures the dependence between Y_{pi} and $Y_{p\,i-1}$ (Equation 10.6) equals the parameter that captures the dependence between $Y_{p\,i-1}$ and Y_{pi} (Equation 10.8).

The joint probability distribution for $\boldsymbol{y}_p$ derived from the conditional distributions of all items i in Equation 10.9 now reads as:

$$\Pr(\boldsymbol{Y}_p = \boldsymbol{y}_p) \tag{10.10}$$

$$= \frac{\exp\left(\sum_{i=1}^I y_{pi}(\theta_p - \beta_i) + \sum_{j<k} y_{pj}y_{pk}\delta_{jk} + \ldots + y_{p1}\cdots y_{pI}\delta_{12\cdots I}\right)}{\sum_{\boldsymbol{s}} \exp\left(\sum_{i=1}^I s_i(\theta_p - \beta_i) + \sum_{j<k} s_j s_k \delta_{jk} + \ldots + s_1 \cdots s_I \delta_{12\cdots I}\right)},$$

where the sum in the denominator is taken over all 2^I possible binary vectors $\boldsymbol{s} = (s_1, \ldots, s_i, \ldots, s_I)$ of length I. See Section 4.2.2 of Chapter 4 for a similar formulation, with ωs instead of δs. This is the (random-effects) loglinear specification of the joint distribution of the response vector (Bishop, Fienberg, & Holland, 1975; Cox, 1972). It is the random-effects specification because of the inclusion of θ_p. In general, each of the δs can be made a function of a random effect. In Equation 10.10, only δ_i is a function of a random effect $(\delta_i = \theta_p - \beta_i)$, but not the pairwise and higher-order dependence parameters. That is why Hoskens and De Boeck (1997) called this model (or submodels of it) the *constant combination interaction model*, with the term 'constant' used to contrast it with models in which pairwise and/or higher-order dependencies are either dependent on θ_p or on some other random effects. The model from Equation 10.10 is the fully parametrized model and meaningful restrictions will be discussed below.

Features of the nonrecursive model

Starting from a model in which feedback loops between responses are allowed, we end up with a different model than when feedback is not allowed. First, in contrast with the recursive models, the joint probability of the nonrecursive model can be written in the loglinear form with a denominator that does not contain the responses on other items. Second and unfortunately, for the nonrecursive case, things are not so straightforward as to include earlier responses as predictors in the predictor matrix $\boldsymbol{W}$. The reason is that there is no factorization that results in a product of simple models, such as the one in Equation 10.1 for the recursive model. Therefore, an easy adaptation of the predictor matrix to achieve conditional independence is not possible.

The probability of a response pattern on a set of items can actually be regarded as a single response to a virtual polytomous item with 2^I categories. In Chapter 3 of this volume we argued that a response to a polytomous item is a multivariate response; in this case we reverse the argument and state that under the nonrecursive model a multivariate binary response can be seen as a response to a polytomous item. A new random variable Y_p^* is introduced to represent the response of person p on the virtual polytomous item; Y_p^* can take values ranging from 0 to $2^I - 1$ so that each different response pattern receives a unique value (assume response pattern $(0,\ldots,0)$ obtains value 0). Because the categories are not ordered, a baseline-category logit model (with 0 as the baseline category) is the appropriate choice for these data. Referring to Equation 3.14 from Chapter 3, we see that the components of the random-effects predictor matrix Z_p (notation from Chapter 3) consists of all possible sum scores on the individual binary items. The logit specific parameters β_{im} are decomposed according to Equation 10.10.

As an example of such a model-translation exercise, consider a nonrecursive model with two items. The probabilities of the four possible response patterns can be deduced from Equation 10.10:

$$\Pr(y_{p1}, y_{p2}) \hspace{4cm} (10.11)$$
$$= \frac{\exp\left(y_{p1}(\theta_p - \beta_1) + y_{p2}(\theta_p - \beta_2) + y_{p1}y_{p2}\delta\right)}{1 + \exp\left(\theta_p - \beta_1\right) + \exp\left(\theta_p - \beta_2\right) + \exp\left(2\theta_p - \beta_1 - \beta_2 + \delta\right)}.$$

Now define a new (virtual) item Y_p^* with four categories by assigning category labels 0, 1, 2 and 3 to the response patterns $(0, 0)$, $(1, 0)$, $(0, 1)$, and $(1, 1)$, respectively. The three baseline-category logits, with category 0 as baseline category, are then

$$\log\left(\frac{\pi_{p1}^*}{1 - \pi_{p1}^* - \pi_{p2}^* - \pi_{p3}^*}\right) = \log\left(\frac{\Pr(1, 0)}{\Pr(0, 0)}\right) = \theta_p - \beta_1,$$

$$\log\left(\frac{\pi_{p2}^*}{1 - \pi_{p1}^* - \pi_{p2}^* - \pi_{p3}^*}\right) = \log\left(\frac{\Pr(0, 1)}{\Pr(0, 0)}\right) = \theta_p - \beta_2,$$

$$\log\left(\frac{\pi_{p3}^*}{1 - \pi_{p1}^* - \pi_{p2}^* - \pi_{p3}^*}\right) = \log\left(\frac{\Pr(1, 1)}{\Pr(0, 0)}\right) = 2\theta_p - \beta_1 - \beta_2 + \delta.$$

It can be seen that this is a baseline-category logit model with predictor matrices for person p:

$$X_p = \begin{pmatrix} 1 & 0 & 0 \\ 0 & 1 & 0 \\ 1 & 1 & -1 \end{pmatrix} \quad \text{and} \quad Z_p = \begin{pmatrix} 1 \\ 1 \\ 2 \end{pmatrix},$$

using the notation from Chapter 3 (X_p for fixed effects, and Z_p for random effects).

This shows that a nonrecursive model can be fitted with software for polytomous items with some restrictions on the item parameters (see also Hoskens & De Boeck, 1997). Note that the specification of X_p and Z_p can easily be understood within the framework of Thissen and Steinberg (1986).

A drawback of analyzing data with nonrecursive models is that the number of possible response patterns (and therefore also the number of categories in the polytomous item) increases at an exponential rate. This makes the approach only feasible for modeling residual dependencies in clusters of a small size.

Model restrictions

The model in Equation 10.10 is the fully parametrized model, but simpler models can be obtained by setting some dependence parameters equal to zero or equal to each other. A common restriction is to set all third- and higher-order interaction parameters equal to zero ($\delta_{ijk} = \ldots = \delta_{12\ldots I} = 0$); this leads to a pairwise dependence model. For a model formulation of this kind based on the partial order of response patterns, see Ip, Wang, De Boeck, and Meulders (2003). A further step is to restrict all pairwise interaction parameters to be equal ($\delta_{ij} = \delta$ for all i and j); then we obtain a model in which the effect of the sum score of the remaining items on a given item is modeled (see also Prentice, 1988; Qu et al., 1987). The latter can be derived easily from Equation 10.9. If all dependence parameters equal zero, the nonrecursive model simplifies to a product of common Rasch models. Therefore, the Rasch model is nested within the nonrecursive model.

Interpretational issues

The same three interpretation issues as for the recursive models are relevant for the nonrecursive models. First, the exact interpretation of the *dependence parameters* depends on the order of association that is captured. For two-way dependence parameters (e.g., δ_{ij}), we have to look at the change in odds for item i if the score on item j is altered keeping the response pattern for the remaining items constant. Consequently, the two-way dependence parameter expresses the conditional log odds ratio for the item pair i and j, given the responses on all other items (denoted as $Y_{pl}, l \neq i, j$):

$$\log \left(\frac{\Pr(11|Y_{pl})\Pr(00|Y_{pl})}{\Pr(10|Y_{pl})\Pr(01|Y_{pl})} \right) = \delta_{ij}.$$

A three-way dependence parameter δ_{ijk} is the difference in the conditional log odds ratios between items i and j if the response on item k changes from 0 to 1:

$$\log \left(\frac{\Pr(11|Y_{pk} = 1, Y_{pl})\Pr(00|Y_{pk} = 1, Y_{pl})}{\Pr(10|Y_{pk} = 1, Y_{pl})\Pr(01|Y_{pk} = 1, Y_{pl})} \right)$$

$$- \log \left(\frac{\Pr(11|Y_{pk} = 0, Y_{pl})\Pr(00|Y_{pk} = 0, Y_{pl})}{\Pr(10|Y_{pk} = 0, Y_{pl})\Pr(01|Y_{pk} = 0, Y_{pl})} \right) = \delta_{ijk}.$$

Similar definitions apply to higher-order dependence parameters. Because the dependence parameters are defined in terms of conditional odds ratios and ratios of conditional odds ratios, they are not directly related to the odds ratios used to construct Figure 10.1, because the latter are marginal log odds ratios (marginal log odds ratios do not result in simple expressions in the nonrecursive model).

Second, the nonrecursive models are *nonreproducible*, although they may be approximated quite well by a logistic model with an additional discrimination parameter (see Tuerlinckx & De Boeck, 2001). Third, *backward learning* is still an issue in nonrecursive models.

10.4   Random-effects models for residual dependencies

Person-specific random effects were introduced to account for the dependence between responses on different items due to clustering of items within persons. For this reason, it seems natural to include random effects as well if additional clustering in the data is present, for instance, due to the presence of testlets. Testlet random-effect models were proposed by Bradlow, et al. (1999) and by Scott and Ip (2002), and a simplified variant of their model will be discussed here.[4]

General model

Assume that the test of I items contains a single group of I_{testlet} items ($I_{\text{testlet}} > 1$) that are related in some way (e.g., because these are questions that follow the same reading paragraph) while the others do not belong to that group (and conditional independence can be assumed for them). Then we define an indicator variable X_{I+1} for the single testlet (it carries the index $I + 1$ because there are I indicators for the single items and this predictor codes for the testlet):

$$X_{i\ I+1} = \begin{cases} 1 & \text{if item } i \text{ belongs to testlet 1,} \\ 0 & \text{otherwise.} \end{cases}$$

---

[4]Note that we will use, unlike Bradlow et al. (1999), a model without a discrimination parameter and a logistic model instead of a probit model. However, the probit model will be discussed in Section 10.5.

From the definition of X_{I+1}, we deduce it is an item predictor because its values change over items but remain constant over persons. The probability of a response y_{pi} now becomes

$$\Pr(Y_{pi} = y_{pi}) = \frac{\exp\left(\theta_{p0} + X_{i\ I+1}\theta_{p1} - \beta_i\right)}{1 + \exp\left(\theta_{p0} + X_{i\ I+1}\theta_{p1} - \beta_i\right)}, \tag{10.12}$$

or $\eta_{pi} = \theta_{p0} + X_{i\ I+1}\theta_{p1} - \beta_i$, where θ_{p1} is the person-specific testlet effect which is normally distributed with mean 0 and standard deviation σ_{θ_1}. The second formulation of the model (with η_{pi}) is used to show the similarity and difference with the other random-effects models discussed in this volume. It is possible to allow for a covariance $\sigma^2_{\theta_0\theta_1}$ between the random intercept θ_{p0} (previously denoted by θ_p) and the testlet effect θ_{p1}, but that is not necessary and it will not be done in this chapter (therefore, we assume, like Bradlow et al. that $\sigma^2_{\theta_0\theta_1} = 0$). As can be seen from the definition, the random-effects testlet model is a multidimensional model (see Chapter 8 in this volume). In the presentation of the testlet model, we included only one additional random effect assuming there was only a single testlet. However, this does not have to be the case and more complicated clustering patterns can be taken into account. This will be illustrated with the verbal aggression data set in which the testlets are actually overlapping.

In the application of the model to the verbal aggression data, we included separate random effects for the three Behavior Types (Curse, Scold, Shout), for the four situations (Bus, Train, Store, Call) and for the two Behavior Modes (Want and Do). However, we did not include random effects for the Situation Type (Self-blame and Other-blame). Because there was also the random intercept θ_{p0}, the final model is a ten-dimensional one. Fitting such a model with a realistic number of quadrature nodes to approximate the integral over the random-effects populations would take a very long time. Therefore we reduced the number of nodes to two per dimension. This is not a common practice and we do not advise its general use; it is done here only to illustrate the effects of including all these random effects while still limiting the computation time (though the PC with 1.8Ghz Pentium IV processor and 512 Mb RAM still ran for over 15 hours). To have a minimal check on our results, we computed the correlation between the Rasch estimates of the difficulty parameters and the estimates under the ten-dimensional model. The correlation proved to be sufficiently large ($r = .999$) for us to be satisfied. We have used the graphical technique presented in Section 10.2 to evaluate how well the ten-dimensional model captures the residual dependencies; the result is shown in Figure 10.2. It can be seen that the model-based plots are almost indistinguishable from the empirical plots. The model clearly takes into account a great deal of the remaining dependencies in the data.

In our application of the random-effects testlet model, we did not allow for covariances between the random effects, which is a drawback of the approach. However, when covariances are present, the computational burden

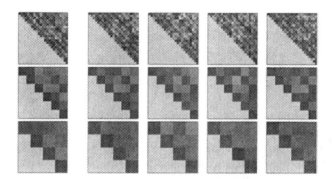

FIGURE 10.2. Log odds ratio plot for the testlet random-effects model. Figures in row 1 contain dependencies between pairs of items; figures in row 2 contain average dependencies based on wanting and doing combined with behaviors; figures in row 3 contain average dependencies based on a common situation. The first figure in each row is derived from the data, the other four stem from data generated from the testlet random-effects model.

becomes even greater due to the inflation of the number of parameters. Haaijer, Vriens, Wansbeek, and Wedel (1998) and Tsai and Böckenholt (2001) proposed to handle this inflation of number of covariance parameters by assuming a factor-analytical model for the covariance matrix of the random effects which may reduce the number of parameters to some extent.

Interpretation issues

The interpretation of the model differs slightly from the interpretation of the conditional models, since the latter were fixed-effects models. Assume two persons p and q with the same value for the random intercept $\theta_{p0} = \theta_{q0}$ who respond to an item i from a test with one testlet. Then their odds of responding correctly differ with a factor $\exp(X_{i\ I+1}\ \theta_{p1} - X_{i\ I+1}\ \theta_{q1})$. If the item does belong to the testlet ($X_{i\ I+1} = 1$), then the difference between the two testlet specific trait values, θ_{p1} and θ_{q1} explains the difference in odds. On the other hand, if the item does not belong to the testlet ($X_{i\ I+1} = 0$), then there is no change in the odds. As for the conditional models, the random-effects testlet model is *nonreproducible*.

10.5   Marginal models for residual dependencies

In many cases, the residual dependencies are considered to be a nuisance and the main interest lies in the marginal probability of 1-response on a given item, $\Pr(Y_{pi} = 1)$, as a function of θ_p (the trait measured through the random intercept) or another characteristic (e.g., Gender or Trait Anger). However, under none of the previous models for residual dependencies are the marginal probabilities reproducible, which means that the univariate marginal probability, $\Pr(Y_{pi} = 1)$, is not a logistic function of θ_p and the relevant item parameters. Moreover, the parameters pertaining to a single item cannot be seen as item difficulties. An alternative is to build a model in which the univariate marginal probabilities are explicitly specified and unaffected by the association structure capturing the residual item dependencies.

A possible model for the purpose of marginal modeling is the *multivariate probit model* (Ashford & Sowden, 1970; Chib & Greenberg, 1998; Lesaffre & Molenberghs, 1991) which is a multivariate extension of the well-known probit model and which has a long but rather unnoticed history in statistical practice. By considering a probit model, we step outside the realm of logistic models and model the probability of a 1-response on an item with the probit or normal-ogive model (see Chapter 1).

Consider two items and assume, as in Chapter 1, that there exists a continuous latent random variable V_{pi} ($i = 1, 2$) which is normally distributed with mean $\theta_p - \beta_i$ and standard deviation σ_ε. The value σ_ε is a scale parameter that cannot be estimated from the data. It is set equal to 1 for simplicity. Assume also that there exists a threshold at 0 and that for $V_{pi} > 0$, a 1-response follows and a 0-response otherwise. Moreover, let θ_p be the random effect associated with person p. All these assumptions are the same as in Chapter 1. It can be shown that θ_p is responsible for a specific correlation structure between the responses in the multivariate probit model. Conditional upon θ_p, the bivariate vector V_p is distributed as follows:

$$\begin{pmatrix} V_{p1} \\ V_{p2} \end{pmatrix} | \theta_p \sim N\left(\begin{pmatrix} \theta_p - \beta_1 \\ \theta_p - \beta_2 \end{pmatrix}, \begin{pmatrix} 1 & 0 \\ 0 & 1 \end{pmatrix} \right),$$

where $N(\boldsymbol{\mu}, \boldsymbol{\Sigma})$ stands for a bivariate normal distribution with mean vector $\boldsymbol{\mu}$ and variance-covariance matrix $\boldsymbol{\Sigma}$. If we integrate over the normal distribution for the random intercept θ_p (with mean 0 and variance σ^2 which was denoted in earlier chapters by σ_θ^2 or $\sigma_{\theta_0}^2$), then we obtain

$$\begin{pmatrix} V_{p1} \\ V_{p2} \end{pmatrix} \sim N\left(\begin{pmatrix} -\beta_1 \\ -\beta_2 \end{pmatrix}, \begin{pmatrix} \sigma^2 + 1 & \sigma^2 \\ \sigma^2 & \sigma^2 + 1 \end{pmatrix} \right)$$
$$\sim N\left(\begin{pmatrix} -\beta_1^* \\ -\beta_2^* \end{pmatrix}, \begin{pmatrix} 1 & \rho \\ \rho & 1 \end{pmatrix} \right),$$

where $\rho = \frac{\sigma^2}{\sigma^2 + 1}$ and $\beta_i^* = \frac{\beta_i}{\sigma^2 + 1}$ (the marginal probability of solving an item i). Thus the continuous latent data are distributed as a bivariate normal distribution with the correlation matrix R in equicorrelated form. The justification of this result can be found in any introductory book on linear mixed models (e.g., Verbeke & Molenberghs, 2000). It is the well-known compound symmetry form from repeated observations ANOVA (see Chapter 1).

Because the latent continuous data V_{p1} and V_{p2} are correlated, the discrete responses Y_{p1} and Y_{p2} will be too. The marginal probability of a 1-response is given by $f_{\text{probit}}^{-1}(-\beta_i^*)$, where f_{probit}^{-1} is the inverse probit link function (see Chapter 1). The model can be easily extended to more than two dimensions, but then one has to work with the multivariate normal density and cumulative distribution function.

Assume now that there exists additional clustering in the test (e.g., questions that are given after a common paragraph of text), then the random-effects probit model as formulated here may leave residual dependencies unexplained. Suppose that we are in the general case of I items and that the first $I_{\text{testlet 1}}$ (with $I_{\text{testlet 1}} < I$) items belong to a testlet and the remaining $I_{\text{testlet 2}} = I - I_{\text{testlet 1}}$ items belong to a second testlet. Furthermore, we assume that we have already inserted a random effect in the probit model, leading to the model presented above (but generalized to I items). We will now include two additional uncorrelated random effects θ_{p1} and θ_{p2}, one for each testlet, both uncorrelated with the random intercept θ_{p0} and normally distributed with mean 0 but with variance τ^2. Then we find that the $I \times I$ correlation matrix R for the continuous latent variables becomes

$$
R = \left(
\begin{array}{ccc|ccc}
1 & \cdots & \rho_1 & \rho_2 & \cdots & \rho_2 \\
\vdots & \ddots & \vdots & \vdots & \ddots & \vdots \\
\rho_1 & \cdots & 1 & \rho_2 & \cdots & \rho_2 \\
\hline
\rho_2 & \cdots & \rho_2 & 1 & \cdots & \rho_1 \\
\vdots & \ddots & \vdots & \vdots & \ddots & \vdots \\
\rho_2 & \cdots & \rho_2 & \rho_1 & \cdots & 1
\end{array}
\right),
$$

now with $\rho_1 = (\sigma^2 + \tau^2)/(\sigma^2 + \tau^2 + 1)$ for two items belonging to the same testlet and $\rho_2 = \sigma^2/(\sigma^2 + \tau^2 + 1)$ for two items belonging to different testlets. Moreover, $\beta_i^* = \beta_i/(\sqrt{\sigma^2 + \tau^2 + 1})$. This model is a random-effects testlet probit model, with an additional random effect included for all items belonging to the same testlet. Actually, it is more closely related to the original testlet model of Bradlow et al. (1999) than the logistic model proposed above because the model of Bradlow et al. was also a probit model. An important difference with the logistic testlet model is that for a probit model, the marginal probability of solving an item i belonging to a testlet but with the testlet random effect (θ_{p1} or θ_{p2}) integrated out, can be easily expressed as:

$$
\eta_{pi}^* = (\theta_{p0} - \beta_i)/\sqrt{\tau^2 + 1},
$$

with $\eta_{pi}^* = f_{\text{probit}}(\pi_{pi}^*)$, and where the asterisk superscript indicates that the values are averaged over the testlet random effect. The model is reproducible because the marginal probabilities (π_{pi}^*) are still normal-ogive functions (independent of the association structure and how many items are involved) and β_i can be interpreted as the item difficulty.

Moreover, we can further marginalize over θ_{p0} in order to derive the marginal probability of a 1-response in the population, $\Pr(Y_i = 1)$, which is again a probit model (see e.g., McCulloch & Searle, 2001):

$$\eta_{pi}^{**} = -\beta_i / \sqrt{\sigma^2 + \tau^2 + 1},$$

with $\eta_{pi}^{**} = f_{\text{probit}}(\pi_{pi}^{**})$, where the double asterisk superscript indicates that the values are averaged over the two random effects. Hence, this formula gives the proportion of 1-responses in the population for a randomly selected individual. If a latent regression on person predictors was part of the random-effects model specification, then we can derive that the effect of the predictor is quantified by the parameter $\vartheta^* = \frac{\vartheta}{\sqrt{\sigma^2 + \tau^2 + 1}}$ (the population-averaged regression coefficient, which is attenuated compared to the person-specific regression coefficient; see Diggle, Heagerty, Liang, & Zeger, 2002).

As long as the structure on the correlation matrix $\boldsymbol{R}$ can be obtained from a random-effects model (which implies that the covariance matrix of the random effects $\boldsymbol{\Sigma}$, is positive definite; see Section 4.6.3 in Chapter 4), the multivariate probit model can be estimated with computer software that allows a random-effects probit analysis (e.g., the procedure NLMIXED from SAS). However, the multivariate probit model can be specified with any arbitrary correlation matrix, also one that cannot be obtained from a simple underlying random-effects model. For example, assume that similar items (with different item parameters) are assessed repeatedly over time. It may be reasonable to assume that the correlation between the latent continuous variables Vs (conditional on θ_{p0}) will diminish with increasing time lag between the observation occasions. The entry in the correlation matrix for the correlation between V_{pi} and $V_{pi'}$ (conditional on θ_{p0}) has then the following form: $\rho^{|i-i'|}$. Fitting such models often requires specialized software.

Despite the indisputable advantage of having a model which leads to reproducible marginals, there are also a few important disadvantages to multivariate probit analysis. First, the nice interpretation of effects in terms of odds ratios, as we had in logit models, is unavailable in probit models. However, because both models are so similar, one could still defend the use of odds ratios as an approximate way of interpreting the probit-based regression coefficients. A second and more serious drawback is that in a frequentist inferential framework, the multivariate probit model is computationally a very demanding model, certainly if the number of items becomes large (the evaluation of a multivariate normal cumulative distribution function is a very computationally intensive task) or if the model cannot be reformulated as a random-effects model. In the latter case, the best way to make inferences about the model is to resort to a Bayesian approach (Chib & Greenberg, 1998).

10.6   Concluding remarks

All methods presented in this chapter try to account for residual dependencies in the data that are not captured by a conditional independence model. Each method is based on different assumptions and none of them can be labeled as uniformly the best method in all situations. In this section we discuss the assets and drawbacks of each method and present some generalizations.

The conditional methods model the probability of a certain response on the current item given the responses on all other items or on some subset of the other items. Within the class of conditional models, we distinguished between recursive and nonrecursive models; both techniques use fixed-effects parameters to account for the dependencies (for random-effects versions, see Chapter 7). Which one of these two can be applied in a given situation depends in the first place on whether there is an *a priori* ordering of the items or not. The recursive models are certainly simpler to apply since they only require the adaptation of the predictor matrix by including the responses on the previous items, as shown in Chapter 7. Once that task is completed, we are back in the conditional independence situation and the traditional estimation tools for conditional independence models can be applied. However, an ordering may not be present. When no 'natural' ordering is available, making an arbitrary choice for a certain ordering and applying a recursive model is probably not a good idea because a different ordering would result in a totally different model. Therefore, if no ordering is available, it might be more reasonable to apply a nonrecursive model.

The greatest disadvantage of the nonrecursive conditional models is that ultimately the joint probability distribution of the responses conditional on the random effect has to be available. If the number of items that are suspected to show residual dependencies is not too large, this is no problem. However, if a testlet contains for instance 10 binary scored items, the testlet is a virtual polytomous item with 1028 categories which is impractical to fit with software for polytomous data. Moreover, it is advisable to restrict the number of parameters in some way (but this is also true for the recursive models). There have been some suggestions not to use the orthodox maximum likelihood estimation procedures for nonrecursive models with many items but instead to apply pseudo-maximum likelihood procedures which are based on the direct product of the conditional distributions in Equation 10.9 (see Arnold et al., 1999; Connolly & Liang, 1988). However, this approach has not yet been studied thoroughly in terms of bias and loss of efficiency of the parameter estimates.

The random-effects approach is very straightforward to apply in the situation where no *a priori* ordering exists. It does not suffer from problems with large cluster sizes, but it has difficulties with a high number of clusters because then the dimensionality of the model may become practically unmanageable. A huge drawback of both random-effects and conditional models is their lack of reproducible univariate marginals. If one is really interested in modeling the probability of a correct response and considers the residual dependencies as a nuisance, it is unfortunate that the marginal inferences from a random-effects model (as displayed in the right-hand branch of Figure 4.4) are strongly influenced by the adopted association structure.

The multivariate probit model has reproducible marginals which is its major advantage. However, the model itself is not a standard model to apply and easy-to-use software is not yet available, certainly not if one wants to fit the more complicated and interesting variants (otherwise, one could use the random-effects logistic testlet model as well). Moreover, the model is computationally hard to handle.

We conclude the chapter with three remarks. First, the different models proposed in this chapter can, of course, be combined in various ways. Instead of having pure recursive and nonrecursive models, one may define an intermediate class of models. For example, if up to a certain item i there is an *a priori* order and no feedback loops, but from then on there are feedback loops indeed, one can construct, for the second set of items given the first, a nonrecursive model and for the first set a recursive model, and both can be combined. Another example is when it would make sense to combine recursive models with random-effects testlet models to model learning between testlets. Still another application of a combined approach is to make the fixed-effects dependence parameter in the conditional dependence models random over persons (Smits & De Boeck, 2003).

Second, we have studied exclusively the case of positive residual dependencies, that is the case that the data show more dependencies than the model can account for. All approaches are suited for this type of residual dependencies. However, negative residual dependencies may also occur (Tuerlinckx, De Boeck, & Lens, 2002). In such a case, the random-effects testlet model is not an appropriate model anymore.

Third, the residual dependence techniques can be applied to many models described in the previous chapters. For instance, we have limited our discussion to the Rasch model for binary data, but the generalization to polytomous data, to multidimensional models and to the inclusion of other types of predictors is relatively straightforward. See for example Hoskens and De Boeck (2001) for a generalization of a conditional model to the multidimensional case. As illustrated in the Exercises, a polytomous extension and a DIF analysis are also possible.

10.7   Exercises

1. A commonly used index for residual dependencies is Yen's Q_3 measure (Yen, 1984). For an item pair i and i', Q_3 is defined as the correlation between the residuals on the two items. The residuals are defined as

$r_{pi} = y_{pi} - \widehat{\Pr}(y_{pi} = 1)$ and $r_{pi'} = y_{pi'} - \widehat{\Pr}(y_{pi'} = 1)$, where $\widehat{\Pr}(y_{pi'} = 1)$ stands for the estimated probability of a correct response for person p on item i', so that $i \neq i'$. Computing the correlation between the r_{pi}s and the $r_{pi'}$s gives the Q_3 for pair (i, i'). Construct a similar plot as in Figure 10.1 using the Q_3 instead.

2. Construct a recursive model for five items with the usual two-way dependencies, as well as a three-way dependence (that is, specify W_p and δ). How should three-way dependence parameters be interpreted?

3. Show that there is no reproducibility in the constant combination interaction model.

4. Show that there is no reproducibility for the random-effects testlet model.

5. Suppose there is only one testlet of I_{testlet} ($I_{\text{testlet}} < I$) items. A marginal probit model with a random intercept and a single random testlet effect is defined. What is the structure of the marginal correlation matrix for the continuous latent random variables V_{pi} and how are the correlations defined?

6. A test contains four items and it is known that items 3 and 4 can be modeled with a constant combination interaction model while learning, as defined in Equation 10.4, takes place from item 1 up to the set of the final two items. Schematically, this can be displayed as follows:

$$1 \rightarrow 2 \rightarrow \left\{ \begin{array}{c} 3 \\ \updownarrow \\ 4 \end{array} \right\}.$$

Set up a model for this data structure.

7. A short test of five similar items is given to normal children and to children with an attention deficit disorder. From previous research it is known that both groups learn while taking the test but it is hypothesized that the attention deficit has a negative effect on learning. Set up a model to test this hypothesis. Assume that the number of previous correct responses drives the learning process. Show the design matrices for a normal and for a disabled child. (This is a model for DIF in the learning parameter.)

8. How would you extend the random-effects model for residual dependencies with binary scored items (Equation 10.12) to the case of polytomous data? Hint: work with cumulative logits.

10.8   References

Arnold, B.C., Castillo, E., & Sarabia, J.M. (1999). *Conditional Specification of Statistical Models*. New York: Springer.

Ashford, J.R., & Sowden, R.R. (1970). Multivariate probit analysis. *Biometrics, 26*, 535–546.

Bahadur, R. (1961). A representation of the joint distribution of responses to n dichotomous items. In H. Solomon (Ed.), *Studies in Item Analysis and Prediction* (pp. 158–168). Palo Alto: Stanford University Press.

Bishop, Y.M., Fienberg, S.E., & Holland, P. (1975). *Discrete Multivariate Analysis*. Cambridge, MA: MIT Press.

Bollen, K.A. (1989). *Structural Equations with Latent Variables*. New York: Wiley.

Bonney, G.E. (1987). Logistic regression for dependent binary observations. *Biometrics, 43*, 951–973.

Bradlow, E.T., Wainer, H., & Wang, X. (1999). A Bayesian random effects model for testlets. *Psychometrika, 64*, 153–168.

Chen, W.H., & Thissen, D. (1997). Local dependence indexes for item pairs using item response theory. *Journal of Educational and Behavioral Statistics, 22*, 265–289.

Chib, S., & Greenberg, E. (1998). Analysis of multivariate probit models. *Biometrika, 85*, 347–361.

Connolly, M.A., & Liang, K.-Y. (1988). Conditional logistic regression results for correlated binary data. *Biometrika, 75*, 501–506.

Cox, D.R. (1972). The analysis of multivariate binary data. *Applied Statistics, 21*, 113–120.

Diggle, P.J., Heagerty, P.J., Liang, K.-Y., & Zeger, S.L. (2002). *Analysis of Longitudinal Data (2nd ed.)*. Oxford: Oxford University Press.

Douglas, J., Kim, H.R., Habing, B., & Gao, F. (1998). Investigating local dependence with conditional covariance functions. *Journal of Educational and Behavioral Statistics, 23*, 129–151.

Efron, B., & Tibshirani, R. (1993). *An Introduction to the Bootstrap*. London: Chapman & Hall.

Fahrmeir, L., & Tutz, G. (2001). *Multivariate Statistical Modeling Based on Generalized Linear Models (2nd ed.)*. New York: Springer.

Fitzmaurice, G.M., Laird, N.M., & Rotnitzky, A.G. (1993). Regression models for discrete longitudinal responses. *Statistical Science, 8*, 284–309.

Gelman, A. (2002). Exploratory data analysis for complex models. Technical report, Department of Statistics, Columbia University.

Gelman, A., Goegebeur, Y., Tuerlinckx, F., & Van Mechelen, I. (2000). Diagnostic checks for discrete-data regression models using posterior predictive simulations. *Applied Statistics, 42,* 247–268.

Haaijer, M.E., Vriens, M., Wansbeek, T.J., & Wedel, M. (1998). Utility covariances and context effects in conjoint MNP models. *Marketing Science, 17,* 236–252.

Hoskens M., & De Boeck, P. (1997). A parametric model for local item dependencies among test items. *Psychological Methods, 2,* 261–277.

Hoskens M., & De Boeck, P. (2001). Multidimensional componential IRT models. *Applied Psychological Measurement, 25,* 19–37.

Ip, E. (2000). Adjusting for information inflation due to local dependence in moderately large item clusters. *Psychometrika, 65,* 73–91.

Ip, E. (2001). Testing for local dependence in dichotomous and polytomous item response models. *Psychometrika, 66,* 109–132.

Ip, E. (2002). Locally dependent latent trait model and the Dutch identity revisited. *Psychometrika, 67,* 367–386.

Ip, E., Wang, J.W, De Boeck, P., & Meulders, M. (2003). Locally dependent latent trait models for polytomous responses. *Psychometrika.* Manuscript accepted for publication.

Jannerone, R.J. (1986). Conjunctive item response theory kernels. *Psychometrika, 51,* 357–373.

Kelderman, H. (1984). Loglinear Rasch model tests. *Psychometrika, 49,* 223–245.

Keller, L.A., Swaminathan, H., & Sireci, S.G. (2003). Evaluating scoring procedures for context-dependent item sets. *Applied Measurement in Education, 16,* 207–222.

Lee, L.-F. (1981). Fully recursive probability models and multivariate loglinear probability models for the analysis of qualitative data. *Journal of Econometrics, 16,* 51–69.

Lesaffre, E., & Molenberghs, G. (1991). Multivariate probit analysis: A neglected procedure in medical statistics. *Statistics in Medicine, 10,* 1391–1403.

Liang, K.-Y., & Zeger, S.L. (1986). Longitudinal data analysis using generalized linear models. *Biometrika, 73,* 13–22.

McCulloch, C.E., & Searle, S.R. (2001). *Generalized, Linear, and Mixed Models.* New York: Wiley.

Nerlove, M., & Press, S.J. (1973). *Univariate and Multivariate Loglinear and Logistic Models* (Report R-1306.) Santa Barbara, CA: Rand Corporation.

Prentice, R.L. (1988). Correlated binary regression with covariates specific to each binary observation. *Biometrics, 44,* 1033–1048.

Qu, Y., Williams, G.W., Beck, G.J., & Goormastic, M. (1987) A generalized model of logistic regression for clustered data. *Communications in Statistics: Theory and Methodology, 16,* 3447–3476.

Rosenbaum, P. (1984). Testing the conditional independence and monotonicity assumptions of item response theory. *Psychometrika, 49*, 425–435.

Rosenbaum, P. (1988). Item bundles. *Psychometrika, 53*, 349–359.

Schmidt, P., & Strauss, R. (1975). The prediction of occupation using multiple logit models. *International Economic Review, 16*, 471–486.

Scott, S., & Ip, E. (2002). Empirical Bayes and item clustering effects in a latent variables hierarchical model: A case study from the National Assessment of Educational Progress. *Journal of the American Statistical Association, 97*, 409–419.

Smits, D.J.M., & De Boeck, P. (2003). Random local item dependencies. Paper presented at the 13th International Meeting and the 68th Annual American Meeting of the Psychometric Society, Cagliari, Italy.

Smits, D.J.M., De Boeck, P., & Hoskens, M. (2003). Examining the structure of concepts: Using interaction between items. *Applied Psychological Measurement, 27*, 415–439.

Thissen, D., & Steinberg, L. (1986). A taxonomy of item response models, *Psychometrika, 51*, 567–577.

Tsai, R.-C., & Böckenholt, U. (2001). Maximum likelihood estimation of factor and ideal point models for paired comparison data. *Journal of Mathematical Psychology, 45*, 795–811.

Tuerlinckx, F., & De Boeck, P. (2001). The effect of ignoring item interaction on the estimated discrimination parameter of the 2PLM. *Psychological Methods, 6*, 181–195.

Tuerlinckx, F., De Boeck, P., & Lens, W. (2002). Measuring needs with the Thematic Apperception Test: A psychometric study. *Journal of Personality and Social Psychology, 82*, 448–461.

van den Wollenberg, A.L. (1982). Two new test statistics for the Rasch model. *Psychometrika, 47*, 123–140.

Verbeke, G., & Molenberghs, G. (2000). *Linear Mixed Models for Longitudinal Data.* New York: Springer.

Verguts, T., & De Boeck, P. (2000). A Rasch model for learning while solving an intelligence test. *Applied Psychological Measurement, 24*, 151–162.

Verhelst, N.D., & Glas, C.A.W. (1993). A dynamic generalization of the Rasch model. *Psychometrika, 58*, 395–415.

Verhelst, N.D., & Glas, C.A.W. (1995). Dynamic generalizations of the Rasch model. In G.H. Fischer & I.W. Molenaar (Eds), *Rasch Models: Foundations, Recent Developments, and Applications.* (pp. 181–201). New York: Springer.

Wainer, H., & Kiely, G.L. (1987). Item clusters and computerized adaptive testing: A case for testlets. *Journal of Educational Measurement, 24*, 185–201.

Wilson, M., & Adams, R.J. (1995). Rasch models for item bundles. *Psychometrika, 60,* 181–198.

Yen, W.M. (1984). Effect of local item dependence on the fit and equating performance of the three-parameter logistic model. *Applied Psychological Measurement, 8,* 125–145.

Yen, W.M. (1993). Scaling performance assessments: Strategies for managing local item dependence. *Journal of Educational Measurement, 30,* 187–213.

Zeger, S.L., & Liang, K.-Y. (1986). Longitudinal data analysis for discrete and continuous outcomes. *Biometrics, 42,* 121–130.

Chapter 11

Mixture Models

Steffen Fieuws
Bart Spiessens
Karen Draney

11.1   Introduction

In all models discussed thus far in this volume, it has been assumed that the random person weights $\boldsymbol{\theta}_p$ follow a normal distribution with mean $\mathbf{0}$ and covariance matrix $\boldsymbol{\Sigma}$:

$$\boldsymbol{\theta}_p \quad \sim \quad N(\mathbf{0}, \boldsymbol{\Sigma}).$$

In most of these models the vector $\boldsymbol{\theta}_p$ reduces to a scalar since only one random weight is considered (e.g., the random intercept in the Rasch model). However, there are situations in which the normality assumption is not justified. When the random weights come from two or more populations, and population membership is known, this feature can be incorporated into the model, as has been shown in earlier chapters. However, if population membership is unknown (i.e., latent), it is not straightforward to incorporate this into the generalized linear mixed model framework discussed thus far. Models which include latent population membership are sometimes referred to in the psychometric literature as *mixture models* (e.g., Mislevy & Verhelst, 1990; Rost, 1990).

Such models have a moderately long history in educational and psychological contexts, with such varied uses as classification into psychological diagnostic groups (Waller & Meehl, 1998), personality assessment (Reise & Gomel, 1995), analysis of strategy use in problem-solving (Mislevy & Verhelst, 1990), detection of random guessing behavior in multiple choice testing (Mislevy & Verhelst, 1990), the use of cognitive strategies (Rijmen & De Boeck, 2003), speededness effects in time-limit tests (Bolt, Cohen, & Wollack, 2002) and developmental stages in task solution (Wilson, 1984, 1989; Draney, 1996).

When random weights are drawn from two or more latent populations, and these populations show systematic differences in their item response behavior, it is important to include this feature in the model. When it is not included, this can affect the estimation of other elements of the model, including the item slopes (e.g., Wilson, 1989; Yen, 1985). In addition, there may be much to be learned from a substantive point of view by examining person membership in latent populations.

The feature that the models described in this chapter have in common is that persons are classified into groups, and these groups are latent, rather than observed. The earliest such models were latent class models, the basic structure of which is summarized in Lazarsfeld and Henry (1968), although there have been many extensions and specifications of these models designed to accommodate the specifics of a given situation (e.g., Croon, 1990; Dayton & Macready, 1976; Formann, 1992; Goodman, 1974; Haberman, 1979; Heinen, 1993; Langeheine, 1988; Meulders, De Boeck, Kuppens & Van Mechelen, 2002; Vermunt, 1997). One of the major features of latent class models is that there is no variability on the person metric (i.e., on the intercept) within a given latent class. Rost (1988) gives as the defining feature of latent class models the characteristic that all persons within a latent class have the same probabilities of answering a set of items correctly, and thus (if considered in an educational context) the same ability or proficiency. Each class is generally represented by only one set of response probabilities.

However, it may not always be the case that all persons within a latent class have a common set of response probabilities; there may be more variation in person responses than can easily be accommodated by such a model. Other approaches have been taken; for example, Gitomer and Yamamoto (1991), in a model they name the 'hybrid model,' assign persons who do not match one of the latent classes within the model to a 'catch-all' latent trait model. More generally, in the last 20 years, a number of models have been developed which are combinations of latent trait and latent class models, such that a latent trait model holds within each latent class.

Mislevy (1984) explored the possibility that the observed population could be composed of two or more latent populations, each with its own distribution for the random intercepts (e.g., each latent population has a normal distribution with its own mean and variance).

The *saltus model* (Wilson, 1984, 1989; Mislevy & Wilson, 1996; Draney, 1996) is a simple example of a mixture model that was originally formulated to describe Piagetian-like developmental hierarchies (the word 'saltus' is Latin for 'leap'). It extends the Rasch item response model to development that occurs in discrete stages or levels. In this model there are different classes or developmental stages in the population to be measured. Items are assumed to represent each one of these stages. Items representing a stage or class are constructed such that only persons at or above that stage are fully equipped to answer these items correctly, and once a person enters the developmental stage with which items are associated, that person gains a substantial advantage in answering those items. The saltus model assumes that all persons in a group answer all items in a manner consistent with membership in that group, but persons within a group may differ by proficiency.

Mislevy and Verhelst (1990) developed a *mixture LLTM model* that is an extension of Fischer's (1983) linear logistic test model (LLTM). They state that within each latent class, the item parameters may be expressed as a function of some smaller number of more basic parameters that reflect the effects of salient characteristics of the items, as in the LLTM. In their examples, they assume that each person is applying one of several possible solution strategies to all items in an item set, and uses the same strategy for all items. Substantive theory must associate the observable features of the items with the probability of success for members of each strategy group. It is not necessary for each of the latent classes to be governed by a LLTM. The model was originally expressed in such general terms that more general item response functions can be used in place of the LLTM model that is discussed in the article. Also, Mislevy and Verhelst (1990) discuss the addition of a group of random guessers, a group for which the probability of a correct response is a fixed constant, generally the reciprocal of the number of response options.

A well-known mixture model in the psychometric literature, is the *mixed Rasch model* described by Rost (1988, 1990). This model assumes that the population being measured is composed of two or more latent subgroups, which are mutually exclusive and exhaustive. Within each of these subgroups, a Rasch model holds across all items. In this model, there is no particular structure for the item parameters in different groups. As Rost states, "...No a priori hypotheses about item difficulties within the latent classes are needed" (Rost, 1990, p. 273). The model provides estimates of both item difficulty for each item and (in a second step) person proficiency for each person within each latent class, as well as the proportion of the sample that falls within each class. Note that the class-specific estimate for a person's proficiency is only meaningful if class membership is likely.

11.2 Mixture model

11.2.1 Formal presentation

We will now formulate the previously discussed models by incorporating finite mixtures of normal distributions. We assume that

$$\boldsymbol{\theta}_p \sim \sum_{r=1}^{R} \pi_r N(\boldsymbol{\mu}_r, \boldsymbol{\Sigma}_r), \tag{11.1}$$

where R is the number of mixture classes. The probability of belonging to class r is π_r, such that $\sum_{r=1}^{R} \pi_r = 1$. Further, $\boldsymbol{\mu}_r$ refers to the means of the random effects in the rth class, and $\boldsymbol{\Sigma}_r$ is the covariance matrix of the random effects in the rth class. Note that the elements in $\boldsymbol{\mu}_r$ are class-specific deviations from the corresponding mean weights; this to ensure that the distribution for the random person weights $\boldsymbol{\theta}_p$ remains centered around zero. Denoting a mean weight by β, $\beta_r = \beta + \mu_r$ then refers to a class-specific mean weight.

Let the density of a multivariate normal distribution with mean $\boldsymbol{\mu}$ and covariance matrix $\boldsymbol{\Sigma}$ be denoted by $\phi(.)$. Denoting Y_{pi} as the response of the pth person on the ith item and the vector $\boldsymbol{y}_p = (y_{p1}, \ldots, y_{pI})'$ as the vector of the observed responses of the pth person ($p = 1, \ldots, P$), the joint density function of $\boldsymbol{y}_p$ can then be written as

$$f_p(\boldsymbol{y}_p) \;\; = \;\; \int f_p(\boldsymbol{y}_p | \boldsymbol{\theta}_p) \phi(\boldsymbol{\theta}_p) \, d\boldsymbol{\theta}_p,$$

when no mixture distribution is used for the random effects (thus, $\boldsymbol{\theta}_p \sim N(\mathbf{0}, \boldsymbol{\Sigma})$). Using a mixture distribution for the random effects in Equation 11.1 and using $\phi_r(.)$ to denote the density of a multivariate normal distribution in class r with mean $\boldsymbol{\mu}_r$ and covariance matrix $\boldsymbol{\Sigma}_r$, the joint density function of $\boldsymbol{y}_p$ becomes

$$f_p(\boldsymbol{y}_p) \;\; = \int f_p(\boldsymbol{y}_p | \boldsymbol{\theta}_p) \sum_{r=1}^{R} \pi_r \phi_r(\boldsymbol{\theta}_p) \, d\boldsymbol{\theta}_p$$

$$= \sum_{r=1}^{R} \pi_r \int f_p(\boldsymbol{y}_p | \boldsymbol{\theta}_p) \phi_r(\boldsymbol{\theta}_p) \, d\boldsymbol{\theta}_p \qquad (11.2)$$

$$= \sum_{r=1}^{R} \pi_r f_{pr}(\boldsymbol{y}_p).$$

It can be seen that the density function of $\boldsymbol{y}_p$ comes from a mixture of densities with class probabilities $\pi_1, \ldots, \pi_R$ and class densities $f_{pr}(\boldsymbol{y}_p)$. These densities are the probabilities of a correct response in a specific class and can be described by models such as the Rasch model, the LLTM model, etc. To see better the relation with the models described in the other chapters of this volume, we express the model for the case of the random intercept (a random intercept per class), and as if we knew the class membership:

$$\eta_{pi} = \sum_{r=1} \alpha_{pr} (\theta_{pr} - \beta_{ir}),$$

where η_{pi} is the logit of the probability of a 1-response for person p (belonging to class r) and item i, where $\alpha_{pr} = 1$ if person p is a member of class r, $\alpha_{pr} = 0$ otherwise ($\Sigma_{r=1}^{R} \alpha_{pr} = 1$); where θ_{pr} is the class-specific random intercept; where β_{ir} is the class-specific difficulty. However, the αs (also called latent observations) will not be estimated but instead the class probabilities function as parameters, as can be seen in Equation 11.2.

Let us now write $\boldsymbol{\pi} = (\pi_1, \ldots, \pi_R)'$, the vector of all class probabilities and $\boldsymbol{\beta}$, the vector containing the class-specific as well as the class-invariant predictor effects. Further, $\boldsymbol{\psi} = (\boldsymbol{\beta}', \text{vec}(\boldsymbol{\Sigma})')'$ where $\text{vec}(\boldsymbol{\Sigma})$ is a vector with all upper-triangular elements of $\boldsymbol{\Sigma}_1, \ldots, \boldsymbol{\Sigma}_R$ stacked on top of each other and $\boldsymbol{\xi} = (\boldsymbol{\psi}', \boldsymbol{\pi}')'$, the vector of all parameters in the model. The following loglikelihood has to be maximized:

$$l(\boldsymbol{\xi}|\boldsymbol{y}) = \sum_{p=1}^{P} \log \left\{ \sum_{r=1}^{R} \pi_r f_{pr}(\boldsymbol{y}_p|\boldsymbol{\psi}) \right\}. \tag{11.3}$$

Owing to the analytical complexity, numerical maximization of this loglikelihood is not straightforward. Therefore, this loglikelihood will be maximized using the Expectation-Maximization algorithm (EM), introduced by Dempster, Laird and Rubin (1977), which is typically used for mixture problems. A description of the EM algorithm – with references to the SAS macro we will use – is given in Section 11.6. How to obtain standard errors and empirical Bayes (EB) estimates is discussed in the Sections 11.7.2 and 11.7.3.

11.2.2 Typology of mixture models

Application of a mixture model is based on an assumption of R classes, but different values of R may be used. For each given number of classes one can then 'detect' what kind these classes are. The classes can be defined on one or more weights of the item predictors (depending on the dimension of the vector $\boldsymbol{\theta}_p$ in Equation 11.1). A simple typology of mixture models will be obtained by considering the number of weights that are used for the definition of the classes and by considering different possibilities for the covariance matrix $\boldsymbol{\Sigma}_r$. This yields simple latent class models, as well as models with different class-specific weights and class-specific covariance matrices. Also, oversimplistic situations will be covered, since they enlighten the formal framework.

The typology will be illustrated using a hypothetical analysis of the verbal aggression data set which is described in Chapter 1. Suppose a very simplistic LLTM for this data set, where besides the constant predictor, the only other predictor is Situation Type. The design matrix $\boldsymbol{X}$ then contains only two columns, one column containing the constant predictor and the other column containing a dummy variable having value 1 for the other-to-blame items and value 0 for the self-to-blame items.

No variability within classes

The (over)simplistic situation of no variability within classes arises when there is only one weight θ_p, following a mixture distribution with the vari-

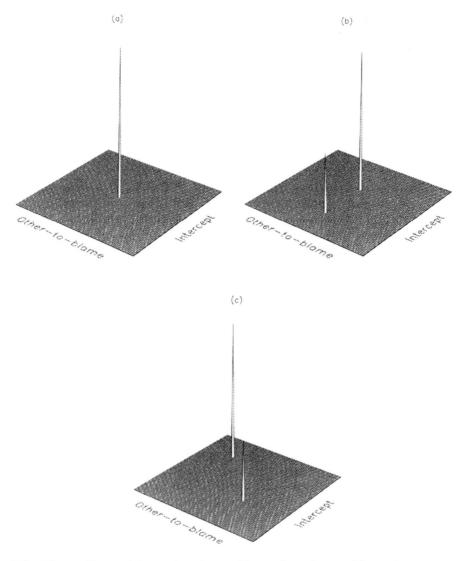

FIGURE 11.1. No variability within classes: (a) one-class solution, (b) two classes defined on one weight, (c) two classes defined on two weights.

ance in each class equal to zero:

$$\theta_p \sim \sum_{r=1}^{R} \pi_r N\left(\mu_r, 0\right). \tag{11.4}$$

This situation corresponds to a simple latent class analysis with R latent classes of persons and no variability between the persons within each latent class. Strictly speaking, since the class-specific normal distributions have no variance, the weight θ_p follows a mixture of R degenerate distributions or has a discrete distribution with R support points. Alternatively, one can say that the weight θ_p is class specific.

A first situation is when θ_p refers to an intercept, such that the distinct classes only differ in a general level of ability or propensity. Of course, items can differ in probability as a function of chosen predictors (item indicators or item properties), but the weights for these predictors are the same in the R classes. For example, the mixture distribution in Equation 11.4 can be used for R classes in the data, each class with its own verbal aggression level, where all persons within a class have the same level. Of course, θ_p can also refer to the weight of a predictor with values varying between items (e.g., Situation Type).

Using two weights to define the classes, instead of one weight, yields the following extension of the mixture in Equation 11.4:

$$ \begin{bmatrix} \theta_{p0} \\ \theta_{p1} \end{bmatrix} \sim \sum_{r=1}^{R} \pi_r N \left(\begin{bmatrix} \mu_{0r} \\ \mu_{1r} \end{bmatrix}, \begin{bmatrix} 0 & 0 \\ 0 & 0 \end{bmatrix} \right). \tag{11.5} $$

μ_{0r} is the class-specific deviation from the intercept and μ_{1r} is the class-specific deviation from the mean slope of the first item property. The class-specific intercept β_{0r} and the class-specific slope β_{1r} are then given by $\beta_{0r} = \beta_0 + \mu_{0r}$ and $\beta_{1r} = \beta_1 + \mu_{1r}$. The covariance matrix Σ is restricted to contain only zeros.

Figure 11.1 represents model types without variability within the classes, where the two weights are an intercept and the slope of an item property. Model type (a) represents a one-class starting point, where all persons have the same verbal aggression level and the same weight for the item property Other-to-blame. As a consequence, two probabilities will occur within the class: one for items relating to a self-to-blame situation and another relating to an other-to-blame situation. This is also true for the model types (b) and (c). Model type (a) implies that neither the propensity nor the sensitivity to the Other-to-blame property is used to distinguish between persons. Model type (b) corresponds to the mixture in Equation 11.4 with the two classes only distinguished by the verbal aggression level, whereas in model type (c) classes are also different with respect to the weight of Other-to-blame, in line with Equation 11.5. Panels (b) and (c) correspond to latent class models discussed in the Introduction.

In these three model types, persons within a class are homogeneous. These models would be oversimplistic in many domains, where differences between persons cannot be captured by such a limited set of fixed values.

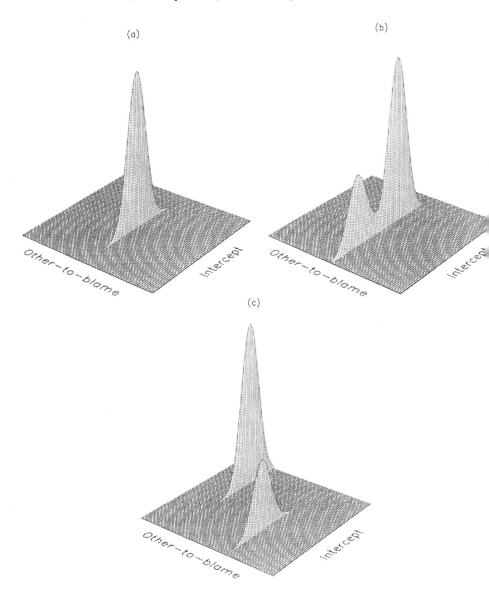

FIGURE 11.2. Variability in one weight within classes: (a) one-class solution, (b) two classes defined on one weight, (c) two classes defined on two weights.

Variability within classes (variability in one weight)

Considering one weight θ_p, and allowing variability between persons within a class results in

$$\theta_p \sim \sum_{r=1}^{R} \pi_r N\left(\mu_r, \sigma_r^2\right). \tag{11.6}$$

A subscript r is added to the variance, indicating that the variability of the random effect can differ between the classes. A simplified model is obtained when this variance is restricted to be equal in all R classes. Applied to the verbal aggression data set, this model type is displayed in panel (b) of Figure 11.2, where the two classes differ in mean verbal aggression level, and persons within a class can also have different levels of verbal aggression. This was the situation explored by Mislevy (1984). As a comparison, panel (a) of the same figure represents the standard LLTM, which is a one-class model with persons having different levels of verbal aggression.

When two weights are considered for the definition of the classes, a common class of models is defined by

$$
\begin{bmatrix} \theta_{p0} \\ \theta_{p1} \end{bmatrix} \sim \sum_{r=1}^{R} \pi_r N \left(\begin{bmatrix} \mu_{0r} \\ \mu_{1r} \end{bmatrix}, \begin{bmatrix} \sigma_{0r}^2 & 0 \\ 0 & 0 \end{bmatrix} \right). \tag{11.7}
$$

The mixture in Equation 11.7 implies that classes differ in mean level of two weights and that there is variability in one weight (the intercept) among persons within a class. As an example, classes not only differ in mean level of verbal aggression but also in mean weight of Other-to-blame. In other words, the effect of Situation Type is class specific. Moreover, within a class there is variability in verbal aggression level, but the weight of Situation Type is the same for all persons within a class. This situation is displayed in panel (c) of Figure 11.2. Both the saltus model (Wilson, 1984, 1989; Mislevy & Wilson, 1996; Draney, 1996) and the LLTM-based mixture models described by Mislevy and Verhelst (1990) correspond to this panel. When replacing the item property Other-to-blame with item indicators, the panel also illustrates the general mixture model described by Rost (1988, 1990). Of course, in the latter case, it will be a high-dimensional figure, one dimension for each item.

Variability within classes (variability in two weights)

A further extension is the most general case where there are no zero variances in Σ, such that there is variability in both weights:

$$
\begin{bmatrix} \theta_{p0} \\ \theta_{p1} \end{bmatrix} \sim \sum_{r=1}^{R} \pi_r N \left(\begin{bmatrix} \mu_{0r} \\ \mu_{1r} \end{bmatrix}, \begin{bmatrix} \sigma_{0r}^2 & \sigma_{01r} \\ \sigma_{01r} & \sigma_{1r}^2 \end{bmatrix} \right). \tag{11.8}
$$

These model types are described in Figure 11.3. Panel (a) illustrates the one-class solution. Panels (b) and (c) describe the mixture model extensions where the classes differ in mean level of one and two weights, respectively. The models illustrated by the latter panels are more complex than most mixture models currently used in the educational and psychological literature.

All discussed model types are summarized in Table 11.1 with a reference to the Figures. The slope in the examples concerns Other-to-blame.

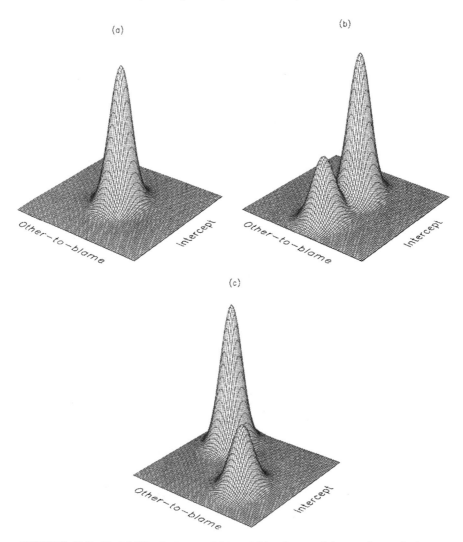

FIGURE 11.3. Variability in two weights within classes: (a) one-class solution, (b) two classes defined on one weight, (c) two classes defined on two weights.

TABLE 11.1. Overview of model types presented in Figures 11.1, 11.2, and 11.3.

Number of classes	Figure	Weight(s) used to define classes	Variability within classes
1	Fig. 11.1 (a)	-	no
2	Fig. 11.1 (b)	intercept	no
2	Fig. 11.1 (c)	intercept and one slope	no
1	Fig. 11.2 (a)	-	in intercept
2	Fig. 11.2 (b)	intercept	in intercept
2	Fig. 11.2 (c)	intercept and one slope	in intercept
1	Fig. 11.3 (a)	-	in intercept and one slope
2	Fig. 11.3 (b)	intercept	in intercept and one slope
2	Fig. 11.3 (c)	intercept and one slope	in intercept and one slope

11.3   Applications of mixture modeling

In this section some specific examples will be given of the discussed typology of mixtures. The results presented are obtained with a SAS macro for mixture modeling. A previously discussed LLTM analysis (see Chapter 2) of the verbal aggression data will serve as a starting point. Briefly, in this LLTM, three item properties (Situation Type, Behavior Type and Behavior Mode) were used, which were coded into four X-variables, complemented with the constant predictor (X_0). Situation Type has been defined using a dummy variable (X_1), with Other-to-Blame coded as 1, and Self-to-Blame as 0. Behavior Type has been coded with two contrasts, one (X_2) comparing Curse and Scold with Shout and another (X_3) contrasting Curse and Shout with Scold. Behavior Mode has been coded as a dummy (X_4), with Do coded as 1, and Want as 0. Note that the order of the predictors is different in the other chapters. The results of this analysis will be referred to as the *one-class model* (see Figure 11.2a). Results are obtained using nonadaptive Gaussian quadrature with 20 quadrature points in the NLMIXED procedure of SAS. As one can see in Table 11.2, the results are the same as reported in Chapter 2. Note that we do not follow the common practice of expressing the effects from the item side in a negative way (see

Chapter 2), but instead these effects will be expressed in a positive way using a plus sign for the effects of the item properties.

TABLE 11.2. Estimates for the one-class LLTM model, and for three two-class LLTM models (verbal aggression data).

	One-class model	Two-class model A	Two-class model B	Two-class model C
Deviance	8232	8231	8158	8160
AIC	8244	8247	8176	8176
BIC	8266	8277	8210	8206
β_0	-.31(.09)			-.32(.06)
β_{01}		.20(.10)	-.17(.12)	
β_{02}		-.83(.11)	-.41(.08)	
β_1	1.03(.06)	1.03(.05)		
β_{11}			2.47(.15)	2.64(.16)
β_{12}			.50(.10)	.50(.09)
β_2	1.36(.05)	1.36(.03)	1.40(.03)	1.41(.03)
β_3	.70(.05)	.70(.04)	.72(.04)	.72(.04)
β_4	-.67(.06)	-.67(.04)	-.69(.04)	-.69(.04)
σ_0^2	1.86(.20)	1.53(.16)	1.30(.10)	1.35(.10)
π_1		.52(.07)	.30(.05)	.27(.04)
π_2		.48(.01)	.70(.05)	.73(.04)

Note: β_0 to β_4 are the overall fixed effects of the item predictors; β_{01} and β_{02}, and β_{11} and β_{12}, are the class-specific weights; σ_0^2 is the variance of the intercept; π_1 and π_2 are the two class probabilities.

An extension of this LLTM model would be to allow different classes of individuals based on their verbal aggression propensity. As a starting example, we will investigate the hypothesis that there are two classes with different levels of propensity and with an equal variance within each class (i.e., σ_0^2). In the remainder, this model will be referred to as *two-class model A* (see Figure 11.2b). The syntax of a SAS macro to fit the two-class model A is presented in Section 11.5.

The deviance of the two-class model A was equal to 8231 and the maximum likelihood estimates can be found in Table 11.2. Note that likelihood-ratio tests may not be used to compare the one-class with the two-class model, because of boundary problems (Böhning, 1999). Model comparison

can be based on other criteria such as the AIC and BIC. Using these criteria, there is no need to reject the one-class model and accept this two-class
model. In other words, a normal distribution as a model for the variability
in propensity should not be replaced by a mixture of two normals.

Note that a special case arises when an analysis with homogeneous classes
is used to capture the variability in propensity (Haertel, 1990). Thus, instead of using one normal distribution for propensity, two or more homogeneous classes are assumed, each with a specific level of propensity, but
without within-class variability. To fit such a latent class model with the
SAS macro, a class-specific weight must be specified, without using the
RANDOMSTAT statement. The latent classes can be defined on the intercept
and/or on other weights. Fitting such a latent class model on the example
data set yields less parsimonious results compared to the one-class model.
Indeed, we found that a (too) high number of classes are needed to mimic
the variability in propensity. Results of these analyses are not reported.

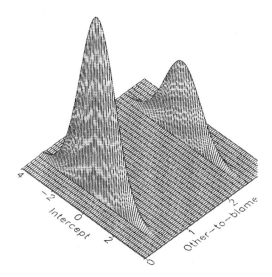

FIGURE 11.4. Distribution of weights used to define classes in the two-class
model B (verbal aggression data).

In the *two-class model B*, the classes are not only defined on the intercept
(as in the A variant), but also on the weight of Situation Type (see Figure
11.2c). Clearly, this model yields an improved fit. The deviance decreases
to 8158 and also the information criteria yield lower values compared to the
one-class model and the two-class model A. The estimates can be found in
Table 11.2. The distinction between the two obtained classes can be seen in
Figure 11.4. The small class represents approximately 30%, the larger class
70%. Figure 11.4 clearly shows that a major distinction between the two
classes is given by the effect of Situation Type. Previous analyses showed

that verbal aggressiveness is higher when others are to blame, compared with situations in which one should blame oneself. In the smaller class this difference is much larger than in the bigger class (2.47 vs .50). This means that there are two types of people: those who do not differentiate very much between other-to-blame situations and self-to-blame situations and those who are clearly more verbally aggressive when others are to blame. Gender is a candidate covariate to explain this distinction for example because one might expect men to be more aggressive than women when others can be blamed. In other words, the heterogeneity detected by the mixture model could reflect the 'forgotten' covariate Gender. However, the distribution of Gender is similar in both classes (26% of the males and 25% of the females are classified in the small class), indicating that the class distinction in the effect of Other-to-blame cannot be captured by Gender.

With respect to propensity, the classes in the two-class model B do not seem to differ much (-.17 vs -.41). Therefore, a two-class model with a common level of propensity, the *two-class model C* has also been fit, yielding a deviance of 8160. Since the deviance increased only a little, and the AIC and BIC values are equal or better, respectively, one may conclude that different intercepts are not needed for the two classes.

The resulting model is in fact equivalent with the saltus model (Mislevy & Wilson, 1996; Wilson, 1989), apart from the fact that in the saltus model each item has its own effect. Let us assume that a subset of items increases or decreases in difficulty from one latent class to the other. This is equivalent to including an item property for the subset, with a weight of zero in one class and a nonzero weight in the other, while the distribution of the random intercept (the propensity) is the same. In the example, the other-to-blame items 'make a leap' from the second and larger class to the first and smaller class (from .50 to 2.64, the values of β_{11} and β_{12} for the two-class model C in Table 11.2).

It is clear that the discussed analysis serves only an illustrative purpose. Many further extensions are possible. The number of classes could be increased, class-specific variances could be assumed whenever variability is allowed and other weights could be included in the definition of the classes.

11.4   Concluding remarks

There are many areas of education and psychology in which mixture models could conceivably be useful; certainly it is not difficult to imagine situations in which two or more populations might respond to an instrument in predictably different ways. Although such populations may often be differentiated based on observable characteristics (gender, socioeconomic status, school district), there are surely times when this is not the case. And yet, there are relatively few applications of the models discussed in the Introduction of this chapter, even in areas of education and psychology, in which they would be highly relevant.

One likely reason for this is the complexity of the models themselves. As mixture models are not members of the standard families of item response models (for example, they are not exponential-family models), their use is doubtless constrained by the lack of widespread existing estimation software. In this chapter we have presented a macro suitable to fit a variety of mixture models within the SAS framework. Of course, other software programs exist for specific models: for example, WINMIRA (von Davier, 2001) for Rost's mixed Rasch model, SALTUS for the saltus model (Draney & Wilson, 1997). There also exist software programs that fit a variety of models, such as ℓEM (Vermunt, 1997), and latent GOLD (Vermunt & Magidson, 2000).

As seen in the examples, mixture models can be tailored to reflect the complexities of a particular experimental design, psychological theory, or instrument structure. Explorations based on different parametrizations can lead us to interesting conclusions about subgroups in the dataset. In this example, although the two groups in the dataset had similar overall levels of aggression, the smaller group was much more likely to be aggressive when someone else was to blame than when they themselves were to blame, while the difference was not as extreme in the larger group. Further exploration of the characteristics of the persons classified into the two groups might lead to new understandings about verbal aggression and why people react as they do. If the classes can be linked to person properties this contributes to the explanatory purpose of modeling. As an example, the detected heterogeneity in effect of the Other-to-blame property could perhaps be linked to another property besides Gender.

Analyses that are more confirmatory than those reported here would also be possible if we had started with specific theories about the latent populations in question, and their relationships to the different item types or item characteristics. This is often the case in fields such as cognitive development.

The use of SAS, and the macro described in Section 11.7.1, open new avenues of exploration using mixture models. Complex models can be developed, such as those in which both overall proficiency, and the particular effect of various item characteristics, differ not only between populations, but within them as well (as displayed in the panels b and c of Figure 11.3).

11.5   Software

The macro we have used in the application is a *SAS macro* for nonlinear and generalized linear mixed models with finite normal mixtures as random-effects distribution. The macro can be downloaded from http://www.med.-

kuleuven.ac.be/biostat/research/software.htm. Details of this macro can be found in Spiessens, Verbeke, and Komárek (2004). The model that is estimated is a LLTM with a mixture of two normals for the intercept (the two-class model A of Table 11.2). The code used for the example is discussed in two steps.

LLTM with a mixture of two normals for the intercept (verbal aggression data)

Code first step

```
data startv;
input parameter$ estimate;
cards;
beta01 -1
beta02 -2
beta1 1.028
beta2 0.703
beta3 1.362
beta4 -0.672
s2 1.5
;
options nonotes;
run;
```

Comments first step

A data set containing starting values for the different parameters in the model has to be created. Starting values were taken from the one-class model (see Table 11.2), except for σ_0^2 which was started a bit smaller than 1.86 because it represents the variance within a class and not the total variance.

Code second step

```
%HetMlmixed(DATA=aggression_dich,OPTIONS=%str(qpoints=5 noad),
PARMS = startv,
SUBJECT = idnr,
RESPONSE = y,
COMPSPEC = x0 ,
PROGRAMSTAT =
%str(eta = theta*x0 + beta01*x01 + beta02*x02 +
beta1*x1 + beta2*x2 + beta3*x3 + beta4*x4;
ex = exp(eta);
p = ex/(1+ex);),
MODELSTAT = %str(y ~ binary(p)),
RANDOMSTAT = %str(theta ~ normal(0,s2)),
```

```
G=2, A=1e08, DECISION=2, STOPRULE=1e-08,
MAXITER=1000, ENDPOST=poster, EB=ebest,
EBmean=%str('beta01','beta02'));
```

Comments second step

1. In the **DATA** statement, the name of the dataset is specified.
2. The **OPTIONS** statement can be used to specify options for NLMIXED. Here, we have used nonadaptive Gaussian quadrature with 5 quadrature points to speed up the algorithm.
3. The data set containing the starting values is given in the **PARMS** statement.
4. The variable containing the identification numbers of the persons (**idnr**) is put in the **SUBJECT** statement.
5. The **RESPONSE** statement contains the name of the response variable (**y**).
6. The class-specific effects that are used in the model are specified in the **COMPSPEC** statement. In this case, **x0** is specified, since classes will be defined only on the intercept.
7. The **PROGRAMSTAT** and **MODELSTAT** statements contain similar programming and modeling statements as used in SAS NLMIXED to fit the one-class model, except now that we specify two different means **beta01** and **beta02**, for **x0** corresponding to the two latent classes. The **RANDOMSTAT** statement is also similar to the **RANDOM** statement of SAS NLMIXED. Here we only have one random weight, **theta** (θ_{p0}), which corresponds to the intercept. Note that in the code for the macro, the model has been parametrized in terms of the class-specific means **beta01** and **beta02** and not in terms of the class-specific deviations **mu01** and **mu02**.
8. The number of classes is specified in the **G** statement.
9. The **DECISION** and **STOPRULE** statements allow one to change the convergence criterion. The default (**DECISION = 2**) is that the algorithm will stop as soon as two successive loglikelihood evaluations are smaller than **STOPRULE**. One can change the stopping criterion to the maximum absolute difference between two successive parameter estimates (**DECISION = 1**) or to the derivative of the loglikelihood in Equation 11.3 (**DECISION = 3**). By default, **STOPRULE = 1e-08**.
10. The multiplication factor C used in Equation 11.13 is specified in the **A** statement.
11. The posterior probabilities and empirical Bayes estimates are written to the SAS datasets **poster** and **ebest**. This is specified in the **ENDPOST** and **EB** statements. The **EBmean** statement is necessary to calculate the EB-estimates.
12. The value of **x0** is one for all observations and **x01** and **x02** are dummy variables indicating class membership. These variables are created by the SAS macro. The weights **beta01** and **beta02** are the class-specific means of the intercept.

13. Note that in the two-class model A the variance of the random weight is assumed to be equal in both classes. To fit a model with different variances, the RANDOMSTAT statement can be adapted as follows: theta $\sim$ normal(0,s21*x01+s22*x02) with s21 and s22 referring to the variance in the first and second class respectively.

11.6   Exercises

1. Do you think it is possible to combine the mixture models of Figure 11.2c and 11.3c, so that the two classes differ as to their structure? Can you describe each class?

2. The symbol α_{pr} is used to indicate class membership, but it functions also like a slope, since it is a multiplicative factor for $(\theta_{pr} - \beta_{ir})$. Explain how the αs can play these two roles and how they can be interpreted.

3. Is the two-class model C represented in one of the figures of the chapter?

4. Estimate the two-class model B with the SAS macro.

5. Adapt the software code in Section 11.5, so that for the two-class model A the difference between the two class means is estimated and can be tested.

11.7   Appendix: Estimation of parameters, standard errors, and random effects

11.7.1   Estimation of parameters

Define the indicator variables $\alpha_{pr}, p = 1, \ldots, P; r = 1, \ldots, R$ as follows:

$$\alpha_{pr} = \begin{cases} 1 & \text{if the } p\text{th person belongs to the } r\text{th class,} \\ 0 & \text{otherwise.} \end{cases}$$

It follows from this definition that $\Pr(\alpha_{pr} = 1) = \pi_r$. The joint loglikelihood function for the observed measurements y and for the vector α of all unobserved α_{pr} equals

$$\begin{aligned} l(\xi|y, \alpha) &= \sum_{p=1}^{P} l_p(\xi|y_p, \alpha_p) \\ &= \sum_{p=1}^{P} \sum_{r=1}^{R} \alpha_{pr} (\log(\pi_r) + \log(f_{pr}(y_p|\psi))). \end{aligned} \tag{11.9}$$

Maximization of $l(\xi|y, \alpha)$ thus not only depends on the observed data y but also on the class variables α_{pr}, which are unknown. Intuitively, a solution is to replace the 'missing' α_{pr} by their expected value, following the EM algorithm. Therefore, the expected value of the log-likelihood $l(\xi|y, \alpha)$, given the observed data y will be maximized. The maximization procedure keeps iterating between two steps, an Expectation step (E-step) and a Maximization step (M-step), until convergence is attained.

In the first step, the E-step, the conditional expected value of the loglikelihood, referred to as the objective function Q, will be calculated. Suppose that $\xi^{(t)}$ is the current estimate of ξ. Then,

$$
\begin{aligned}
Q(\xi|\xi^{(t)}) &= E(l(\xi|y, \alpha)|y, \xi^{(t)}) \\
&= \sum_{p=1}^{P} \sum_{r=1}^{R} E(\alpha_{pr}|y_p, \xi^{(t)})(\log(\pi_r) \\
&\quad + \log(f_{pr}(y_p|\psi))),
\end{aligned} \tag{11.10}
$$

where

$$
E(\alpha_{pr}|y_p, \theta^{(t)}) = \left. \frac{\pi_r^{(t)} f_{pr}(y_p|\xi^{(t)})}{\sum_{r=1}^{R} \pi_r^{(t)} f_{pr}(y_p|\psi^{(t)})} \right|_{\xi^{(t)}} \equiv \pi_{pr}(\xi^{(t)}).
$$

Here, $\pi_{pr}(\xi)$ is the posterior probability of the pth person belonging to the rth class. It can be seen that the E-step actually reduces to calculating the posterior probabilities. Note that compared to Equation 11.9 the unknown variables α_{pr} are replaced in Equation 11.10 by their expected value.

In the second step of the algorithm, the M-step, the objective function $Q(\xi|\xi^{(t)})$ has to be maximized with respect to ξ in order to get the updated parameter vector $\xi^{(t)}$. It can be seen from Equation 11.10 that the objective function can be written as a sum of two parts:

$$
\begin{aligned}
Q(\xi|\xi^{(t)}) &= Q_1(\pi|\xi^{(t)}) + Q_2(\psi|\xi^{(t)}) \\
&= \sum_{p=1}^{P} \sum_{r=1}^{R} \pi_{pr}(\xi^{(t)}) \log(\pi_r) \tag{11.11} \\
&\quad + \sum_{p=1}^{P} \sum_{r=1}^{R} \pi_{pr}(\xi^{(t)}) \log\{f_{pr}(y_p|\psi)\}.
\end{aligned}
$$

Maximizing the first part of Equation 11.11 results in updating the class probabilities in the following way:

$$
\pi_r^{(t+1)} = \frac{1}{P} \sum_{p=1}^{P} \pi_{pr}(\xi^{(t)}).
$$

The updated estimate of the rth class probability is the average of the posterior probabilities in this class.

The second part of Equation 11.11 is more difficult to maximize, since it requires numerical procedures such as Newton-Raphson. We will now explain how standard software, such as the NLMIXED procedure of SAS, can be used to maximize this part of the objective function. We want to maximize

$$Q_2(\psi|\xi^{(t)}) = \sum_{p=1}^{P}\sum_{r=1}^{R} \pi_{pr}(\xi^{(t)}) \log\{f_{pr}(y_p|\psi)\}, \qquad (11.12)$$

with respect to ψ. A first key idea is that if the posterior probabilities $\pi_{pr}(\xi^{(t)})$ were integers, this would be the loglikelihood for the homogeneous model based on observations from $\sum_{p=1}^{P}\sum_{r=1}^{R}\pi_{pr}(\xi^{(t)})$ individuals. A second key idea is that maximization of an objective function is equivalent to maximizing this objective function multiplied by a constant. Thus maximization of Equation 11.12 is equivalent to maximizing

$$C.Q_2(\psi|\xi^{(t)}) = \sum_{p=1}^{P}\sum_{r=1}^{R} C.\pi_{pr}(\xi^{(t)}) \log\{f_{pr}(y_p|\psi)\}$$

$$= \sum_{p=1}^{P}\sum_{r=1}^{R} c_{pr}(\xi^{(t)}) \log\{f_{pr}(y_p|\psi)\}, \qquad (11.13)$$

where C is an arbitrary constant and $c_{pr}(\xi^{(t)}) = C.\pi_{pr}(\xi^{(t)})$. By taking C sufficiently large, and by rounding off the numbers c_{pr} to integers, Equation 11.13 can be maximized as if it were a loglikelihood coming from an homogeneous model with $\sum_{p=1}^{P}\sum_{r=1}^{R} c_{pr}$ persons. This will be an approximation to maximizing the loglikelihood in Equation 11.12. The larger C, the better this approximation will be. However, in practice, we would have to multiply our dataset C times, which would increase the computation time substantially. Fortunately, the SAS procedure NLMIXED provides a REPLICATE statement which can be used when modeling data sets where different persons have identical data. The use of this REPLICATE statement allows us to increase C without affecting the computation time, such that the loglikelihood in Equation 11.12 can be approximated with an arbitrarily close degree of accuracy.

The algorithm will iterate between the E-step and M-step until the difference between two successive loglikelihood evaluations in Equation 11.3 is smaller than some small value ϵ, that is until

$$|l(\xi^{(t)}|y) - l(\xi^{(t+1)}|y)| < \epsilon.$$

In practice one often uses $\epsilon = 1e - 08$ as stopping criterion. The maximum likelihood estimate of ξ is denoted by $\hat{\xi}$.

11.7.2   Standard errors

One of the drawbacks of the EM algorithm is that it does not provide standard errors automatically. For this, one would have to calculate the observed information matrix: the inverse of the second derivative of the loglikelihood in Equation 11.3. One of the reasons for using the EM algorithm was to avoid this calculation.

Louis (1982) provides a procedure to approximate this observed information matrix $\mathcal{I}(\boldsymbol{\xi}, \boldsymbol{y})$. For finite mixture models, it can be shown (McLachlan & Krishnan, 1997) that $\mathcal{I}(\boldsymbol{\xi}, \boldsymbol{y})$ can be approximated by the empirical observed information matrix

$$\mathcal{I}_e = \sum_{p=1}^{P} s(\boldsymbol{y}_p, \widehat{\boldsymbol{\xi}}) s'(\boldsymbol{y}_p, \widehat{\boldsymbol{\xi}}),$$

where

$$s(\boldsymbol{y}_p, \widehat{\boldsymbol{\xi}}) = E\left\{ \frac{\partial l_p(\boldsymbol{\xi} | \boldsymbol{y}_p, \boldsymbol{\alpha}_p)}{\partial \boldsymbol{\xi}} | \boldsymbol{y}_p \right\}.$$

It can be seen that this approximation can be expressed in terms of the conditional expectation of the gradient of the loglikelihood in Equation 11.13, evaluated at $\widehat{\boldsymbol{\xi}}$. The computation of the second order derivative of this loglikelihood is not needed.

11.7.3 Empirical Bayes estimation

The EB estimates in the SAS procedure NLMIXED are defined as the mode of $f_p(\boldsymbol{\theta}_p | \boldsymbol{y}_p, \boldsymbol{\xi}) \propto f_p(\boldsymbol{y}_p | \boldsymbol{\theta}_p, \boldsymbol{\xi}) \phi(\boldsymbol{\theta}_p)$, the posterior distribution of the random effects, conditional on $\boldsymbol{y}_p$. However, because of the possible multimodality of the random-effects distribution under the heterogeneous model, this definition is no longer suitable. The posterior distribution of $\boldsymbol{\theta}_p$ can also be written as

$$f_p(\boldsymbol{\theta}_p | \boldsymbol{y}_p, \boldsymbol{\xi}) = \sum_{r=1}^{R} \pi_{pr}(\boldsymbol{\xi}) f_{pr}(\boldsymbol{\theta}_p | \boldsymbol{y}_p, \boldsymbol{\psi}),$$

where $f_{pr}(\boldsymbol{\theta}_p | \boldsymbol{y}_p, \boldsymbol{\psi})$ is the posterior density function of $\boldsymbol{\theta}_p$, conditional on the fact that $\boldsymbol{\theta}_p$ was sampled from class r in the mixture.

Therefore, it is natural to calculate the EB estimates under the heterogeneous model as

$$\widehat{\boldsymbol{\theta}}_p = \sum_{r=1}^{R} \pi_{pr}(\boldsymbol{\xi}) \widehat{\boldsymbol{\theta}}_{pr},$$

where $\widehat{\boldsymbol{\theta}}_{pr}$ are the EB estimates of the random effects for the pth person in the rth class.

11.8 References

Böhning, D. (1999). *Computer-Assisted Analysis of Mixtures and Applications : Meta-analysis, Disease Mapping and Others*. London: Chapman & Hall.

Bolt, D.M., Cohen, A.S., & Wollack, J.A. (2002). Item parameter estimation under conditions of test speediness: Application of a mixture Rasch model with ordinal constraints. *Journal of Educational Measurement, 39*, 331–348.

Croon, M. (1990). Latent class analysis with ordered latent classes. *British Journal of Mathematical and Statistical Psychology, 43*, 171–192.

Dayton, C.M. & Macready, G.B. (1976). A probabilistic model for validation of behavioral hierarchies. *Psychometrika, 41*, 189–204.

Dempster, A.P., Laird, N.M., & Rubin, D.B. (1977). Maximum likelihood from incomplete data via the EM algorithm, *Journal of the Royal Statistical Society, Series B, 39*, 1–38.

Draney, K. (1996). The polytomous saltus model: A mixture model approach to the diagnosis of developmental differences. Unpublished Ph.D. thesis, UC, Berkeley.

Draney, K., & Wilson, M. (1997). PC-Saltus [Computer program]. Berkeley Evaluation and Assessment Center Research Report, UC Berkeley.

Fischer, G.H. (1983). Logistic latent trait models with linear constraints. *Psychometrika, 48*, 3–26.

Formann, A.K. (1992). Linear logistic latent class analysis for polytomous data. *Journal of the American Statistical Association, 87*, 476–486.

Gitomer, D.H. & Yamamoto, K. (1991). Performance modeling that integrates latent trait and class theory. *Journal of Educational Measurement, 28*, 173–189.

Goodman, L.A. (1974). The analysis of systems of qualitative variables when some of variables are unobservable; Part I- A modified latent structure approach. *American Journal of Sociology, 79*, 1179–1259.

Haberman, S.J. (1979). *Analysis of Qualitative Data. Vol.2: New Developments*. New York: Academic Press.

Haertel, E. (1990). Continuous and discrete latent structure models for item response data. *Psychometrika, 55*, 477–494.

Heinen, A.G.J. (1993). *Discrete Latent Variable Models*. Tilburg: Tilburg University Press.

Langeheine, R. (1988). New developments in latent class theory. In R. Langeheine & J. Rost (Eds), *Latent Trait and Latent Class Models* (pp. 77–108). New York: Plenum Press.

Lazarsfeld, P.F. & Henry, N.W. (1968). *Latent Structure Analysis*, Boston: Houghton-Mifflin.

Louis, T.A. (1982). Finding the observed information matrix when using the EM algorithm. *Journal of the Royal Statistical Society, Series B, 44,* 226–233.

McLachlan, G.J. & Krishnan, T. (1997). *The EM Algorithm and Extensions.* New York: Wiley.

Meulders, M., De Boeck, P., Kuppens, P., & Van Mechelen, I. (2002). Constrained latent class analysis of three-way three-mode data. *Journal of Classification, 19,* 277–302.

Mislevy, R.J. (1984). Estimating latent distributions. *Psychometrika, 49,* 359–382.

Mislevy, R.J. & Verhelst, N. (1990). Modeling item responses when different persons employ different solution strategies. *Psychometrika, 55,* 195–215.

Mislevy, R.J. & Wilson, M. (1996). Marginal maximum likelihood estimation for a psychometric model of discontinuous development. *Psychometrika, 61,* 41–71.

Reise, S.P., & Gomel, J.N. (1995). Modeling qualitative variation within latent trait dimensions: Application of mixed measurement of personality assessment. *Multivariate Behavioral Research, 30,* 341–358.

Rijmen, F. & De Boeck, P. (2003). A latent class model for individual differences in the interpretation of conditonals. *Psychological Research, 67,* 219–231.

Rost, J. (1988). Test theory with qualitative and quantitative latent variables. In R. Langeheine & J. Rost (Eds), *Latent Trait and Latent Class Models* (pp. 147–171). New York: Plenum Press.

Rost, J. (1990). Rasch models in latent class analysis: An integration of two approaches to item analysis. *Applied Psychological Measurement, 14,* 271–282.

Spiessens, B., Verbeke, G., & Komárek, A. (2004). A SAS macro for the classification of longitudinal profiles using mixtures of normal distributions in nonlinear and generalised linear mixed models. Manuscript submitted for publication.

Vermunt, J.K. (1997). lEM. A general program for the analysis of categorical data. Tilburg University, The Netherlands.

Vermunt, J.K. (1997). *Loglinear Models of Event Histories.* Thousand Oaks, CA: Sage.

Vermunt, J.K., & Magdison, J. (2000). *Latent-GOLD.* Belmont, MS: Statistical Innovations.

von Davier, M. (2001). WINMIRA 2001. *Latent Class Analysis, Dichotomous and Polytomous Rasch Models.* St. Paul, MN: Assessment Systems.

Waller, N.G., & Meehl, P. (1998). *Multivariate Taxomatric Procedures.* Thousand Oaks, CA: Sage.

Wilson, M. (1984). A psychometric model of hierarchical development. Unpublished Ph.D. thesis, University of Chicago.

Wilson, M. (1989). Saltus: A psychometric model of discontinuity in cognitive development. *Psychological Bulletin, 105,* 276–289.

Yen, W. (1985). Increasing item complexity: A possible cause of scale shrinkage for unidimensional item response theory. *Psychometrika, 50,* 399–410.

Part IV: Estimation and software

Chapter 12

Estimation and software

Francis Tuerlinckx
Frank Rijmen
Geert Molenberghs
Geert Verbeke
Derek Briggs
Wim Van den Noortgate
Michel Meulders
Paul De Boeck

12.1   Introduction

The aim of this last chapter is threefold. First, we want to give the reader
further insights into the estimation methods for the models presented in this
volume. Second, we want to discuss the available software for the models
presented in this volume. We will not sketch all possibilities of the software,
but only those directly relevant to item response modeling as seen in this
volume. Third, we want to illustrate the use of various programs for the
estimation of a basic model, the Rasch model, for the verbal aggression
data.

12.2   General description of estimation algorithms

In this section we give a brief overview of the most common estimation
methods for the item response models discussed in this volume. It is not
our purpose to explain these methods in great detail but rather to lay out
the fundamental ideas and discuss some advantages and drawbacks. The
content of this section is closely related to theoretical material presented
in Chapter 4.

12.2.1   Introduction

The Rasch model will be the central example for which the various estimation methods will be explained. The generalization of the methods
presented to more dimensions and other models is straightforward. Our
discussion in this section is restricted to 2-level models (i.e., no level be-

yond the persons, see Chapter 5), but most of the methods presented can be generalized to models with more than just two levels.

The Rasch model has been introduced in Chapter 2:

$$\eta_{pi} = \theta_p - \beta_i, \tag{12.1}$$

where $\eta_{pi} = \text{logit}(\pi_{pi})$, and where $p = 1, \ldots, P$ indexes persons and $i = 1, \ldots, I$ indexes items.

The model from Equation 12.1 contains two different kinds of parameters: βs, which are fixed-effects parameters representing the item difficulties, and θs, which are person parameters. In Chapter 2 the person parameter was seen as a random effect, but there are in fact three possible ways to look at the person-specific parameters, each with consequences for the estimation methods and inferences one can make.

Joint maximum likelihood estimation

In a first approach, the person parameters can be viewed as *fixed effects*, having the same status as the item parameters β_i. To estimate the parameters of the model with fixed person and item parameters, one computes the following likelihood:

$$L_{\text{JML}}(\boldsymbol{\beta}, \boldsymbol{\theta}) = \prod_{p=1}^{P} \prod_{i=1}^{I} \Pr(Y_{pi} = y_{pi}),$$

which is then maximized jointly with respect to item and person parameters (all item and person parameters are collected in the vectors $\boldsymbol{\beta}$ and $\boldsymbol{\theta}$, respectively). This method is called joint maximum likelihood (JML) estimation.

A major disadvantage associated with JML is that the estimators of the item parameters are not consistent (Neyman & Scott, 1948). The reason is that the number of parameters increases at the same rate as the sample size increases because each new person implies a new parameter. The inconsistency of item parameter estimators is a problem from both descriptive and explanatory points of view. In a descriptive research context, one often wants to calibrate a measurement instrument and inconsistent estimators may jeopardize a valid calibration. From an explanatory point of view, inconsistent estimators may pose a threat to valid inferences about what determines the item difficulties.

Conditional maximum likelihood estimation

In a conditional inference approach, the conditional probabilities of the response pattern are derived using the sufficient statistics. For the Rasch model, the sufficient statistic for a person-specific effect θ_p is the sum score, $s_p = \sum_{i=1}^{I} y_{pi}$ (Andersen, 1980). From the definition of sufficient statistics it follows that, after conditioning, the probability of observing a response pattern does not depend on the person-specific effect, but only on the sufficient statistic. Consequently, the person-specific effects disappear from the so-called conditional likelihood:

$$L_{\mathrm{CML}}(\beta) = \prod_{p=1}^{P} \Pr(Y_{p1} = y_{p1}, \ldots, Y_{pI} = y_{pI} | s_p).$$

The conditional likelihood is maximized with respect to β. This method is known as the conditional maximum likelihood (CML) method.

Unlike JML, CML estimators are consistent and asymptotically normally distributed (Andersen, 1970). However, there are also a few disadvantages to the conditional framework. First, from a measurement perspective it is an undesirable situation that no inferences are possible on the persons. A possible solution is to consider the item parameters after estimation as known quantities, and to plug them into the joint likelihood and optimize the latter with respect to the person parameters. However, this method does not recognize the uncertainty in the item estimates. Second, CML may not be the most efficient method, because the conditional likelihood is maximized rather than the full likelihood. If the distribution of the sufficient statistics depends on the item parameters, then not all information regarding the latter is used, because this distribution is not part of the likelihood. However, asymptotically, the loss of information is negligible; see Molenaar (1995) for a discussion. Third, for models without sufficient statistics for the person parameters, the CML method cannot be applied. This is the case for models that are not GLMMs, such as the 2PL model, but an exception is the MIRID (Chapter 9).

Marginal maximum likelihood estimation

A third possibility is to consider the person-specific effects as independent random draws from a density defined over the population of persons, denoted by $g(\theta_p|\psi)$, which is characterized by a vector of unknown population parameters, ψ, that have to be estimated together with fixed-effects parameters β_i. This has been the perspective taken in this volume. The marginal likelihood is formed by integrating with respect to the random effects:

$$L_{\mathrm{MML}}(\beta, \psi) = \prod_{p=1}^{P} \int_{-\infty}^{+\infty} \prod_{i=1}^{I} \Pr(Y_{pi} = y_{pi}|\theta_p) g(\theta_p|\psi) d\theta_p \qquad (12.2)$$

and this likelihood is then maximized with respect to β and ψ. If the density g is discrete, the integral must be replaced with a sum. In the psychometric literature the method based on maximizing Equation 12.2 is known as the marginal maximum likelihood (MML) method. In the following, we will refer only to MML estimation, so we will drop the subscripts of the likelihood and use $L(\beta, \psi)$ to refer to the MML likelihood.

Three special cases of the MML approach can be distinguished: nonparametric, semiparametric and parametric, depending on the assumptions one makes about the unobserved population density of the random effects. (1) Under the most general approach, the *nonparametric maximum likelihood estimation* or *fully semi-parametric estimation method* (Heinen, 1996), no assumptions are made about $g(\theta_p|\psi)$ – it is left completely unspecified. Laird (1978) has shown that in this case the estimate of the cumulative distribution function $G(\theta_p|\psi)$ is a step function with a finite number of steps. (2) In the *semi-parametric estimation method* (Heinen, 1996), the location of the steps are assumed to be known but the probability masses at these fixed nodes have to be estimated. (3) In the *parametric estimation method*, the population density $g(\theta_p|\psi)$ is taken to be a parametric density for which the parameters have to be estimated. For most models presented in this book, the population density $g(\theta_p|\psi)$ is assumed to be normal with zero mean and unknown variance.

By assuming that the person-specific parameters are a random sample from a parametric population distribution, the original item response model (such as the one in Equation 12.1) is extended with an additional component. If the model fails to fit the data, this misfit can be the result of the fact that the assumed population distribution does not adequately describe the true distribution of random effects. In Chapter 11 an approach is described with a mixture of normals as a population distribution for the random effects which allows for more flexibility in fitting the distribution.

Note that for a model with crossed random effects (see Chapter 6), the dimension of integration is the sum of the number of persons and the number of items, whereas in Equation 12.2 the dimensionality is only one. As a consequence, some of the approximative methods discussed below (e.g., the Laplace approximation) may not be accurate (Shun & McCullagh, 1995), and (approximative) numerical integration may not be feasible. Bayesian methods may be used instead, as illustrated in Chapter 6.

12.2.2   *Optimizing the marginal likelihood with a normal random-effects distribution*

In this section we give an overview of the most common estimation methods that are used with a normal random-effects distribution. We start with some notation. The normal random-effects distribution is denoted by $\phi(\theta_p|\mu_\theta, \sigma_\theta^2)$, where μ_θ is the mean (by convention fixed to 0) and σ_θ^2 is the unknown variance. The probability of the response pattern y_p as generated by person p on the set of I items and conditional on θ_p, is denoted by $\Pr(y_p|\beta, \theta_p)$, where β is the vector of dimension I containing the fixed effects (one per item). For the Rasch model, $\Pr(y_p|\beta, \theta_p) = \prod_{i=1}^{I} \Pr(y_{pi}|\beta, \theta_p)$ (with $\Pr(y_{pi} \mid \beta, \theta_p) = \pi_{pi}$ if $y_{pi} = 1$), but this is not the case if the conditional independence assumption does not hold (as for some models described in Chapters 7 and 10).

The marginal likelihood that has to be optimized can now be written as follows:

$$L(\boldsymbol{\beta}, \sigma_\theta^2) = \prod_{p=1}^{P} L_p(\boldsymbol{\beta}, \sigma_\theta^2) = \prod_{p=1}^{P} \int \Pr(\boldsymbol{y}_p | \boldsymbol{\beta}, \theta_p) \phi(\theta_p | 0, \sigma_\theta^2) d\theta_p, \quad (12.3)$$

where $L_p(\boldsymbol{\beta}, \sigma_\theta^2)$ is the contribution of person p to the marginal likelihood. To facilitate the numerical maximization, it is common to take the logarithm of the marginal likelihood. For the sake of clarity, we have dropped the limits of integration in Equation 12.3 and in the remainder of the section.

For all the item response models considered in this volume (with the exception of some models mentioned in Chapter 4), the integral appearing in the marginal likelihood is intractable which means that it has no analytical or closed-form solution. This is unlike the integral from the linear mixed model.

There are two general types of solutions to the problem of the intractable integral. The first one is to approximate the integral with numerical integration techniques. The second solution is to approximate the integrand, so that the integral of the approximation does have a closed-form solution. Apart from the type of approximation, the problem is a standard optimization problem for which many good introductory texts are available (Bunday, 1984; Everitt, 1987; Gill, Murray, & Wright, 1981; Lange, 1999).

12.2.3   Approximation to the integral

A major advantage of the methods that rely on the approximation to the integral is that they can be applied to all models from this volume, with the exception of the models from Chapter 6 for which a Bayesian analysis is definitely better suited.

In this method, a numerical approximation to the likelihood in Equation 12.3 is maximized. Roughly speaking there are four different ways of approximating the integral, and they can be classified in a two-by-two table. The first dimension is direct versus indirect maximization. Indirect maximization means that the maximization problem is transferred to another function for which it can be shown that as a by-product of its maximization the marginal likelihood is also maximized. A prominent example is the EM algorithm. The second dimension is the deterministic versus stochastic nature of the numerical approximation to the intractable integral.

In what follows, direct and indirect maximization will be discussed in two separate sections and the deterministic and stochastic variants will be considered within each section.

Direct maximization

When applying direct maximization techniques, the intractable integral in Equation 12.3 is numerically approximated and then this numerical approximation is maximized. A first possibility is to approximate the integral by means of a numerical integration rule; this constitutes the deterministic approach. In the unidimensional case, the integral is then replaced by a single finite sum of rectangular areas that approximate the area under the integrand. Because the random effects are assumed to be normally distributed, the Gauss-Hermite (GH) quadrature (Abramowitz & Stegun, 1974) is most commonly chosen, called *Gaussian quadrature* in this volume. The Gaussian quadrature approximation is as follows (Naylor & Smith, 1982):

$$L_p(\boldsymbol{\beta}, \sigma_\theta^2) \quad = \quad \int \Pr(\boldsymbol{y}_p|\boldsymbol{\beta}, \theta_p)\phi(\theta_p|0, \sigma_\theta^2)d\theta_p \qquad (12.4)$$

$$\approx \quad \sum_{m=1}^{M} \Pr(\boldsymbol{y}_p|\boldsymbol{\beta}, \sqrt{2}\sigma_\theta q_m)\frac{w_m}{\sqrt{\pi}}, \qquad (12.5)$$

where q_m and w_m are the mth quadrature node and weight, respectively. The nodes of a Gaussian quadrature are optimally spaced and weighted so that with M nodes the approximation is exact if the function $\Pr(\boldsymbol{y}_p|\boldsymbol{\beta}, \theta_p)$ is polynomial of degree $2M - 1$ or less. Nodes and weights can be found in Abramowitz and Stegun (1974).

In a standard Gaussian quadrature approximation the nodes are rescaled (and recentered, but the latter does not have an effect because of the zero population mean) such that they cover the range of the normal population distribution. However, this rescaling is identical for every person p, which is not always the most accurate thing to do. To see this, we go back to the form of the integrand, $\Pr(\boldsymbol{y}_p|\boldsymbol{\beta}, \theta_p)\phi(\theta_p|0, \sigma_\theta^2)$. The integrand is actually the (unnormalized) posterior distribution of θ_p given the data and fixed-effects parameters. If the data for person p are extreme (e.g., almost all ones or zeros), then the posterior distribution of θ_p will also be extreme and may deviate strongly from the population distribution, which puts more mass in the region where the moderate θ_p values are located.

Consequently, it might be more appropriate to apply an individual rescaling and recentering. That is the basic idea behind adaptive Gaussian quadrature (Pinheiro & Bates, 1995). For each person, the empirical Bayes estimate of θ_p (i.e., $\hat{\theta}_p$) is computed together with the asymptotic variance of this estimate. Both quantities are computed given the current estimates of the fixed effects and given the data. Then the contribution of person p to the marginal likelihood is rewritten in the following form:

$$L_p(\boldsymbol{\beta}, \sigma_\theta^2) \quad = \quad \int \Pr(\boldsymbol{y}_p|\boldsymbol{\beta}, \theta_p)\phi(\theta_p|0, \sigma_\theta^2)d\theta_p$$

$$= \quad \int \frac{\Pr(\boldsymbol{y}_p|\boldsymbol{\beta}, \theta_p)\phi(\theta_p|0, \sigma_\theta^2)}{\phi(\theta_p|\hat{\theta}_p, \hat{\tau}_p^2)}\phi(\theta_p|\hat{\theta}_p, \hat{\tau}_p^2)d\theta_p,$$

where $\hat{\tau}_p^2$ is the asymptotic variance of the empirical Bayes estimate. In this case, $\phi(\theta_p|\hat{\theta}_p, \hat{\tau}_p^2)$ is the distribution that determines the position and the weights of the quadrature points instead of $\phi(\theta_p|0, \sigma_\theta^2)$. This means that the empirical Bayes estimate $\hat{\theta}_p$ needs to be added to the node q_m, and the node must be multiplied by $\sqrt{2}\hat{\tau}_p$.

Adaptive Gaussian quadrature needs fewer quadrature nodes, because, as explained in Chapter 4, it is better concentrated in the informative region of the continuum. The price to pay is that empirical Bayes estimates have to be computed at each step of the optimization algorithm, which may be very time-consuming. That is the main reason why in many chapters the nonadaptive or regular Gaussian quadrature rule was used. In defense of this, recall that, for the basic models in Chapter 2, and for several other models in the subsequent chapters, adaptive Gaussian quadrature was used, and gave similar results, with differences not larger than reported in Section 12.4.2. However, this may not be true in general. For an interesting study investigating the number of quadrature nodes for logistic random-effects models, see Lesaffre and Spiessens (2001).

Several algorithms are available for maximization of the approximated likelihood function obtained from adaptive or nonadaptive Gaussian quadrature. Some well-known methods to accomplish this are the Newton–Raphson technique and Fisher scoring.

The previous two methods made use of a fixed or deterministic set of nodes and weights. An alternative is to use Monte Carlo integration. The integral over the random-effects distribution can be viewed as an expectation of the function $\Pr(\boldsymbol{y}_p|\boldsymbol{\beta}, \theta_p)$ over the normally distributed random variable θ_p:

$$L_p(\boldsymbol{\beta}, \sigma_\theta^2) \;=\; \int \Pr(\boldsymbol{y}_p|\boldsymbol{\beta}, \theta_p)\phi(\theta_p|0, \sigma_\theta^2)d\theta_p = \mathrm{E}\left(\Pr(\boldsymbol{y}_p|\boldsymbol{\beta}, \theta_p)\right).$$

An expectation can be estimated by drawing a random sample and computing the sample average. This means that M values of θ_p are drawn from the population distribution and then the following quantity is calculated:

$$L_p(\boldsymbol{\beta}, \sigma_\theta^2) \approx \frac{1}{M} \sum_{m=1}^{M} \Pr(\boldsymbol{y}_p|\boldsymbol{\beta}, \theta_p^{(m)}). \tag{12.6}$$

with $\theta_p^{(m)}$ as the value of θ_p at node m. This simple Monte Carlo procedure is the stochastic equivalent of the Gaussian quadrature with common re-centering and rescaling (i.e., nonadaptive). Adaptive Gaussian quadrature has a stochastic counterpart as well (Pinheiro & Bates, 1995), but now the draws of θ_p come from the distribution $\phi(\theta_p|\hat{\theta}_p, \hat{\tau}_p^2)$.

Indirect maximization

In an indirect maximization method the optimization of the (log)likelihood is transferred to another function for which it can be shown that a maximization results in an increase in the original marginal likelihood. The most common indirect maximization algorithm that is applied in the context of random-effects models is the *Expectation-Maximization (EM) algorithm* (Dempster, Laird, & Rubin, 1977).

In the EM algorithm, the collection of random effects from all persons $\theta = (\theta_1, \ldots, \theta_P)$ are considered as missing data and, together with the observed data $y = (y'_1, \ldots, y'_P)'$, they form the complete data. The random effects are missing and thus not observed, so that in each cycle of the algorithm, one starts with computing the expected value of the complete data loglikelihood, given the observed data and given the estimates of the fixed effects β^{old} and $\sigma_\theta^2{}^{\text{old}}$ from the previous cycle, and the observed data. This is called the E-step. Then the expected loglikelihood is maximized, which is called the M-step. Each iteration of the EM algorithm consists of an E-step followed by an M-step, and that is continued until convergence.

The expectation of the complete data loglikelihood, $\ell_C(\beta, \sigma_\theta^2)$, is defined as follows:

$$
\begin{aligned}
&\mathrm{E}\left(\ell_C(\beta, \sigma_\theta^2)|y, \sigma_\theta^2{}^{\text{old}}, \beta^{\text{old}}\right) \\
&= \mathrm{E}\left(\log \prod_{p=1}^{P}\left(\Pr(y_p|\beta, \theta_p)\phi(\theta_p|0, \sigma_\theta^2)\right)|y, \sigma_\theta^2{}^{\text{old}}, \beta^{\text{old}}\right) \\
&= \sum_{p=1}^{P} \mathrm{E}\left(\log\left(\Pr(y_p|\beta, \theta_p)\phi(\theta_p|0, \sigma_\theta^2)\right)|y, \sigma_\theta^2{}^{\text{old}}, \beta^{\text{old}}\right) \qquad (12.7) \\
&= \sum_{p=1}^{P} \int\left(\log\left(\Pr(y_p|\beta, \theta_p)\right) + \log\left(\phi(\theta_p|0, \sigma_\theta^2)\right) h(\theta_p|y, \sigma_\theta^2{}^{\text{old}}, \beta^{\text{old}})\right) d\theta_p,
\end{aligned}
$$

where $h(\theta_p|y, \sigma_\theta^2{}^{\text{old}}, \beta^{\text{old}})$ is the conditional density of the random effects given the observed data, the current estimates of the fixed parameters, and the variance of the random-effects distribution. After computing the expected complete data loglikelihood (the E-step), it is maximized with respect to β and σ_θ^2 (the M-step).

It can be seen from Equation 12.7 that the intractable integral has not disappeared from the expected complete data loglikelihood. Thus, the integral still has to be approximated with a Gaussian quadrature or with Monte Carlo integration (the latter leading to a Monte Carlo EM algorithm; see Tanner, 1996, and McCulloch & Searle, 2001).

If we are left with the same problem that we have tried to avoid, why use the EM algorithm? The EM algorithm offers three advantages. First, the algorithm guarantees that in every iteration the marginal loglikelihood (the log of Equation 12.3) increases, although the algorithm does not directly maximize it (Lange, 1999; McLachlan & Krishnan, 1997). This makes the algorithm numerically very stable. This is not guaranteed, however, when the integral is only an approximation. Second, the expected complete data loglikelihood from Equation 12.7 is written as the sum of a part pertaining to the fixed-effect parameters and a part pertaining to the variance parameter. This means that the estimation of both sets of parameters can be done separately in the M-step which reduces the dimensionality of the optimization problem. Third, the M-step in the EM algorithm has closed-form solutions for some parameters. For the variance components under a normal distribution, such a closed-form solution is available. For parameters that do not have a closed-form solution, one has to rely in the M-step on an iterative optimization method, using for example the Newton-Raphson method.

A disadvantage of the EM algorithm is that the convergence to the maximum is usually not very fast, especially in the neighborhood of the maximum of the marginal likelihood. Modifications of the original EM algorithm have been presented to accelerate convergence or to facilitate the computation of the maximization step; see McLachlan and Krishnan (1997) and Tanner (1996) for an overview.

In the context of traditional item response modeling with only the item indicators as item predictors, the application of the EM algorithm has another major advantage as has been shown by Bock and Aitkin (1981). To illustrate this point, we consider the Rasch model; but the same is true for the 2PL model. The vector with item parameters β can be subdivided into I disjoint subsets of parameters (in this case individual parameters), $\beta_1, \ldots, \beta_I$, each pertaining to a single item. Given the random effect θ_p, there is conditional independence, and consequently, the expected loglikelihood can be written as a sum of independent terms, one for each item, and each can be maximized separately. This property allows one to analyze data sets with a large number of items (e.g., 50 or more) which would be otherwise impossible. The same property still holds with person predictors in the model. The person part of the regression model can be seen as the non-zero mean of the normal distribution and therefore the regression coefficients can be estimated again separately from the item difficulties (Adams, Wilson, & Wang, 1997; Wu, Adams, & Wilson, 1998). This advantage explains the popularity of MML estimation with EM in the field of psychometrics.

12.2.4 Approximation to the integrand

The goal of approximating the integrand is to obtain an expression so that the integral of the approximation has a closed-form solution. Two types of techniques will be discussed: Laplace's method and a class of methods called the quasi-likelihood methods.

Laplace's method

In Laplace's method (Tierny & Kadane, 1986), we take the integrand of the contribution of person p to the marginal likelihood, $\Pr(\boldsymbol{y}_p|\boldsymbol{\beta}, \theta_p)\phi(\theta_p|0, \sigma_\theta^2)$, and write it as $\exp(\log\left(\Pr(\boldsymbol{y}_p|\boldsymbol{\beta},\theta_p)\phi(\theta_p|0,\sigma_\theta^2)\right))$. Next, we approximate the exponent by a quadratic Taylor series expansion about its maximum $\hat{\theta}_p$ (which is again the empirical Bayes estimate for θ_p). Because the approximation to the exponent is quadratic in θ_p, the approximation to the integrand will be proportional to a normal distribution and the integral can be solved explicitly. The result is then:

$$L_p(\boldsymbol{\beta},\sigma_\theta^2) = \int \Pr(\boldsymbol{y}_p|\boldsymbol{\beta},\theta_p)\phi(\theta_p|0,\sigma_\theta^2)d\theta_p \approx \Pr(\boldsymbol{y}_p|\boldsymbol{\beta},\hat{\theta}_p)\phi(\hat{\theta}_p|0,\sigma_\theta^2)\sqrt{2\pi}\hat{\tau}_p,$$

where $\hat{\tau}_p$ is the square root of the asymptotic variance of the empirical Bayes estimate.

The empirical Bayes estimate $\hat{\theta}_p$ as well its variance $\hat{\tau}_p^2$ depend on the unknown parameters $\boldsymbol{\beta}$ and σ_θ^2, so that in order to obtain $\hat{\theta}_p$ and $\hat{\tau}_p^2$ one needs to know the value of $\boldsymbol{\beta}$ and σ_θ^2. There are two options to solve this problem. First, one can use the estimates for $\boldsymbol{\beta}$ and σ_θ^2 obtained from the previous iteration of the algorithm in order to obtain empirical Bayes estimates, as in adaptive Gaussian quadrature. Adaptive Gaussian quadrature with a single node is equivalent to this version of Laplace's method. Once the empirical Bayes estimates are available, the Laplace approximation can be maximized with respect to $\boldsymbol{\beta}$ and σ_θ^2. This method is not used except when one wants to apply Laplace's method through adaptive quadrature with one node, as mentioned in the SAS manual (SAS Institute, 1999). The second option is to acknowledge explicitly the dependency of $\hat{\theta}_p$ and $\hat{\tau}_p^2$ on the unknown parameters $\boldsymbol{\beta}$ and σ_θ^2 and to find the empirical Bayes estimates and fixed-effects estimates jointly. This is the option that is commonly implemented.

Raudenbush, Yang, and Yosef (2000) proposed an extension of Laplace's method by including also higher order terms in the Taylor approximation to $\log\left(\Pr(\boldsymbol{y}_p|\boldsymbol{\beta},\theta_p)\phi(\theta_p|0,\sigma_\theta^2)\right)$. Raudenbush et al. (2000) argue that six terms are sufficient for an accurate approximation. They call their method Laplace6.

Quasi-likelihood approaches

Because estimation methods for linear mixed models are well-established, several researchers have tried to approximate the models for categorical data by a linear mixed model so that the estimation methods for the latter class of models can be applied. The two most popular approaches here are the *penalized quasi-likelihood* (PQL; Breslow & Clayton, 1993; Schall, 1991; Stiratelli, Laird, & Ware, 1984) and *marginal quasi-likelihood* (MQL; Goldstein, 1991). There are also several extensions proposed of both methods (MQL2, PQL2, and corrected PQL).

Breslow and Clayton (1993) introduced the names PQL and MQL. The term quasi-likelihood methods is used because the methods require only the specification of a mean and variance for the observations and there is no need to spell out explicitly the distribution of the data. In a GLM framework, the same terminology is used for the estimation of models where only means and variances are specified. Although PQL and MQL are classified here as methods that approximate the integrand, they can also be explained as approximations to the data. That is also the perspective we take for didactical reasons.

In both PQL and MQL, the response function (i.e., the inverse link function) is approximated by a linear Taylor series expansion. For PQL, the expansion is about the current estimates of the fixed-effect regression coefficients and about the empirical Bayes estimates for the random effects. For MQL, the expansion is also about the current estimates of the fixed-effect regression coefficients, but about 0 for the random effects. It can be shown that applying this linear approximation of the response function leads to a linear mixed model for a linear transformation of the original data y. The parameters of this model can be estimated and the estimates can in turn be used to update the linear approximation. The algorithm cycles between these two steps until convergence.

Because the PQL and MQL methods rely on a number of approximations, for which it is hard to assess the accuracy, one should not be surprised to learn that the methods often do not work very well. The original data are transformed in PQL and MQL, and then they are considered as normally distributed such that a linear mixed model estimation routine can be applied. Consequently, the methods will perform poorly when the original data are far from normal, which is the case for binary data. This was confirmed by Breslow and Clayton (1993) in a simulation study for PQL and MQL. Rodríguez and Goldman (1995) came to the same conclusion for MQL. A bias towards zero was found for the fixed effects and/or variance component estimates. Similar results are reported in Section 12.4. Breslow and Lin (1995) demonstrated that there is also an asymptotic downward bias for the regression coefficients estimated with PQL.

Another factor affecting the quality of the quasi-likelihood methods is the number of items given to the persons. The reason is that in a linear mixed model, the estimates of the fixed-effects parameters are only affected by the observations through the sufficient statistics of the fixed-effect parameters, which are linear combinations of the data. Hence, it is the distribution of the sufficient statistics of the fixed effects that should be close to normal. For a large number of items or sufficiently continuous data, this is not problematic but for fewer items or with less sufficiently continuous data, the normality approximation can be poor. Thus, it is expected that PQL and MQL perform less well if the number of items is small, or if the data are binary, or both.

Moreover, MQL uses a linear Taylor approximation around the current fixed effects and zeros for the random effects. As a consequence, if the random-effect variances are large, this method will lead to less accurate results. Rodríguez and Goldman (1995) have confirmed this hypothesis in a simulation study.

To overcome some of the problems of PQL and MQL, there have been attempts to improve both methods. PQL2 and MQL2 make use of second-order (as opposed to first-order) Taylor expansions of the response function. Breslow and Lin (1995), and Lin and Breslow (1996) present a bias-corrected version of PQL. Comparing the different quasi-likelihood methods, Rodríguez and Goldman (1995) show that MQL2 performs only slightly better than MQL in terms of bias but Goldstein and Rasbash (1996) demonstrate that PQL2 leads to a substantial improvement over PQL. In a recent simulation study by Browne and Draper (2003), it appears that PQL2 leads to much better results than MQL (the authors did not use PQL).

Unfortunately, the quasi-likelihood methods have been investigated only for GLMMs, and for NLMMs with normally distributed error (Wolfinger & Lin, 1997) (and thus continuous variables). It is unclear how they perform for other nonlinear mixed models such as the 2PL model.

As a final disadvantage to the quasi-likelihood methods, note that the deviance measure produced by using PQL or MQL methods cannot be used for model testing. These methods are based only on assumptions about the first and second moments of the data (mean and variance), which is acceptable when estimating the parameters but not for testing. Testing the model requires reference distributions for the test statistics and for this purpose one must specify the full distribution of the data, not only their first and second moments.

Of the methods we discussed for an approximation of the integrand, only PQL and PQL2 are used in this volume, more in particular in Chapter 5 and in Section 12.4.

12.2.5   Bayesian estimation

An important feature of the previously discussed estimation methods is that they are developed within a frequentist framework of statistical inference. An alternative is to consider Bayesian estimation methods. The major advantage of the Bayesian framework is that modern computer-intensive techniques, known as Markov chain Monte Carlo (MCMC) methods (Gelman, Carlin, Stern, & Rubin, 2004; Tanner, 1996; Zeger & Karim, 1991), can often make the parameter estimation problem less complex. For models with more than two levels of random effects or models with crossed random effects, Bayesian estimation methods can be very practical. A Bayesian estimation method is used in Chapter 6, for models with crossed effects.

Classical (maximum likelihood) and Bayesian approaches differ in several respects:

First, classical approaches clearly distinguish between fixed and random effects (parameters of interest and nuisance variables) whereas Bayesian approaches consider all effects to be essentially random. As discussed before, classical approaches involve a two-stage approach for parameter estimation.

In a first stage, fixed effects are obtained by maximizing the integrated likelihood (MML) or the conditional likelihood (CML) of fixed-effect parameters. In a second stage, person parameters are estimated by maximizing their posterior distribution assuming (first-stage) estimates of fixed effects are true. In contrast, Bayesian approaches use sampling-based MCMC algorithms such as the Gibbs sampler (Geman & Geman, 1984; Gelfand & Smith, 1990) and the Metropolis algorithm (Metropolis & Ulam, 1949; Metropolis et al., 1953) to obtain a sample of the entire posterior distribution of all model parameters in one stage. To guarantee the propriety of the posterior distribution it is necessary to specify a prior distribution for all model parameters. For person parameters and location parameters a normal distribution can be used whereas for discrimination parameters a lognormal distribution (allowing for only positive values) is often specified.

Second, classical approaches yield standard errors of parameters that are based on an asymptotic normal approximation to the likelihood (or posterior) whereas Bayesian approaches yield posterior intervals of parameters that are also valid in small samples.

Third, monitoring convergence is more straightforward when using a classical approach than when using a Bayesian approach to approximate the entire posterior. A popular maximization algorithm such as the EM algorithm has the strong property of increasing the likelihood at each iteration and converging to a stationary point of the parameter space. For popular MCMC algorithms such as the Gibbs sampler it is known that, under mild regularity conditions, the simulated sequences converge to the true posterior distribution, but assessing whether convergence has been attained is a difficult problem (for an overview, see Cowles & Carlin, 1996).

Fourth, when using a classical approach for estimation, it is straightforward to check whether a necessary condition for (local) identifiability of the model is satisfied (i.e., evaluate whether the Hessian in the estimated point is negative definite). In contrast, such a check is not available when using a Bayesian approach for parameter estimation.

12.3   Software

12.3.1   Comparative description of the programs

Several programs are available to estimate the models that are presented in this volume. On the one hand there is software available with the specific purpose to estimate item response models. Among these programs, most can estimate models with the propensity as a random variable (based on the MML formulation of the models). Most of the specific-purpose programs use indirect maximization (with EM). Examples are BILOG (Zimowski, Muraki, Mislevy & Bock, 1995), ConQuest (Wu, Adams & Wilson, 1998), MULTILOG (Thissen, Chen & Bock, 2002), OPLM (Verhelst, Glas & Verstralen, 1994). We will not further discuss these item response modeling programs, because, in line with the framework in this volume, we want to stress item response models as instantiations of broader categories of models.

On the other hand, there is a more general kind of software with an initially different or broader kind of purpose: for multilevel models, generalized linear and nonlinear mixed models and structural equation models. We will restrict the discussion to the programs of the multilevel type and the mixed models type. Note that the S-PLUS module nlme (Pinhero & Bates, 2000) can be used for nonlinear mixed models with Gaussian outcomes (continuous variables) but not for categorical data. However, also most structural equation software can handle ordered-category (including binary) data, for example LISREL (Jőreskog & Sőrbom, 2003), and Mplus (Muthén & Muthén, 2003).

As far as the software from the *multilevel tradition* is concerned, there are two major programs: MLwiN, and HLM, and they will both be discussed in the following. As far as the *generalized linear and nonlinear mixed models tradition* is concerned, SAS has a macro, called GLIMMIX which uses the procedure MIXED for linear mixed models to estimate generalized linear mixed models, and it has also a separate procedure, called NLMIXED, for the estimation of generalized linear and nonlinear mixed models. Based on STATA, a program called GLLAMM is also available for similar purposes. Some stand-alone programs are available: VARCL from the multilevel tradition, and MIXOR/MIXNO from the biostatistical mixed models tradition. EGRET (Cytel Software Corporation, 2000) stems also from the latter tradition and can handle also quite different models, such as survival models. VARCL (Longford, 1993) and EGRET (Cytel Software Corporation, 2000) will not be discussed further here, as they are restricted to binary data for item reponse models.

The two traditions, the multilevel tradition and the mixed models tradition, differ as to their specialization (nested designs and linear models for the former, and nonlinear link functions for the latter), which explains why the multilevel programs often use linearization techniques to approximate the integrand, while the programs from the mixed models tradition use (approximative) numerical integration.

The following programs: MLwiN, HLM, GLIMMIX, NLMIXED, GLLAMM, and MIXOR/MIXNO, will be first compared in general terms concerning the item response models that they can estimate and the estimation methods they use, and then more specific characteristics of each will be described.

Programs and models

The general features concerning the models that can be estimated are the following. Table 12.1 records the features of each of the programs listed above (the keywords within parentheses are used in Table 12.1).

TABLE 12.1. Kind of models that can be estimated by six programs.

Program	level	crossed	dist	linear	reg	link	poly
MLwiN	more	cross	normal	linear	man	both	poly
HLM	more	cross	normal	linear	man	logit	poly
GLIMMIX	more	cross	normal	nonlin	man	both	bin
NLMIXED	two	no	normal	nonlin	man	both	poly
GLLAMM	more	no	normal	nonlin	lat	both	poly
			discrete				
MIXOR/	two	no	normal	nonlin	man	both	poly
MIXNO			uniform				

- Levels of random effects (level)

The item response models we have discussed always have at minimum two levels: (1) observations within persons, and (2) persons. The random element of the first level is covered by the random component of the model (e.g., the Bernoulli distribution). The persons constitute the second level, which is commonly treated as a level with random effects. Most item response models that are discussed in this volume are 2-level models. But a higher *number of levels* is possible. As shown in Chapter 5, one can easily add levels, (3) for groups of persons, and for (4) sets of groups, etc.

- Crossed random effects (crossed)

When random effects are introduced on both sides, for persons and for items, a model with *crossed random effects* is obtained. Crossed random effects occur whenever factors that are crossed in a design have effects that are random over the levels they have in the design. For example, the factors Person and Item are commonly crossed in item response data, and they may have effects that are random over their levels (i.e., individual persons and items, respectively). It is also possible that two types of person groups are crossed, for example schools and the neighborhoods where the students live.

- Distribution of random effects (dist)

For the distribution of random effects, four possibilities can be distinguished: a standard distribution, an unspecified distribution, a mixture distribution, and conditioning out the distribution. The most common standard distribution is the normal distribution. No other standard distributions for item response models are used in this volume. For standard distributions, a *parametric estimation method* is used (see Section 12.2.1). An unspecified distribution implies that the distribution needs to be approached through the estimation of probabilities of a set of nodes on a line (one-dimensional) or a grid (multidimensional) without prespecified weights for the nodes. This is in fact a mixture of peak distributions. These are *non-parametric* or *semi-parametric estimation methods*, as mentioned in Section 12.2.1, and called here 'discrete distributions.' A *mixture distribution* is a mixture of standard distributions. Two cases are described in this volume: peak distributions (with zero variance) and normal distributions (see Chapter 11) . If a sufficiently large number of normal distributions is used, any shape of distribution can be approached reasonably well. Finally, when the *conditional maximum likelihood method* is used for estimation, as explained in Section 12.2.2, then the distribution is conditioned out. The distribution does not matter, since one conditions on the sufficient statistics. This is equivalent to a saturated model for the distribution.

• Linearity of the systematic component (linear)
The systematic component (structural part) of a model is a function of predictors with η_{pi} as the function value. The function is linear in all GLMMs (e.g., the LLTM). The most common case of nonlinearity in this volume is that the model includes a product of two parameters, also called a *bilinear term*, such as $\alpha_i\theta_p$ in the 2PL model. The product can also be one of an item weight and a person parameter, as in the 2PL model, or of two item parameters, as in the MIRID. A more complicated form of nonlinearity occurs in the 3PL model. It depends on the program which kind of nonlinearity can be handled (see Section 12.3.2).

• Type of latent regression (reg)
Two types latent regression may be distinguished. In a first case one or more *manifest person variables* are regressed on η_{pi}, or one could say on θ_p. Such variables are actually treated as a set of constant values, and are assumed to be error-free. In fact, this type of regression is nothing more than using person predictors, but we have used the term 'latent regression' in Chapter 2 for the case person properties are used as predictors. The second kind of latent regression is one where one or more *latent person variables* (random effects) are regressed on one or more other latent variables (random variables), as when $\theta_{pk'}$ is regressed on θ_{pk}. Such models imply restrictions on the covariance structure of the random effects. They are also a way to deal with predictors with error.

• Link function (link)
The two link functions we have discussed in this volume are the *logit link* and the *probit link*. For multicategorical data, adaptations of these are needed.

• Polytomous items (poly)
The number of values Y_{pi} can have determines whether the items are *di-*

chotomous (binary data) or *polytomous* (multicategorical). When the data are polytomous, the categories can be ordered or not. As explained in Chapter 3, various options are available, based on adjacent odds (PCMs), cumulative odds (GRMs), etc.

It can be seen from Table 12.1 that the software for multilevel models can handle more than two levels ('more' in Table 12.1, 5 by default for MLwiN but more if wanted, 3 for HLM) and also crossed random effects ('cross' in Table 12.1), while the typical software that was written for GLMMs and NLMMs, such as NLMIXED and MIXOR/MIXNO cannot ('two' in Table 12.1). On the other hand, the latter can handle both nonlinear and linear systematic components ('nonlin' in Table 12.1), while the former cannot ('linear' in Table 12.1). Of the other two programs, GLIMMIX resembles the multilevel programs, and GLLAMM combines most good features of both. All programs use the normal distribution for random effects ('normal' in Table 12.1), but GLLAMM also allows for a discrete distribution ('discrete' in Table 12.1). Except for HLM, all programs can handle both the logit and probit link functions ('both' in Table 12.1, 'logit' if only logit link). All can handle binary as well as multicategorical data ('poly' in Table 12.1), except for GLIMMIX (bin' in Table 12.1). For latent regression, only GLLAMM is really suited for latent variable regression ('lat' in Table 12.1), while all other programs concentrate on external manifest variables as predictors ('man' in Table 12.1). However, any program that can estimate multidimensional models, and allows one to express one random effect as a function of another, can also be used for the purpose of latent regression with latent variables. When one can express covariance parameters of the random effects as a function of other such parameters, then a confirmatory analysis is also possible. We have tried this with success in a small simulation study with the NLMIXED procedure from SAS, for the case where two random effects are partly determined by a common third random effect and the correlation between the first two stems only from the shared influence from the third.

Estimation

Next, the programs are compared in terms of the estimation methods they use. The features we will consider are the following:

• Approximation of the integral
The direct maximization is performed using *Gaussian quadrature*, adaptive or nonadaptive, as explained in Section 12.2.3. The adaptive method is superior as shown in Chapter 4 of this volume, but for our application, the difference is minimal. One reason for the small difference is that a relatively large number of observations is made for each person (24 item responses compared with only 7 observations in the onychomycosis data that are an-

alyzed in Chapter 4). The alternative is an indirect method, using the *EM algorithm* as in most programs that are specifically written for the estimation of item response models.

- Approximation of the integrand

Here we distinguish between the *Laplace6* method and quasi-likelihood approaches, such as *MQL* and *PQL* (see Section 12.2.4), further extended into MQL2 and PQL2. The PQL method outperforms the MQL method, and MQL2 and PQL2 are improvements on MQL and PQL, respectively, for reasons explained in Section 12.2.4.

- Note on QL methods

The QL methods are based on a linear approximation as explained in Section 12.2.4. This makes these methods more similar to those used for linear mixed models. An important distinction in the estimation of the latter is made between restricted maximum likelihood (REML) and full maximum likelihood (ML). With ML, the fixed effects and the variance components (covariance structure) are estimated simultaneously (with all degrees of freedom), but with REML the loss of degrees of freedom involved in estimating the fixed effects is taken into account. A simple example is the estimation of the variance in a normal population. Either the number of persons in the sample is used in the numerator (ML method) or the same number minus one (REML). One degree of freedom is lost, because the mean, a fixed effect, takes one degree of freedom. The ML estimators are biased, while the REML estimators are not. The difference is especially important when the number of fixed effects is large. For example, in the Rasch model where each item has its own fixed effect.

When the restricted approach used in the context of a linear approximation of a GLMM, two remarks are of importance. First, although the merits of ML and REML are documented for LMMs, they are much less clear for the linear approximations in the estimation of models with a nonlinear link function. Second, although the term 'maximum likelihood' is still used (ML, REML), one should not forget that QL methods do not maximize the likelihood of the data, but of a linear approximation instead.

- Bayesian estimation methods

Only one of the programs we discuss offers the possibility of a Bayesian estimation. Many of the models presented in this volume can be estimated using standard software for MCMC simulation such as BUGS (Spiegelhalter, Thomas, Best & Lunn, 2003).

It can be seen from Table 12.2, that the multilevel programs use methods to approximate the integrand (Laplace6 and QL methods) while the programs for mixed models use approximations of the integral (adaptive or nonadaptive). In only one program (MLwiN), is a Bayesian estimation method available (Metropolis Hastings within Gibbs).

TABLE 12.2. Estimation methods that are available in six programs.

Program	Approximation integral	Approximation integrand	Bayesian
MLwiN	no	PQL, PQL2, MQL, MQL2	yes
HLM	no	Laplace6, PQL	no
GLIMMIX	no	PQL and MQL	no
NLMIXED	adaptive/ nonadaptive	no	no
GLLAMM	adaptive nonadaptive	no	no
MIXOR/MIXNO	nonadaptive	no	no

12.3.2 Specifics of the programs

For each program we will first describe some specific features that have not yet been discussed in the comparative description of the programs. They concern data and models, and estimation. Second, we describe data format and commands. A typical data format is what we will call the *vertical string format*. This means that the item responses (the observations) are organized in one long string, with a separate row per response of a person on an item, so that the length of the string is the number of persons multiplied by the number of items. Missing data make the string shorter, with a different number of observations per person. For a discussion of the implications, see Section 4.8. The values of the predictors for each individual response are then specified on the same row. Information for how to set up the different programs to estimate the Rasch model as in Section 12.4 is given on the website specified in the Preface. Third, we will also inform the reader on the availability of the programs and where one can find more information. Our discussion of the software is restricted to its use for item response modeling: to categorical data and models with a logit or probit link.

MLwiN

MLwiN (Goldstein et al., 1998) is the successor of an earlier program MLn. It is designed for multilevel modeling, but it can also be used for item response modeling.

• Models and estimation
Although MLwiN cannot estimate NLMMs, it is possible to work with a discrimation parameter following an estimation procedure based on alternating the estimation of the propensities and the item discrimination

parameters described by Woodhouse (1991).

Goldstein and Rasbash (1996) show that the inclusion of a second-order term in the approximate procedures (MQL and PQL) proposed by Breslow and Clayton (1993) seriously reduces the bias inherent to these procedures. The adapted procedures are called MQL2 and PQL2. Both the original procedures (MQL and PQL) and the adapted ones (MQL2 and PQL2) are available in MLwiN. For accuracy of estimation, PQL2 is the best of these procedures, but for complex models PQL2 sometimes fails to converge, unless one starts from good initial values. Therefore it is recommended to use MQL first (without extra-binomial variance) and to use the MQL estimates as initial values for PQL2. Because the approximation of the integrand is based on a linearization of the dependent variable, iterative generalized least squares (IGLS) and its REML version (RIGLS) can be used, as proposed by Goldstein (1989).

- Data format and commands

MLwiN makes use of worksheets. These worksheets contain the data. After a run of the program, the worksheets also contain the selected options and model specifications, and the results. If one does not want a worksheet to be overwritten in the next run, one should save it under a different name, to be inspected later, or to start from in later sessions. A MLwiN session starts with retrieving an existing worksheet or with creating a new worksheet by entering data or by importing data from an ASCII-file. The program makes use of a statistical environment that is useful to prepare the data (e.g., by sorting) and for other purposes.

MLwiN can be used in three modes. The first is based on a graphical interface of windows. The commands that are needed can be chosen by pointing to and clicking on the commands that are displayed on the screen. The second mode is the command mode, typing in the commands one needs. This has to be repeated for each new run. The third mode consists of using a batch file containing the commands, so that one can reuse (parts of) the command set.

- Availability and information

MLwiN can be ordered from the website of the Centre for Multilevel Modeling at the Institute of Education in London: http://multilevel.ioe. ac.uk. The models and estimation methods are described in Goldstein (2003) and Goldstein et al. (1998).

HLM

HLM is a program for multilevel modeling that can also be used for the estimation of item response models. A recent update is HLM5 (Raudenbush, Bryk, Cheong & Congdon, 2000).

• Models and estimation
The specification of the model is nicely parallel to the formulation of a GLMM: (1) the sampling model, (2) the link function, and (3) the structural model. When the link function is nonlinear, Raudenbush et al. (2000) use the term *hierarchical generalized linear model* (HGLM). The models that can be estimated are restricted to GLMMs. For example, the 2PL cannot be estimated.

HLM provides MQL and PQL. Because HLM also makes use of a linear approximation, two variants are available for estimation: the ML variant and the REML variant. In addition to MQL and PQL a sixth-order approximation to the likelihood based on a Laplace transform is also available (Laplace6) (for binary data and 2-level models). Raudenbush et al. (2000) investigated the qualities of this estimation method and found that it is quite accurate.

• Data format and commands
Two separate input files are required: one for the items and one for the persons. The item file has a vertical string format, and contains one row per pair of a person and an item: with the observations and with the item predictors, and if there are such predictors, the person-by-item predictors as well. The person file has as many rows as there are persons and is used for the person predictors. The two files are linked through an ID for each person in both files. These files may be prepared in one of the common software packages. They are transformed by the program into a 'sufficient statistics matrix' (SSM) file. HLM can also be used in three modes: with a Windows interface, a command mode (answering questions on a prompt), and a batch mode.

• Availability and information
Full versions of HLM are available for purchase from `http://www.ssicen tral.com` or `http://www.assess.com` with restricted versions available for students for free. The HLM software supplements the HLM book first published by Bryk and Raudenbush (1992) and revised by Raudenbush and Bryk (2002).

GLIMMIX

GLIMMIX is a SAS macro that makes use of the MIXED procedure from SAS for linear mixed models, in order to estimate GLMMs. It is based on an algorithm proposed by Wolfinger and O'Connell (1993). Altough GLIMMIX can handle only binary data, we discuss the program here because it is an alternative for the NLMIXED procedure within SAS, and because it is used in one of the previous chapters.

• Models and estimation
An important limitation is that GLIMMIX cannot be used for multicategorical data. GLIMMIX uses PQL by default, but MQL is also available. Because GLIMMIX is based on the MIXED procedure it also benefits from the interesting features of this procedure. For example, both ML and REML are supported, and serial correlations can be dealt with.

• Data format and commands
The data set must be structured as a univariate data set (vertical string format) with one column for the responses and further columns for the predictors. However, one item indicator variable is used, indicating the number of each item, instead of binary item indicators. SAS will implicitly generate a set of binary item indicators. The body of the macro consists of syntax from the MIXED procedure surrounded by statements specific to the GLMM settings, to define the error structure and the link function. Batch mode is used for the commands.

• Availability and information
The macro can be downloaded from the homepage of SAS: `ftp://ftp.sas.com/techsup/download/stat`. It requires SAS version 6.08 or higher. The files are named `glmmXXX.sas`, where `XXX` refers to the version of SAS. Further information regarding the MIXED procedure statements and the GLIMMIX macro can be found in Littell, Milliken, Stroup, and Wolfinger (1996).

NLMIXED procedure of SAS

The NLMIXED procedure is a very general procedure for GLMMs and NLMMs (SAS Institute, 1999).

• Models and estimation
NLMIXED adopts a very large variety of functions in the structural part of the model, so that, for example, the 3PL model can be estimated. Its major limitation is that it can handle only one level of random effects (i.e., 2-level data). Because it uses Gaussian quadrature, the procedure takes quite a lot of time, especially when the number of persons is high. Often good initial values are required when the models are complicated. Convergence problems occur now and then, as well as negative variance estimates. For the latter problem, it sometimes helps to reparameterize the model using a fixed variance, but a free overall discrimination value.

• Data format and commands
The data need to be imported into SAS and organized in a vertical string format, in an array with as many rows as the number of persons times the number of items. For each observation, the values of the predictors need

to be specified in the following columns. The data have to be sorted by person. Batch mode is used for the commands.

• Availability and information
The NLMIXED procedure is available from version 8.0 of SAS onwards. It is part of the software product SAS/STAT. See http://support.sas.com/software/release 82/. Information on SAS/STAT can be found at http://support.sas.com/rnd/app/da/stat.html.

GLLAMM

Generalized linear latent and mixed models (GLLAMM) (Rabe-Hesketh, Pickles, & Skrondal, 2001) is a program written as part of the statistical software package STATA. It combines features of a program for generalized linear mixed models and for structural equation models.

• Models and estimation
In comparison with the NLMIXED procedure from SAS, GLLAMM is not limited to 2-level data, it can estimate discrete distributions (semi-parametric estimation) for random effects, and it can be used in an elegant way for structural equations modeling, so that one can regress random person effects on other random person effects. In comparison with the NLMIXED procedure, GLLAMM is limited only in that effects other than linear and bilinear person effects (unweighted and weighted θs, respectively) need to be fixed. For example, a random-effect guessing parameter is not possible. In comparison to the multilevel software, GLLAMM is limited mainly in that it cannot deal with crossed random effects. To conclude, GLLAMM combines the main attractive features of three traditions: multilevel modeling, generalized linear mixed models, and structural equation modeling, but some models that are specific to the software from these traditions are lacking. GLLAMM shares with the NLMIXED procedure its direct maximization through adaptive or nonadaptive Gaussian quadrature, and therefore can be very slow.

• Data format and commands
Before running GLAMM, the data must be imported into STATA and formatted into the vertical string format, with item responses stacked within respondents. On each row, the values of the predictors must be given for the corresponding observed response. Data in the format of a person-by-item array can be reshaped with a STATA command. GLLAMM works with STATA command files and thus uses batch mode for the commands.

• Availability and information
The program can be downloaded for free at http://www.gllamm.org. Purchasing information for STATA can be found at http://www.stata.com.

Information on the program can be found in the manual (Rabe-Hesketh et al., 2001) which can be downloaded from the same website as the program. For the models and estimation methods, see Rabe-Hesketh, Pickles, and Skrondal (2002, in press), and Skrondal and Rabe-Hesketh (2003).

MIXOR/MIXNO

MIXOR (Hedeker & Gibbons, 1996) is a program for generalized linear mixed models applied to 2-level ordered-category data, including binary data. MIXNO (Hedeker, 1999) is the corresponding program for nominal data.

• Models and estimation
The forms of nonlinearity in the structural part that the programs can handle is limited to bilinearity (as in the 2PL model). For the estimation, Gaussian quadrature is used, but only in its nonadaptive version. Unlike the previous two programs Fisher scoring is used for the maximization of the marginal likelihood. It is worth noting that the covariance structure of the random effects is not estimated, but that the program relies on a Cholesky decomposition, from which the covariance matrix is calculated (without standard errors).

• Data format and commands
The input data file must be a standard text file (ASCII), with a vertical string format with items nested within persons: one row per response of a person to an item, including the response in question and the corresponding values of the predictors. For the commands, batch mode is used.

• Availability and information
The programs are in the public domain and can be downloaded from http://tigger.uic.edu/~hedeker/mix.html. Manuals containing various examples can be downloaded from the same location. A basic descriptive article is the one by Hedeker and Gibbons (1994).

12.4 Applications

12.4.1 Options and results

All six programs were applied to the verbal aggression data set (binary data) for the estimation of the Rasch model as described in Chapter 2. The options chosen for the different programs are the following:

  MLwiN: PQL2 (with RIGLS),
  HLM: PQL (with ML),
  GLIMMIX: PQL (with REML),
  NLMIXED: nonadaptive Gaussian quadrature (20 nodes),

GLAMM: nonadaptive Gaussian quadrature (20 nodes),

MIXOR: nonadaptive Gaussions quadrature (20 nodes).

We also utilized other options for some of the programs, but the results of these options are not reported in Table 12.3, and only discussed in the text.

TABLE 12.3. Results of applying the six programs for estimation of the Rasch model. Estimates of item parameters and their standard errors and of the variance of the intercept and its standard error (verbal aggression data).

	Items			ML-wiN	HLM	GLIM-MIX	NL-MIXED	GL-LAMM	MIXOR
1	Bus	Want	Curse	-1.22	-1.17	-1.17	-1.22	-1.23	-1.23
				(.16)	(.22)	(.16)	(.16)	(.16)	(.19)
2	Bus	Want	Scold	-.56	-.54	-.54	-.57	-.57	-.57
				(.15)	(.21)	(.15)	(.15)	(.15)	(.18)
3	Bus	Want	Shout	-.08	-.08	-.08	-.09	-.09	-.08
				(.15)	(.21)	(.15)	(.15)	(.15)	(.17)
4	Train	Want	Curse	-1.74	-1.67	-1.67	-1.75	-1.76	-1.75
				(.17)	(.22)	(.17)	(.17)	(.17)	(.20)
5	Train	Want	Scold	-.71	-.68	-.68	-.71	-.71	-.71
				(.15)	(.21)	(.15)	(.15)	(.15)	(.19)
6	Train	Want	Shout	-.01	-.01	-.01	-.02	-.02	-.02
				(.15)	(.21)	(.15)	(.15)	(.15)	(.18)
7	Store	Want	Curse	-.53	-.51	-.51	-.53	-.54	-.53
				(.15)	(.21)	(.15)	(.15)	(.15)	(.17)
8	Store	Want	Scold	.69	.66	.66	.68	.68	.68
				(.16)	(.21)	(.15)	(.15)	(.15)	(.17)
9	Store	Want	Shout	1.53	1.46	1.46	1.52	1.52	1.52
				(.17)	(.22)	(.17)	(.17)	(.17)	(.19)
10	Call	Want	Curse	-1.08	-1.03	-1.03	-1.09	-1.09	-1.09
				(.16)	(.21)	(.16)	(.16)	(.16)	(.18)
11	Call	Want	Scold	.35	.33	.33	.34	.34	.34
				(.15)	(.21)	(.15)	(.15)	(.15)	(.17)
12	Call	Want	Shout	1.04	1.00	1.00	1.04	1.04	1.04
				(.16)	(.21)	(.16)	(.16)	(.16)	(.19)
13	Bus	Do	Curse	-1.22	-1.17	-1.17	-1.23	-1.23	-1.23
				(.16)	(.22)	(.16)	(.16)	(.16)	(.19)
14	Bus	Do	Scold	-.39	-.37	-.37	-.40	-.39	-.40
				(.15)	(.21)	(.15)	(.15)	(.15)	(.19)
15	Bus	Do	Shout	.87	.83	.83	.87	.87	.87
				(.16)	(.21)	(.15)	(.16)	(.16)	(.18)
16	Train	Do	Curse	-.87	-.83	-.83	-.87	-.88	-.88
				(.16)	(.21)	(.15)	(.15)	(.16)	(.18)
17	Train	Do	Scold	.06	.05	.05	.05	.06	.05
				(.15)	(.21)	(.15)	(.15)	(.15)	(.18)
18	Train	Do	Shout	1.48	1.42	1.42	1.48	1.48	1.48
				(.17)	(.22)	(.16)	(.17)	(.17)	(.20)
19	Store	Do	Curse	.21	.20	.20	.21	.21	.21
				(.15)	(.21)	(.15)	(.15)	(.15)	(.17)
20	Store	Do	Scold	1.50	1.44	1.44	1.50	1.50	1.50
				(.17)	(.22)	(.17)	(.17)	(.17)	(.19)
21	Store	Do	Shout	2.96	2.84	2.84	2.97	2.97	2.98
				(.23)	(.27)	(.22)	(.23)	(.23)	(.25)
22	Call	Do	Curse	-.71	-.68	-.68	-.71	-.71	-.71
				(.15)	(.21)	(.15)	(.15)	(.15)	(.18)
23	Call	Do	Scold	.38	.37	.37	.38	.38	.38
				(.15)	(.19)	(.15)	(.15)	(.15)	(.18)
24	Call	Do	Shout	1.99	1.91	1.91	2.00	2.00	2.00
				(.18)	(-)	(.18)	(.18)	(.18)	(.20)
	Variance of the intercept			1.87	1.69	1.70	1.98	1.98	1.98[a]
				(.17)	(.15)	(.17)	(.21)	(.21)	(-)

Note a: The standard deviation is estimated, rather than the variance, and this standard deviation has a standard error of .07.

Table 12.3 shows the parameter estimates and their standard errors. The parameter estimates displayed are for the item parameters (in the minus parametrization – higher means lower logit values), and the variance of the random intercept.

HLM is different from the rest, in that $I - 1$ item indicators are used (23 instead of 24), plus a constant predictor. This yields 23 estimates of the item effects, with the effect of the 24th item (i.e., the reference item) fixed to 0. In order to derive item parameter values for the same parametrization as used for the other programs, one must add the effect of the constant predictor to each of the 23 estimated item effects and to the constrained value 0 for the 24th item. The standard errors reported in Table 12.3 are those of the 23 estimates before the reparametrization, which explains why no standard error is given for the reference item (item 24). However, these standard errors are no longer valid after the reparametrization. The item parameter estimates after reparametrization are the sum of two estimates: an item-specific estimate and an estimate of the effect of the constant predictor. The variance of this sum depends on the variance of each of the terms (var_i and var_c, respectively) and on their covariance ($covar_{ic}$). The new standard errors are the square root of $var_i + var_c + 2covar_{ic}$. When this formula is applied, the resulting standard errors have values that are about equal to those obtained with most other programs.

12.4.2   Discussion of the results

As can be seen in Table 12.3, the results are highly similar for all six programs. For the three programs that make use of Gaussian quadrature (NLMIXED, GLLAMM, MIXOR), the estimates are nearly identical. The only difference is the somewhat higher SE of the estimates from MIXOR. Note that in general the SEs are slightly larger for more extreme estimates. This makes sense because these estimates are based on less information.

Note that when an adaptive procedure was used for the Gaussian quadrature with NLMIXED, the results were again highly similar, with differences that were not larger than .01 for the item parameter estimates and the standard errors (these results are not shown in Table 12.3). However, the estimated variance was somewhat smaller: 1.92 (.20) instead of 1.98 (.21). GLAMM also has the possibility to use adaptive Gaussian quadrature.

The results we obtained for the other three programs diverge a little more among one another, and also differ slightly from those we already discussed. In fact, the estimates of the item parameters are identical for HLM and GLIMMIX. The estimates for the variance differ only slightly for these two programs. All estimates (of the item parameters and the variance) are somewhat less extreme than those obtained with Gaussian quadrature. This is due to the well-known downward bias of PQL. For both HLM and GLIMMIX, a PQL method was used.

The bias is much smaller and hardly noticeable in the item parameters when MLwiN is used (with PQL2), as may be noted in Table 12.3. For the variance, values between the estimates with PQL and Gaussian quadrature are obtained (1.87 is greater than 1.69 and 1.70, and less than 1.98). The better results must be attributed to the PQL2 method, since when MLwiN is used with PQL instead, the MLwiN estimate of the variance is also 1.70. On the other hand, when the Laplace6 method is used for HLM, the estimate of the variance is 1.92. This latter value is identical to the value of the variance estimate we obtained when using adaptive quadrature. This is perhaps not surprising since adaptive quadrature "can be thought of alternatively as the form of 'm-order Laplace approximation' " (Liu & Pierce, 1994, p. 626).

Note that for MLwiN and GLIMMIX a restricted approach was used (the analogon of REML for linear mixed models). When the equivalent of a full maximum likelihood method was used, the downward bias was a little bit larger, but the differences were never larger than .01.

Finally, note that the standard errors of the item parameter estimates are somewhat larger when HLM is used, but this must be attributed to the fact that they are actually the standard errors for the estimates of the corresponding 23 item effects, with item 24 as the reference level.

The results are very clear. The estimations based on Gaussian quadrature for numerical integration (NLMIXED, GLLAMM, MIXOR) agree with one another very well. The methods that are based on an approximation of the integrand also show a high degree of convergence when PQL is used (MLwiN, HLM, GLIMMIX). They also show a moderate downward bias. However, this bias is largely reduced for the PQL2 method (MLwiN), or when Laplace6 is chosen (HLM). For the sake of completeness, we can add that when a Bayesian estimation was carried out (using BUGS), the results were nearly identical to those of the Gaussian quadrature methods.

We do not claim any generality for the findings from these results, since only one data set was analyzed based on only one model. An extensive simulation study would be a better basis for a generalization. However, the results are in line with the expectations.

12.5   References

Abramowitz, M., & Stegun, I. (1974). *Handbook of Mathematical Functions.* New York: Dover Publications.

Adams, R.J., Wilson, M.R., & Wang, W. -C. (1997). The multidimensional random coefficients multinomial logit model. *Applied Psychological Measurement, 21,* 1–23.

Andersen, E.B. (1970). Asymptotic properties of conditional maximum-likelihood estimators. *Journal of the Royal Statistical Society, Series B, 32,* 283–301.

Andersen, E.B. (1980). *Discrete Statistical Models with Social Science Applications.* Amsterdam: North-Holland.

Bock, R.D., & Aitkin, M. (1981). Marginal maximum likelihood estimation of item parameters: An application of the EM algorithm. *Psychometrika,*

46, 443–459.

Breslow, N.E. and Clayton, D.G. (1993). Approximate inference in generalized linear mixed models. *Journal of the American Statistical Association, 88*, 9–25.

Breslow, N.E., & Lin, X. (1995). Bias correction in generalised linear mixed models with a single component of dispersion. *Biometrika, 82*, 81–91.

Browne, W.J., & Draper, D. (2003). A comparison of Bayesian and likelihood-based methods for fitting multilevel models. Manuscript submitted for publication.

Bryk, A.S., & Raudenbush, S.W. (1992). *Hierarchical Linear Models: Applications and Data Analysis Methods.* London: Sage.

Bunday, B.D. (1984). *Basic Optimisation Methods.* London: Edward Arnold.

Cowles, K., & Carlin, B. P. (1996). Markov chain Monte Carlo convergence diagnostics: A comparative review. *Journal of the American Statistical Association, 91*, 883-904.

Cytel Software Corporation (2000). *EGRET for Windows*, User Manual.

Dempster, A.P., Laird, N.M., and Rubin, D. B. (1977). Maximum likelihood from incomplete data via the EM algorithm (with discussion). *Journal of the Royal Statistical Society, Series B, 39*, 1–38.

Everitt, B.S. (1987). *Optimisation Methods and their Applications in Statistics.* London: Chapman & Hall.

Gelfand, A. E., & Smith, A. F. M. (1990). Sampling based approaches to calculating marginal densities. *Journal of the American Statistical Association, 85*, 398–409.

Gelman, A., Carlin, J.B., Stern, H.S., and Rubin, D.B. (2004). *Bayesian Data Analysis.* London: Chapman and Hall.

Geman, S., & Geman, D. (1984). Stochastic relaxation, Gibbs distributions and the Bayesian restoration of images. *IEEE Transactions on Pattern Analysis and Machine Intelligence, 6*, 721–741.

Gill, P.E., Murray, W., & Wright, M.H. (1981). *Practical Optimization.* New York: Academic Press.

Goldstein, H. (1989). Restricted unbiased iterative generalized least squares estimation. *Biometrika, 76*, 622–623.

Goldstein, H. (1991). Nonlinear multilevel models, with an application to discrete response data. *Biometrika, 78*, 45–51.

Goldstein, H. (2003). *Multilevel Statistical Models (3rd ed.).* London: Arnold.

Goldstein, H. & Rasbash, J. (1996). Improved approximations for multilevel models with binary responses. *Journal of the Royal Statistical Society A, 159*, 505–513.

Goldstein, H., Rasbash, J., Plewis, I., Draper, D., Browne, W., Yang, M., Woodhouse, G., & Healy, M. (1998). *User's Guide to MLwiN.* Multilevels Models Project, University of London.

Hedeker, D. (1999). MIXNO: A computer program for mixed-effects nominal logistic regression. Computer software and manual.

Hedeker, D., & Gibbons, R.D. (1994). A random-effects ordinal regression model for multilevel analysis. *Biometrics, 50*, 933–944.

Hedeker, D., & Gibbons, R.D. (1996). MIXOR: A computer program for mixed-effects ordinal regression analysis. *Computer Methods and Programs in Biomedicine, 49*, 157–176.

Heinen, T. (1996). *Latent Class and Discrete Latent Trait Models: Similarities and Differences.* Thousand Oaks, CA: Sage.

Jöreskog, K.G. & Sörbom, D. (2003). *LISREL 8.5 for Windows.* Lincolnwood, IL: Scientific Software.

Laird, N.M. (1978). Nonparametric maximum likelihood estimation of a mixing distribution. *Journal of the American Statistical Association, 73*, 805–811.

Lange, K. (1999). *Numerical Methods for Statisticians.* New York: Wiley.

Lesaffre, E., & Spiessens, B. (2001). On the effect of the number of quadrature points in a logistic random-effects model: an example. *Applied Statistics, 50*, 325–335.

Lin, X. and Breslow, N.E. (1996). Bias correction in generalized linear mixed models with multiple components of dispersion. *Journal of the American Statistical Association, 91*, 1007–1016.

Littell, R., Milliken, G., Stroup, W., & Wolfinger, R. (1996). *SAS System for Mixed Models.* Cary, NC: SAS Institute Inc.

Liu, Q., & Pierce, D.A. (1994). A note on Gauss-Hermite quadrature. *Biometrika, 81*, 624–624.

Longford, N.T. (1993). *Random Coefficients Models.* Oxford: Clarendon Press.

McCulloch, C.E., & Searle, S.R. (2001). *Generalized, Linear, and Mixed Models.* New York: Wiley.

McLachlan, G.J. & Krishnan, T. (1997). *The EM Algorithm and Extensions.* New York: Wiley.

Metropolis, N. & Ulam, S. (1949) The Monte Carlo Method. *Journal of the American Statistical Association, 44*, 335–341.

Metropolis, N., Rosenbluth, A.W., Rosenbluth, M.N., Teller, A.H. & Teller, E. (1953). Equation of state calculations by fast computing machines. *Journal of Chemical Physics, 21*, 1087–1092.

Molenaar, I. (1995). Estimation of item parameters. In G.H. Fischer & I. Molenaar (Eds), *Rasch Models. Foundations, Recent Developments and Applications* (pp. 39-57). New York: Springer.

Muthén, B., & Muthén, L. (2003). *Mplus version 2.14.* Los Angeles, CA: Muthén & Muthén.

Naylor, J.C., & Smith, A.F.M. (1982). Applications of a method for the efficient computation of posterior distributions. *Applied Statistics, 31,* 214–225.

Neyman, J., & Scott, E.L. (1948). Consistent estimates based on partially consistent observations. *Econometrica, 16,* 1–32.

Pinheiro, P.C. and Bates, D.M. (1995). Approximations to the log-likelihood function in the nonlinear mixed-effects model. *Journal of Computational and Graphical Statistics, 4,* 12–35.

Pinheiro, P.C. and Bates D.M. (2000). *Mixed-Effects Models in S and S-PLUS.* New-York: Springer.

Rabe-Hesketh, S., Pickles, A., & Skrondal, A. (2001). GLLAMM Manual. Technical Report 2001/01. Department of Biostatistics and Computing, Institute of Psychiatry, King's College, University of London.

Rabe-Hesketh, S., Skrondal, A., & Pickles, A. (2002). Reliable estimation of generalized linear mixed models using adaptive quadrature. *The Stata Journal, 2,* 1–21.

Rabe-Hesketh, S., Skrondal, A., & Pickles, A. (in press). Generalized multilevel structural equation modeling. *Psychometrika.*

Raudenbush, S.W., Yang, M.-L., & Yosef, M. (2000). Maximum likelihood for generalized linear models with nested random effects via high-order, multivariate Laplace approximation. *Journal of Computational and Graphical Statistics, 9,* 141–157.

Raudenbush, S.W., Bryk, A.S., Cheong, Y., & Longdon, R.T. (2000). *HLM5: Hierarchical Linear and Nonlinear Modeling.* Chicago: Scientific Software International.

Raudenbush, S.W., & Bryk, A.S. (2002). *Hierarchical Linear Models. Applications and Data Analysis Methods.* Newbury Park, CA: Sage.

Rodríguez, G. and Goldman, N. (1995). An assessment of estimation procedures for multilevel models with binary responses. *Journal of the Royal Statistical Society A, 158,* 73–89.

SAS Institute (1999). *SAS Online Doc (Version 8)* (software manual on CD-Rom). Cary, NC: SAS Institute Inc.

Schall, R. (1991). Estimation in generalised linear models with random effects. *Biometrika, 78,* 719–727.

Shun, Z., & McCullagh, P. (1995). Laplace approximation of high dimensional integrals. *Journal of the Royal Statistical Society B, 57,* 749–760.

Skrondal, A., & Rabe-Hesketh, S. (2003). Multilevel logistic regression for polytomous data and rankings. *Psychometrika, 68,* 267-287.

Spiegelhalter, D., Thomas, A., Best, N. & Lunn, D. (2003). *BUGS: Bayesian inference using Gibbs sampling.* MRC Biostatistics Unit, Cambridge, England. www.mrc-bsu.cam.ac.uk/bugs/

Stiratelli, R., Laird, N., and Ware, J.H. (1984). Random-effects model for serial observations with binary response. *Biometrics, 40,* 961–971.

Tanner, M.A. (1996). *Tools for Statistical Inference (3rd ed.)*. New York: Springer.

Thissen, D., Chen, W.-H, & Bock, R.D. (2002). *MULTILOG7*. Lincolnwood, IL: Scientific Software.

Tierny, L., & Kadane, J.B. (1986). Accurate approximations for posterior moments and marginal densities. *Journal of the American Statistical Association, 81*, 82–86.

Verhelst, N.D., & Glas, C.A.W., & Verstralen, H.H.F.M. (1994). *One Parameter Logistic Model* (computer program and manual). Arnhem, The Netherlands: CITO.

Wolfinger, R.D., & Lin, X. (1997). Two Taylor-series approximation methods for nonlinear mixed models. *Computational Statistics and Data Analysis, 25*, 465–490.

Wolfinger, R., & O'Connell, M. (1993). Generalized linear mixed models: A pseudo-likelihood approach. *Journal of Statistical Computing and Simulation, 48*, 233–243.

Woodhouse, G. (1991). Multilevel item response models. In R. Prosser, J. Rasbash, & H. Goldstein (Eds.), *Data Analysis with ML3* (pp. 19–43). London: Institute of Education.

Wu, M.L., Adams, R.J., & Wilson, M. (1998). *ACER Conquest*. Hawthorn, Australia: ACER Press.

Zeger, S.L. and Karim, M.R. (1991). Generalised linear models with random effects: a Gibbs sampling approach; *Journal of the American Statistical Association, 86*, 79–102.

Zimowski, M., Muraki, E., Mislevy, R.J., & Bock, R.D. (1995). *BILOG-MG: Multiple-Group Item Analysis and Test Scoring*. Chicago, IL: Scientific Software.

Afterword (regarding the verbal aggression data)

The verbal aggression data set has been repeatedly analyzed throughout this volume for illustrative reasons. Various aspects of the data have been revealed, but there was no point in the text where it was our aim to find the ultimate 'best' fitting model for the data. Nor have we tried to combine the various findings into one improved model by paying attention to cross-chapter model selection. Nevertheless, we have learned much about the data from the different chapters, so that an integrative summary of the results for this data set might prove to be both interesting and educative.

On the *item side*, the effects of the items can be quite well explained with the item properties that were used. If the correlation between the Rasch model item parameter estimates and those calculated from the LLTM parameter estimates is used as an effect size for the relative fit of the two models, then the LLTM did very well. However, the goodness of fit of the LLTM was lower than that of the Rasch model, based on statistical significance. Perhaps some improvement on the LLTM can be obtained by exploring interactions between the item properties, and also some improvement can be gained by using the crossed random-effects model with item properties from Chapter 6. Note also that a strong relation was found between the item effects of the do-items and the want-items (see Chapter 9).

On the *person side*, there is evidence that a unidimensional structure does not suffice. As shown in Chapters 8 and 10, a multidimensional model is required in terms of statistical significance testing, although the gains in terms of effect sizes were less clear. It seems that every level of the factors in the item design is a separate though correlated source of individual differences, in line with the results from Chapter 1 where the data were analysed with a linear mixed model. This means the structure has a rather high dimensionality. As a further complication, it is possible that mixture distributions are needed instead of a normal distribution for the different dimensions (random effects), as may be inferred from Chapter 11 (for the effect of Other-to-blame vs Self-to-blame). Gender and Trait Anger each also seem to play a role in explaining the individual differences. As for Gender, the effect is more clearly evident when the three-valued data are used.

As far as *person-by-item interactions* are concerned, there seems to be some DIF, meaning that females are more inhibited than males to actually display blaming behaviors in frustrating situations. This DIF cannot be explained as a dimension-specific effect of Gender in the case where blaming and doing are included as separate dimensions (random effects), since the DIF is evident in the conjunction of both (blaming *and* doing). As an alternative to random effects, one may consider dependence models, as in Chapter 7. It was found there that doing is clearly related to wanting, but that the association depends on the behavior under consideration. The association is not as strong for blaming behaviors than for expressive behaviors, perhaps because inhibition plays less of a role for the latter. This is again a complication for a simple multidimensional model, because it means that the correlation between two types of items differs depending on an item property. A common type of person-by-item interaction is that a second item parameter can improve the goodness of fit, as in the 2PL. This is also the case for our data set, as shown in Chapter 8. However, if this is done for all dimensions that would be needed to capture all dependencies, then a very complex model would be obtained.

In sum, at the end of this volume we have no final best model for the verbal aggression data. It was not our explicit aim to obtain such a model, but having gone through the various chapters, it seems that a very complex and high-dimensional model would be required, although it is unclear yet exactly what all of the elements of this model would need to be. Especially in the case where mixture distributions were required in a high-dimensional space, in addition to other complexities, it would be a difficult task to estimate the ultimate model and to compare it for its goodness of fit with many other somewhat less complicated models. We leave it as an open challenge to find an all-encompassing model. We may have opened Pandora's box by the broadness of the framework, which should not have been a surprise knowing the complexities of the psychological reality we were seeking to model. One possible way to keep the complexities under control would be to investigate how well one can trust a wrongly specified (too simple) model for inferences on some aspects of the data, or which approaches can be used to make simplifying assumptions about aspects one is not directly interested in. Examples of the latter approaches are marginal modeling (as discussed in Chapters 4 and 10), and multivariate probit models (discussed in Chapter 10).

Paul De Boeck & Mark Wilson

Index

Breinigsville, PA USA
27 December 2010
251934BV00015B/3/A